D0481884

A WORLD TREASURY OF

Proverbs

from twenty-five languages

A WORLD TREASURY OF

Proverbs

from twenty-five languages

AFRICAN	GERMAN	POLISH
ARABIC	GREEK	PORTUGUESE
CHINESE	HEBREW	ROUMANIAN
DANISH	HUNGARIAN	RUSSIAN
DUTCH	ITALIAN	SPANISH
ENGLISH	JAPANESE	SWEDISH
FRENCH	LATIN	TURKISH
GAELIC	NORWEGIAN	YIDDISH
	PERSIAN	

COLLECTED BY HENRY DAVIDOFF

Random House, New York

FIRST PRINTING

PUBLISHED SIMULTANEOUSLY IN CANADA
BY RANDOM HOUSE OF CANADA LIMITED

MANUFACTURED IN THE UNITED STATES OF AMERICA
BY THE HADDON CRAFTSMEN, INC., SCRANTON, PA.

Designed by Robert Josephy

FOREWORD

THE first problem that meets the ambitious collector of proverbs is the difficulty of defining his search. Any fairly complete dictionary will give him a list of synonyms for "Proverb" that will contain such words as "Adage," "Aphorism," "Apothegm," "Axiom," "Maxim," "Quotation," "Saying," and others. Without going into detailed discussion of the somewhat subtle differences among these words, it will be enough to say that the title-page of this collection, emphasizing just "Proverbs," will sufficiently indicate what the editor included.

In the very nature of the case it became necessary to impose an arbitrary limit on the material to be collected. One of the problems that arose is the question of authorship. For the most part anonymity seems to be an inevitable attribute of the typical proverb in every language; yet some of them are definitely known to have been first created by a specific writer and have been on the tongues of men for a long time. Especially is this true of the sayings of the old Greek and Latin authors.

Another problem—mechanical in nature—is the limit of length to be imposed. The editor decided that, since "pithiness" is almost inseparable from proverbial lore, the extreme length beyond which no proverb was to be included is twenty words.

With these and other limitations in mind, the editor offers the following collection of well over 15,000 proverbs and sayings from twenty-five languages as a fairly complete exhibit of the world's proverbial lore. Two indexes—of subjects and authors—have been added.

It almost goes without saying that, since this collection is intended for English-speaking readers, more than half the proverbs and sayings included are from English and American sources. The following bibliography indicates most of these sources as well as the collections of proverbs in other languages:

APPERSON *English Proverbs and Proverbial Phrases* (1929)
BERNSTEIN *Yüdische Sprichwörter und Redensarten* (1908)
BILLAUDEAU *French Idioms, Sayings and Proverbs* (1903)
BOHN'S *Handbook of Proverbs* (1855)
BRIDGE *Cheshire Proverbs* (1917)
CAMDEN *Remaines Concerning Britaine* (1614, etc.)
CHRISTY *Proverbs, Maxims and Phrases of All Ages* (1888)
CLARKE *Paroemiologia* (1639)
COTGRAVE *Dictionary* [Ed. by Howell] (1650)
D'ISRAELI *Curiosities of Literature* (1823)
DRAXE *Collection of . . . Latin Words and Phrases* (1612)
DRAXE *A Treasury of Ancient Adagies and Prouerbs* (1616)
ERASMUS *Adagia* (c. 1500)
FERGUSSON *Scottish Proverbs* (1641)
FLORIO *First Fruits* (1578)
FLORIO *Second Fruits* (1581)
FRANKLIN *Poor Richard's Almanac* (1733-1758)
FULLER *Gnomologia: Adagies and Proverbs* (1732)
HALL *Contemplations* (1612-1615)
HAZLITT *English Proverbs and Proverbial Phrases* (1869)
HENDERSON *Scottish Proverbs* (1832)
HERBERT *Outlandish Proverbs* (1640)
HERBERT *Jacula Prudentum* (1651)
HEYWOOD *Dialogue Conteining Proverbes* (1546)
HISLOP *Scottish Proverbs* (1862)
HOWELL *Proverbs: Lexicon Tetraglotton* (1659)
KELLY *Complete Collection of Scottish Proverbs* (1721)
LEAN *Collecteana . . . Proverbs, etc.* 4 vols. (1902-1904)
Proverbial Literature—A Bibliography (Ed. by Bonser) (1930)
RAMSAY *Scots Proverbs* (1737)
RAY *English Proverbs* (1670, etc.)
SKEAT *Early English Proverbs* (1910)
SMITH *The Oxford Dicitionary of English Proverbs* (1935)
STANFORD *Houres of Recreation* (1572)
STEPNEY *Spanish Schoolmaster* (1591)
SYRUS *Publilius—Sententiae* (c. 40 B.C.)
SWIFT *Polite Conversation* (c. 1720)

TAYLOR *The Proverb* (1931)
TILLEY *Elizabethan Proverb Lore* (1926)
TORRIANO *Italian Proverbs . . .* trans. into English (1666)
WILSON *Arte of Rhetorique* (1553—Revis. Edn. 1560)

Finally, here are some statistics that may be of interest to those who might want to know the exact number of sayings included from specific writers most frequently cited:

English

Shakespeare	376
Emerson	66
Pope	55
Bacon	53
Chaucer	52
Franklin	45
Johnson	38
Dryden	36
Blake	29
Young	28
Milton	27
Byron	22
Tennyson	21
Swift	20

Latin

Horace	42
Ovid	31
Vergil	25
Seneca	23

Greek

Homer	30

French

La Rochefoucauld	47
Voltaire	37
Montaigne	36

German

Goethe	33

Italian

Dante	11

Spanish

Cervantes	20

Russian

Tolstoy	10

H. D.

A WORLD TREASURY OF

Proverbs

from twenty-five languages

When not attributed, the proverbs are from English and American folklore. Otherwise, the foreign-language source or the actual author is given immediately after each proverb.

ABILITY

And all may do what has by man been done. *(Young)*
Everyone excels in something in which another fails. *(Latin)*
No one knows what he can do till he tries. *(Latin)*
They can because they think they can. *(Vergil)*
We cannot all do all things. *(Vergil)*

ABSENCE

Absence makes the heart grow fonder. *(T. H. Bayly)*
Absence sharpens love, presence strengthens it.
Distance sometimes endears friendship, and absence sweeteneth it.
He that is absent is soon forgotten.
Heart soon forgets what the eye sees not.
Long absent, soon forgotten.
Our hours in love have wings; in absence, crutches. *(C. Cibber)*
The rarer seen, the less in mind. *(B. Googe)*
What the eye does not see, the heart does not grieve for.
Absence diminishes little passions and increases great ones. *(La Rochefoucauld)*
Achilles absent was Achilles still. *(Homer)*
Out of sight, out of mind. *(Homer)*
Absence is the enemy of love. *(Italian)*
Distance makes the heart less fond. *(Claudian)*
Friends, though absent, are still present. *(Cicero)*
Greater things are believed of those who are absent. *(Tacitus)*
Let no one be willing to speak ill of the absent. *(Propertius)*
The absent shall not be made heir. *(Latin)*
Never was the absent in the right. *(Spanish)*

ABSENT-MINDED

You look for the horse you ride on. *(Russian)*

ABSTINENCE
Abstinence is the mother of competence. *(S. Hutchins)*
It is easier to abstain than to restrain. *(French)*
To abstain that we may enjoy. *(Rousseau)*

ABUNDANCE
Abundance, like want, ruins man. *(Franklin)*

ABUSE
The best things may be abused. *(Lyly)*

ACCIDENT
Accidents will occur in the best-regulated families. (*Dickens*)
Nothing under the sun is accidental. (*Lessing*)
There's many a slip 'twixt the cup and the lip. *(Palladas)*

ACCOUNTS
He that gains well and spends well needs no account book.
Short reckonings are soon cleared.
Short reckonings make long friends.

ACHE
Every heart hath its own ache.
The tongue ever turns to the aching tooth.
Better a finger off than aye wagging. *(-aching) (Scottish)*

ACQUAINTANCE
Short acquaintance brings repentance.

ACTION
Action is the proper fruit of knowledge.
Actions speak louder than words.
Brave actions never want a trumpet.
Great actions speak great minds. *(Fletcher)*
That action is best which procures the greatest happiness for the greatest numbers. *(Hutchinson)*
For the sake of one good action a hundred evil ones should be forgotten. *(Chinese)*
Who acts not when he should, acts not when he would. *(French)*

ACTORS
The strolling tribe; a despicable race. *(C. Churchill)*

ADAM

In Adam's fall
We sinnèd all. *(New Eng. Primer)*

ADDER

If the adder could hear, and the blindworm could see,
Neither man nor beast would ever go free.

ADVANTAGE

Every advantage has its disadvantage. *(Latin)*

ADVENTURE

Who seeks adventure finds blows.

ADVERSITY

Adversity is the first path to truth. *(Byron)*
Adversity makes a man wise, not rich.
Many can bear adversity but few contempt.
Sweet are the uses of adversity. *(Shakespeare)*
There is no education like adversity. *(Disraeli)*
Adversity tries virtue. *(Arabian)*
Adversity flatters no man. *(French)*
Adversity is the touchstone of friendship. *(French)*
Adversity is the trial of courage. *(French)*
In adversity a man is saved by hope. *(Menander)*
Adversity has no friends. *(Tacitus)*
Adversity reminds men of religion. *(Livy)*
Gold is tried by fire, brave men by adversity. *(Seneca)*

ADVICE

Advice comes too late when a thing is done.
Advice is something the wise don't need and fools won't take.
Advice: the smallest current coin. *(Bierce)*
Advise none to marry or go to war.
Advice when most needed is least heeded.
Fools need Advice most, but wise Men only are the better for it. *(Franklin)*

Give advice to all; but be security for none.
Give neither counsel nor salt till you are asked for it.
Good advice is beyond price.
He that will not be counselled cannot be helped.
If the counsel be good, no matter who gave it.

Short sede, good rede.
We may give Advice, but we cannot give conduct.
In the multitude of counsellors there is safety. *(Proverbs)*
When error is committed, good advice comes too late. *(Chinese)*
Advice after mischief is like medicine after death. *(Danish)*
A good advice is as good as an eye in the hand. *(French)*
Advisers are not payers. *(French)*
He asks advice in vain who will not follow it. *(French)*
Nothing is given so freely as advice. *(French)*
Less advice and more hands. *(German)*
One can advise comfortably from a safe port. *(Schiller)*
In giving advice, seek to help, not to please, your friend. *(Solon)*
He who counsels aids. *(Plautus)*
It is bad advice that cannot be altered. *(Latin)*
Nobody can give you wiser advice than yourself. *(Cicero)*
Whatever advice you give, be brief. *(Horace)*
When we are well, it is easy to give good advice to the sick. *(Terence)*
Worthless is the advice of fools. *(Latin)*
Advice whispered is not worth a pea. *(Spanish)*
Hazard not your wealth on a poor man's advice. *(Spanish)*
When the rabbit has escaped comes advice. *(Spanish)*
Ask advice, but use your own common sense. *(Yiddish)*

AFFECTION
Affection is a coal that must be cool'd;
  Else, suffer'd, it will set the heart on fire. *(Shakespeare)*
As the rolling stone gathers no moss, so the roving heart gathers no affection. *(Jameson)*
Talk not of wasted affection, affection never was wasted. *(Longfellow)*
When affection only speaks,
  Truth is not always there. *(Middleton)*
Affection bends the judgment to her ply. *(Dante, trans. Cary)*

AFFLICTION
Affliction, like the iron-smith, shapes as it smites.
To bear other people's afflictions, everyone has courage and enough to spare. *(Franklin)*
The afflicted person is sacred. *(Ovid)*

AFRICA
Africa always brings something new. *(Aristotle)*

AGE

A head that's white
  To maids brings no delight.
Age and wedlock tame man and beast.
Age is like love, it cannot be hid. *(Dekker)*
A young man will be wiser by and by;
  An old man's wit may wander ere he die. *(Tennyson)*
Age is rarely despised but when it is contemptible. *(Johnson)*
Age should think, and youth should do.
Age will not be defied. *(Bacon)*
All would live long, but none would be old. *(Franklin)*
An old man is a bed full of bones.
Crabbèd age and youth cannot live together. *(Shakespeare)*
He that would be old long must be old betimes.
It is hard to put old heads on young shoulders.
Many foxes grow gray, but few grow old. *(Franklin)*
No wise man ever wished to be younger. *(Swift)*
Of young men die many; of old escapes not any.
Old age makes us wiser and more foolish.
Old be, or young die.
Old men for counsel, young men for war.
The autumn of the beautiful is beautiful. *(Bacon)*
The more thy years, the nearer thy grave.
They who would be young when they are old, must be old when they are young.
We do not count a man's years, until he has nothing else to count. *(Emerson)*
Some fall into their "anecdotage." *(Disraeli)*
When age is jocund it makes sport for death.
When old age is evil, youth can learn no good.
When the age is in, the wit is out. *(Shakespeare)*
Women and music should never be dated. *(Goldsmith)*
Youth is a blunder; manhood a struggle; old age a regret. *(Disraeli)*
The beauty of old men is the gray head. *(Proverbs)*
With the ancient is wisdom; and in length of years understanding. *(Job)*
Your old men shall dream dreams, your young men shall see visions. *(Joel)*
When old men are not upright, they teach their sons to be rogues. *(Chinese)*
Age is a sorry travelling companion. *(Danish)*

Age makes many a man white but not better. *(Danish)*
A man is as old as his arteries. *(French)*
Few people know how to be old. *(La Rochefoucauld)*
If youth but knew; if old age could! *(Etienne)*
Old age is a tyrant who forbids, upon pain of death, all pleasures of youth. *(La Rochefoucauld)*
Old age plants more wrinkles in the mind than in the face. *(Montaigne)*
One is as old as one's heart. *(d'Houdetot)*
The hell of women is old age. *(La Rochefoucauld)*
The oldest man that ever lived died at last. *(Gaelic)*
Old age comes uncalled. *(German)*
Old people see best in the distance. *(German)*
The old forget, the young don't know. *(German)*
The old man who dances furnishes the devil fine sport. *(German)*
Age is more just than youth. *(Aeschylus)*
It is always in season for the old to learn. *(Aeschylus)*
Nobody loves life like an old man. *(Sophocles)*
Old age and the wear of time teach many things. *(Sophocles)*
Old age is the harbor of all ills. *(Bion)*
Old men are twice children. *(Greek)*
The old age of an eagle is better than the youth of a sparrow. *(Greek)*
What else is an old man but voice and shadow? *(Euripides)*
Youth is a garland of roses, age is a crown of thorns. *(Hebrew)*
Age steals away all things, even the mind. *(Vergil)*
An angelic boyhood becomes a satanic old age. *(Erasmus)*
How rare to find old age and happiness in one! *(Seneca)*
Life is most delightful when it is on the downward slope. *(Seneca)*
No one is so old as to think he cannot live one more year. *(Cicero)*
Old age has disgraces of its own; do not add to them the shame of vice. *(Cato)*
Old age is itself a disease. *(Terence)*
Old age, more to be feared than death. *(Juvenal)*
Who steals an old man's supper, does him no harm. *(Spanish)*
When an old man cannot drink, prepare his grave. *(Spanish)*

AGE, THE GOLDEN

The golden age never was the present age. *(Franklin)*
We must not look for a golden age in an iron age.
The age of gold was the age when gold did not rule. *(Lézay-Marnésia)*

AGREEMENT

An ill agreement is better than a good judgment.
Fools bite one another, but wise men agree together.
Good wits jump.

AGUE

An ague in the spring is physic for a king.

ALE

Ale sellers should not be tale-tellers.
As he brews so shall he drink. *(Jonson)*
Everyone has a penny to spend at a new ale-house.
Good ale is meat, drink, and cloth.
Good ale will make a cat speak.
He that buys good ale buys nothing else.
When the ale is in, the wit is out.

ALMOST

"Almost" was never hanged.
"Almost" never killed a fly. *(German)*

ALMS

Alms are the golden key that opens the gates of Heaven.
The little alms are the good alms. *(French)*
Better give nothing than stolen alms. *(German)*
Alms are the salt of riches. *(Hebrew)*
Alms never make poor. *(Italian)*

ALONE

A man alone is either a saint or a devil. *(Burton)*
Better be alone than in bad company.
A wise man is never less alone than when alone. *(Latin)*
It is not good to be alone even in Paradise. *(Yiddish)*

AMBITION

Ambition is no cure for love. *(Scott)*
Ambition is the growth of every clime. *(Blake)*
Ambition is the mind's immodesty. *(D'Avenant)*
Ambition is the only power that combats love. *(Cibber)*
Ambition obeys no law but its own appetite.
Ambition often spends foolishly what Avarice had wickedly collected.

Black ambition stains a public cause. *(Pope)*

He will shoot higher who shoots at the sun than he who aims at a tree. *(Sidney)*

. . . fling away ambition:
By that sin fell the angels. *(Shakespeare)*

Hew not too high lest the chips fall in thine eye.

Low ambition and the thirst of praise. *(Cowper)*

Men do not heed the rungs by which they climb. *(Masefield)*

Men would be Angels, Angels would be Gods. *(Pope)*

Nothing humbler than Ambition, when it is about to climb. *(Franklin)*

The trap to the high-born is ambition.

Vaulting ambition . . . o'erleaps itself. *(Shakespeare)*

Virtue is chok'd with foul ambition. *(Shakespeare)*

Would you rise in the world, veil ambition with the forms of humanity. *(Chinese)*

The wise man is cured of ambition by ambition. *(La Bruyère)*

There is no eel so small but it hopes to become a whale. *(German)*

Ambition destroys its possessor. *(Hebrew)*

I would rather be the first man here than the second at Rome. *(Caesar)*

AMERICA

America first.

America means opportunity, freedom, power. *(Emerson)*

Don't give up the ship. *(Capt. Lawrence, 1813)*

E Pluribus Unum. [*Motto*]

Equal rights for all, special privileges for none. *(Jefferson)*

Good Americans, when they die, go to Paris. *(Appleton)*

I only regret that I have but one life to lose for my country. *(Nathan Hale)*

If anyone attempts to haul down the American flag, shoot him on the spot. *(Dix)*

Millions for defense, but not one cent for tribute. *(Pinckney)*

. . . our country, right or wrong. *(Decatur)*

The hope of all who suffer,
The dread of all who wrong. *(Whittier)*

Wake up, America. *(Gardner, 1916)*

AMUSEMENT

Amusement is the happiness of those who cannot think. *(Pope)*

We are not amused. *(Queen Victoria)*

ANCESTRY

All blood is alike ancient.
He's a chip o' the old block.
High buildings have a low foundation.
I don't know who my grandfather was; I am much more concerned to know who his grandson will be. *(Abr. Lincoln)*
There's nobbut three generations atween clog and clog. *(Lancashire prov.)*

When Adam dolve and Eve span
 Who was then the gentleman? *(John Ball)*
. . . where the bull and cow are both milk-white,
 They never do beget a coal-black calf. *(Shakespeare)*
He who serves well of his country has no need of ancestors. *(Voltaire)*
I am my own ancestor. *(Marshal Junot)*
Every king springs from a race of slaves, and every slave has had kings among his ancestors. *(Plato)*
Ancestral glory is, as it were, a lamp to posterity. *(Sallust)*
The brave are born from the brave and good. *(Horace)*
He is well-born who is by nature well fitted for virtue. *(Seneca)*

ANGEL

Be not forgetful to entertain strangers: for thereby some have entertained angels unawares. *(New Test., Hebr.)*
A ministering angel shall my sister be. *(Shakespeare)*
Angels are bright still, though the brightest fell. *(Shakespeare)*
We are ne'er like angels till our passion dies. *(Dekker)*

ANGER

A soft answer turneth away wrath: but grievous words stir up anger. *(Old Test., Prov.)*

An angry man stirreth up strife. *(Old Test., Prov.)*
Anger resteth in the bosom of fools. *(Old Test., Prov.)*
He that is slow to wrath is of great understanding. *(Old Test., Prov.)*
Let not the sun go down upon your wrath. *(New Test., Ephesians)*
Anger is as useless as the waves of the ocean without wind. *(Chinese)*
A man in a passion rides a mad horse.
Anger edgeth valor.
Anger and haste hinder good counsel.
Anger is never without a Reason, but seldom with a good One. *(Franklin)*

Anger makes dull men witty but it keeps them poor. *(Bacon)*

Anger punishes itself.
Anger warms the Invention, but overheats the Oven. *(Franklin)*
Angry men seldom want woe.
Beware the fury of a patient man. *(Dryden)*
Come not between the dragon and his wrath. *(Shakespeare)*
Dread the anger of the dove.
Let anger's fire be slow to burn.
Short folk are soon angry.
The dog bites the stone, not him that throws it.
The flame of anger, bright and brief,
  Sharpens the barb of love. *(Landor)*
When a man grows angry, his reason rides out.
When anger blinds the eye, truth disappears.
When angry, count a hundred.
When angry, count four; when very angry, swear. *(Mark Twain)*
Anger is a bad counsellor. *(French)*
Anger without power is folly. *(German)*
Master anger. *(Periander)*
The pain of anger punishes the fault. *(Homer)*
Anger renders the man insane and the prophet dumb. *(Hebrew)*
Anger is a short madness. *(Horace)*
Anger manages everything badly. *(Statius)*
Even a fly has anger. *(Latin)*
Fury and anger carry the mind away. *(Vergil)*
However weak the hand, anger gives it strength. *(Ovid)*
It is hidden wrath that harms. *(Seneca)*
Like fragile ice anger in time passes away. *(Ovid)*
The greatest remedy for anger is delay. *(Seneca)*
Anger is a fool. *(Yiddish)*

ANSWER

A soft answer turneth away wrath. *(Old Test., Prov.)*
No answer is also an answer. *(Danish)*
Who answers suddenly knows little.
Not all words require an answer. *(Italian)*

ANT

None preaches better than the ant, and she says nothing. *(Franklin)*
What would the ant do if it had the head of a bull? *(German)*
The ant has wings to its hurt. *(Spanish)*

ANTIQUITY

Remove not the ancient landmark. *(Old Test., Prov.)*
Antiquity is not always a mark of verity.
To look back to antiquity is one thing; to go back to it another. *(C. C. Colton)*

Veneration of antiquity is congenial to the human mind. *(Burke)*
Antiquity surrenders, defeated by new things. *(Lucretius)*
We praise the past, but use our present years. *(Ovid)*

ANVIL

The anvil fears no blows.
When you are an anvil, hold you still;
  When you are a hammer, strike your fill.
It is better to be the hammer than the anvil. *(French)*
Thou must . . . be either hammer or anvil. *(Goethe)*
A good anvil does not fear the hammer. *(Italian)*
The anvil lasts longer than the hammer. *(Italian)*

APE

An ape is an ape, a varlet's a varlet though he be clad in silk and scarlet.
An old ape has an old eye.
Apes are never more beasts than when they wear men's clothes.
Every monkey will have his gambols.
The higher the ape goes, the more he shows his tail.
Though he endeavor all he can,
  The ape will never be a man. *(G. Wither)*
. . . Women, dying maids, lead apes in hell.
The old monkey gets the apple. *(French)*
An ape will be an ape though clad in purple. *(Latin)*

APPEARANCE

Judge not according to the appearance. *(New Test., John)*
A grave and majestic outside is the palace of the soul. *(Chinese)*
A beautiful face is a silent commendation. *(Bacon)*
All things are less dreadful than they seem.
Always scorn appearances and you always may. *(Emerson)*
An honest good look covereth many faults.
Habit maketh no monk, ne wearing of gilt spurs maketh no knight. *(Chaucer)*

Mellow nuts have hardest rind.

Men are valued not for what they are, but for what they seem to be. *(Bulwer-Lytton)*
Never judge from appearances.
O what a goodly outside falsehood hath! *(Shakespeare)*
One must not hang a man by his looks.
They take chalk for cheese.
Appearances are very deceitful. *(French)*
Don't judge a tree by its bark. *(French)*
Dirt glitters as long as the sun shines. *(Goethe)*
Look to the mind, not to the outward appearance. *(Aesop)*
Even virtue is fairer in a fair body. *(Vergil)*
Seem not greater than thou art. *(Latin)*
Things are not always what they seem. *(Phaedrus)*
We are deceived by the appearance of right. *(Horace)*
All that glitters is not gold. *(Cervantes)*

APPETITE

Appetite don't regulate de time o' day. *(American Negro)*
Put a knife to thy throat, if thou be a man given to appetite. *(Old Test., Prov.)*
He who cheats his appetite avoids debt. *(Chinese)*
A good appetite is the best sauce.
A mortified appetite is never a wise companion.
All things require skill but an appetite.
God sendeth and giveth both mouth and meat.
New dishes beget new appetites.
Poor men want meat for their stomachs, rich men stomachs for their meat.
What one relishes, nourishes.
Where reason rules, appetite obeys.
Appetite comes with eating. *(French)*
A stomach that is seldom empty despises common food. *(Horace)*
It is the sign of an over-nice appetite to toy with many dishes. *(Seneca)*
Let the appetites be subject to reason. *(Cicero)*
Seek an appetite by hard toil. *(Horace)*
The full stomach turns from the honey of Hybla. *(Petronius)*
There's no stomach a hand's breadth bigger than another. *(Cervantes)*
One always has a good appetite at another's feast. *(Yiddish)*

APPLAUSE

Applause: the echo of a platitude. *(Bierce)*
Applause is the spur of noble minds, the end and aim of weak ones.

The applause of the crowd makes the head giddy . . . *(Steele)*
The applause of the people is a blast of air.
Applause is the root of abuse. *(Japanese)*
. . . no man will disown the wish to earn the applause of men. *(Persius)*

APPLE
A goodly apple rotten at the heart. *(Shakespeare)*
All the evil in the world was brought in by means of an apple.
An apple a day keeps the doctor away.
An apple may happen to be better given than eaten.
He pares his apple that will cleanly feed.
She is lost with an apple, and won with a nut.
The apples on the other side of the wall are the sweetest.
The apple falls not far from the tree. *(Yiddish)*
The best apple is taken by the pig. *(Yiddish)*
What's the good of a fair apple, if it has a worm in its heart? *(Yiddish)*

APPROPRIATENESS
Being on sea, sail; being on land, settle.

APRIL
April showers bring May flowers.
April weather, rain and sunshine both together.
When April blows his horn, 'tis good for hay and corn.
When beans are in flower, fools are in power.

ARCADIA
I too was born in Arcadia. *(Latin)*

ARCHER
A good archer is not known by his arrow but by his aim.
The archer that shoots badly has a lie ready. *(Spanish)*

ARCHITECTURE
Houses are built to live in, and not to look on . . . *(Bacon)*
When we build, let us think that we build forever. *(Ruskin)*
Every man is the architect of his own fortune. *(French)*
Architecture is frozen music. *(Goethe)*
To build many houses is the readiest road to poverty. *(Greek)*

ARGUMENT

A contentious man will never lack words.
A knock-down argument; 'tis but a word and a blow. *(Dryden)*
A noisy man is always in the right.
Debate destroys dispatch. *(Denham)*
I am not arguing with you—I am telling you. *(Whistler)*
It were endless to dispute upon everything that is disputable.
Men may be convinced, but they cannot be pleased, against their will. *(Johnson)*
Treating your adversary with respect is giving him an advantage to which he is not entitled. *(Johnson)*
You have not converted a man because you have silenced him.
The arguments of the strongest have always the most weight. *(French)*
There are two sides to every question. *(Greek)*
Do not investigate facts by the light of arguments, but arguments by the light of facts. *(Greek)*
In a heated argument we are apt to lose sight of the truth. *(Latin)*

ARM

Stretch your arm no farther than your sleeve. *(French)*

ARMS

Arms carry peace. *(Italian)*
Let arms give place to the gown. *(Cicero)*
Arms and money require good hands. *(Spanish)*

ARMY

Terrible as an army with banners. *(Old Test., Song of Songs)*
An army, like a serpent, goes on its belly. *(Napoleon)*
Two armies are two bodies which meet and try to frighten each other. *(Napoleon)*

ARROGANCE

Supple knees feed arrogance.

ARROW

Two arrows in the quiver are better than one, and three are better still.
Not every sort of wood is fit to make an arrow. *(French)*
One arrow does not bring down two birds. *(Turkish)*

ART

Art hath an enemy called ignorance. *(Jonson)*
Art is long, life short, experience deceiving. *(Brathwaite)*

Art is not a thing: it is a way.
Art is power.
Art is the path of the creator to his work. *(Emerson)*
Art may err, but nature cannot miss. *(Dryden)*
Art never expresses anything but itself. *(Wilde)*
Art strives for form, and hopes for beauty. *(Bellows)*
As the sun colors flowers so does art color life. *(Lubbock)*
Great art is an instant arrested in eternity. *(Huneker)*
New arts destroy the old. *(Emerson)*
All the arts are brothers; each one is a light to the others. *(Voltaire)*
Art for art's sake. *(Coussin)*
Art is either a plagiarist or a revolutionist. *(Gauguin)*
Art holds fast when all else is gone. *(German)*
Art is far feebler than necessity. *(Aeschylus)*
Art is long, life is short. *(Hippocrates)*
Let each man exercise the art he knows. *(Aristophanes)*
Art is a shadow of Divine perfection. *(Michelangelo)*
It is a poor art that does not maintain the artisan. *(Italian)*
Nature is the art of God. *(Dante)*
All art is but imitation of nature. *(Seneca)*
Art counterfeits chance. *(Ovid)*
The perfection of art is to conceal art. *(Quintillian)*
That which takes effect by chance is not an art. *(Seneca)*
To whiten ivory by ink is to spoil nature by art. *(Latin)*

ARTIST
A great artist can paint a great picture on a small canvas.
A man may be an artist though he have not his tools about him.
An artist is a dreamer consenting to dream of the actual world. *(Santayana)*
Artists, like the Greek gods, are only revealed to one another. *(Wilde)*
Every artist was first an amateur. *(Emerson)*
Every artist writes his own autobiography. *(H. Ellis)*
Nothing can come out of the artist that is not in the man.
Scratch an artist and you surprise a child. *(Huneker)*
The artist needs no religion beyond his work. *(Hubbard)*
The poison of the honey-bee
 Is the artist's jealousy. *(Blake)*
The great artist is the simplifier. *(Amiel)*
Good material often stands idle for want of an artist. *(Seneca)*

ASHES

Under white ashes are often glowing embers. *(Italian)*

ASK

Ask much to have a little.
Lose nothing for asking.
He who is afraid of asking is ashamed of learning. *(Danish)*
Do not ask a blind man which is the right way. *(German)*
Asking costs little. *(Italian)*
Never ask of him who has, but of him who wishes you well. *(Spanish)*
Better ask ten times than go astray once. *(Yiddish)*

ASPIRATION

He shoots higher, that threatens the moon, than he that aims at a tree. *(Herbert)*
He that stays in the valley shall never get over the hill.
Heaven is not reached at a single bound.
Hitch your wagon to a star. *(Emerson)*
No bird soars too high if he soars with his own wings. *(Blake)*
The desire of the moth for the star . . . *(Shelley)*
'Tis not what man Does which exalts him, but what man Would do. *(Browning)*
Too low they build, who build beneath the stars. *(Young)*
Who digs hills because they do aspire,
  Throws down one mountain to cast up a higher. *(Shakespeare)*
Man is complete and upstanding only when he would be more than man. *(Unamuno)*

ASS

A dull ass near home needs no spur.
A thistle is a fat salad for an ass's mouth.
An ass is beautiful to an ass, and a pig to a pig.
An ass is but an ass, though laden with gold.
An ass loaded with gold climbs to the top of a castle.
An ass often carries gold on his back, yet feeds on thistles.
Asses die and wolves bury them.
Better strive with an ill ass than carry the wood one's self.
Every ass loves to hear himself bray.
Every ass thinks himself worthy to stand with the King's horses.
Give an ass oats and he runs after thistles.
He that makes himself an ass, must not take it ill if men ride him.
I had rather ride an ass that carries me than a horse that throws me.
Never went out ass, and came home horse.

The ass loaded with gold still eats thistles.
The ass that brays most eats least.
The ass that carrieth wine drinketh water.
The ass thinks one thing, and he that rides him another.
The braying of an ass does not reach heaven.
What good can it do an ass to be called a lion?
When all tell thee thou art an ass, 'tis time for thee to bray.
For a stubborn ass a sharp goad. *(French)*
Ail asses do not go on four feet. *(German)*
Make yourself an ass and everyone will lay a sack on you. *(German)*
One ass names another "Longears." *German)*
The ass and his driver do not think alike. *(German)*
The ass of a King is still but an ass. *(German)*
An ass laden with gold can enter the gates of any city. *(Greek)*
If one, two or three tell you you are an ass, put on a bridle. *(Hebrew)*
A braying ass eats little hay. *(Italian)*
A living ass is better than a dead doctor. *(Italian)*
Who washes an ass's head loses both labor and soap. *(Italian)*
A man who cannot beat his ass beats the saddle. *(Latin)*
An ass to an ass is a beauty. *(Latin)*
Hay is more acceptable to an ass than gold. *(Latin)*
Lay the burden on the slow-paced ass. *(Latin)*
The ass is known by his ears. *(Latin)*
What has an ass to do with a lyre? *(Lucian)*
When the ass bears too light a load, he wants to lie down. *(Russian)*
An ass endures his burden, but not more than his burden. *(Spanish)*
Honey is not for the ass's mouth. *(Cervantes)*
Other folks' burdens kill the ass. *(Cervantes)*
The ass knows well in whose face he brays. *(Spanish)*
The ass of many owners is eaten by wolves. *(Spanish)*

ATHEISM
The fool hath said in his heart, There is no God. *(Old Test., Psalms)*
Atheism is rather in the lip than in the heart of man. *(Bacon)*
By night an atheist half-believes in God. *(Young)*
Some are atheists only in fair weather.
The devil divides the world between atheism and superstition. *(Herbert)*
The infidels of one age have been the aureoled saints of the next. *(Ingersoll)*
A man cannot become an atheist merely by wishing it. *(Napoleon)*
Atheism is the last word of theism. *(Heine)*

AUCTION

At an auction keep your mouth shut. *(Spanish)*

AUDIENCE

Fit audience find, though few. *(Milton)*

AUGUST

Dry August and warm
  Doth harvest no harm.

AUTHORITY

Authority forgets a dying King. *(Tennyson)*

Though authority be a stubborn bear, yet he is oft led by the nose with gold. *(Shakespeare)*

AUTUMN

The melancholy days are come, the saddest of the year. *(Bryant)*

Dread autumn, harvest season of the Goddess of Death. *(Horace)*

AVARICE

A covetous man does nothing well till he dies.

Avarice and happiness never saw each other.

Avarice is the root of all evil.

Avarice is the vice of declining years.

Avarice, the spur of industry. *(Hume)*

Covetousness breaks the sack.

Excess of wealth is cause of covetousness.

He'd drive a louse a mile for the skin and tallow of 'en.

He would skin a flint.

It is not want but abundance that makes avarice.

Money lies nearest them that are nearest their graves. *(Wm. Penn)*

The devil lies brooding in the miser's chest.

There's no getting blood out of a turnip.

The more a man has, the more he desires. *(Italian)*

He who covets is always poor. *(Latin)*

Poverty is in want of much, avarice of everything. *(Latin)*

The love of pelf increases with the pelf. *(Juvenal)*

The miser . . . fears to use his gains. *(Horace)*

The miser is as much in want of what he has as of what he has not. *(Latin)*

To greed, all nature is insufficient. *(Seneca)*

AWARD

A lean Award is better than a fat Judgment.

B

BABY
Out of the mouth of babes and sucklings hast thou ordained strength. *(Old Test., Psalms)*
Every baby born into the world is a finer one than the last.
When God sends babies he sends penny loaves.
A baby is an angel whose wings decrease as his legs increase. ***(French)***

BACCHUS
Bacchus hath drowned more than Neptune.
If you make Bacchus your god, Apollo will not keep you company.
When Bacchus pokes the fire, Venus sits by the oven. ***(German)***

BACHELOR
An old bachelor is only the half of a pair of scissors.
Bachelors' fare: bread and cheese, and kisses. ***(Swift)***
Bachelors' wives and maids' children are well taught.
Praise a wife, but remain a bachelor. ***(Italian)***

BAD
Bad men leave their mark wherever they go. ***(Chinese)***
Putrid flesh is all of a flavor. ***(Chinese)***
A bad tree does not yield good apples. ***(Danish)***
Nothing so bad but it might have been worse.
Into the mouth of a bad dog often falls a good bone. ***(French)***
What is bad for one is good for another. ***(French)***
A bad reaper never gets a good sickle. ***(Gaelic)***
There is nothing so bad but may be of some use. ***(German)***
Bad is the wool that cannot be dyed. ***(Italian)***
Bad mind, bad heart. ***(Terence)***

BAIT
The bait hides the hook.

BAKER
Be not a baker if your head be of butter. *(Spanish)*

BALD
A bald head is soon shaven.
Hair and hair makes the carle's head bare.

BARBER
The barber learns to shave on the orphan's face. *(Arabian)*
A barber learns to shave by shaving fools.
. . . a barber's chair . . . fits all buttocks. *(Shakespeare)*
One barber shaves not so close but another finds work.
He is a poor barber that has but one comb. *(Italian)*
The bad barber leaves neither hair nor skin. *(Spanish)*

BARGAIN
One word will not settle a bargain. *(Chinese)*
A bargain's a bargain.
A good bargain is a pick-purse.
The rule for a bargain: "Do other men, for they would do you."
It takes two to make a bargain.
Make every bargain clear and plain,
  That none may afterwards complain.
Make the best of a bad bargain.
The second word makes the bargain.
The timely buyer hath cheaper his fire.
No one will get a bargain he does not ask for. *(French)*
It is an ill bargain where no man wins. *(Latin)*
Without drink bargains can't be hastened. *(Latin)*
A bargain is always dear. *(Yiddish)*

BARK
Barking dogs seldom bite.
His bark is worse than his bite.

BASHFUL
Bashfulness is of no use to the needy. *(Dutch)*
It is only the bashful that lose. *(French)*
Bashfulness is an enemy to poverty. *(Latin)*
If you are bashful, you'll have no children. *(Yiddish)*

BASTARD
When a mother calls her child "bastard!"—you may believe her. *(Yiddish)*

BEANS

Be it weal or be it woe,
  Beans blow before May doth go.

BEAR

As savage as a bear with a sore head.
He must have iron nails that scratcheth with a bear.
One thing thinketh the bear, but another thinketh his leader. *(Chaucer)*
The bear wants a tail and cannot be a lion.
Tho' the bear be gentle, don't bite him by the nose.
An old bear is slow in learning to dance. *(German)*
Make sure of the bear before you sell his skin. *(Aesop)*

BEARD

If the beard were all, a goat might preach. *(Danish)*
The beard creates lice, not brains. *(Gr. Anth.)*
It is not the beard that makes the philosopher. *(Italian)*

BEAST

A righteous man regardeth the life of his beast. *(Old Test., Prov.)*
Nature teaches beasts to know their friends. *(Shakespeare)*
The beast dead, the venom dead. *(French)*
Who goes a beast to Rome, a beast returns. *(Italian)*
There is no beast so savage but it sports with its mate. *(Spanish)*

BEATING

A stick is soon found to beat a dog.
If you beat spice it will smell the sweeter.
A woman, an ass, and a walnut tree
  Bring the more fruit, the more beaten they be.

BEAUTY

As a jewel of gold in a swine's snout, so is a fair woman which is without discretion. *(Old Test., Prov.)*
Beauty is a fading flower. *(Old Test., Prov.)*
Favor is deceitful, and beauty is vain. *(Old Test., Prov.)*
He hath made every thing beautiful in his time. *(Old Test., Eccles.)*
Everything has its beauty but not everyone sees it. *(Confucius)*
A good face needs no band and a pretty wench no land.
A poor beauty finds more lovers than husbands.
A thing of beauty is a joy forever. *(Keats)*

All heiresses are beautiful.
All orators are dumb, when beauty pleadeth. *(Shakespeare)*
Beauté sans bonté, blessed were never. *(Langland)*
Beauty and folly are old companions.
Beauty and honesty seldom agree.
Beauty blemished once forever's lost. *(Shakespeare)*
Beauty buys no beef.
Beauty carries its dower in its face.
Beauty draws more than oxen.
Beauty draws us with a single hair. *(Pope)*
Beauty has no inheritance.
Beauty has wings, and too hastily flies.
Beauty in distress is much the most affecting beauty. *(Burke)*
Beauty is but a blossom.
Beauty is but skin deep.
Beauty is in the eye of the beholder.
Beauty is its own excuse for being. *(Emerson)*
Beauty is not caused,
It is. *(E. Dickinson)*
Beauty is Nature's coin, must not be hoarded. *(Milton)*
Beauty is potent, but money is omnipotent.
Beauty is the child of love.
Beauty is the flower of virtue.
Beauty is truth, truth beauty. *(Keats)*
Beauty provoketh thieves sooner than gold. *(Shakespeare)*
Beauty without bounty avails not.
Good looks buy nothing in the market.
She that is fair hath half her portion.
There is no excellent beauty that hath not some strangeness in the proportion. *(Bacon)*
Where beauty is, there will be love.
Beauty without virtue is a flower without perfume *(French)*
Here below, the beautiful is the useful. *(French)*
We seize the beautiful and reject the useful. *(La Fontaine)*
Beauty is as good as ready money. *(German)*
Beauty opens locked doors. *(German)*
Every woman would rather be beautiful than good. *(German)*
Beauty is a natural superiority. *(Plato)*
Beauty is a short-lived reign. *(Socrates)*
Beauty is an evil in an ivory setting. *(Theocritus)*
Beauty is another's good. *(Bion)*

Beauty is the flower of chastity. *(Zeno)*
Beauty is the gift of God. *(Aristotle)*
What is beautiful is good, and who is good will soon also be beautiful. *(Sappho)*
When the candles are out all women are fair. *(Plutarch)*
Beauty is the purgation of superfluities. *(Michelangelo)*
She who is born a beauty is born betrothed. *(Italian)*
Beautiful enough if good enough. *(Latin)*
Beauty and wisdom are rarely conjoined. *(Petronius)*
Dear to the heart of girls is their own beauty. *(Ovid)*
Rare is the union of beauty and modesty. *(Juvenal)*
We cannot divide beauty into dollars. *(Polish)*
A strange illusion to suppose that beauty is goodness. *(Tolstoy)*

BED
As you make your bed, so you must lie on it.
Early to bed and early to rise,
  Makes a man healthy, wealthy and wise.
Bed is a medicine. *(Italian)*

BEE
A dead bee makes no honey.
Bees that have honey in their mouths have stings in their tails.
Every bee's honey is sweet.
Honey is sweet, but the bee stings.
One bee makes no swarm.
Where bees are, there will be honey.
From the same flower the bee extracts honey and the wasp gall. *(Italian)*

BEER see *ALE*

BEG
Better it is to die than to beg. *(Apocrypha)*
Beg from beggars and you'll never be rich.
Who is not ashamed to beg soon is not ashamed to steal. *(German)*
That costs dear which is bought with begging. *(Italian)*
He that asks faintly begs a denial. *(Latin)*
Better to beg than steal, but better to work than beg. *(Russian)*

BEGGAR
A beggar pays a benefit with a louse.
A beggar's scrip is never filled.

A lordly taste makes a beggar's purse.
A shameless beggar must have a short denial.
Beggars breed and rich men feed.
Beggars mounted run their horse to death. *(Shakespeare)*
Beggars should be no choosers.
Better to die a beggar than live a beggar.
If wishes were horses, beggars would ride.
One beggar is woe that another by the door should go.
Set a beggar on horseback and he will ride a gallop.
When it rains porridge the beggar has no spoon. *(Danish)*
A beggar's estate lies in all lands. *(Dutch)*
Better a living beggar than a dead emperor. *(French)*
Beggar is jealous of beggar. *(Greek)*
The beggar's wallet has no bottom. *(Italian)*
The beggar may sing before the thief. *(Juvenal)*
God rejoices when one beggar scratches another. *(Yiddish)*

BEGIN

Better is the end of a thing than the beginning thereof.
(Old Test., Eccles.)
Everything is difficult at first. *(Chinese)*
All glory comes from daring to begin.
Better never begin than never make an end.
Each goodly thing is hardest to begin. *(Spenser)*
Everything must have a beginning.
Good beginning maketh good ending.
Good to begin well, better to end well.
He who begins many things, finishes but few.
Such beginning, such end.
The beginning is the hardest.
The first step is as good as half over.
The hardest step is that over the threshold.
Things bad begun make strong themselves by ill. *(Shakespeare)*
What begins with tow won't end with silk.
It is only the first step that counts. *(French)*
Things are always at best in their beginning. *(Pascal)*
The beginning of the dollar is the bank shilling. *(German)*
A bad beginning makes a bad ending. *(Greek)*
Beware beginnings. *(Greek)*
The beginning is half the whole. *(Greek)*
For a web begun God sends thread. *(Italian)*

Well begun is half done. *(Horace)*
Whatever begins, also ends. *(Latin)*
The beginnings of all things are small. *(Cicero)*

BEHAVIOR
Let every man be swift to hear, slow to speak . . . *(New Test., James)*
Neither crow nor croak.
Walk groundly, talk profoundly, drink roundly, sleep soundly.
Nothing is more adroit than irreproachable conduct. *(French)*
Behavior is the mirror in which everyone shows his image. *(Goethe)*
If not seemly, do it not; if not true, say it not. *(Greek)*
Bad conduct soils the finest ornament more than filth. *(Plautus)*
As the occasion, so the behavior. *(Cervantes)*

BEHIND
Look before or you'll find yourself behind.

BELIEF
Blessed are they that have not seen, and yet have believed. *(New Test., John)*
Lord, I believe; help thou mine unbelief. *(New Test., Mark)*
Believe not all that you see nor half what you hear.
Believe well and have well.
Believing where we cannot prove. *(Tennyson)*
Each man's belief is right in his own eyes.
He does not believe that does not live according to his belief.
He that believes all, misseth; he that believes nothing, hits not.
Man prefers to believe what he prefers to be true. *(Bacon)*
Quick believers need broad shoulders.
What a man desires he easily believes.
A belief is not true because it is useful. *(Amiel)*
Nothing is so firmly believed as that which we least know. *(Montaigne)*
Who quick believes late repents. *(German)*
Who knows much believes the less. *(Italian)*
No storm harms a man who believes. *(Ovid)*
I believe because it is impossible. *(Tertullian)*
I will not believe it until I have read it. *(Martial)*
They can conquer who believe they can. *(Vergil)*

BELL
While the great bells are ringing, no one hears the little ones. *(Danish)*
A crackt bell can never sound well.

Bells call others, but themselves enter not the church.
If you love not the noise of bells, why do you pull the ropes?
Who hears but one bell hears one sound. *(French)*

BELLY
Evil beasts, slow bellies. *(New Test., Titus)*
Whose God is their belly. *(New Test., Philippians)*
The belly gives no credit. *(Danish)*
A belly full of gluttony will never study willingly.
A full belly is the mother of all evil.
A full belly makes a dull brain.
A full belly neither fights nor flies well.
An empty belly hears nobody.
Better belly burst than good liquor be lost.
Better fill a man's belly than his eye.
He who does not mind his belly will hardly mind anything else.
The belly hates a long sermon.
The belly is not filled with fair words.
The belly robs the back.
The belly thinks that the throat has been cut.
The eye is bigger than the belly.
When the belly is full, the bones are at rest.
When the belly is full, the mind is amongst the maids.
A full belly counsels well. *(French)*
No clock is more regular than the belly. *(French)*
What avails it to have our bellies full of meat if it be not digested? *(Montaigne)*
The belly is a bad adviser. *(German)*
A gross belly does not produce a refined mind. *(Greek)*
Do not mourn the dead with the belly. *(Homer)*
It is hard to argue with the belly, since it has no ears. *(Cato)*
When pain swells the belly, it matters not what else goes well. *(Persian)*
The belly carries the legs, and not the legs the belly. *(Spanish)*
If the belly is empty, sleep comes not. *(Yiddish)*

BEND
Better bend than break.
Better bend the neck than bruise the forehead.
Best to bend while it is a twig.
Oaks may fall when reeds brave the storm.

BENEFIT

Benefits please, like flowers, when they are fresh.
Benefits turn poison in bad minds.
The last benefit is the most remembered.
When befriended, remember it; when you befriend, forget it. *(Franklin)*
Write injuries in dust, benefits in marble.
He who confers a benefit on anyone loves him better than he is beloved. *(Aristotle)*
Benefits are only agreeable as long as one can repay them. *(Latin)*
Benefits are traced on the sand and injuries are graven on brass. *(Latin)*
To accept a benefit is to sell one's freedom. *(Latin)*
When you confer a benefit on a worthy man you oblige all men. *(Latin)*

BEST

The best manure is under the farmer's foot. *(Danish)*
The best pears fall into the pig's mouth.
The best things in life are free.
The best always goes first. *(Italian)*
The best is cheapest. *(Italian)*
The best cloth has uneven edges. *(Spanish)*

BETRAY

He won't betray in whom none will confide. *(Congreve)*
He who will betray pipes sweet. *(German)*

BETTER

Better a blind horse than an empty halter. *(Danish)*
Better coarse cloth than the naked thighs. *(Danish)*
Better a bare foot than none at all.
Better fifty years of Europe than a cycle of Cathay. *(Tennyson)*
Better half an egg than an empty shell.
Better to say "Here it is" than "There it was."
Better to wear out than to rust out.
The better is the enemy of the good. *(French)*
Better be the head of a cat than the tail of a lion. *(Italian)*
Better a red face than a black heart. *(Portuguese)*

BEWARE

Beware of him whom God hath marked.
Beware of no man more than of thyself.

BIBLE
All is not Gospel that thou dost speak.
Brown bread and the Gospel is good fare.
The music of the Gospel leads us home.
The history of every individual man should be a Bible. *(Novalis)*

BID
Be not too hasty to outbid another.

BIND
Bind so as you may unbind.
Fast bind, fast find.

BIOGRAPHY
Biography is the only true history. *(Carlyle)*
Biography—one of the new terrors of death. *(Arbuthnot)*

BIRD
A bird may be caught by a snare that will not be shot. *(Danish)*
However high a bird may soar, it seeks its food on earth. *(Danish)*
Birds in their little nests agree. *(Watts)*
Birds of a feather flock together.
Each bird loves to hear himself sing.
It is a foul bird that defileth his own nest.
. . . Kill two birds with one stone.
Old birds are not caught with chaff.
The bird that can sing and won't sing must be made to sing.
The early bird catches the worm.
The shell must break before the bird can fly.
To fright a bird is not the way to catch her.
Even when the bird walks one feels that it has wings. *(French)*
Birds of prey do not sing. *(German)*
A bird in the hand is worth two in the bush. *(Greek)*
Such bird, such song. *(Latin)*
Birds of prey do not flock together. *(Portuguese)*
Better a sparrow in the hand than a vulture on the wing. *(Spanish)*
Little bird, little nest. *(Spanish)*
There are no birds this year in last year's nest. *(Spanish)*
A bird is known by his feathers. *(Yiddish)*

BIRTH
No man can help his birth. *(Danish)*
A man is not completely born until he be dead. *(Franklin)*

He was born with a silver spoon in his mouth.
I wept when I was born, and every day shows why.
Our birth made us mortal, our death will make us immortal.
No one is born with an axe in his hand. *(German)*
Blest are those who were never born to see the sun. *(Greek)*
High birth is a poor dish at table. *(Italian)*
He who is born, yells; he who dies is silent. *(Russian)*
Naked was I born, naked I am; I neither lose nor gain. *(Cervantes)*

BIT
Bit by bit the plate is filled. *(Yiddish)*

BITE
The greatest barkers are not the greatest biters.
He who can lick can bite. *(French)*
If you cannot bite never show your teeth. *(French)*
Don't make the bite larger than the mouth. *(German)*
The biter is sometimes bit. *(Italian)*

BLAB
He that is a blab is a scab.

BLACK
A black hen will lay a white egg.
A black plum is as sweet as a white.
As black as a crow.
Black will take no other hue.
Every white will have its black; every sweet its sour.
Two blacks do not make a white.
Above black there is no color; above salt no savor. *(Italian)*
The pot called the kettle black. *(Cervantes)*

BLADE
The blade wears out the sheath.

BLAME
He must be pure who would blame another. *(Danish)*

BLESSING
Blessed is he that cometh in the name of the Lord. *(New Test.)*
Out of the same mouth proceedeth blessing and cursing.
(New Test., James)

A double blessing is a double grace. *(Shakespeare)*

Blessings ever wait on virtuous deeds.
Go in God's name, so ride no witches.
They have need of a blessing that kneel to a thistle.
No human blessing lasts forever. *(Plautus)*
Nothing is blessed in every respect. *(Horace)*

BLIND

Can the blind lead the blind? shall they not both fall into the ditch? *(New Test., Luke)*
The sky is not less blue because the blind man does not see it. *(Danish)*
A blind man will not thank you for a looking-glass.
A pebble and a diamond are alike to a blind man.
Better be blind than to see ill.
Better eyesore than all blind.
Better half blind than have both eyes out.
Better one-eyed than stone blind.
Folk ofttimes are most blind in their own cause.
In the kingdom of the blind men, the one-eyed is king.
None so blind as those who won't see.
The blind eat many a fly.
What matters it to a blind man that his father could see?
A blind man can sometimes find corn. *(French)*
When the blind man carries the banner, woe to those who follow. *(French)*
He is indeed blind who cannot see the sun. *(Italian)*
Blind men should judge no colors. *(Latin)*
The eyes are blind when the mind is elsewhere. *(Latin)*
He is blind enough who sees not through a sieve. *(Cervantes)*
Among the blind close your eyes. *(Turkish)*

BLISS

Bliss is the same in subject or in king. *(Pope)*
The bliss e'en of a moment still is bliss.

BLOCKHEAD

He who deals with a blockhead will have need of much brains. *(Spanish)*

BLOOD

The blood is the life. *(Old Test., Deuter.)*
All blood is alike ancient.
Blood is thicker than water.

Blood will have blood.
Human blood is all of a color.
You come of good blood and so does a black pudding.
Noble and ignoble blood is of the same color. *(German)*
Blood does not wash blood away. *(Russian)*

BLOT
Cleaning a blot with a blotted finger makes a greater blot. *(Chinese)*

BLOW
If you don't succeed with one blow don't hesitate to deliver two.
The first blow makes the wrong, the second makes the fray.
The first blow is as good as two. *(Italian)*
It's easier to get a blow than to give one. *(Yiddish)*

BLOWING
Blow not against the hurricane.
He that blows in the fire will get sparks in his eyes. *(German)*

BLUNDER
It is worse than a crime: it is a blunder . . . *(French)*

BLUSH
Blushes are badges of imperfection. *(Wycherley)*
Blushing is either a sign of guilt or of ill-breeding.
The man that blushes is not quite a brute.
When guilty men begin to blush, it is a sign of grace.
Innocence is not accustomed to blush. *(Molière)*
Men blush less for their crimes than for their weaknesses. *(French)*
Whoso blushes is guilty already. *(French)*
Blushing is the hue of virtue. *(Greek)*
The blush is beautiful, but it is sometimes inconvenient. *(Goldoni)*
He blushes: all is well. *(Latin)*
I would rather see a young man blush than turn pale. *(Cato)*
Rather bring the blood into a man's cheek than let it out of his body. *(Tertullian)*
Better a blush on the cheek than a spot in the heart. *(Spanish)*

BOAST
A vaunter and a liar are near akin.
Empty barrels make the most noise.
Great boast and small roast.
He changes a fly into an elephant.

He that boasts of his own knowledge proclaims his ignorance.
It out-herods Herod. *(Shakespeare)*
Where boasting ends there dignity begins. *(Young)*
Great boasters, little doers. *(French)*
Believe a boaster as you would a liar. *(Italian)*
They can do least who boast loudest. *(Latin)*
It's good to whip a boaster. *(Yiddish)*

BOAT
Little boats must keep the shore, large ships may venture more.
The boat goes but sorrily without oars. *(Italian)*

BODY
Our vile body. *(New Test., Philippians)*
A little body often harbors a great soul.
If anything is sacred, the human body is sacred. *(Whitman)*
Our bodies are our gardens, to which our wills are gardeners. *(Shakespeare)*
The body is an affliction of the soul. *(Greek)*
Death alone discloses how insignificant are the puny bodies of men. *(Latin)*
Who can put trust in strength of body? *(Juvenal)*

BOLDNESS
A bold man never wants a weapon.
As bold as Beauchamp.
As bold as blind Bayard. *(Chaucer)*
Be not too bold with your betters.
Bold knaves thrive, without one grain of sense,
  But good men starve for want of impudence. *(Dryden)*
Boldness is an ill keeper of promise.
Fearless minds climb soonest unto crowns. *(Shakespeare)*
Great boldness is seldom without some absurdity. *(Bacon)*
He most prevails who nobly dares.
It is a bold mouse that breeds in the cat's ear.
Naught venture naught have.
What action is to the orator, that is boldness to the public man. *(Bacon)*
To dare, and again dare, and forever dare! *(Danton)*
Boldness has genius, power, and magic in it. *(Goethe)*
Boldness ever meets with friends. *(Homer)*
Boldness leads a man to heaven and to hell. *(Greek)*

Boldness is a bulwark. *(Latin)*
By boldness great fears are concealed. *(Latin)*
Fortune assists the bold. *(Latin)*
God himself favors the bold. *(Latin)*
No one reaches a high position without boldness. *(Latin)*

BONE

Broken bones well set become stronger.
He that gives thee a bone would not have thee die.
The nearer the bone the sweeter the meat.
What is bred in the bone will out in the flesh.
Bones for those who come late. *(Latin)*

BOOK

Every age hath its book. *(Koran)*
Of making many books there is no end. *(Old Test., Eccles.)*
Something is learned every time a book is opened. *(Chinese)*
A book may be as great a thing as a battle. *(Disraeli)*
A book that is shut is but a block.
A good book is the precious life-blood of a master spirit . . . *(Milton)*
A wicked book is the wickeder because it cannot repent.
Books are a guide in youth and an entertainment for age.
Books are a triviality. Life alone is great. *(Carlyle)*
Books are ships which pass through the vast seas of time. *(Bacon)*
Books are the blessed chloroform of the mind.
Books cannot always please, however good,
  Minds are not ever craving for their food. *(Crabbe)*
Books give not wisdom where was none before . . .
Books are . . . for wisdom, piety, delight, or use. *(Denham)*
Books teach us very little of the world. *(Goldsmith)*
Books, the children of the brain.
Have thy study full of books, than thy purse full of money.
Judge not a book by its cover.
My Book and Heart
  Shall never part. *(New Eng. Primer)*
No furniture so charming as books.
Nothing so old as a new book.
Some books are lies frae end to end. *(Burns)*
That is a good book which is opened with expectation and closed
    with profit. *(A. B. Alcott)*
The best companions are the best books.

The books which help you most are those which make you think the most. *(Parker)*
Books . . . the monument of vanished minds.
The virtue of books is to be readable. *(Emerson)*
There is no frigate like a book
To take us lands away . . . *(E. Dickinson)*
We cannot learn men from books.
We profit little from books we do not enjoy.
Wear the old coat and buy the new book.
When the mind wakes, books are set aside as impertinent. *(Emerson)*
Who, without books, essays to learn,
Draws water in a leaky urn. *(Dobson)*
A book is never a masterpiece; it becomes one. *(Goncourt)*
All the world may know me by my book, and my book by me. *(French)*
The multitude of books is making us ignorant. *(Montaigne)*
Word by word the great books are written. *(Voltaire)*
A big book is a great evil. *(Greek)*
There is no worse robber than a bad book. *(Italian)*
A room without books is a body without a soul. *(Latin)*
Beware of the man of one book. *(Latin)*
I can study my books at any time, for they are always disengaged. *(Cicero)*
No book is so bad but some profit may be gleaned from it. *(Latin)*
The reader's fancy makes the fate of books. *(Pliny the Elder)*
Books and friends should be few and good. *(Spanish)*

BOOR
A boor remains a boor though he sleeps on silken bolsters. *(Danish)*

BORE
A bore is a man who, when you ask him how he is, tells you. *(B. L. Taylor)*
All men are bores except when we want them.
Bore: a person who talks when you want him to listen. *(Bierce)*
The secret of being a bore is to tell everything. *(Voltaire)*
We often pardon those who bore us, but never those whom we bore. *(La Rochefoucauld)*
The well-bred man should never consent to become a bore. *(Ovid)*

BORROW
A borrowed cloak does not keep one warm. *(Arabian)*
Be not made a beggar by banqueting upon borrowing. *(Apocrypha)*

The borrower is the servant of the lender. *(Old Test., Prov.)*
Better buy than borrow.
Borrowed garments never fit well.
Creditors have better memories than debtors.
Have a horse of thine own and thou may'st borrow another.
He that borrows must pay again with shame or loss.
He that goes a-borrowing goes a-sorrowing.
I had rather ask of my fire brown bread, than borrow of my neighbor white.
If you would know the value of a ducat, try to borrow one.
Let us . . . live within our income, even if we have to borrow the money to do it. *(Art. Ward)*
Neither a borrower nor a lender be. *(Shakespeare)*
Pay with the same dish you borrow.
Borrowing is not much better than begging. *(German)*
Borrowing thrives but once. *(German)*
Who readily borrows, readily lies. *(German)*
Borrowing is the mother of trouble. *(Hebrew)*
Borrow from yourself. *(Latin)*
He who does not have to borrow lives without cares. *(Yiddish)*

BOSTON
A Boston man is the east wind made flesh.
Boston is a state of mind. *(Mark Twain)*
Boston State-house is the hub of the solar system. *(O. W. Holmes)*

BOUGH
The boughs that bear most hang lowest.

BOURBONS
They have learned nothing and forgotten nothing. *(de Panat)*

BOW
Draw not your bow until your arrow is fixed.
Have two strings to your bow.
When the bow is too much bent it breaks.
The bow that is always bent slackens or breaks. *(Spanish)*

BOY
Boys will be boys.
Boys will be men one day.
The sweetest roamer is a boy's young heart.

When the boy is growing he has a wolf in his belly. *(German)*
Once a man twice a boy. *(Latin)*

BRAG
Brag is a good dog, but Holdfast is a better.
His calves are bulls at the butchers and his bulls are calves at the tanners. *(French)*

BRAIN
De price of your hat ain't de measure of your brain. *(American Negro)*
If the brain sows not corn it plants thistles.
The brains don't lie in the beard.
The head gray, and no brains yet.
An empty brain is the devil's shop. *(French)*
All the brains are not in one head. *(Italian)*
Half a brain is enough for him who says little. *(Italian)*

BRANCH
The branch is seldom better than the stem. *(Danish)*
The highest branch is not the safest root.
The old branch breaks if bent.

BRANDY
Brandy is lead in the morning, silver at noon, gold at night *(German)*

BRAVE
None but the brave deserve the fair. *(Dryden)*
Many are brave when the enemy flies. *(Italian)*
To a brave man every soil is his country. *(Ovid)*
There were brave men before Agamemnon. *(Horace)*
The brave man's word is a coat of mail. *(Turkish)*

BREAD
Cast thy bread upon the waters: for thou shalt find it after many days. *(Old Test., Eccles.)*
Give us this day our daily bread. *(New Test., Matthew)*
Man doth not live by bread only. *(Old Test., Deut.)*
Man shall not live by bread alone. *(New Test., Matthew)*
What man is there of you, whom if his son ask bread, will he give him a stone. *(New Test., Matthew)*
Acorns were good till bread was found.
Better half a loaf than no bread.

Bread and cheese be two targets against death.
Bread is the staff of life.
Eaten bread is forgotten.
His bread is buttered on both sides.
I won't quarrel with my bread and butter.
Of all smells, bread; of all tastes, salt.
They that have no other meat,
  Bread and butter are glad to eat.
What bread men break is broke to them again.
Whose bread I eat, his song I sing. *(German)*
Others' bread has seven crusts. *(Italian)*
Bread and circus games. *(Juvenal)*
Another's bread costs dear. *(Spanish)*
I know well what I say when I ask for bread. *(Spanish)*
A knife is soon found for bread. *(Yiddish)*
If you have bread, don't look for cake. *(Yiddish)*
When God gives us bread, men will supply the butter. *(Yiddish)*

BREAKFAST
A clean fast is better than a dirty breakfast. *(Gaelic)*

BREATH
Save your breath to cool your porridge.

BREEDING
Better unborn than unbred.
Birth is much, but breeding is more.
He is not well bred, that cannot bear ill-breeding in other.
Vipers breed vipers.
What is bred in the bone will not out of the flesh.
Bad bird—bad egg. *(German)*
What is born of a cat will catch mice. *(Italian)*

BREVITY
Let thy speech be short, comprehending much in few words.
(Apocrypha)
Use not vain repetitions. *(New Test., Matthew)*
Brevity is the soul of wit.
It is better to be brief than tedious. *(Shakespeare)*

BREW
If you brew well you may drink well.

BRIBE
A bribe will enter without knocking.
All those men have their price. *(Walpole)*
Bribery and theft are first cousins.
Few men have virtue to withstand the highest bidder. *(Washington)*
He refuseth the bribe, but putteth forth his hand.
Honesty stands at the gate and knocks, and bribery enters in.
A greased mouth cannot say no. *(Italian)*
Bribes buy both gods and men. *(Latin)*

BRIDE
He who has the luck brings home the bride. *(German)*
The weeping bride makes a laughing wife. *(German)*
A bonny bride is soon buskit. *(-kissed) (Scottish)*
At the wedding feast the least eater is the bride. *(Spanish)*
If everyone seek a handsome bride, what will become of the ugly ones? *(Yiddish)*

BRIDGE
Bridges were made for wise men to walk over, and fools to ride over.
Let every man praise the bridge that carries him over.
Never cross a bridge until you come to it.
That is a bad bridge that is shorter than the stream. *(German)*

BRIGHT
He is only bright that shines by himself.

BROOK
Before you drink at a brook, it is well to know its source.

BROOM
A bad broom leaves a dirty room.
A new broom sweeps clean.

BROTHER
Am I my brother's keeper? *(Old Test., Genesis)*
Let brotherly love continue. *(New Test., Hebrews)*
Own brothers keep careful accounts. *(Chinese)*
The younger brother hath the more wit.
A brother is a friend given by nature. *(French)*
Though they are brothers their pockets are not sisters. *(Turkish)*

BUILD

The stone which the builders refused is become the headstone of the corner. *(Old Test., Psalms)*

Building and marrying of children are great wasters.

Building is a sweet impoverishing.

He builded better than he knew.

To build is to be robbed.

First build your house and then think of your furniture. *(Hebrew)*

It is easier to pull down than to build. *(Latin)*

BULL

Like a red rag to a bull.

The bull must be taken by the horns. *(French)*

BULLET

Every bullet has its billet.

BULLY

A bully is always a coward.

A drubbed bully never says anything about the matter. *(French)*

BURDEN

Bear ye one another's burdens. *(New Test., Galatians)*

An ass endures his burden, but not more than his burden.

Every horse thinks his own pack heaviest.

Let every pedlar carry his own pack.

Light burden is heavy if far borne.

None knows the weight of another's burden.

Take up the White Man's burden. *(Kipling)*

The back is shaped to the burden.

God gives the shoulder according to the burden. *(German)*

The burden is equal to the horse's strength. *(Hebrew)*

It is base to flinch under a burden. *(Latin)*

Light grows the burden which is well borne. *(Ovid)*

Place the burden on the slow-paced ass. *(Latin)*

The burden is light on the shoulder of another. *(Russian)*

It is other people's burdens that kill the ass. *(Spanish)*

BUSINESS

Seest thou a man diligent in his business? he shall stand before kings. *(Old Test., Prov.)*

A man without a smiling face must not open a shop. *(Chinese)*

Fuel is not sold in a forest, nor fish on a lake. *(Chinese)*
Business is business.
Business is the salt of life.
Curses on the man who business first designed.
Drive thy business or it will drive thee.
Everybody's business is nobody's business.
Everyone lives by selling something.
He who thinks his business below him, will always be above his business.
Ill ware is never cheap.
Keep thy shop and thy shop will keep thee.
Mind your till and till your mind.
The citizen is at his business before he rises.
There is nothing more requisite in business than despatch. *(Addison)*
Without business, debauchery.
You cannot live by selling ware for words.
Business before pleasure. *(French)*
Business is other people's money. *(French)*
Everyone knows his own business. *(French)*
The sign brings customers. *(French)*
Business tomorrow. *(Greek)*
The market is a place set apart where men may deceive each other. *(Greek)*
Tell everybody your business and they will do it for you. *(Italian)*
A tradesman thou! and hope to go to Heav'n? *(Persius, trans. Dryden)*
Good merchandise finds a ready buyer. *(Latin)*
How happy the life unembarrassed by the cares of business. *(Latin)*
The playthings of our elders are called business. *(St. Augustine)*
Let every man mind his own business. *(Spanish)*

BUSY
As busy as a bee.
As busy as a hen with one chick.
Busy will have bands.
Ever busy, ever bare.
I have eggs on the spit.
I have other eggs to fry.
I have other fish to fry.
To be too busy gets contempt.
To the boiling pot the flies come not.
None so busy as those who do nothing. *(French)*

BUTTER
Boil stones in butter and you may sup the broth.
Butter is mad twice a year.
Butter is gold in the morning, silver at noon, lead at night.
She looks as if butter would not melt in her mouth.
Who carries butter on his head should not walk in the sun. *(Yiddish)*

BUTTERFLY
Who breaks a butterfly upon a wheel? *(Pope)*

BUY
Don't buy everything that's cheap. *(Chinese)*
Buy at a fair, but sell at home.
Don't buy a pig in a poke.
He that blames would buy.
There are more foolish buyers than foolish sellers.
Don't buy a cat in a bag. *(German)*
He who buys the broom can also buy the handle. *(Italian)*
The buyer needs a hundred eyes, the seller not one. *(Italian)*
Let the buyer beware. *(Latin)*

BYGONE
Let bygones be bygones.

CABBAGE
Cabbage twice cooked is death. *(Greek)*

CAESAR
Render unto Caesar the things which are Caesar's. *(New Test., Matthew)*
I come to bury Caesar, not to praise him. *(Shakespeare)*
Imperious Caesar, dead and turn'd to clay,
  Might stop a hole to keep the wind away. *(Shakespeare)*
Not that I loved Caesar less, but that I loved Rome more. *(Shakespeare)*
What millions died—that Caesar might be great! *(Campbell)*
Caesar's wife must be above suspicion. *(Plutarch)*
Hail Caesar, we who are about to die salute thee! *(Latin)*
Either Caesar or nothing. *(Borgia motto)*

CAGE
A fine cage won't feed the bird. *(French)*

CAKE
Every cake hath its make.
You can't eat your cake and have it.

CALAMITY
Calamity is the test of integrity.
Calamity is virtue's opportunity. *(Latin)*

CALF
A lean calf forgets to skip.
The greatest calf is not the sweetest veal.
The butcher's calves are all cows; the tanner's cows are all calves. *(French)*
A change of pasture makes fat calves. *(Spanish)*

CALM

A calm is welcome after a storm.
The calmest husbands make the stormiest wives.
A calm portends a storm. *(Italian)*

CALUMNY

Be thou as chaste as ice, as pure as snow, thou shalt not escape calumny. *(Shakespeare)*
Calumnies are answered best with silence.
Hurl your calumnies boldly; something is sure to stick.
There are calumnies against which even innocence loses courage. *(French)*
Lying calumny alarms no one except the liar. *(Latin)*

CAMEL

The camel carries sugar but eats thorns. *(Arabian)*
The camel that travels often to Mecca will return lame at last. *(Arabian)*
'Tis the last feather that breaks the camel's back.
Everything with a crooked back is not a camel. *(German)*
A mangy camel bears the load of many camels. *(Greek)*
The camel going to seek horns lost his ears. *(Turkish)*

CANDLE

Neither do men light a candle, and put it under a bushel . . . *(New Test., Matthew)*
You may light another candle by your own without loss. *(Danish)*
A candle lights others and consumes itself.
Choose neither a woman nor linen by candle-light.
. . . consuming, like a candle on both ends, between wine and women.
He that is worst may still hold the candle.
Light not a candle to the sun.
At the foot of the candle it is dark. *(Persian)*
The candle does not give light to itself. *(Turkish)*

CANDOR

Open rebuke is better than secret love. *(Old Test., Prov.)*
He that speaketh what he will shall hear what he would not.
I hate him that my vices telleth me. *(Chaucer)*
Plain-dealing is a jewel, and he that useth it shall die a beggar.
Speak boldly, and speak truly, shame the devil.
There is no wisdom like frankness.

Be not ashamed to say what you are not ashamed to think. *(Montaigne)*
Speak out, hide not thy thoughts. *(Homer)*
To call a fig a fig, and a skiff a skiff. *(Greek)*
He calls a spade a spade. *(Erasmus)*

CAP
If the cap fits, wear it.

CARDS
Damn your cards, they are the devil's books.
I would cheat my own father at cards.
It is courtesy at cards to let the loser have his word.
The cards are ill shuffled till I have a good hand. *(Swift)*
There be that can pack the cards, and yet cannot play well. *(Bacon)*
When in doubt, win the trick. *(Hoyle)*

CARE
Care and not fine stables makes a good horse. *(Danish)*
Care's an enemy to life. *(Shakespeare)*
Care is beauty's thief.
Care is no cure.
"Care not" would have it.
Fretting cares make gray hairs.
What is past my help is past my care.
Want of care admits despair.
A pound of care will not pay an ounce of debt. *(French)*
Care killed a cat. *(French)*
Banish care from your mind.
Behind the horseman sits black care. *(Horace)*
Light cares speak, great ones are silent. *(Seneca)*
A man does not die of care: he dries up. *(Russian)*
Other folk's care killed the ass. *(Spanish)*
Another's cares will not rob you of sleep. *(Yiddish)*

CAREFUL
Good take heed Doth surely speed.
He looks not well to himself that looks not over.

CARELESS
Throw not the child out with the bath. *(Danish)*
A careless watch invites the vigilant foe.

CARESS
A caress is better than a career.

CARRION
No carrion will kill a crow.
The carrion which the eagle has left feeds the crow. *(Latin)*

CART
The best cart may overthrow.
To make the cart go you must grease the wheels. *(Italian)*

CARTHAGE
Carthage must be destroyed. *(Cato)*

CASE
A rotten case abides no handling. *(Shakespeare)*

CASK
A cask is easily set rolling.
Every cask smells of the wine it holds. *(Italian)*
The full cask makes no noise. *(Italian)*
The cask savors of the first fill. *(Latin)*

CASTLE
Better a castle of bones than of stones.
Castles are forests of stone.
Castles in the air cost a vast deal to keep up.
Easy to keep the castle that was never beseiged.
There is more pleasure in building castles in the air than on the ground. *(Gibbon)*

Thou shalt make castles then in Spain,
And dream of joy, all but in vain. *(Chaucer)*

CAT
The cat steals the rice and the dog comes and eats it. *(Chinese)*
When cat and mouse agree the farmer has no chance. *(Danish)*
A baited cat may grow as fierce as a lion.
A cat has nine lives.
A cat may look on a king.
An old cat laps as much milk as a young.
An old cat sports not with her prey.
By scratching and biting cat and dog come together.
Cats eat what hussies *(-housewives)* spare.

Cats hide their claws.
Keep no more cats than will catch mice.
Let the cat wink and the mouse will run.
The cat in gloves catches no mice.
The cat invites the mouse to a feast.
The cat will after kind.
The cat would eat fish and would not wet her feet.
The more you rub the cat on the rump, the higher she sets her tail.
There are more ways of killing a cat than choking her with cream.
When the cat's away, the mice will play.
Who is born of a cat will run after mice.
A good cat deserves a good rat. *(French)*
At night all cats are gray. *(French)*
When I play with my cat, who knows whether I do not make her more sport than she makes me. *(Montaigne)*
Singed cats live long. *(German)*
A cat that licks the spit is not to be trusted with roast meat. *(Italian)*
How can the cat help it if the maid be a fool? *(Italian)*
Don't look for five feet on a cat. *(Spanish)*
They whip the cat if our mistress does not spin. *(Spanish)*
Who shall hang the bell about the cat's neck? *(Spanish)*
If the cat had wings she'd choke all the birds in the air. *(Yiddish)*
If you play with a cat, you must not mind her scratch. *(Yiddish)*
Two cats in one bag cannot have peace. *(Yiddish)*

CAT'S PAW
Take the chestnuts out of the fire with the cat's paw.
Burn not thy fingers to snuff another man's candle. *(French)*
Draw the snake out of the hole with another's hand. *(Spanish)*

CATCH
Catch that catch may.
Catch the bear before you skin him.
When we think to catch we are sometimes caught. *(Spanish)*

CAUSE
Everything must have a cause. *(Chinese)*
The best cause requires a good pleader. *(Dutch)*
A bad cause will be supported by bad men.
A good cause makes a stout heart and a strong arm.
A man is a lion in his own cause.

A noble cause doth ease a grievous case.
Everything is the cause of itself. *(Emerson)*
It is a bad cause that none dare speak on.
They never fail who die in a great cause. *(Byron)*
To know truly is to know by causes. *(Bacon)*
What follows conforms to what went before. *(Greek)*
When the cause is lost, words are useless. *(Italian)*
A bad cause should be silent. *(Latin)*
It is a bad cause that asks for mercy. *(Latin)*
The causes of events are more interesting than the events themselves. *(Cicero)*

CAUTION
Caution is the mother of tender beer glasses. *(Dutch)*
He that looks not before, finds himself behind.
Lock the stable door before the steed is stolen.
He who sees not the bottom let him not pass the water. *(Italian)*

CEMETERY
A piece of a churchyard fits everybody.
From the cemetery no one is brought back. *(Yiddish)*

CENSURE
Censure and scandal are not one.
First look at home, then censure me.
The pot calls the kettle black.
Censure pardons the ravens but rebukes the doves. *(Latin)*

CEREMONY
Ceremony is the smoke of friendship. *(Chinese)*
Ceremony is not Civility, nor Civility Ceremony.
Excess of ceremony shows want of breeding.

CERTAIN
As sure as death.
Never take anything for granted.
Nothing is certain but death and taxes. *(Franklin)*
Nothing is certain but the unforeseen.
Quit not certainty for hope.
Sure as God made little apples.
He is a fool who leaves certainties for uncertainties. *(Greek)*
It is certain because it is impossible. *(Tertullian)*

CHAFF

There is no wheat without chaff.

CHAIN

Chains of gold are stronger than chains of iron.
The chain is no stronger than its weakest link.

CHAIR

A rickety chair will not serve as a seat. *(Danish)*
For want of a wise man a fool is set in the chair.

CHALK

Chalk and cheese.
Chalk is no shears.

CHANCE

A chance may win what by mischance was lost.
Chance governs all.
He who leaves nothing to chance will do few things ill, but he will do very few things. *(Halifax)*
Let me stand to the main chance.
Something must be left to chance.
Too late to grieve when the chance is past.
Chance is a nickname of Providence. *(French)*
Chance is blind . . . *(French)*
He that waits for chance is never sure of his dinner. *(French)*
Nothing must be left to chance. *(French)*
Blind chance sweeps the world along. *(Greek)*
Chance contrives better than we ourselves. *(Greek)*
Chance fights ever on the side of the prudent. *(Greek)*
Chances rule men and not men chances. *(Greek)*
The dice of Zeus have ever lucky throws. *(Greek)*
Chance and valor are blended in one. *(Latin)*
Chance dispenses life with unequal justice. *(Latin)*
Chance is another master. *(Latin)*
Probabilities direct the conduct of the wise man. *(Latin)*
What chance has made yours is not really yours. *(Latin)*
Whom chance often passes by, it finds at last. *(Latin)*

CHANGE

Who would be constant in happiness must often change. *(Chinese)*
All things change them to the contrary. *(Shakespeare)*

Change doth unknit the tranquil strength of men. *(M. Arnold)*
Change is not made without inconvenience . . .
Change lays not her hand upon truth.
Change of pasture makes fat calves.
Fools are fain of flitting.
Things do not change; we change. *(Thoreau)*
The more it changes, the more it is the same thing. *(French)*
We have changed all that. *(French)*
Change in all things is sweet. *(Greek)*
There is nothing permanent except change. *(Greek)*
All things change, nothing perishes. *(Latin)*
Times change and we change with them. *(Latin)*

CHAOS
And the earth was without form and void. *(Old Test., Genesis)*

CHARACTER
Character is much easier kept than recovered.
Character is what you are in the dark. *(D. L. Moody)*
Character must be kept bright as well as clean.
I am as bad as the worst, but thank God I am as good as the best. *(Whitman)*
No man can climb out beyond the limitations of his own character. *(J. Morley)*
There is a great deal of unmapped country within us.
A man shows his character by what he laughs at. *(German)*
. . . Character is nurtured midst the tempests of the world. *(Goethe)*
Character is destiny. *(Greek)*
Character is habit long continued. *(Greek)*
Our characters are the result of our conduct. *(Greek)*
Put more trust in character than in an oath. *(Greek)*
To a bad character good doctrine avails nothing. *(Italian)*
A man's own character is the arbiter of his fortune. *(Latin)*
It matters not what you are thought to be, but what you are. *(Latin)*

CHARITY
Cast thy bread upon the waters, for thou shalt find it after many days. *(Old Test., Eccles.)*
Charity shall cover the multitude of sins. *(New Test., I Peter)*
He that hath pity upon the poor lendeth unto the Lord. *(Old Test., Prov.)*

Alas! for the rarity
  Of Christian charity
  Under the sun! *(Hood)*
Charity and Pride have different aims, yet both feed the poor.
Charity begins, but doth not end, at home.
Charity covereth a multitude of sins.
Charity excuseth not cheating.
Charity is a virtue of the heart, not of the hands.
Did universal charity prevail, earth would be a heaven, and hell a fable. *(C. C. Colton)*
Great almsgiving lessens no man's living.
He serves the poor with a thump on the back with a stone.
He steals a sheep and gives back the trotters.
He that feeds upon charity has a cold dinner and no supper
He that gives to be seen will relieve none in the dark.
It is better that ten drones be fed than one bee be famished.
The living need charity more than the dead.
True charity, a plant divinely nurs'd. *(Cowper)*
With malice toward none; with charity for all. *(Lincoln)*
With one hand he put a penny in the urn of poverty, with the other took a shilling out.
Better one "take it" than two "you will have it." *(French)*
Rather not to live at all than to live by alms. *(French)*
Who gives me small gifts will have me live. *(French)*
She plays whore for apples and then bestows them upon the sick. *(Hebrew)*
Charity begins at home. *(Latin)*
He gives twice who gives quickly. *(Latin)*
He is truly great who hath a great charity. *(à Kempis)*
Do good and ask not for whom. *(Yiddish)*

CHARM

Charms strike the sight, but merit wins the soul.
There are charms made only for distant admiration.
Charm costs no more than disgust. *(Yiddish)*

CHASTISE

Chastise thy son while there is hope.
He who chastises one threatens a hundred. *(Italian)*

CHASTITY

Who can find a virtuous woman? for her price is far above rubies. *(Old Test., Prov.)*

Dear to heaven is saintly chastity. *(Milton)*
I will find you twenty lascivious turtles ere one chaste man. *(Shakespeare)*
If she seem not chaste to me,
  What care I how chaste she be. *(Raleigh)*
An unattempted woman cannot boast of her chastity. *(Montaigne)*
There are few good women who are not weary of their trade. *(La Rochefoucauld)*
A woman who has sacrificed her chastity will hesitate at no other iniquity. *(Tacitus)*
By no art can chastity, once injured, be made whole. *(Ovid)*
Chaste is she whom no one has asked. *(Latin)*
The most cautious pass for the most chaste. *(Spanish)*

CHATTER
Her tongue runs like the clapper of a mill.
Your tongue runs before your wit.
He hath eaten the hen's rump. *(Italian)*
Chattering will not make the pot boil. *(Turkish)*

CHEAP
Cheap things are not good, good things are not cheap. *(Chinese)*
Cheap and nasty.
Cheap bargains are dear.
The cheap buyer takes bad meat.
The best is the cheapest. *(French)*
Do you want to buy cheap; buy of a needy fool. *(Spanish)*

CHEAT
He is most cheated who cheats himself. *(Danish)*
Cheat, and the cheese will show.
Cheat me in the price but not in the goods.
He hath taken my horse and left me the tether.
He is not cheated who knows he is being cheated.
He that will cheat at play will cheat you any way.
Heads, I win; tails, you lose.
If you are cheated by a great man, lose your money, and say nothing.
In the kingdom of the cheater, the wallet is carried before.
Three things are men most likely to be cheated in: a horse, a wig, and a wife. *(Franklin)*
Who cheateth in small things is a fool; in great ones, a rogue.
A skilful cheat needs no assistant. *(German)*

It is fair and just to cheat the cheater. *(Spanish)*
If you've cheated him of his birthright, at least give him the mess of lentils. *(Yiddish)*

CHEERFUL
A cheerful look makes a dish a feast.
The sign of wisdom is a continual cheerfulness. *(French)*
Cheerful company shortens the miles. *(German)*

CHEESE
Cheese digests everything but itself.
Cheese and bread make the cheek red. *(German)*

CHESHIRE
Cheshire born and Cheshire bred,
Strong i' th' arm and weak i' th' head.

CHICKEN
Large chickens will not eat small grain. *(Chinese)*
Children and chicken must always be picking.
Count not your chickens till they are hatched.
The hen's eyes are with her chickens. *(French)*

CHILDREN
Even a child is known by his doing. *(Old Test., Prov.)*
He that spareth his rod hateth his son. *(Old Test., Prov.)*
Suffer the little children to come unto me . . . *(New Test., Mark)*
Train up a child in the way he should go . . . *(Old Test., Prov.)*
A pet child has many names. *(Danish)*
Children and drunkards speak truth. *(Danish)*
A burnt child dreads the fire.
A spoilt child never loves its mother.
Ask the mother if the child be like the father.
Bachelors' wives and maids' children are well taught.
Better a little chiding than a great heart-break.
Better a snotty child than his nose wiped off.
Children and fools have merry lives.
Children and fools must not play with edged tools.
Children are certain cares but uncertain comforts.
Children are poor men's riches.
Children are the keys of Paradise.
Children have wide ears and long tongues.

Children learn to creep ere they can go.
Children pick up words as pigeons peas . . .
Children should be seen and not heard.
Children suck the mother when they are young, and the father when they are old.
Children, when they are little, make parents fools; when they are great they make them mad.
For a little child a little mourning.
Give a child his will and he'll turn out ill.
Happy is he that is happy in his children.
He that cockers his child provides for his enemy.
He that has no children knows not what is love.
He that has children, all his morsels are not his own.
He that wipes the child's nose kisseth the mother's neck.
Hold your hands off other folks' bairns, till you get some of your own.
How sharper than a serpent's tooth it is
  To have a thankless child. *(Shakespeare)*
Ill bairns are best heard at home.
It is a wise child that knows its own father.
It is better to have one plough going than two cradles.
Just as the twig is bent the tree's inclined. *(Pope)*
Late children, early orphans.
Let thy child's first lesson be obedience . . .
Little children, little sorrows; big children, big sorrows.
Small pitchers have wide ears.
Speak when you are spoken to, come when you are called.
Teach your child to hold his tongue; he'll learn fast enough to speak.
The child is father of the man. *(Wordsworth)*
The child says nothing but what is heard by the fire.
The sports of children satisfy the child
Unruly children make their sire stoop.
Where children stand still, they have done some ill.
Where children are not, heaven is not.
Children have more need of models than of critics. *(French)*
When the child is christened come godfathers enough. *(French)*
Better the child should cry than the father. *(German)*
Our neighbor's children are always the worst. *(German)*
What the parents spin the children must reel. *(German)*

You can do anything with children if you only play with them. *(German)*
Children are to be deceived with comfits and men with oaths. *(German)*
Gold must be beaten, and a child scourged. *(Hebrew)*
Little children are little sorrows, but great joys. *(Italian)*
Children bring with them innumerable cares. *(Latin)*
Children, drunkards and fools cannot lie. *(Latin)*
It is better to bind children by respect than by fear. *(Latin)*
Children are a torment and nothing more. *(Russian)*
If the child does not cry, the mother does not understand it. *(Russian)*
When the child cuts its teeth, death is on the watch. *(Spanish)*
He that does not beat his child will later beat his own breast. *(Turkish)*
When a child stumbles, a good angel puts his hands under. *(Yiddish)*

CHILDHOOD

Childhood and youth are vanity. *(Old Test., Eccles.)*
The days of childhood are but days of woe.
Childhood is the sleep of reason. *(Rousseau)*

CHIMNEY

Where the chimney smokes the meal is being cooked. *(Danish)*
A smokey chimney and a scolding wife are two bad companions.
Every chimney smells of smoke. *(Yiddish)*

CHOICE

God offers to every man the choice between truth and repose. *(Emerson)*
He that comes first to the hill, may sit where he will.
If I be hanged, I'll choose my gallows.
Where bad is the best, naught must be the choice.
While between two stools, my tail goes to the ground.
You must take the fat with the lean.
There is small choice in rotten apples. *(Spanish)*

CHOP

If you chop wood, splinters will fall. *(Yiddish)*

CHRIST

Behold the man! [*Ecce homo.*] *(New Test., John)*
Whose shoe's latchet I am not worthy to unloose. *(New Test., John)*
Thou hast conquered, O Galilean! *(Emperor Julian)*

CHRISTIANITY

Through this sign thou shalt conquer. *(Emperor Constantine)*

CHRISTMAS

A hot Christmas makes a fat churchyard.
After Christmas comes Lent.
Christmas comes but once a year.

CHURCH

Let the church have leave to stand in the churchyard.
No sooner is a temple built to God, but the Devil builds a chapel hard by.
The itch of disputation will prove the scab of the church.
The churches must learn humility as well as teach it.
The nearer the church, the farther from God.
A church is God between four walls. *(French)*

CIRCLE

Circles though small are yet complete.
Every man is the center of a circle whose circumference he cannot pass.

CIRCUMSTANCES

Circumstances alter cases.
Man is the creature of circumstance.

CITY

A city that is set on a hill cannot be hid. *(New Test., Matthew)*
In cities vice is hidden with most ease . . .
God made the country and man made the town. *(Cowper)*
God the first garden made, and the first city Cain. *(Cowley)*
The chicken is the country's, but the city eats it.
Cities are the sink of the human race. *(Rousseau)*
A great city, a great solitude. *(Greek)*
Cities should be walled with the courage of their dwellers. *(Greek)*
It is the men who make the city, not walls or ships. *(Greek)*
Do not dwell in a city where a horse does not neigh nor a dog bark. *(Hebrew)*
Do not dwell in a city whose governor is a physician. *(Hebrew)*
Unless the Lord keepeth the city, the watchman waketh in vain. *(Motto of Edinburgh) (Latin)*

CIVILITY

Civility opens gates to the bad as well as to the good.
There is nothing that costs less than civility. *(Spanish)*

CIVILIZATION

Civilization degrades the many to exalt the few. *(A. B. Alcott)*
Civilization is the making of civil persons. *(Ruskin)*
Civilization is paralysis. *(Gauguin)*

CLAMOR

Much cry and little wool.

CLAY

We are clay in the hands of the potter.
Unless the clay be well pounded, no pitcher can be made. *(Latin)*

CLEANLINESS

Cleanliness is the key of prayer. *(Arabian)*
Be thou clean. *(New Test., Luke)*
Empty, swept, and garnished. *(New Test., Matthew)*
He that toucheth pitch shall be defiled therewith. *(Apocrypha)*
Clean heels, light meals.
Cleanliness is a fine life-preserver.
One keep-clean is better than ten make-cleans.
Have not only clean hands, but clean minds. *(Greek)*
Poverty comes from God, but not dirt. *(Hebrew)*
Cleanliness is next to godliness. *(Latin)*
Unless the vessel is clean, what you pour into it turns sour. *(Latin)*

CLEMENCY

Clemency alone makes us equal to the gods. *(Greek)*
Sometimes clemency is cruelty, and cruelty clemency. *(Italian)*

CLEVER

Be good, sweet maid, and let who can be clever. *(Kingsley)*
Too clever is dumb.
Cleverness is serviceable for everything, sufficient for nothing. *(French)*
Don't be so clever; cleverer ones than you are in jail. *(Russian)*
He who would be too clever make a fool of himself. *(Yiddish)*
What's the use of cleverness, if foolishness serves? *(Yiddish)*

CLIMB

He that never climbed never fell.
He who would climb the ladder must begin at the bottom.

If thy heart fail thee, do not climb at all.
He that climbs high falls heavily. *(German)*

CLOAK
An old cloak makes a new jerkin.
When clouds are seen, wise men put on their cloaks. *(Italian)*
A cloak is not made for a single shower of rain. *(Italian)*
Under a good cloak may be a bad man. *(Spanish)*
You can't make a good cloak out of bad cloth. *(Spanish)*

CLOCK
A clock that stands still is better than one that goes wrong. *(Yiddish)*

CLOTHES
It's hard to make clothes fit a miserable man. *(American Negro)*
The cowl does not make the monk. *(Latin)*
Who arrays himself in other men's garments is stripped on the highway. *(Spanish)*

CLOUD
Behold, there ariseth a little cloud out of the sea, like a man's hand. *(Old Test., I Kings)*

Not all clouds bring rain. *(Dutch)*
After black clouds, clear weather.
Every cloud has a silver lining.
If there were no clouds, we should not enjoy the sun.
One cloud is enough to eclipse all the sun.
When clouds appear, wise men put on cloaks.
The clouds—the only birds that never sleep. *(French)*

CLOWN
Give a clown your finger, and he will take your hand.
The more you court a clown the statelier he grows. *(Spanish)*

CLOUT
Better a clout than a hole out.

CLUMSY
His fingers are all thumbs.

COAL
. . . to send coals to Newcastle.

COAT
Cut your coat according to your cloth.
The coat is quite new; only the holes are old. *(Russian)*
You can't get warm on another's fur coat. *(Yiddish)*

COBBLER
Let not the cobbler go beyond his last. *(Latin)*
All cobblers go barefoot. *(Latin)*

COCK
The cock often crows without a victory. *(Danish)*
A cock is bold on his own dunghill. *(Latin)*
A cock that sings untimely must have his head cut off. *(Turkish)*

COCKROACH
A cockroach is always wrong when arguing with the chicken.

CODDLE
He that cockers his child, provides for his enemy.
He that is suffered to do more than is fitting, will do more than is lawful.

COLD
A dog's nose and a maid's knees are always cold.
Let them that be cold blow at the coal.
Stuff a cold and starve a fever.
What keeps out the cold keeps out the heat. *(Italian)*
Everyone feels the cold according as he is clad. *(Spanish)*

COLT
A ragged colt may make a good horse.
The best colt needs breaking.
You may break a colt but not an old horse.
There is no colt but breaks some halter. *(Italian)*

COMFORT
Is there no balm in Gilead? *(Old Test., Jeremiah)*
Thy rod and thy staff they comfort me. *(Old Test., Psalms)*
When I break my leg it is no comfort to me that another has broken his neck. *(Danish)*
The comforter's head never aches. *(Italian)*

COMING
Coming, and so is Christmas.
What comes seldom comes sharp.

COMMAND
He commands enough that obeys a wise man.
He that cannot obey cannot command.
He who demands does not command. *(Italian)*
It is a fine thing to command though it be but a herd of cattle. *(Spanish)*

COMMERCE
Commerce is the great civilizer.
Honor sinks where commerce long prevails. *(Goldsmith)*
No nation was ever ruined by trade. *(Franklin)*
The merchant has no country. *(Jefferson)*

COMMON
As common as a barber's chair.
Whatever is common is despised.

COMPANION
Two are better than one. *(Old Test., Eccles.)*
A man knows his companion in a long journey and a little inn.
A merry companion is music in a journey.
Birds of a feather flock together.
Like will to like.
A merry companion is a wagon in the way. *(Latin)*
He is known by his companions. *(Latin)*

COMPANY
Evil communications corrupt good manners. *(New Test., I Corinth.)*
Keep company with good men and good men you'll learn to be. *(Chinese)*

A crowd is not company.
Better your room than your company.
Company in misery makes it light.
Company keeps your rind from growing too coarse and rough.
For want of company, welcome trumpery.
Go not to hell for company.
Good company is a good coach.
Ill company is like a dog, who dirts those most whom he loves.

Present company excepted.
Take the tone of the company you are in.
The company makes the feast.
Two is company, three is a crowd.
Two is company, three is none.
We know a man by the company he keeps.
Company in distress makes trouble less. *(French)*
The best company must part. *(French)*
Every man is like the company he is wont to keep. *(Greek)*
If you live with a lame person you will learn to limp. *(Greek)*
Like to like; jackdaw to jackdaw. *(Greek)*
Shun evil company. *(Solon)*
He that lies down with dogs will rise up with fleas. *(Latin)*
He who goes with wolves will learn to howl. *(Spanish)*
Tell me what company you keep, and I'll tell you who you are. *(Spanish)*
With merry company the dreary way is endured. *(Spanish)*
No road is long with good company. *(Turkish)*
The smaller the company, the greater the feast. *(Yiddish)*

COMPARISON
Comparisons are odious.
Comparisons are odorous. *(Shakespeare)*
Nothing is good or bad but by comparison.
Comparisons make enemies of our friends. *(Greek)*

COMPENSATION
. . . the last shall be first. *(New Test., Matthew)*
He that eats the hard shall eat the ripe.
On the fall of an oak every man gathers wood. *(Greek)*
If I have lost the ring I still have the fingers. *(Italian)*
If you rightly bear your cross it will bear you. *(Latin)*

COMPETITION
In the grave, dust and bones jostle not for the wall.
The only competition worthy a wise man is with himself.
Competition makes a horse-race. *(Latin)*

COMPLAIN
Constant complaints never get pity.
He that bewails himself hath the cure in his hands.
The worst wheel of the cart creaks most. *(Latin)*
A tarrowing bairn was never fat. *(Scottish)*

COMPLEXION
Cold of complexion, good of condition.

COMPLIMENT
Compliments cost nothing, yet many pay dear for them.
I can live for two months on a good compliment. *(Mark Twain)*
When quality meets, compliments pass.

COMPROMISE
A lean compromise is better than a fat law-suit.
All great alterations in human affairs are produced by compromise.
Stretch your legs according to the length of your coverlet.

COMPULSION
He that complies against his will,
Is of his own opinion still. *(Butler)*

CONCEAL
That which covers thee discovers thee. *(Spanish)*

CONCEIT
Seest thou a man wise in his own conceit? there is more hope of a fool than of him. *(Old Test., Prov.)*
Conceit is God's gift to little men.
Conceit is the finest armor a man can wear.
Conceit in weakest bodies strongest works. *(Shakespeare)*
Conceit may puff a man up, but never prop him up.
Conceited goods are quickly spent.
Every man has a right to be conceited until he is successful. *(Disraeli)*
He is so full of himself that he is quite empty.
He that falls in love with himself, will have no rivals.
He thinks his farthing good silver.
She holds up her head like a hen drinking.

CONDITION
Condition makes, condition breaks.

CONDUCT
Conduct is three-fourths of our life and its largest concern. *(M. Arnold)*
Be with a man deaf and hearing, silent and speaking. *(Hebrew)*

CONFESSION
A fault confessed is half redressed.
A generous confession disarms slander.

Confess and be hanged.
I own the soft impeachment.
It is a foolish sheep that makes the wolf his confessor.
Open confession is good for the soul.
Confession of our faults is the next thing to innocence. *(Latin)*

CONFIDENCE
Confidence is a plant of slow growth.
Men cannot be forced into trust.
Skill and confidence are an unconquered army.
Confidence does more to make conversation than wit. *(French)*
Confidence should arise from beneath, and power descend from above. *(French)*
God save me from those I confide in. *(French)*
Confident because of our caution. *(Greek)*
Confidence begets confidence. *(Latin)*

CONQUER
He went forth conquering and to conquer. *(New Test., Rev.)*
Conquer thyself. *(Chinese)*
To joy in conquest is to joy in the loss of human life. *(Chinese)*
He that will conquer must fight.
Rats and conquerors must expect no mercy in misfortune.
See the conquering hero comes!
The free can conquer but to save.
The honor of the conquest is rated by the difficulty. *(French)*
We triumph without glory when we conquer without danger. *(French)*
Conquered, we conquer. *(Latin)*
I came, I saw, I conquered. [*Veni, vidi, vici.*] *(Caesar)*
He is twice a conqueror, who can restrain himself in the hour of victory. *(Latin)*
The conquering cause was pleasing to the gods. *(Latin)*
The conqueror may please the conquered according to his pleasure. *(Latin)*
They conquer who believe they can. *(Latin)*

CONSCIENCE
An evil deed has a witness in the bosom. *(Danish)*
A burdened conscience will never need a hangman.
A clear conscience can bear any trouble.
A good conscience is a continual feast.

A good conscience is a soft pillow.
A guilty conscience never thinks itself safe.
A man's conscience tells him what is honor.
A quiet conscience sleeps in thunder.
An evil conscience breaks many a man's neck.
Conscience does make cowards of us all . . . *(Shakespeare)*
Conscience is but the pulse of reason. *(Coleridge)*
Conscience is the voice of God in the soul.
It is always term time in the court of conscience.
Keep conscience clear, then never fear.
No hell like a bad conscience.
Some make a conscience of spitting in the church, yet rob the altar.
Trust that man in nothing who has not a conscience in everything.
A guilty conscience needs no accuser. *(French)*
He who has no conscience has nothing. *(French)*
The conscience of the dying belies their life. *(French)*
It is neither safe nor prudent to do aught against conscience. *(Luther)*
The worm of conscience consorts with the owl. *(Schiller)*
Conscience is a god to all mortals. *(Greek)*
A clear conscience is a wall of brass. *(Latin)*
A scar on the conscience is the same as a wound. *(Latin)*
A good conscience is God's eye. *(Russian)*
A bad conscience is a snake in one's heart. *(Yiddish)*

CONSEQUENCE

He that bulls the cow must keep the calf.

CONSERVATIVE

A conservative government is an organized hypocrisy. *(Disraeli)*
A conservative is a man who is too cowardly to fight and too fat to run. *(E. Hubbard)*

CONSISTENCY

A foolish consistency is the hobgoblin of little minds . . . *(Emerson)*
Consistency, thou art a jewel.
I would always have one play but one thing. *(Shakespeare)*
. . . to run with the hare and hold with the hound.
Inconsistency is the only thing in which men are consistent.
It is often consistency to change the mind. *(Italian)*

CONSTANT

Constant dropping wears the stone. *(Old Test., Job)*
Constancy is the foundation of virtues. *(Bacon)*
Constant in nothing but inconstancy. *(Pope)*
True as the needle to the pole.
Ever the same. [*Semper eadem.*] [*Motto of Queen Elizabeth*] *(Latin)*

CONTEMPLATION

He that contemplates on his bed hath a day without a night.
Wisdom's best nurse, Contemplation. *(Milton)*

CONTEMPT

Contempt is Failure's share.
Contempt is the sharpest reproof.
Contempt will sooner kill an injury than revenge.
Some evils are cured by contempt.

CONTENT

He who is content can never be ruined. *(Chinese)*
He that cannot get bacon must be content with cabbage. *(Danish)*
A contented mind is a continual feast.
A mind content both crown and kingdom is.
Better a little with content than much with contention.
Content is all.
Content is happiness.
Content is the philosopher's stone that turns all it touches into gold.
Content lodges oftener in cottages than in palaces.
Content with little, enough is as good as a feast.
Nature with little is content.
No chance is evil to him that is content.
Our content is our best having. *(Shakespeare)*
Take the goods the gods provide thee.
Take things as they come.
What better fare than well content?
Content surpasses wealth. *(French)*
When we have not what we like, we must like what we have. *(French)*
Who is well seated should not budge. *(German)*
Contentment is an impregnable fortress. *(Greek)*
Think not on what you lack as much as on what you have. *(Greek)*
He has enough who is content. *(Italian)*
Contented with your lot, you will live wisely. *(Latin)*
No man is content with his lot. *(Latin)*

Remain within your own sphere. *(Latin)*
The best of blessings—a contented mind. *(Latin)*
If you haven't a capon, feed on an onion. *(Spanish)*
Since we have loaves, let us not look for cakes. *(Spanish)*

CONTENTION
Religious contention is the Devil's harvest. *(French)*

CONTROL
Rule lust, temper the tongue, and bridle the belly.
The ship that will have no rudder must have a rock. *(Italian)*

CONVERSATION
A man's conversation is the mirror of his thoughts. *(Chinese)*
Conversation makes one what he is.
Let all thy converse be sincere.
Many can argue, not many converse.
Who converses not knows nothing.
A man is not better than his conversation. *(German)*

CONVINCE
A man may be confuted and yet not convinced.

COOK
All are not cooks who carry long knives. *(Dutch)*
A bad cook licks his own fingers.
A cook is known by his knife.
Cooks are not to be taught in their own kitchen.
Every cook commends his own sauce.
God sends meat and the devil sends cooks.
'Tis by his cleanliness a cook must please.
Too many cooks spoil the broth.

COOKING
A fat kitchen, a lean will.
First catch your hare then cook it.
The discovery of a new dish does more for the happiness of man than the discovery of a star. *(Brillat-Savarin)*
In a house where there is plenty, supper is soon cooked. *(Spanish)*
If you cook with straw, the food stays raw. *(Yiddish)*

COPY
None but blockheads copy each other. *(Blake)*

COQUETRY

Coquetry is the champagne of love.

Women know not the whole of their coquetry. *(La Rochefoucauld)*

CORD

The cord breaks at last by the weakest pull. *(Spanish)*

CORPORATION

Corporations have neither souls to be saved nor bodies to be kicked. *(Lord Eldon)*

CORRECTION

For whom the Lord loveth he correcteth. *(Old Test., Prov.)*

Correction brings fruit. *(Dutch)*

CORRUPTION

Corruption wins not more than honesty. *(Shakespeare)*

The best things corrupted become the worst. *(Latin)*

COSMOPOLITAN

All the world is the fatherland of a noble soul. *(Geek)*

I am a citizen of the world. *(Diogenes)*

He has no home whose home is everywhere. *(Latin)*

One's country is wherever one is well off. *(Latin)*

The whole world is a man's birthplace. *(Latin)*

COST

What costs little is little esteemed.

The cost takes away the taste. *(French)*

COUNSEL

To give counsel to a fool is like throwing water on a goose. *(Danish)*

Counsel breaks not the head.

Counsel will make a man stick his own mare.

Give neither counsel or salt until you are asked for it.

Good counsel has no price.

He that will not be counselled cannot be helped.

If the counsel be good, no matter who gave it.

Keep your own counsel.

Good counsel never comes too late. *(German)*

Happy counsels flow from sober feasts. *(Homer)*

Counsel is nothing against love. *(Italian)*

Come not to the counsel uncalled. *(Latin)*

Though you are a prudent old man, do not despise counsel. *(Spanish)*

COUNT
Count not your chickens before they are hatched.
He that reckons without his host, must reckon over again. *(French)*

COUNTRY
A country man may be as warm in kersey as a king in velvet.
My country, right or wrong. *(Decatur)*
The country is lyric—the town dramatic.
God made the country, and man made the town. *(Latin)*

COUPLE
Every couple is not a pair.

COURAGE
If you do not enter a tiger's den, you cannot get his cubs. *(Chinese)*
A man of courage never wants weapons.
Bravery never goes out of fashion.
Courage is the most common and vulgar of the virtues. *(Melville)*
Courage mounteth with occasion. *(Shakespeare)*
Courage scorns the death it cannot shun. *(Dryden)*
Courage should have eyes as well as arms.
Faint heart never won fair lady.
It is easier to use a gun than to show courage.
None but the brave deserve the fair. *(Dryden)*
The test of courage is to bear defeat without losing heart.
Where there is a brave man, there is the thickest of the fight.
A short sword for a brave man. *(French)*
Brave men are brave from the first. *(French)*
Rage avails less than courage. *(French)*
You can't answer for your courage if you have never been in danger. *(French)*
All are brave when the enemy flies. *(Italian)*
He is master of another man's life, who is indifferent to his own. *(Italian)*
Who has not courage should have legs. *(Italian)*
Courage in danger is half the battle. *(Latin)*
Courage is that virtue which champions the cause of right. *(Latin)*
Even savage animals, if kept shut up, forget their courage. *(Latin)*
Fortune favors the brave. *(Latin)*
The brave are born from the brave. *(Latin)*
True courage grapples with misfortune. *(Latin)*
A stout heart breaks bad luck. *(Spanish)*
It is courage that wins, and not good weapons. *(Spanish)*

COURT

A friend in court is better than a penny in purse.
At court everyone for himself.
Far from court, far from care.
He that would rise at court, must begin by creeping.
Leave the court ere the court leave thee.
Whoso liveth in court shall die in the straw.
Who has seen the court has seen the world. *(French)*
At court there are many hands but few hearts. *(German)*

COURTESY

All doors open to courtesy.
Courtesy costs nothing.
Full of courtesy, full of craft.
He that asks a courtesy promises a kindness.
Courtesy on one side never lasts long. *(French)*
Do not limp before the lame. *(French)*
Cap in hand never did anyone harm. *(Italian)*
Courtesy is cumbersome to them that ken it not. *(Scottish)*
Lip courtesy pleases much and costs little. *(Spanish)*
The courteous learns his courtesy from the discourteous. *(Turkish)*

COURTIER

The courtier is cringing and servile in adversity. *(Chinese)*
A young courtier, an old beggar.
The greatest favorites are in most danger of falling.
A courtier should be without feeling and without honor. *(French)*

COURTING

Courting and wooing bring dallying and doing.

COUSIN

Call me cousin, but cozen me not.

COVER

Who covers you discovers you. *(Spanish)*

COVET

All covet, all lose.
Covetous men live drudges to die wretches.
Covetousness often starves other vices.

The world is too small for the covetous. *(Latin)*
Those who covet much want much. *(Latin)*
Covetousness bursts the bag. *(Spanish)*

COW

It is well that wicked cows have short horns. *(Dutch)*
Milk the cow but don't pull off the udder. *(Dutch)*
A cow is good in the field, but we turn her out of a garden.
A lowing cow soon forgets her calf.
A red cow gives good milk.
All is not butter that comes from the cow.
Barley straw is good fodder when the cow gives water.
If you sell the cow you sell her milk too.
Let him who owns the cow take her by the tail.
Many a good cow hath an evil calf.
The cow licks no strange calf.
The cow knows not what her tail is worth till she has lost it.
Who'd keep a cow, when he may have a quart of milk for a penny?
The cow from afar gives plenty of milk. *(French)*
The old cow thinks she never was a calf. *(French)*
The cows that low most give the least milk. *(German)*
Milk the cow which is near. *(Greek)*
Bring the cow to the hall and she'll run to the byre. *(Scottish)*
A dead cow gives no milk. *(Yiddish)*
What use is a cow that gives plenty of milk, if she kicks the pail over? *(Yiddish)*

COWARD

To see what is right and not to do it is the part of a coward. *(Chinese)*

A coward's fear can make a coward valiant.
Cowards are cruel.
Cowards die many times before their deaths . . . *(Shakespeare)*
Cowards in scarlet pass for men of war.
Ever will a coward show no mercy.
Make a coward fight and he will kill the devil.
Many would be cowards if they had courage enough.
There grows no herb to heal a coward heart.
Better be a coward than foolhardy. *(French)*
It is the misfortune of worthy people that they are cowards. *(Voltaire)*
One coward makes ten. *(German)*

The coward threatens only when he is safe. *(German)*
Cowards do not count in battle; they are there, but not in it. *(Greek)*
Cowards' weapons neither cut nor pierce. *(Italian)*
He that has no heart let him have heels. *(Italian)*
Strength avails not a coward. *(Italian)*
Who cannot strike the ass may strike the saddle. *(Italian)*
A coward calls himself cautious and a miser thrifty. *(Latin)*
Hidden valor is as bad as cowardice. *(Latin)*
Coward against coward, the assailant conquers. *(Spanish)*

CRAB
You can never bring a crab to walk straight.

CRAFT
Everyone is a thief in his own craft. *(Dutch)*
No one masters his craft the first day.
Be not ashamed of your craft. *(German)*

CRAFTY
A crafty knave needs no broker.
Craft against craft makes no living.
Craft bringeth nothing home.
Cunning craft is but the waste of wisdom.

CRAVE
Nothing have, nothing crave.
What the eye sees not, the heart craves not. *(Spanish)*

CREAM
If you take off the cream, what remains is sour milk. *(Yiddish)*

CREDIT
He that is hasty to give credit is light minded. *(Old Test., Prov.)*
Better take eight hundred than sell for a thousand on credit. *(Chinese)*
Credit cuts off customers. *(Chinese)*
Buyin' on credit is robbin' next year's crop. *(American Negro)*
Credit lost is like Venice-glass broken.
He that has lost his credit is dead to the world.
Men pay severely who require credit.
No man ever lost his credit but he who had it not.
Who sells on credit has much custom but little money. *(German)*
Credit is dead; bad pay killed it. *(Italian)*
A poor man has no credit. *(Latin)*

He who loses credit can lose nothing further. *(Latin)*
Ah, take the cash and let the credit go. *(Omar Khayyám)*

CREDITOR
Creditors have better memories than debtors. *(Spanish)*

CREED
From the dust of creeds out-worn. *(Shelley)*
Orthodoxy is my doxy; heterodoxy is another man's doxy. *(Warburton)*
Put your creed into your deed. *(Emerson)*
We love the precepts for the teacher's sake.

CRIME
Crimes may be secret, yet not secure.
He acts the third crime that defends the first.
He that doth what he should not, shall feel what he would not.
The greater the man the greater the crime.
The contagion of crime is like that of the plague. *(French)*
We easily forget crimes known only to ourselves. *(French)*
A man may thrive on crime, but not for long. *(Greek)*
Criminals are punished that others may be amended. *(Italian)*
Heaven takes care that no man secures happiness by crime. *(Italian)*
Crime must be concealed by crime. *(Latin)*
Every man enjoys his own crimes. *(Latin)*
If you share your friend's crime, you make it your own. *(Latin)*
It is unlawful to overcome crime by crime. *(Latin)*
No crime is founded upon reason. *(Latin)*
No one lives who is without a crime. *(Latin)*
Successful crime is called virtue. *(Latin)*
Who is content with one crime only? *(Latin)*
Who profits by a crime commits the crime. *(Latin)*

CRIPPLE
A cripple may catch a hare.
Halt not before a cripple.

CRITIC
A critic is a legless man who teaches running.
An unsuccessful author turns critic.
Critics are like brushers of noblemen's clothes.
It is rarely that an author is hurt by his critics.

No critic has ever settled anything. *(S. Johnson)*
A critic is a man whose watch is five minutes ahead of other people's watches. *(Sainte-Beuve)*
A good critic is he who relates the adventures of his soul among masterpieces. *(A. France)*

CRITICISM
Blame is safer than praise.
Blame-all and praise-all are two blockheads.
Chatting to chiding is not worth a chute.
It is easier to be critical than to be correct.
The sting of reproof is the truth of it.
Criticism is easy; art, difficult. *(French)*
Criticism of our contemporaries is not criticism; it is conversation. *(Lemaître)*
Really to stop criticism one must die. *(French)*
They damn what they do not understand. *(Latin)*

CROCODILE TEARS
It is the Wisdome of Crocodiles, that shed teares, when they would devoure. *(Bacon)*

CROOKED
Crooked iron may be straightened with a hammer. *(Danish)*
Crooked logs make straight fires.
If the staff be crooked, the shadow cannot be straight.
To make a crooked stick straight, we bend it the contrary way. *(French)*
A crooked log is not to be straightened. *(Latin)*

CROSS
Crosses are ladders that lead to heaven.
Every cross has its own inscription.
No cross—no crown.
Everyone in this world has his cross. *(French)*
Everyone thinks his own cross is heaviest. *(Italian)*

CROSSING
Cross the stream where it is ebbest.

CROW
Crows are black all the world over. *(Chinese)*
An evil crow—an evil egg.

Crows are never the whiter for washing themselves.
Report makes the crows blacker than they are.
The black crow thinks her own birds white.
The crow doth sing as sweetly as the lark.
When neither is attended. *(Shakespeare)*
To shoot at crows is powder flung away.
When the crow flies her tail follows.
Old crows are hard to catch. *(German)*
One crow does not make a winter. *(German)*
If the crow could feed in quiet, he would have more meat. *(Latin)*
The crow, stripped of her stolen colors, excites our ridicule. *(Latin)*
An old crow croaks not for nothing. *(Russian)*

CROWD
A crowd is not company.
Two is company—three is a crowd.
He who does not mix with the crowd knows nothing. *(Spanish)*

CROWN
A crown is no cure for the headache.
Uneasy lies the head that wears a crown. *(Shakespeare)*
All laws are broken to obtain a crown. *(Spanish)*

CRUELTY
A man of cruelty is God's enemy.
Cruelty ever proceeds from a vile mind . . .
Cruelty is a tyrant that is always attended with fear.
Cruelty is more cruel if we defer the pain.
I must be cruel, only to be kind. *(Shakespeare)*
Oh, 'tis cruelty to beat a cripple with his own crutches!
Cowardice is the mother of cruelty. *(French)*
A cruel heart ill suits a manly mind. *(Greek)*
Clemency is the remedy for cruelty. *(Latin)*
Your cruelty is our glory. *(Tertullian)*

CRUST
It is an ill dog that deserves not a crust. *(Latin)*

CRY
Don't cry before you are hurt.
It is no use crying over spilled milk.

CUCKOLD
Let every cuckold wear his own crown.
The cuckold is the last that knows of it.

CUCKOO
The cuckoo builds not for himself.

CUNNING
As cunning as a dead pig, but not half so honest.
Contrivance is better than force.
Cunning is no burden.
Cunning proceeds from want of capacity.
One man may be more cunning than another, but not more cunning than everybody else.
The weak in courage is strong in cunning.
We take cunning for a sinister or crooked wisdom. *(Bacon)*
Where force hath failed, policy often hath prevailed.
The greatest cunning is to have none. *(French)*
The most cunning are the first caught. *(French)*

CUP
A full cup must be carried steadily.
While drinking from one cup, look not into another. *(Hebrew)*

CUPID
Cupid is a blind gunner.
Some Cupid kills with arrows, some with traps. *(Shakespeare)*

CUR
Brabbling curs never want sore ears.

CURE
No cure, no pay. *(Chinese)*
A desperate disease must have a desperate cure.
Good language cures great sores.
Past cure, past care.
The cure may be worse than the disease.
To fear the worst oft cures the worst.
What can't be cured must be endured.
The purse of the patient protracts the disease. *(German)*

CURIOSITY

He that peeps in at his neighbor's window may chance to lose his eyes. *(Arabian)*

Be not curious in unnecessary matters. *(Apocrypha)*
He that bites on every weed must needs light on poison.
He who peeps through a hole may see what will vex him.
Too much curiosity lost Paradise.
Curiosity is born of jealousy. *(French)*
Avoid a questioner, for he is also a tattler. *(Latin)*
Let curiosities alone. *(Latin)*

CURSE

Don't curse the crocodile's mother before you cross the river. *(African Negro)*
Cussin' de weather is mighty po' farming. *(American Negro)*
A thousand curses never tore a shirt. *(Arabian)*
A curse will not strike out an eye unless a fist goes with it. *(Danish)*
Curse and be cursed!
Curses are the devil's language.
Curses, like chickens, come home to roost.
I shall curse you with book and bell and candle. *(Malory)*
The lips that curse shall want bread. *(Polish)*

CUSTOM

Custom is the plague of wise men and the idol of fools.
Custom meets us at the cradle and leaves us only at the grave.
Custom reconciles us to everything.
Nice customs curtsey to great kings. *(Shakespeare)*
Once a use and ever a custom.
The deadliest foe to love is custom.
Tyrant custom makes a slave of reason.
A cake and a bad custom ought to be broken. *(French)*
Custom is a deceiving schoolmistress. *(French)*
So many countries, so many customs. *(French)*
A good custom is surer than law. *(Greek)*
Choose what is best; custom will make it agreeable and easy. *(Greek)*
We are more sensible of what is done against custom than against nature. *(Greek)*
Custom is a second nature. *(Latin)*
Custom is a tyrant. *(Latin)*
Custom is the master of all things. *(Latin)*

Never can custom conquer nature. *(Latin)*
A custom breaks a law. *(Yiddish)*

CUT
Cut and come again.
Cut not the bough that thou standest upon.

CYNIC
A cynic is a man who knows the price of everything and the value of nothing. *(Wilde)*
Cynicism is intellectual dandyism. *(Meredith)*

DAINTIES

Dear bought and far fetched are dainties for ladies.
Who dainties love shall beggars prove.

DAISY

The daisy's for simplicity.
The Rose has but a summer-reign,
  The Daisy never dies. *(Montgomery)*

DANCE

We have piped unto you, and ye have not danced.
(New Test., Matthew)

A dance is a measured pace . . .
All are not merry that dance lightly.
Dancing is the child of Music and of Love.
He dances well to whom Fortune pipes.
In dance the hand hath liberty to touch . . .
Jack shall pipe, and Jill shall dance.
The dancer must pay the piper.
The greater the fool the better the dancer.
The poetry of the foot. *(Dryden)*
They love dancing well that dance barefoot upon thorns.
Those move easiest who have learned to dance. *(Pope)*
'Twas surely the devil that taught women to dance.
When you go to dance, take heed whom you take by the hand.
If we pay for the music, we will join in the dance. *(French)*
An old man dancing is a child in mind. *(Greek)*
He who dances well goes from wedding to wedding. *(Spanish)*

DANGER

He that loveth danger shall perish therein. *(Apocrypha)*
As soon as there is life there is danger.

Danger and delight grow on one stalk.
Danger deviseth shifts; wit waits on fear. *(Shakespeare)*
Danger is next neighbor to security.
Danger itself is the best remedy for danger.
Danger, the spur of great minds.
Danger well past remembered works delight.
Danger will wink at opportunity.
Dangers bring fears, and fears more dangers bring.
Dangers foreseen are the soonest prevented.
Don't halloo till you're out of the woods.
He that brings himself into needless dangers, dies the devil's martyr.
He that fears danger in time seldom feels it.
He that would sail without danger must never come on the main sea.
If the danger seems slight, then is the time to beware.
It is no jesting with edged tools.
The danger past and God forgotten.
There is no person who is not dangerous for someone. *(French)*
Where there is no danger there is no glory. *(French)*
A danger is never overcome without danger. *(Latin)*
Between the devil and the deep sea. *(Latin)*
Danger comes the sooner when despised. *(Latin)*
He is happy whom other men's perils make wary. *(Latin)*
He who dares dangers overcomes them before he incurs them. *(Latin)*
Sweet is danger. *(Latin)*
The danger that is nearest we least dread. *(Latin)*
Without danger the game grows cold. *(Latin)*
Fear the goat from the front, the horse from the rear, and man from all sides. *(Russian)*
He must have iron nails that scratches a bear. *(Russian)*
He who sees danger perishes in it. *(Spanish)*

DARKNESS

Darkness which may be felt. *(Old Test., Exodus)*
Men loved darkness more than light, because their deeds were evil. *(New Test., John)*
All colors will agree in the dark.
He sees enough who doth his darkness see.
He that gropes in the dark finds what he would not.
He that runs in the dark may well stumble.
In darkness there is no choice.
It is always darkest just before the dawn.

It is sure to be dark if you shut your eyes.
At night all cats are gray. *(French)*
By candle-light a goat is lady-like. *(French)*

DARLING
Better an old man's darling, than a young man's warling.

DAUGHTER
An undutiful daughter will prove an unmanageable wife.
He that would the daughter win, must with the mother first begin.
Judge the daughter by the mother. *(Latin)*
Daughters and dead fish are no keeping wares. *(Scottish)*
Twa daughters and a back door are three stark thieves. *(Scottish)*
A daughter married is a daughter lost. *(Spanish)*
He who has daughters is always a shepherd. *(Spanish)*
Who does not beat his daughters, will one day strike his knees in vain. *(Turkish)*

DAWN
It is always darkest just before the day dawneth.
When God sends the dawn, he sends it for all. *(Cervantes)*

DAY
My days are swifter than a weaver's shuttle. *(Old Test., Job)*
Sufficient unto the day is the evil thereof. *(Old Test., Prov.)*
Every day cannot be a feast of lanterns. *(Chinese)*
A bad day never had a good night.
A day to come shows longer than a year that's gone.
As the days lengthen the cold strengthens.
Be the day never so long, at length cometh evensong.
Better the day, better the deed.
Day breaks not, it is my heart. *(Donne)*
Every day brings its bread with it.
Every dog has his day.
Every man hath his ill day.
He never broke his hour who kept his day.
Hide me from day's garish eye. *(Milton)*
Long it is to the ending of the day . . .
No day passeth without some grief.
One of these days is none of these days.
Only that day dawns to which we are awake. *(Thoreau)*
The day has eyes, the night has ears.

The day is short and the work is much.
The long days are no happier than the short ones.
The longest day will have an end.
Think in the morning. Act in the noon. Eat in the evening. Sleep in the night. *(Blake)*
Think that day lost whose low descending sun
Views from thy hand no worthy action done.
We have seen better days. *(Shakespeare)*
What one day gives, another takes.
My days have gone a-wandering. *(Villon)*
Though the fool waits, the day does not. *(French)*
In the evening one may praise the day. *(German)*
Every day in thy life is a leaf in thy history. *(Greek)*
One day is equal to every day. *(Greek)*
A day differs not a whit from eternity. *(Seneca)*
Day is pushed out by day. *(Latin)*
Each day is the scholar of yesterday. *(Latin)*
Every day should be passed as if it were to be our last. *(Latin)*
No day without its line. *(Latin)*
On a good day good words must be spoken. *(Latin)*
One day well spent is better than an eternity of error. *(Latin)*
The next day is never so good as the day before. *(Latin)*

DEAF

None so deaf as those who won't hear.

DEATH

And I looked, and behold a pale horse: and his name that sat on him was Death. *(New Test., Revelation)*
Death and life are in the power of the tongue. *(Old Test., Job)*
For dust thou art, and unto dust shalt thou return. *(Old Test., Genesis)*
He giveth his beloved sleep. *(Old Test., Psalms)*
I shall go the way whence I shall not return. *(Old Test., Job)*
Judge none blessed before his death. *(Apocrypha)*
Let me die the death of the righteous. *(Old Test., Numbers)*
Let the dead bury their dead. *(New Test., Matthew)*
Make little weeping for the dead, for he is at rest. *(Apocrypha)*
O death, where is thy sting? O grave, where is thy victory? *(New Test., I Corinth.)*
O that they would consider their latter end. *(Old Test., Deut.)*
The king of terrors. *(Old Test., Job)*

The Lord gave, and the Lord hath taken away; blessed be the name of the Lord. *(Old Test., Job)*
The righteous hath hope in his death. *(Old Test., Psalms)*
There is no discharge in that war. *(Old Test., Eccles.)*
There the wicked cease from troubling; and there the weary be at rest. *(Old Test., Job)*
We all do fade as a leaf. *(Old Test., Isaiah)*
We have made a covenant with death. *(Old Test., Isaiah)*
Weep ye not for the dead, neither bemoan him. *(Old Test., Jerem.)*
Who shall deliver me from the body of this death? *(New Test., Romans)*
Yea, though I walk through the valley of the shadow of death, I shall fear no evil. *(Old Test., Psalms)*
Yet a little sleep, a little slumber, a little folding of the hands to sleep. *(Old Test., Prov.)*
Death does not blow a trumpet. *(Danish)*
Few have luck, all have death. *(Danish)*
A dead man feels no cold.
A death-bed is a detector of the heart.
A dying man can do nothing easy. *(Franklin's last words)*
A fair death honors a whole life.
A man can die but once: we owe God a death. *(Shakespeare)*
A sudden death is but a sudden joy.
All that lives must die.
As dead as a door-nail.
As dead as a herring.
As dead as Queen Anne.
As soon as a man is born he begins to die.
Come, gentle death, the ebb of care . . .
Death aims with fouler spite at fairer marks.
Dead men tell no tales.
Death and marriage make term day.
Death borders upon our birth, and our cradle stands in the grave.
Death has many doors to let out life.
Death is a pleasant road that leads to fame.
Death is but a path that must be trod
If man would ever pass to God. *(Parnell)*
Death is here and death is there,
Death is busy everywhere. *(Shelley)*
Death is only an incident in life.
Death is still working like a mole . . .

Death is the grand leveller.
Death loves a shining mark . . .
Death makes equal the high and low.
Death, of all pain the period.
Death opens the gate of Fame and shuts the gate of Envy after it.
Death takes no bribes.
Death will seize the doctor too . . .
Death's day is doom's day.
Death foreseen comes not.
Golden lads and girls all must,
  As chimney-sweepers, come to dust. *(Shakespeare)*
God help the fools who count on death for gain.
Happy he who dies before he calls for death to take him away.
He doth sin that doth belie the dead. *(Shakespeare)*
He that died half a year ago is as dead as Adam.
He that fears death lives not.
He that once is born, once must die.
He that would die well must always look for death.
How sweet is death to those who weep . . . *(Moore)*
I have a rendezvous with death . . . *(Seeger)*
In the midst of life we are in death. *(Bk. of Com. Prayer)*
It is as natural to die as to be born.
It is not death but dying which is terrible.
It is the lot of men but once to die.
Let us eat and drink, for tomorrow we shall die.
Men fear death, as children fear to go in the dark.
Men may live fools, but fools they cannot die.
Nothing so sure as death.
O eloquent, just, and mighty Death! *(Raleigh)*
Never any weary traveler complained that he came too soon to his journey's end.
O Death! the poor man's dearest friend . . . *(Burns)*
Old men go to death, but death comes to young men.
Peace, rest, and sleep are all we know of death.
Six feet of earth make all equal.
Speak not of a dead man at table.
That fatal sergeant Death spares no degree.
That sweet sleep which medicines all pain. *(Shelley)*
The dead are soon forgotten.
The dead have few friends.

The doors of death are ever open.
The first breath is the beginning of death.
The good die early and the bad die late.
The ripest fruit falls first.
The undiscover'd country from whose bourne
  No traveler returns. *(Shakespeare)*
Then is it best . . . to dyen when that he is best of name. *(Chaucer)*
They died well that live well.
They that live longest must die at last.
They who teach us to die well, have taught few to die willingly. *(Johnson)*
'Tis ours to bear, not to judge the dead.
To be content with death may be better than to desire it. *(Sir T. Browne)*
To die would be an awfully big adventure. *(Barrie)*
To every man upon this earth
  Death cometh soon or late. *(Macaulay)*
To live in hearts we leave behind is not to die.
We weep when we are born, not when we die.
When death puts out the flame, the snuff will tell
  If we are wax or tallow, by the smell. *(Franklin)*
Whom God loveth best, those he taketh soonest.
Whom the gods love die young no matter how long they live. *(Hubbard)*
As soon dies the calf as the cow. *(French)*
Death is the receipt for all evils. *(French)*
Death pays all debts. *(French)*
From the day of your birth you begin to die as well as to live. *(French)*
It is only the dead who do not return. *(French)*
Neither the sun nor death can be regarded without flinching. *(French)*
Rome can give no dispensation from death. *(French)*
The dead are always in the wrong. *(French)*
There's no dying by proxy. *(French)*
To die quickly is a privilege. *(French)*
When one is dead it is for a long time. *(French)*
When the snake is dead, his venom is dead. *(French)*
All men are born richer than they die. *(German)*
Never the grave gives back what it has won. *(German)*
The dead ride fast. *(German)*
Account ye no man happy till he die. *(Greek)*
All, soon or late, are doom'd that path to tread. *(Homer, trans. Pope)*

Better to die once for all than to live in continual terror. *(Greek)*
Dead men bite not. *(Greek)*
Death is a debt we must all pay. *(Greek)*
Death rather than a toilsome life. *(Greek)*
Death takes no denial. *(Greek)*
He but sleeps the holy sleep. *(Greek)*
Men hate death unjustly; it is the greatest defense against their many ills. *(Greek)*
Nobly to die were better than to save one's life. *(Greek)*
Not death is dreadful but a shameful death. *(Greek)*
Praise day at night and life at end. *(Greek)*
The whole earth is a sepulchre for famous men. *(Greek)*
To die well is the chief part of virtue. *(Greek)*
We count it death to falter, not to die. *(Greek)*
Whom the gods love die young. *(Greek)*
A dead man does not make war. *(Italian)*
A good death does honor to a whole life. *(Italian)*
Death foreseen never comes. *(Italian)*
Death spares neither pope nor beggar. *(Italian)*
It takes four living men to carry one dead man out of the house. *(Italian)*
Me dead, the world is dead. *(Italian)*
Six feet of earth make all men equal. *(Italian)*
Black death summons all things under the sway of its law. *(Latin)*
Death defies the doctor. *(Latin)*
Death is rest from labor and misery. *(Latin)*
Death is shameful in flight, glorious in victory. *(Latin)*
Death is sometimes a gift. *(Latin)*
Death lays his impious touch on all things rare. *(Latin)*
Death levels all things. *(Latin)*
Death o'ertakes the man who flees. *(Latin)*
Death—the gate of life. *(Latin)*
Forgetfulness and silence are the privileges of the dead. *(Latin)*
He went over to the majority. *(Latin)*
He who you say has passed away has simply posted on ahead. *(Latin)*
Him who is dead honor with remembrance, not with tears. *(Latin)*
It is uncertain where death may await thee, therefore expect it everywhere. *(Latin)*
Live mindful of death. *(Latin)*
Neither dread your last day nor desire it. *(Latin)*

Pale Death, with impartial step, knocks at the poor man's cottage and at the palaces of kings. *(Horace)*
Remember you must die. [*Memento mori*] *(Latin)*
Speak nothing but good of the dead. [*De mortuis . . .*] *(Latin)*
The fear of death is worse than death itself. *(Latin)*
The life of the dead is in the memory of the living. *(Latin)*
The timid and the brave alike must die. *(Latin)*
The slayer soon follows the slain. *(Latin)*
There is no man who does not die his own death. *(Latin)*
There is no medicine against death. *(Latin)*
This day . . . is the birthday of eternity. *(Latin)*
To die without fear of death is a desirable death. *(Latin)*
To whom life was heavy, the earth is light. *(Polish)*
Death does not take the old but the ripe. *(Russian)*
When you die, even your tomb shall be comfortable. *(Russian)*
Death devours lambs as well as sheep. *(Spanish)*
There is a remedy for everything but death. *(Spanish)*
Death is a black camel which kneels at every man's gate. *(Turkish)*
A good death is better than a bad life. *(Yiddish)*
Death is no chooser. *(Yiddish)*
Death reveals the truth. *(Yiddish)*
No one dies before his time. *(Yiddish)*
No one needs a calendar to die. *(Yiddish)*
The Angel of Death has many eyes. *(Yiddish)*
The young may—the old must. *(Yiddish)*

DEBT

Owe no man anything, but to love one another. *(New Test., Romans)*
A hog upon trust grunts till he's paid for.
A man in debt is caught in a net.
A poor man's debt makes a great noise.
A pound of care pays not a dram of debt.
Better go to bed supperless than to rise in debt.
Debt is the mother of folly and crime.
Debt is the worst poverty.
Debtors are liars.
He has but a short Lent that must pay money at Easter.
He that gets out of debt grows rich.
He who oweth is all in the wrong.
Industry pays debts, Despair increases them.
Loans and debts make worries and frets.

Never spend your money before you have it.
Out of debt, out of danger.
Pay what you owe, and what you're worth you'll know.
Speak not of my debts, unless you mean to pay them.
That is but an empty purse that is full of other men's money.
The first vice is running in debt.
Debt is the worst kind of poverty. *(French)*
He is rich enough who owes nothing. *(French)*
He that pays his debts increases his wealth. *(French)*
The debts go to the next heir. *(German)*
Debts turn freemen into slaves. *(Greek)*
A light debt makes a debtor; a heavy one, an enemy. *(Italian)*
Without debt, without care. *(Italian)*
A debt and gratitude are different things. *(Latin)*
Debt is a grievous bondage to an honorable man. *(Latin)*
A sick man sleeps, but not a debtor. *(Spanish)*
Only a dog has no debts. *(Yiddish)*
You can't pay your debts with tears. *(Yiddish)*

DECEIT

Let no man deceive you with vain words. *(New Test., Ephesians)*
Deceit invites deceit.
He cries wine and sells vinegar.
He that once deceives is ever suspected.
If a man deceives me once, shame on him; if he deceives me twice, shame on me.
If the world will be gulled, let it be gulled. *(Burton)*
O what a tangled web we weave,
When first we practice to deceive! *(Scott)*
One dupe is as impossible as one twin.
The deceits of the world, the flesh, and the devil. *(Bk. of Com. Prayer)*
The easiest person to deceive is one's self.
There's a twofold pleasure in deceiving the deceiving.
Thou hast a crooked tongue, holding with hound and running with hare.
Water in the one hand, fire in the other.
We never are but by ourselves deceived.
Who hath deceived thee as often as thyself?
Who makes the fairest show means most deceit. *(Shakespeare)*
Dissimulation is a coward's virtue. *(French)*
Distrust justifies deceit. *(French)*

One may outwit another, but not all the others. *(French) (cf. Lincoln)*
The surest way to be deceived is to think one's self more clever than others. *(French)*
We are usually deceived by that which we love. *(Molière)*
Who would not be deceived must have as many eyes as hairs on his head. *(German)*
Deceive the deceivers. *(Latin)*
My tongue may swear, but I act as I please. *(Latin)*

DECENCY

Decency is Indecency's Conspiracy of Silence. *(G. B. Shaw)*
Immodest words admit of no defense,
For want of decency is want of sense. *(Roscommon)*

DECISION

He that handles a nettle tenderly is soonest stung.
The door must either be shut or open.
Who shall decide, when doctors disagree?
He who considers too much will perform little. *(German)*
Swift decisions are not sure. *(Greek)*
Settled once, settled forever. *(Latin)*
The die is cast. [*Jacta alea est.*] *(Latin)*
When you decide, let it be once for all. *(Latin)*

DECORUM

Let them cant about decorum
Who have characters to lose. *(Burns)*
Observe decorum even in your sport. *(Latin)*

DEED

Men loved darkness rather than light, because their deeds were evil. *(New Test., John)*

A deed well done pleaseth the heart.
A noble deed is a step toward God.
An ill deed cannot bring honor.
Better not do the deed than weep it done.
Black deeds lean on crutches made of slender reeds.
Deeds not words.
Do deeds worth praise and tell you them at night. *(Shakespeare)*
Do noble things, not dream them, all day long. *(Kingsley)*
Do well and right, and let the world sink.
Goodly is he that goodly doeth.

Great things are done when men and mountains meet . . .*(Blake)*
Handsome is that handsome does.
He hath nothing done that doth not all.
How far that little candle throws his beams!
So shines a good deed in a naughty world. *(Shakespeare)*
If you'd have it done, Go: if not, Send.
Ill deeds are doubled with an evil word.
Let us do or die. *(Burns)*
Our deeds determine us, as much as we determine our deeds.
Our deeds are sometimes better than our thoughts.
The reward for a good deed is to have done it.
The shortest answer is doing.
Unnatural deeds do breed unnatural troubles. *(Shakespeare)*
We know better than we do.
We live in deeds, not years.
What is well done is done soon enough.
Whatever is worth doing at all is worth doing well.
What's done, cannot be undone.
Living requires less life than doing. *(French)*
Great soul, great deed. *(German)*
Only deeds give strength to life. *(German)*
A good man makes no noise over a good deed. *(Greek)*
What we have to learn to do we learn by doing. *(Greek)*
Deeds are males, words are females. *(Italian)*
Many things, base in the doing, please when done. *(Latin)*
Men do not value a good deed unless it brings a reward. *(Latin)*
No deed that sets an example of evil brings joy to the doer. *(Latin)*
Nobody enters his good deeds in his day-book. *(Latin)*
The deed is forgotten but its results remain. *(Latin)*
The deeds of men never deceive the gods. *(Latin)*
The gods see the deeds of the righteous. *(Latin)*
Every man is the son of his own works. *(Spanish)*

DEEP

Deep calleth unto deep. *(Old Test., Psalms)*

DEFECT

Knot in de plank will show through de whitewash. *(American Negro)*

DEFENSE

Defense, not defiance.
Millions for defense but not one cent for tribute. *(Pinckney)*
The best defense is an offense.

DEFILE
It is a foul bird that defiles its own nest. *(Latin)*
A dead dog will defile a cistern filled with rose-water *(Persian)*

DELAY
A delay is better than a disaster.
Delay in vengeance gives a heavier blow.
Delay is preferable to error.
Delays are not denials.
Desires are nourished by delays.
Dull not device by delay.
We hate delay and yet it makes us wise.
You may delay, but Time will not.
Delay is a great procuress. *(Latin)*
Every delay that postpones our joys is long. *(Latin)*
There is danger in delay. *(Latin)*
When a man's life is at stake, no delay is too long. *(Latin)*
He who delays, gathers. *(Spanish)*

DELIGHT
The soul of sweet delight can never be defiled. *(Blake)*
'Tis never too late for delight.

DEMAGOGUE
Demagogues are the mob's lackies. *(Greek)*

DEMAND
Demand creates supply.
To a hasty demand a leisurely supply.

DEMOCRACY
A perfect democracy is the most shameless thing in the world. *(Burke)*
Democracy become a government of bullies tempered by editors. *(Emerson)*
Democracy gives every man the right to be his own oppressor. *(Lowell)*
Democracy is direct self-government, over all the people, for all the people, by all the people. *(Th. Parker, 1858)*
Democracy substitutes election by the incompetent many for appointment by the corrupt few. *(G. B. Shaw)*
Envy is the basis of democracy. *(B. Russell)*
The world must be made safe for democracy. *(W. Wilson)*
The only remedy against democracy is soldiers. *(von Merchel)*
Democracy is better than tyranny. *(Periander)*

Go thou, and first establish democracy in thy household. *(Greek)*
It is not good that the few should be governed by the many. *(Homer)*
Democracy is more cruel than wars or tyrants. *(Seneca)*

DEMURE
As demure as if butter would not melt in her mouth. *(French)*

DENY
He who denies all confesses all. *(Italian)*

DEPENDENCE
Dependence is a poor trade.
He who depends on another dines ill and sups worse.
The bitter bread of dependence . . .

DESCENT
Every beggar is descended from some king, and every king from some beggar.
No man is a thousand descents from Adam.
He who boasts of his descent is like the potato; the best part of him is under ground. *(French)*

DESERVING
Use every man after his desert, and who would 'scape whipping? *(Shakespeare)*
What is deservedly suffered must be borne with calmness. *(Latin)*

DESIRE
Go home and make a net if you desire to get fishes. *(Chinese)*
Desires are nourished by delays.
Desire hath no rest.
First deserve and then desire.
He begins to die that quits his desires.
He that desires but little has no need of much.
Humble hearts have humble desires.
It often happens that desire outlives performance.
Our desires may undo us.
Sooner murder an infant in its cradle than nurse unacted desires. *(Blake)*
The desire of the moth for the star . . . *(Shelley)*
The fewer desires, the more peace.
The sea hath bounds, but deep desire hath none. *(Shakespeare)*
We live in our desires, not in our achievements.

You must learn to desire what you would have.
Learn to level down your desires rather than level up your means. *(Greek)*
His own desire leads every man. *(Latin)*
There is no desire for what is unknown. *(Latin)*
We desire nothing so much as what we ought not to have. *(Latin)*
Desire beautifies what is ugly. *(Spanish)*
Heaven favors good desires. *(Spanish)*

DESPAIR
Out of the depths have I cried unto thee, O Lord. [*De profundis . . .*] *(Old Test., Psalms)*
An evil counselor is despair.
Despair and confidence both banish fear.
Despair defies even despotism.
Despair gives courage to a coward.
Despair ruins some, presumption many.
He soonest loses that despairs to win.
The name of the Slough was Despond. *(Bunyan)*
What do the damned endure but despair?
Despair doubles our strength. *(French)*
Despair has often gained battles. *(French)*
Despair aggravates our weakness. *(French)*
Never despair. [*Nil desperandum.*] *(Horace)*
Desperate diseases must have desperate cures. *(Latin)*

DESPISE
A man must make himself despicable before he is despised. *(Chinese)*
Do not despise an insignificant enemy or a slight wound. *(German)*

DESTINY
It is wise to submit to destiny. *(Chinese)*
A man's destiny is always dark.
No one can be more wise than destiny.
We are what we must and not what we would be.
When a thing is shapen, it shall be. *(Chaucer)*
One meets his destiny often in the road he takes to avoid it. *(French)*
No man of woman born can shun his destiny. *(Greek)*
The destiny assigned to every man is suited to him. *(Greek)*
What will be, will be. *(Italian)*
Each man suffers his own destiny. *(Latin)*

DETERMINATION
Sink or swim.
To him who is determined it remains only to act. *(Italian)*

DEVIL
Get thee behind me, Satan. *(New Test., Matthew)*
Resist the devil, and he will flee from you. *(New Test., James)*
It is not easy to walk on the devil's ice. *(Danish)*
Better keep the devil at the door than turn him out of the house.
Better sit still than rise to meet the devil.
Better the devil you know than the devil you don't know.
Cast a bone in the devil's teeth.
Devils are not so black as they are painted.
Every devil has not a cloven hoof.
Give the devil his due.
He must have a long spoon that shall eat with the devil.
He must needs go that the devil drives.
He that hath shipped the devil must make the best of him.
He that takes the devil into his boat must carry him over the sound.
If the devil catch a man idle, he'll set him at work.
If you have swallowed the devil, you may swallow his horns.
It is easier to raise the devil than to lay him.
Never hold a candle to the devil.
Once a devil, always a devil.
One had as good eat the devil as the broth he's boiled in.
Pride made the devil, and the devil made sin.
Renounce the devil and all his works. *(Bk. Com. Prayer)*
The devil always leaves a stink behind him.
The devil bides his day.
The devil can cite Scripture for his purpose. *(Shakespeare)*
The devil is God's ape.
The devil is never far off.
The devil is not so black as he is painted.
The devil rides upon a fiddlestick.
The devil sometimes speaks the truth.
The devil will take his own.
The prince of darkness is a gentleman. *(Shakespeare)*
There is the devil to pay.
We shall know the devil by his horns.
What is got under the devil's back is spent under his belly.
When the devil was sick, he would be a monk . . .

When the devil grows old he turns hermit. *(French)*
Devils must be driven out with devils. *(German)*
Raise no more devils than you can lay. *(German)*
The devil catches most souls in a golden net. *(German)*
Each man for himself and the devil for all. *(Italian)*
He that is afraid of the devil does not grow rich. *(Italian)*
The devil corrects sin. *(Italian)*
Where the devil cannot put his head he puts his tail *(Italian)*
Talk of the devil and he'll appear. *(Latin)*
The devil take the hindmost. *(Latin)*
The virtue of the devil is in the loins. *(Latin)*
The devil lurks behind the cross. *(Spanish)*

DEVOTION
Devotion, mother of obedience.
Devotion has mastered the hard way. *(Latin)*

DIAMOND
Better a diamond with a flaw than a pebble without. *(Chinese)*
A barley-corn is better than a diamond to a cock.
A diamond is valuable tho' it lie on a dunghill.
Diamond cut diamond.

DICE
The best throw of the dice is to throw them away.
The devil is in the dice.

DIE
Never say die.
To live in the hearts we leave behind us is not to die.
We die as we live. *(Turkish)*

DIFFERENCE
Different sores must have different salves.
Distinction without a difference.
It makes a difference whose ox is gored.
The difference is wide that the sheets will not decide.
The difference 'twixt Tweedledum and Tweedledee.
Different times, different manners. *(Latin)*
There's some difference between Peter and Peter. *(Spanish)*

DIFFICULTY
He who accounts all things easy will have many difficulties. *(Chinese)*
All things are difficult before they are easy.

Difficulty is the daughter of idleness.
Many things difficult to design prove easy to performance.
Nothing is difficult to a willing mind.
It is difficulties which show what men are. *(Greek)*
The best things are most difficult. *(Greek)*
Nothing is so easy but it becomes difficult when done reluctantly. *(Latin)*
The greater the difficulty, the greater the glory. *(Latin)*
Through difficulties to the stars. [*Per aspera ad astra.*] *(Latin)*
What is worth while must needs be difficult. *(Latin)*

DIGESTION
A good digestion turneth all to health.
Things sweet to taste prove in digestion sour. *(Shakespeare)*
Unquiet meals make ill digestions.

DIGNITY
Our dignity is not what we do, but what we understand.
The easiest way to dignity is humility.
Beneath one's dignity. [*"Infra dig."*] *(Latin)*
It is easier to grow in dignity than to make a start. *(Latin)*

DILEMMA
Between hawk and buzzard.
Between the beetle [*-hammer*] and the block.
Between the devil and the deep sea.
Between wind and water.
Go forward and fall, go backward and mar all.
Between Scylla and Charybdis. *(Greek)*
Between the hammer and the anvil. *(Latin)*
Between two stools one goes to the ground. *(Latin)*
Flying from the bull he fell into the river. *(Spanish)*

DILIGENCE
Seest thou a man diligent in his business? he shall stand before kings. *(Old Test., Prov.)*
To perfect diligence nothing is difficult. *(Chinese)*
Diligence overcomes difficulties, sloth makes them.
The diligent hand maketh rich.
The diligent spinner has a large shift.
Diligence is the mother of good luck. *(French)*

DINING

A dinner lubricates business.
After dinner sit a while, after supper walk a mile.
At a round table there's no dispute of place.
At dinner my man appears.
Dinner cannot be long where dainties want.
He that hath a good dinner knows better the way to supper.
I value not your bill of fare; give me your bill of company. *(Swift)*
The more, the merrier; the fewer, the better fare.
Who depends upon another man's table often dines late.
Better is a dinner of herbs where love is, than a stalled ox and hatred therewith. *(Old Test., Prov.)*
A warmed-up dinner was never worth much. *(French)*
Better a good dinner than a fine coat. *(French)*
He sups ill who eats all at dinner. *(French)*
Seven make a banquet; nine make a clamor. *(Latin)*

DIPLOMACY

A diplomat is a man who remembers a woman's birthday and forgets her age.
Diplomacy is easy on the brain but hell on the feet.
Ambassadors are the eye and ear of the state. *(Italian)*

DIRECTNESS

Let your yea be yea; and your nay, nay. *(New Test., James)*

DIRT

Dirt show de quickest on de cleanest cotton. *(American Negro)*
Dirt defies the king.
Dirt is matter out of place.
Dirt is the dirtiest upon the fairest spot.
Dirt parts company.
He that deals in dirt has aye foul fingers.
He that falls into the dirt, the longer he stays there the fouler he is.
He that flings dirt upon another dirties himself most.
You must eat a peck of dirt before you die.
You stout and I stout, who shall carry the dirt out?
Never cast dirt into the fountain of which you have sometime drunk. *(Hebrew)*
Fling dirt enough, and some will stick. *(Latin)*

DISAPPOINTMENT

Nothing is so good as it seems beforehand.

DISCONTENT

A discontented man knows not where to sit easy.
A man's discontent is his worst evil.
Discontent is the first step in progress.
Let thy discontents be thy secrets.
Admiring others' lots, we hate our own. *(Latin)*

DISCORD

If a house be divided against itself, that house cannot stand. *(New Test., Mark)*
The whole concord of the world consist in discord. *(Latin)*

DISCOVER

That which covers thee discovers thee.

DISCRETION

An ounce of discretion is worth a pound of wit.
Courage would fight, but Discretion won't let him.
Discreet women have neither eyes nor ears.
Discretion is the better part of valour.
He that fights and runs away
  May live to fight another day. *(Butler)*
O discretion, thou art a jewel!
While the discreet advise, the fool does his business.
You may give a man office, but you cannot give him discretion.
As a jewel of gold in a swine's snout, so is a fair woman which is without discretion. *(Old Test., Prov.)*
Know not what you know, and see not what you see. *(Latin)*
Shoot not beyond the mark. *(Latin)*

DISCUSSION

Discussion is the anvil on which the spark of truth is struck.

DISEASE

Cure the disease, and kill thy patient.
Diseases are the tax on ill pleasures.
Disease will have its course.
Each season has its own disease.
Feed a cold and starve a fever.
He who was never sick dies the first fit.
Illness makes a man a scoundrel. *(S. Johnson)*
Loathsome canker lives in sweetest bud. *(Shakespeare)*

Sickness comes on horseback, but goes away on foot.
Sickness is catching.
Sickness is felt, but health not at all.
We classify disease as error . . . *(Mrs. Eddy)*
There is no curing a sick man who believes himself in health. *(French)*
There is no mortal whom sorrow and disease do not touch. *(Greek)*
Disease is not of the body but of the place. *(Latin)*
Meet the disease on its way. *(Latin)*
To hide disease is fatal. *(Latin)*
The beginning of health is to know the disease. *(Spanish)*

DISGRACE
Disgraces are like cherries, one draws another.
Better not live at all than live disgraced. *(Greek)*
A wise and good man can suffer no disgrace. *(Latin)*
Disgrace is deathless. *(Latin)*

DISHONEST
By hook or by crook.
Nothing is profitable which is dishonest. *(Latin)*

DISILLUSION
There's not a joy the world can give like that it takes away. *(Byron)*

DISLIKE
I do desire we may be better strangers. *(Shakespeare)*
What you dislike for yourself do not like for me. *(Spanish)*

DISPUTE
Dispute the price but don't dispute the weight. *(Chinese)*
Disputations leave truth in the middle and party at both ends.
He who disputes with the stupid must have sharp answers. *(German)*
There is no disputing about tastes.
[*De gustibus non est disputandum.*] *(Latin)*

DISTANCE
Far away fowls have aye fair feathers.
Far behind must follow faster.
Far from eye, far from heart.
Far shooting never killed bird.
'Tis distance lends enchantment to the view. *(Campbell)*
From a distance it is something; near by it is nothing. *(French)*

Far from Jupiter, far from thunder. *(Latin)*
Respect is greater from a distance. *(Latin)*

DISTRUST
Distrust is poison to friendship.
Distrust that man who tells you to distrust.
Distrust yourself, and sleep before you fight.
Hear all men speak; but credit few or none.
Remember to distrust.
Distrust is the mother of safety. *(French)*

DIVIDE
Who divides honey with the bear gets the lesser share. *(Italian)*

DIVIDED INTEREST
Divide and rule. *(Latin)*
If you run after two hares, you will catch neither. *(Latin)*

DIVINE
It is a good divine that follows his own teachings. *(Shakespeare)*
Divine ashes are better than earthly meal. *(Italian)*
Divine favors were never too late. *(Italian)*

DIVORCE
Divorce, the public brand of shameful life.
Divorce is the sacrament of adultery. *(French)*

DO
Do as you would be done by. *(New Test., trans. by Wyclif)*
It is easier to know how to do than it is to do. *(Chinese)*
All may do what has by man been done.
Do as I say, not as I do.
Do as you may if you can't do as you would.
Do the likeliest and God will do the best.
Do the next thing.
Do well and have well.
Do what you ought and come what can.
If you would have a thing well done, do it yourself.
That which is well done is twice done.
There is a right and a wrong way to do everything.
They that do nothing learn to do ill.
No man can do nothing and no man can do everything. *(German)*
When a thing is done, make the best of it. *(German)*

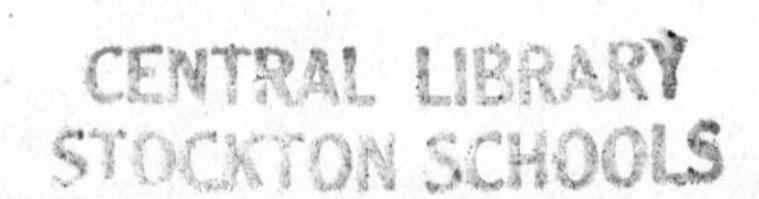

He who cannot do always wants to do. *(Italian)*
What is done cannot be undone. *(Italian)*
To do two things at once is to do neither. *(Latin)*
We do as we can, since we can't do as we would. *(Latin)*
What should be done must be learned from one who does it. *(Latin)*
Whatever you do, do with all your might. *(Latin)*

DOCTOR

Physician, heal thyself. *(New Test., Luke)*
They that be whole need not a physician, but they that are sick. *(New Test., Matthew)*
An ignorant doctor is no better than a murderer. *(Chinese)*
The doctor can cure the sick, but he cannot cure the dead. *(Chinese)*
A man who is his own doctor has a fool for his patient.
A skilful leech is better far
  Than half a hundred men of war. *(Butler)*
After death the doctor.
An old physician, and a young lawyer.
Beware of the young doctor and the young barber.
Doctors disagree.
Every doctor has his favorite disease.
Few physicians live well.
God heals and the doctor takes the fee.
He's the best physician that knows the worthlessness of most medicines.
Honor a physician before thou hast need of him.
If the doctor cures, the sun sees it; if he kills, the earth hides it.
In a good surgeon, a hawk's eye; a lion's heart; and a lady's hand.
Leeches kill with license.
One doctor makes work for another.
Physicians are the cobblers—rather the botchers of men's bodies.
Though the patient die, the doctor is paid.
While the doctors consult, the patient dies.
Better pay the baker than the doctor. *(French)*
Better pay the butcher than the doctor. *(French)*
Happy the doctor who is called in at the end of the disease. *(French)*
The doctor is more to be feared than the disease. *(French)*
A new doctor, a new grave-digger. *(German)*
Every doctor thinks his pills the best. *(German)*
Do not dwell in a city whose governor is a physician. *(Hebrew)*
From the physician and lawyer keep not the truth hidden. *(Italian)*
No good doctor ever takes physic. *(Italian)*

A physician is nothing but a consoler of the mind. *(Latin)*
Every man at thirty is either a fool or a physician. *(Latin)*
He's a fool that makes his doctor his heir. *(Latin)*
In fleeing diseases you fall into the hands of doctors. *(Latin)*
The doctor cannot prescribe by letter; he must feel the pulse. *(Latin)*

DOCTRINE

Carried about with every wind of doctrine. *(New Test., Ephesians)*
. . . prove their doctrines orthodox,
By apostolic blows and knocks. *(Butler)*
Doctrines are nothing but the skin of truth set up and stuffed. *(Beecher)*
Live to explain thy doctrine by thy life.

DOG

A living dog is better than a dead lion. *(Old Test., Eccles.)*
The dog is turned to his own vomit again. *(New Test., II Peter)*
A dog is a dog whatever his color. *(Danish)*
The dog's kennel is not the place to keep a sausage. *(Danish)*
A bad dog never sees the wolf.
A cursed dog should be short tied.
A dog will bark ere he bite.
A dog will not cry if you beat him with a bone.
A dog's nose is ever cold.
A gentle hound should never play the cur.
A good dog deserves a good bone.
A staff is quickly found to beat a dog.
A waking dog afar off barks at a sleeping lion.
An old dog cannot change his way of barking.
Barking dogs never bite.
Better to have a dog fawn on you than bark at you.
Dogs are fine in the field.
Dogs bark as they are bred.
Dogs begin in jest and end in earnest.
Dogs gnaw bones because they cannot swallow them.
Dogs have teeth in all countries.
Dogs run away with the whole shoulders.
Dogs that put up many hares kill none.
Dogs wag their tails, not for you, but for your bread.
Every dog has his day.
Give a dog an ill name and hang him.
He that keeps another man's dog, shall have nothing left him but the line.

He that lieth down with dogs, shall rise up with fleas.
His bark is worse than his bite.
Hungry dogs will eat dirty puddings.
If you wish the dog to follow you, feed him.
It is a hard winter when dog eats dog.
It is hard to teach an old dog new tricks.
Killing the dog does not cure the bite.
Let dogs delight to bark and bite . . . *(Watts)*
Let sleeping dogs lie.
Look not for musk in a dog's kennel.
Love me, love my dog.
Old dogs bark not for nothing.
The slowest barker is the surest biter.
When a dog is drowning, everyone offers him drink.
A man who wants to drown his dog says he is mad. *(French)*
A snappish cur never wants a sore ear. *(French)*
The more I see of men, the more I admire dogs. *(French)*
A bashful dog never fattens. *(German)*
What! keep a dog and bark myself. *(German)*
When the dog is awake the shepherd may sleep. *(German)*
Like a dog in the manger. *(Greek)*
A hair of the dog cures the bite. *(Italian)*
A kitchen dog was never good for the chase. *(Italian)*
Cut off the dog's tail, he remains a dog. *(Italian)*
Every dog is a lion at home. *(Italian)*
The dog that licks ashes is not to be trusted with flour. *(Italian)*
Beat the dog before the lion. *(Latin)*
Beware of a silent dog and still water. *(Latin)*
The wild boar is often held by a small dog. *(Latin)*
Dogs bark and the wind carries it away. *(Russian)*
A lean dog gets nothing but fleas. *(Spanish)*
The dog that kills wolves is killed by wolves. *(Spanish)*
Try that bone on some other dog. *(Spanish)*
The dog barks and the caravan passes. *(Turkish)*
Don't send a dog to the butcher's for meat. *(Yiddish)*
Don't show a beaten dog the stick. *(Yiddish)*
Every dog in his own yard. *(Yiddish)*
Give a dog your finger, and he'll want your whole hand. *(Yiddish)*
If you are a dog, don't be a pig too. *(Yiddish)*
Let a dog bark, and you go on your way. *(Yiddish)*

DOLLAR

The almighty dollar, that great object of universal devotion . . . *(W. Irving)*

DONKEY

If you cannot drive an ox drive a donkey.
Like a donkey between two bundles of hay. *(Latin)*

DOOMSDAY

A thousand pounds and a bottle of hay, is all one thing at doomsday.

DOOR

At open doors dogs come in.
The back door robs the house.
A door must be either open or shut. *(French)*
Every door may be shut but death's door. *(Italian)*
When one door shuts another opens. *(Spanish)*

DOUBT

He that doubteth is damned. *(New Test., Romans)*
An honest man can never surrender an honest doubt.
Doubt makes the mountain which faith can move.
He that casteth all doubts shall never be resolved.
There lives more faith in honest doubt,
  Believe me, than in half the creeds. *(Tennyson)*
Through doubt error acquires honor . . .
To doubt is safer than to be secure.
When in doubt do nowt.
When in doubt win the trick.
Who never doubted never half believed.
The first step towards philosophy is incredulity. *(Diderot)*
Who knows nothing doubts nothing. *(French)*
The wise are prone to doubt. *(Greek)*
Doubt charms me no less than knowledge. *(Dante)*
To believe with certainty we must begin with doubting. *(Polish)*

DOVE

Oh that I had wings like a dove . . . *(Old Test., Psalms)*
Doves will peck in safeguard of their brood. *(Shakespeare)*
Who hawks at eagles with a dove?

DOWN

He that is down can fall no lower.
He that is down, down with him.
Look down, and you'll see how high up you are. *(Yiddish)*

DOWRY

A great dowry is a bed full of brambles.
He who gets a dowry with his wife, sells himself for it.
He who marries for money, earns it.
Old woman's gold is not ugly.

DREAM

All men of action are dreamers.
Dream of a funeral and you hear of a marriage.
Dreamer of dreams, born out of my due time . . . *(W. Morris)*
Dreams go by contraries.
Foolish men have foolish dreams.
Love's dreams prove seldom true.
None thrives for long upon the happiest dreams.
The more a man dreams, the less he believes.
You eat, in dreams, the custard of the day.
Who lives in a silver bed has golden dreams. *(German)*
Dreams are from Zeus. *(Greek)*

DRESS

Silk was invented so that woman could go naked in clothes. *(Arabian)*
The woman shall not wear that which pertaineth unto man.
(Old Test., Deut.)
They sewed fig-leaves together and made themselves aprons.
(Old Test., Gen.)
Clothes make the man. *(Dutch)*
A civil habit oft covers a good man.
A peasant's dress befits a peasant's fortune.
A sweet disorder in the dress
  Kindles in clothes a wantonness. *(Herrick)*
Avoid any particular character in your dress. *(Chesterfield)*
Beauty when most unclothed is clothed best.
Costume is not dress. *(Whistler)*
Eat to please thyself, but dress to please others.
Fine clothes is never out of fashion.
Fine dressing is a foul house swept before the doors.
Fine feathers make fine birds.

Good clothes open doors.
If all the world went naked, how could we tell the kings?
In dress consult your purse before your fancy.
It's not the skirt that ruins papa, it's the chiffon ruffles.
Let him who has a threadbare soul wear new garments.
Let thy attire be comely but not costly.
No fine clothes can hide the clown.
Plain without pomp, rich without show. *(Dryden)*
Set not thy sweet heart on proud array. *(Shakespeare)*
That man is best dressed whose dress no one observes.
The hood makes not the monk, nor the apparel the man.
The tailor makes the man.
We are all Adam's children, but silk makes the difference.
Without black velvet breeches, what is man?
Dress slowly when you are in a hurry. *(French)*
In your own country, your name; in other countries, your dress. *(Hebrew)*
The white coat does not make the miller. *(Italian)*
Though manners make, yet apparel shapes. *(Italian)*
A negligent dress is becoming to men. *(Latin)*
If she is beautiful, she is overdressed. *(Latin)*
A stick dressed up does not look like a stick. *(Spanish)*
Dress does not give knowledge. *(Spanish)*
He who has but one coat cannot lend it. *(Spanish)*
The dress does not make the friar. *(Spanish)*
The outer dress covers the petticoat. *(Yiddish)*

DRIFT

Drift is as bad as unthrift.

DRINK

Woe unto them that rise up early in the morning, that they may follow strong drink. *(Old Test., Isaiah)*
Good drink drives out bad thoughts. *(Dutch)*
A hair of the dog that bit us last night
Ale in, wit out.
As deep drinketh the goose as the gander.
As they brew, so let them drink.
Bacchus hath drowned more than Neptune.
Better belly burst than good drink lost.
Candy is dandy, but liquor is quicker. *(O. Nash)*
Cobblers and tinkers are the best ale-drinkers.

Drink afterwards less and go home by daylight.
Drink and drowth come seldom together.
Drink does not drown Care, but waters it . . .
Drinking is the soldier's pleasure. *(Dryden)*
Drink down all unkindness.
Drink makes men hungry or it makes them lie.
Drink only with the duck. [*i.e. water*]
Drink wine and have the gout; drink none, and have the gout.
Drunken days have all their tomorrows.
Drunken men never take harm.
Ever drunk, ever dry.
Go not for every thirst to the pot.
He is drinking at the *Harrow* when he should be at the plow.
He that drinks well, sleeps well.
He that goes to bed thirsty, rises healthy.
He was hanged that left his drink behind him.
"It's a long time between drinks."
Long quaffing maketh a short life.
Much drinking, little thinking.
There is no deceit in a brimmer.
They drink with impunity, or anybody who invites them.
They never taste who always drink.
To drink healths is to drink sickness.
To drink like a funnel.
When the wine is in, the wit is out.
Whiskey is a bad thing—especially bad whiskey.
Thirst comes with drinking, when the wine is good. *(French)*
Thirst departs with drinking *(French)*
Who has drunk will drink. *(French)*
Thousands drink themselves to death before one dies of thirst. *(German)*
If you cannot carry your liquor when you are young, you will be a water-carrier when you are old. *(Greek)*
Never go out to drink on a winter night. *(Greek)*
When the wine is in, murder will out. *(Hebrew)*
A man cannot whistle and drink at the same time. *(Italian)*
Drink wine and let the water go to the mill. *(Italian)*
A hot drink is as good as an overcoat. *(Latin)*
Wisdom is clouded by wine. *(Latin)*
Only what I drink is mine. *(Polish)*
Under a bad cloak there is often a good drinker. *(Spanish)*

DRIVE

Drive gently over the stones.
Drive the nail that will go.
It is better driving a flock than one.

DROP

Constant dropping wears the stone.
The last drop makes the cup flow over.
The whole ocean is made up of little drops.
Drop by drop fills the tub. *(French)*

DROWN

A drowning man will catch at a straw.
Good swimmers are oftmost drowned.
Pour not water on a drowned mouse.
When a dog is drowning, everyone offers him a drink.
A drowning man will catch on to the edge of a sword. *(Yiddish)*
You can be drowned even at the shore. *(Yiddish)*

DRUNKENNESS

Licker talks mighty loud w'en it gits loose from de jug. *(American Negro)*
The best cure for drunkenness is, while sober, to see a drunken man. *(Chinese)*
A drunkard can soon be made to dance. *(Danish)*
A drunken night makes a cloudy morning.
A drunkard's purse is his bottle.
Drinking takes the drunkard first out of society, then out of the world.
Drunkards have a fool's tongue and a knave's heart.
He that killeth a man when he is drunk shall be hanged when he is sober.
It is kindness to lead the sober; a duty to lead the drunk.
Let the drunkard alone and he will fall of himself.
The drunkard's joy is the sober man's woe.
What is in the heart of the sober, is on the tongue of the drunkard.
What the sober man thinks the drunkard tells. *(French)*
The wise drunkard is a sober fool. *(German)*
Better to trip with the feet than with the tongue. *(Greek)*
Drunkards beget drunkards. *(Greek)*
No fool is silent over his cups. *(Greek)*
The drunkard is always talking of wine. *(Italian)*
Drunkenness does not create vice; it merely brings it into view. *(Latin)*

Drunkenness is voluntary madness. *(Latin)*
I would appeal to Philip, but to Philip sober. *(Latin)*
What soberness conceals, Drunkenness reveals. *(Latin)*
A drunken woman is only herself. *(Russian)*
The drunken don't think their own thoughts. *(Russian)*
For ilka man that's drunk's a lord. *(Burns)*
There's a special Providence watches ower drunk men and bairns. *(Scottish)*
A young drunkard, an old pauper. *(Yiddish)*
There's no bad brandy for a drunkard. *(Yiddish)*

DUE
Give the devil his due.
Who loses his due gets no thanks.

DUST
He that blows in the dust, fills his eyes with it.

DUTY
Duty before pleasure.
Duty determines destiny.
Duty is what one expects from others. *(O. Wilde)*
God never imposes a duty without giving the time to perform it.
Stern Daughter of the voice of God. *(Wordsworth)*
To do my duty in that state of life unto which it shall please God to call me. *(Bk. Com. Prayer)*
Do well the duty that lies before you. *(Greek)*
Slight not what is near through aiming at what is far. *(Greek)*
In doing what we ought we deserve no praise. *(Latin)*
It is an honor to have remembered one's duty. *(Latin)*

DWARF
A dwarf on a giant's shoulders sees farther of the two. *(Latin)*

EAGLE

Wheresoever the carcass is, there will the eagles be gathered together. *(New Test., Matthew)*

Eagles do not breed doves.

Eagles fly alone.

The eagle never lost so much time as when he submitted to learn of the crow. *(Blake)*

The eagle suffers little birds to sing . . .

You cannot fly like an eagle with the wings of a wren.

When the eagle is dead, the crows pick out his eyes. *(German)*

No need to teach an eagle to fly. *(Greek)*

The eagle does not make war against frogs. *(Italian)*

Eagles catch no flies. *(Latin)*

EAR

He that hath ears to hear, let him hear. *(New Test., Mark)*

The ear trieth words as the mouth tasteth meat. *(Old Test., Job)*

Cities are taken by ears.

Give every man thy ear, but few thy voice. *(Shakespeare)*

One pair of ears draws a hundred tongues.

Little pitchers have great ears.

The hearing ear is close to the speaking tongue.

Walls have ears.

The ear is the road to the heart. *(French)*

Ears are eyes to the blind. *(Greek)*

We have two ears and one mouth that we may listen the more and talk the less. *(Greek)*

If your ear burns, someone is talking about you. *(Latin)*

In at one ear and out at the other. *(Latin)*

Let the ear despise nothing, nor yet believe anything forthwith. *(Latin)*

Even a boot has ears. *(Yiddish)*

EARLY
Early to bed and early to rise,
  Makes a man healthy, wealthy, and wise.
Get a name to rise early, and you may lie all day.
Go to bed with the lamb, and rise with the lark.
The early bird catches the worm.
The morning hour has gold in its mouth. *(German)*
He who does not rise with the sun does not enjoy the day. *(Spanish)*
Out early and watch, labor and catch. *(Spanish)*
Early to bed, and early to get married. *(Yiddish)*

EARTH
Of the earth, earthy. *(New Test., I Corinth.)*
One generation passeth away, and another generation cometh; but the earth abideth forever. *(Old Test., Eccles.)*
Speak to the earth, and it shall teach thee. *(Old Test., Job)*
The earth is the Lord's, and the fulness thereof. *(Old Test., Psalms)*
The heaven is my throne, and the earth is my footstool. *(Old Test., Isaiah)*
Earth's the best shelter.
He findeth God who finds the earth He made.
The earth produces all things, and receives all again.
The little O, the earth. *(Shakespeare)*
The poetry of earth is never dead. *(Keats)*
The earth is a host who murders his guests. *(Persian)*

EARTHQUAKE
The earth-ox changes his burden to the other shoulder. *(Chinese)*

EAST
Easterly winds and rain bring cockles here from Spain.
Oh, East is East, and West is West, and never the twain shall meet. *(Kipling)*
From the East comes light, from the West, law. *(Latin)*

EASTER
At Easter let your clothes be new, or else be sure you will it rue.
Easter so longed for is gone in a day.
You keep Easter when I keep Lent.
Jesus is risen today . . . *(Latin)*

EASY
It is easy to manage when fortune favors. *(Danish)*
It is not easy to know your butter in another man's cottage. *(Danish)*

As easy as lying.
Easy come, easy go.
It is easier to pull down than to build up.
Nothing is easy to the unwilling.

EAT

Gather up the fragments that remain, that nothing be lost.
(New Test., John)
Leave off first for manners' sake. *(Apocrypha)*
Let us eat and drink; for tomorrow we shall die. *(Old Test., Isaiah)*
Strong meat belongeth to them that are of full age. *(New Test., Hebr.)*
Take no thought for your life, what ye shall eat, or what ye shall drink. *(New Test., Matthew)*
Take thine ease, eat, drink and be merry. *(New Test., Luke)*
Whether therefore ye eat, or drink, or whatever ye do, do all to the glory of God. *(New Test., I Corinth.)*
A man must eat though every tree were a gallows. *(Dutch)*
Better bide the cooks than the medicines.
By suppers more have been killed than *Galen* ever cured.
Eat, and welcome; fast, and heartily welcome.
Eat at pleasure, drink by measure.
Eat enough and it will make you wise.
Eat less and drink less, and buy a knife at Michaelmas.
Eat peas with the king, and cherries with the beggar.
Eat thy meat, and drink thy drink, and stand thy ground.
Eat till you sweat and work till you freeze.
Eat-well is Drink-well's brother.
Eat when you're hungry, and drink when you're dry.
Eat without surfeit; drink without drunkenness.
Eat your fill and pouch none.
Eating and drinking wants but a beginning.
Feed by measure and defy the physician.
He hath eaten me out of house and home.
He that banquets every day never makes a good meal.
He that eats well should do his duty well.
It is good to be merry at meat.
Lazy folks' stomachs don't get tired.
Many dishes make many diseases.
Never spare the parson's wine, nor the baker's pudding.
The proof of the pudding is in the eating.
The table robs more than a thief.

The way to a man's heart is through his stomach.
There is no love sincerer than the love of food.
They say fingers were made before forks, and hands before knives.
To lengthen thy life, lessen thy meals.
Unquiet meals make ill digestions.
We never repent of having eaten too little.
Who dainties love shall beggars prove.
Who will eat the kernel of the nut must break the shell.
Young children and chickens would ever be eating.
Breakfast makes good memory. *(Rabelais)*
Eating and drinking takes away one's stomach. *(French)*
He who eats too much knows not how to eat. *(French)*
One may be surfeited by eating tarts. *(French)*
Tell me what you eat, and I will tell you what you are. *(French)*
As a man eats so he works. *(German)*
One does not eat acorns when he has pearls. *(German)*
One is what he eats. *(German)*
A rich man, when he will; a poor man, when he can. *(Greek)*
Eat to live, not live to eat. *(Greek)*
At table it becomes no one to be bashful. *(Latin)*
Manners in eating count for something. *(Latin)*
Stop short of your appetite. *(Latin)*
Their sole reason for living lies in their palate. *(Latin)*
What is food to one may be poison to another. *(Latin)*
You require flesh if you want to be fat. *(Latin)*
He who eats the meat, let him pick the bone. *(Spanish)*
If you eat it for supper, you can't have it for breakfast. *(Spanish)*
Not with whom you are bred, but with whom you are fed. *(Spanish)*
Who eats his dinner alone must saddle his horse alone. *(Spanish)*
Eat the fruit and don't inquire about the tree. *(Turkish)*

EAVESDROPPER

Eavesdroppers never hear any good of themselves. *(French)*

EBB

Every flow hath its ebb.

ECHO

Echo is the voice of the reflection in the mirror.
Our echoes roll from soul to soul. *(Tennyson)*

ECONOMY

A good saver is a good server.
Economy is a great revenue.
Of saving cometh having.
Spare at the spigot and let out at the bung-hole.
Spare well and have well.
Take care of the pence, and the pounds will take care of themselves.
That penny is well spent that saves a groat.
Without frugality none can be rich, and with it very few would be poor.
Economy is the wealth of the poor and the wisdom of the rich. *(French)*
A farthing saved is twice earned. *(Italian)*
Economy is too late at the bottom of the purse. *(Latin)*
Frugality embraces all the other virtues. *(Latin)*
Frugality is a handsome income. *(Latin)*
Frugality is misery in disguise. *(Latin)*

EDUCATION

A person may be educated beyond his intelligence.
Better build schoolrooms for "the boy,"
  Than cells and gibbets for "the man." *(E. Cook)*
Education makes the man.
Genius without education is like silver in the moon.
He that brings up his son to nothing, breeds a thief.
Nothing so much worth as a mind instructed.
Self-education is fine when the pupil is a born educator.
The Common School is the greatest discovery ever made by man. *(H. Mann)*
The only really educated men are self-educated.
The secret of education lies in respecting the pupil. *(Emerson)*
'Tis education forms the common mind;
  Just as the twig is bent the tree's inclined. *(Pope)*
What sculpture is to a block of marble, education is to the soul.
Nature has always been stronger than education. *(French)*
Public instruction should be the first object of government. *(Napoleon)*
Too much and too little education hinders the mind. *(French)*
Educated men are as much superior to the uneducated as the living are to the dead. *(Greek)*
Education is an ornament in prosperity and a refuge in adversity. *(Greek)*

Only the educated are free. *(Greek)*
The foundation of every society is education of its youth. *(Greek)*
The roots of education are bitter, but the fruit is sweet. *(Greek)*
There is no royal road to geometry. *(Euclid)*
Education leads to an immortal treasure. *(Latin)*
Education is the poor man's haven. *(Latin)*
It is only the ignorant who despise education. *(Latin)*

EEL
All that breed in the mud are not eels.
An eel held by the tail is not yet caught.
Mud chokes no eels.
You cannot hide an eel in a sack.

EFFICIENT
He kills two birds with one stone.

EFFORT
He that blows hardest bears away the horn.

EGG
Eggs and oaths are easily broken. *(Danish)*
A black hen lays a white egg.
An evil crow, an evil egg.
But one egg, and that addled.
It is very hard to shave an egg.
Put all your eggs in one basket—and watch the basket. *(Mark Twain)*
The more the eggs, the worse the hatch.
Omelettes are not made without breaking eggs. *(French)*
A wild goose never laid a tame egg. *(Gaelic)*
He who treads on eggs must tread lightly. *(German)*
As full as an egg is of meat. *(Italian)*
There are many that will have both the egg and the hen. *(Italian)*
He that would have eggs must endure the cackling of hens. *(Latin)*
A hen will sit on one egg. *(Spanish)*
Do not venture all your eggs in one basket. *(Spanish)*
The egg would be wiser than the hen. *(Yiddish)*

EGOISM
Every man is of importance to himself.
He that is giddy thinks the world turns round. *(Shakespeare)*
We talk little if we do not talk of ourselves.

When a man tries himself, the verdict is in his favor.
Who venerate themselves, the world despise.
It is difficult to esteem a man as highly as he would wish. *(French)*
The egoist does not tolerate egoism. *(French)*
I easily regain favor with myself. *(Latin)*

EGYPT

And they spoiled the Egyptians. *(Old Test., Exodus)*
The land of Egypt, when we sat by the fleshpots . . .
(Old Test., Exodus)

ELEPHANT

The elephant is not won with anger.
Slow as the elephant.
The elephant does not feel a flea-bite. *(Italian)*
An elephant does not catch mice. *(Latin)*

ELOQUENCE

Eloquence is the child of knowledge.
He that has not silver in his purse, should have silk on his tongue.
True eloquence scorns eloquence. *(Pascal)*
Eloquence avails nothing against the voice of gold. *(Latin)*
Everyone is eloquent in his own cause. *(Latin)*
He is eloquent enough for whom truth speaks. *(Latin)*
It is the heart which makes men eloquent. *(Latin)*
Often there is eloquence in a silent look. *(Latin)*
Their own eloquence is fatal to many. *(Latin)*

EMPTY

De stopper get de longest rest in de empty jug. *(American Negro)*
An empty sack cannot stand upright.
Empty chambers make foolish maids.
Empty vessels make the greatest sound.
Empty hands allure no hawks. *(Latin)*

END

Let us do evil that good may come. *(New Test., Romans)*
The end is not yet. *(New Test., Matthew)*
The end of a thing is better than the beginning. *(Old Test., Eccles.)*
All's well that ends well.
As a thing begins, so ends it still.
Everything hath an end.

Everything hath an end, and a pudding hath two.
He who wills the end wills the means.
In the end things will mend.
Let the end try the man.
The end makes all equal.
The end tries all.
The longest day has an end.
There's a divinity that shapes our ends,
  Rough-hew them how we will. *(Shakespeare)*
Who keeps one end in view makes all things serve.
In everything consider the end. *(French)*
Remember the end. *(Greek)*
The end of a corsair is to drown. *(Italian)*
Look at the end. *(Latin)*
The end crowns the word. *(Latin)*
The result justifies the deed. *(Latin)*
When the end is lawful, the means are also lawful.
[*Jesuit motto, 1650*] *(Latin)*

ENDURE

He that shall endure unto the end, the same shall be saved.
(New Test., Matthew)
Bear and forbear.
Every lot is to be overcome by endurance.
He that endures is not overcome. *(Chaucer)*
What is bitter to endure may be sweet to remember.
What can't be cured were best endured.
Nothing befalls any man which he is not fitted to endure. *(Greek)*

ENEMY

No man is without enemies. *(Arabian)*
A man's foes shall be they of his own household. *(New Test., Matthew)*
If thine enemy be hungry, give him bread to eat. *(Old Test., Prov.)*
Rejoice not over the greatest enemy being dead. *(Apocrypha)*
He who feeds a wolf strengthens his enemy. *(Danish)*
A man cannot be too careful in the choice of his enemies. *(O. Wilde)*
A man has many enemies when his back is to the wall.
A man's greatness can be measured by his enemy.
An enemy may chance to give good counsel.
An enemy's mouth seldom speaks well.
Do not under-value an enemy by whom you have been worsted.
Every wise man dreadeth his enemy. *(Chaucer)*

In an enemy spots are soon seen.
Love your enemies, for they tell you your faults. *(Franklin)*
Make your enemy your friend.
My nearest and dearest enemy.
One enemy can do more hurt than ten friends can do good.
One enemy is one too many.
Once an enemy, always an enemy.
Though thy enemy be a mouse, yet watch him like a lion.
Who shows mercy to an enemy denies it to himself.
None but myself ever did me any harm. *(Napoleon)*
There is no little enemy.
Little enemies and little wounds are not to be despised. *(German)*
One foe is too many; and a hundred friends too few. *(German)*
Even from a foe a man may learn wisdom. *(Greek)*
He that gives honor to his enemy is like to an ass. *(Hebrew)*
Your enemy makes you wise. *(Italian)*
Do not speak ill of an enemy, but think it. *(Latin)*
Enmity is anger watching the opportunity for revenge. *(Latin)*
Fortune can give no greater advantage than discord among the enemy. *(Latin)*
His must be a very wretched fortune who has no enemy. *(Latin)*
It is well to learn even from an enemy. *(Latin)*
Man is his own worst enemy. *(Latin)*
No tears are shed when an enemy dies. *(Latin)*
The body of a dead enemy always smells sweet. *(Latin)*
Be my enemy, but go to my mill. *(Spanish)*
For a fleeing enemy make a golden bridge. *(Spanish)*
Of enemies the fewer the better. *(Spanish)*
Take heed of enemies reconciled, and of meat twice boiled. *(Spanish)*
Be thy enemy an ant, see in him an elephant. *(Turkish)*
Water sleeps, the enemy wakes. *(Turkish)*
Better a good enemy than a bad friend. *(Yiddish)*

ENGLAND

A nation of shopkeepers. *(S. Adams, 1776)*
An acre in Middlesex is better than a principality in Utopia. *(Macaulay)*
An Englishman does not travel to see Englishmen.
An Englishman loves a lord.
An Englishman thinks he is moral when he is only uncomfortable. *(G. B. Shaw)*

An old and haughty Nation proud in arms. *(Milton)*
England expects every man to do his duty. *(Nelson)*
England is the mother of parliaments. *(Bright)*
England, with all thy faults, I love thee still. *(Cowper)*
Every Englishman's house is his castle.
God and my right. [*Motto of Richard I*]
Hearts of oak are our ships,
  Hearts of oak are our men. *(Garrick)*
His Majesties dominions on which the sun never sets.
No Englishman is ever fairly beaten. *(G. B. Shaw)*
Pudding and beef make Britons fight.
Rule, Britannia, rule the waves;
  Britons never will be slaves. *(Thomson)*
St. George was for England: St. Denis was for France.
  Sing *Honi soit qui mal y pense.*
The English are the stupidest in speech, the wisest in action. *(Carlyle)*
The self-complaisant British sneer.
What should they know of England who only England know? *(Kipling)*
When two Englishmen meet their first talk is of the weather.
Ah! perfidious Albion! *(French)*
Drunk as an Englishman. *(French)*
England is a good land, and a bad people. *(French)*
In this country they put an admiral to death from time to time to encourage the others. *(Voltaire)*
The English amuse themselves sadly. *(French)*
The English never value anything until they lose it. *(French)*
Not only England, but every Englishman, is an island. *(Novalís)*
Silence—a conversation with an Englishman. *(Heine)*
England is the paradise of women, the purgatory of men, and the hell of horses. *(Italian)*
In England there are sixty different religions and only one sauce. *(Italian)*
Not Angles, but Angels. *(Pope Gregory I)*
The English are the best at weeping and the worst at laughing. *(Latin)*

ENOUGH
Enough to keep the wolf from the door.
Enough to make a cat speak.
Enough to make a saint swear.
He is wise that knows when he's well enough.
Leave well enough alone.

Enough is as good as a feast. *(Greek)*
There is never enough where nothing is left. *(Italian)*

ENTHUSIASM

Every production of genius must be the production of enthusiasm. *(D'Israeli)*
He that burns most, shines most.
Two dry sticks will burn a green one.
He freezes who does not burn. *(Latin)*

ENVY

Envy and wrath shorten the life. *(Apocrypha)*
Envy does not enter an empty house. *(Danish)*
A man shall never be enriched by envy.
An envious man is a squint-eyed fool.
Bad eyes never see any good.
Envy is the sincerest form of flattery.
Envy's a coal comes hissing hot from hell.
Envy never enriched any man.
Envy, the living, not the dead, doth bite . . . *(Lovelace)*
Expect not praise without envy until you are dead.
I envy no man, no, not I,
  And no man envies me. *(MacKay)*
Men always hate most what they envy most.
Nothing sharpens sight like envy.
The envious man shall never want woe.
The green sickness. *(Shakespeare)*
Envy goes beyond avarice. *(French)*
The envious die, but envy never. *(French)*
Envy is the sorrow of fools. *(German)*
As rust corrupts iron, so envy corrupts man. *(Greek)*
Envy slays itself by its own arrows. *(Greek)*
It is better to be envied than pitied. *(Greek)*
A brave man is able to bear envy. *(Latin)*
Envy has no holidays. *(Latin)*
I would rather my enemies envy me than I envy them. *(Latin)*
Nothing can allay the rage of biting envy. *(Latin)*
Our neighbor's crop seems better than our own. *(Latin)*
The envious grow thin at others' prosperity. *(Latin)*
The envious heart procures mickle smart. *(Scottish)*
Your cracked jug seems better to me than my sound one. *(Spanish)*

EPIGRAM

No epigram contains the whole truth.

Somewhere in the world there is an epigram for every dilemma. *(van Loon)*

What is an epigram? A dwarfish whole
Its body brevity, and wit its soul. *(Coleridge)*

EPITAPH

Gravestones tell truths scarce forty years. *(Sir T. Browne)*

In lapidary inscriptions a man is not upon oath. *(Johnson)*

EQUALITY

All men are equal before the natural law.

We hold these truths to be self-evident, that all men are created equal . . . *(Jefferson)*

Equality begins in the grave. *(French)*

Equality breeds no war. *(Greek)*

We are all born equal, and distinguished alone by virtue. *(Latin)*

All fingers are equal in the clenched fist. *(Russian)*

In the bath-house all are equal. *(Yiddish)*

ERROR

When the learned man errs, he errs with a learned error. *(Arabian)*

The last error shall be worse than the first. *(New Test., Matth.)*

Who can discern his errors? *(Old Test., Psalms)*

An error cannot be believed sincerely enough to make it a truth. *(Ingersoll)*

Error cannot be defended but by error.

Error is a hardy plant that flourishes in every soil.

Error is worse than ignorance.

Errors, like straws, upon the surface flow;
He who would search for pearls, must dive below. *(Dryden)*

Error lives ere reason can be born. *(Congreve)*

. . . error, wounded, writhes in pain,
And dies among her worshippers. *(Bryant)*

He who errs quickly is quick in correcting his error.

Honest error is to be pitied, not ridiculed.

If the wise erred not, it would go hard with fools.

No man prospers so suddenly as by others' errors.

One error breeds twenty more.

There is no anguish like an error of which we are ashamed.

Yesterday's errors let yesterday cover.

You conquer error by denying its verity. *(Mrs. Eddy)*
Love truth, but pardon error. *(French)*
The shortest errors are always the best. *(French)*
Erring is not cheating. *(German)*
Truth belongs to the man, error to his age. *(Goethe)*
No one who lives in error is free. *(Greek)*
The wisest of the wise may err. *(Greek)*
Error is no payment. *(Italian)*
Who errs in the tens errs in the thousands. *(Italian)*
Error is prolific. *(Latin)*
I would rather err with Plato than perceive the truth with others. *(Cicero)*
To err is human. *(Latin)*
Error is the force that welds men together. *(Tolstoy)*
Him who errs forgive once but never twice. *(Spanish)*
Who errs and mends, commends himself to God. *(Spanish)*

ESCAPE

The mouse that has but one hole is quickly taken. *(Latin)*

ESTATE

The bones of a great estate are worth the picking.
He who walks daily over his estate finds a coin each time. *(Hebrew)*

ETERNITY

Eternity has no gray hairs.
Eternity is written in the skies.
In the presence of eternity, the mountains are as transient as the clouds.
Eternity consists of opposites. *(Latin)*

EUROPE

Better fifty years of Europe than a cycle of Cathay. *(Tennyson)*

EVIDENCE

Some circumstantial evidence is very strong, as when you find a trout in the milk. *(Thoreau)*

EVIL

For everyone that doeth evil hateth the light. *(New Test., John)*
Recompense to no man evil for evil. *(New Test., Romans)*
Sufficient unto the day is the evil thereof. *(New Test., Matthew)*

Evil conduct is the root of misery. *(Chinese)*
All spirits are enslaved which serve things evil. *(Shelley)*
Bear with evil and expect good.
Better good afar off than evil at hand.
By excess of evil, evil dies.
Evil communications corrupt good manners.
Evil got, evil spent.
Evil is soon learned.
Evil is wrought by want of thought
  As well as want of heart. *(Hood)*
Evils must be cured by their contraries.
Evil shall have that evil well deserves. *(Chaucer)*
Man creates the evil he endures.
None but the base in baseness do delight.
Of evil grain no good seed can come.
Of one ill come many.
Of two evils choose the least.
To a mortal man no evil is immortal.
All evils are equal when they are extreme.
Evil is easy and has infinite forms. *(Pascal)*
Evil often triumphs but never conquers.
Evil to him who evil thinks. [*Honi soit qui mal y pense.*]
The fear of one evil may lead one into a worse.
We believe no evil till the evil's done.
Doing evil to avoid an evil cannot be good. *(German)*
Who does not punish evil invites it. *(German)*
Of evils we must choose the least. *(Greek)*
Never do evil that good may come of it. *(Italian)*
The worse the evil, the calmer we face it. *(Italian)*
Evil is fittest to consort with evil. *(Latin)*
No one becomes at once completely vile. *(Latin)*
No time is too brief for the wicked to accomplish evil. *(Latin)*
One evil rises out of another. *(Latin)*
Submit to the present evil, lest a greater one befall you. *(Latin)*
The authors of great evils know best how to remove them. *(Latin)*
The best-known evils are the most tolerable. *(Latin)*
An evil life is a kind of death. *(Spanish)*
The evil which issues from thy mouth falls into thy bosom. *(Spanish)*

EXAGGERATE
We always weaken whatever we exaggerate. *(French)*

EXAMPLE

Follow example in drawing your calabash. *(Chinese)*
A good example is the best sermon.
Example is a lesson that all men can read.
Example is the school of mankind, and they will learn at no other. *(Burke)*
Example prevails more than precept.
Where the dam leaps over, the kid follows.
Why doth one man's yawning make another yawn?
Words but direct, example must allure.
Example is the greatest of all seducers. *(French)*
Nothing more contagious than a bad example. *(French)*
Precept begins, example accomplishes. *(French)*
The path of precept is long; that of example short. *(Latin)*
They do more harm by their evil example than by their actual sin. *(Latin)*
What is shown by example, men think they may justly do. *(Latin)*

EXCEPTION

The exception proves [i.e. *tests*] the rule. *(Latin)*

EXCESS

Nothing in excess. *(Greek)*
Every excess becomes a vice. *(Latin)*

EXCHANGE

A fair exchange is no robbery.

EXCUSE

Accusing the times is but excusing ourselves.
Better a bad excuse, than none at all.
Don't make excuses—make good.
We easily find a staff to beat a dog.
He who excuses himself accuses himself. *(French)*
Pretexts are not wanting when one wishes to use them. *(Italian)*
How pitiable is he who cannot excuse himself! *(Latin)*
I readily find excuses for myself. *(Latin)*
Make excuses for another, never for yourself. *(Latin)*

EXERTION

Lambs don't run into the mouth of the sleeping wolf. *(Danish)*
Roast pigeons don't fly through the air.
No pear falls into a shut mouth. *(Italian)*

EXILE

Exiles feed on hope. *(Greek)*

He suffers exile who denies himself to his country. *(Latin)*

No exile from his country ever escaped from himself. *(Latin)*

EXPECTATION

Blessed is he who expects nothing, for he shall never be disappointed.

Count not your chickens before they are hatched.

God send you readier meat than running hares.

Gut no fish till you get them.

EXPENSE

Beware of little expenses: a small leak will sink a great ship. *(Franklin)*

Cut your coat according to your cloth.

EXPERIENCE

He knows the water best who has waded through it. *(Danish)*

An ounce of wit that's bought is worth a pound that's taught.

Experience is good if not bought too dear.

Experience, the child of Thought; Thought, the child of Action.

Experience is the father of wisdom, and memory the mother.

Experience is the mother of knowledge.

Experience keeps a dear school, yet fools will learn in no other. *(Franklin)*

He complains wrongfully on the sea that twice suffers shipwreck.

He is wise that can beware by another's harms.

He returns wisest that comes home whipt with his own follies.

It is costly wisdom that is bought by experience.

Once bit, twice shy.

Put an old cat to an old rat.

Sad experience leaves no room for doubt. *(Pope)*

The burnt child fears the fire.

Wise men learn by others' harm; fools by their own.

I know by my own pot how the others boil. *(French)*

Each believes naught but his experience. *(Greek)*

He that has been bitten by a serpent is afraid of a rope. *(Hebrew)*

Experience is the mother of all things. *(Italian)*

A scalded dog fears cold water. *(Italian)*

The frog in the well knows nothing of the great ocean. *(Japanese)*

A shipwrecked man fears every sea. *(Latin)*

Believe him who has experienced it. [*Experto credite.*] *(Latin)*

Experience is the teacher of fools. *(Latin)*

Happy is he who gains wisdom from another's mishap. *(Latin)*
He may bear a bull that hath borne a calf. *(Latin)*
He who suffers, remembers. *(Latin)*
You shall know by experience. *(Latin)*

EXPERT
An expert is one who knows more and more about less and less.

EXPLANATION
I wish he would explain his explanation. *(Byron)*
The unknown is explained by what is still more unknown. *(Latin)*

EXTRAVAGANCE
Silks and satins put out the kitchen fire.
Who dainties love, shall beggars prove.

EXTREME
Extremes in nature equal ends produce. *(Pope)*
Man's extremity is God's opportunity.
Extremes meet. *(French)*
Extremity of right is wrong. *(Latin)*

EYE
If thine eye offend thee, pluck it out, and cast it from thee.
(New Test., Matthew)
The eye is not satisfied with seeing. *(Old Test., Eccles.)*
The eyes of a fool are in the ends of the earth. *(Old Test., Prov.)*
The light of the body is the eye. *(New Test., Matthew)*
An evil eye can see no good. *(Danish)*
What the eye sees not, the heart craves not. *(Dutch)*
A rolling eye, a roving heart.
A small hurt in the eye is a great one.
All looks yellow to a jaundiced eye.
Better eye out than always ache.
It does not hurt weak eyes to look into beautiful eyes. *(Emerson)*
Love's tongue is in the eyes.
Never rub your eyes but with your elbow.
The eye is a shrew.
The eye is bigger than the belly.
The eye is the pearl of the face.
The eye of the master will do more work than both hands.
The eye that sees all things else, sees not itself.

The eyes have one language everywhere.
The heart's letter is read in the eyes.
The present eye praises the present object. *(Shakespeare)*
What the eye sees not, the heart rues not.
Who has only one eye, guards it well. *(French)*
The ear is less trustworthy than the eye. *(Greek)*
The eyes are as ignorant as the ears are knowing. *(Greek)*
The master's eye makes the horse fat. *(Greek)*
If the eye do not admire, the heart will not desire. *(Italian)*
The eye is blind if the mind is absent. *(Italian)*
The eyes serve for ears to the deaf. *(Italian)*
Four eyes see more than two. *(Latin)*
Love is allured by gentle eyes *(Ovid)*
The ears can endure an injury better than the eye. *(Latin)*
The eyes do not go wrong if the mind rules them. *(Latin)*
There are voice and words in a silent look. *(Latin)*
What I can see with my eyes, I point out with my finger. *(Spanish)*
If you don't look with the eye, you will lose out of the pocket. *(Yiddish)*
One eye has more faith than two ears. *(Yiddish)*
Out of the eye, out of the heart. *(Yiddish)*
The eye is small, yet it sees the whole world. *(Yiddish)*

FACE

A face that only a mother could love.
A fair face is half a fortune.
A good face needs no band . . . and a pretty wench no land.
All men's faces are true, whatsome'er their hand are. *(Shakespeare)*
Human face divine. *(Milton)*
In the faces of men and women I see God. *(Whitman)*
It is good that a man's face gives his tongue leave to speak.
Man is read in his face.
May the man be damned and never grow fat
  Who wears two faces under one hat.
The face is ofttimes a true index of the heart.
The tartness of his face sours grapes. *(Shakespeare)*
There is a garden in her face
  Where roses and white lilies grow. *(Campion)*
There's no art to find the mind's construction in the face. *(Shakespeare)*
Where the face is fair there need no colors.
Your face doth testify what you be inwardly.
A comely face is a silent recommendation. *(Latin)*
Men's faces are not to be trusted. *(Latin)*
Often a silent face has voice and words. *(Latin)*
The face is the portrait of the mind; the eyes, its informers. *(Latin)*
The face is the index of the heart. *(Latin)*
When the disposition is friendly, the face pleases. *(Latin)*
Your face betrays your years. *(Latin)*
A face that resembles nothing but itself. *(Russian)*
An ugly face should not curse the mirror. *(Russian)*
A face like a benediction. *(Spanish)*
Everyone is satisfied with his own face. *(Yiddish)*

FACT

Facts alone are wanted in life. *(Dickens)*
Facts are stubborn things.
Facts do not cease to exist because they are ignored.
No facts are sacred; none are profane. *(Emerson)*
You can't alter facts by filming them over with romance.

FAILURE

Thou art weighed in the balance and found wanting.
(Old Test., Daniel)

A living failure is better than a dead masterpiece.
Failure teaches success.
Give me the heart to fight and lose.
He is good that failed never.
He who never fails will never grow rich.
In the lexicon of youth . . . there is no such word as "fail."
(Bulwer-Lytton)

There is not a fiercer hell than failure in a great object.
They went forth to battle but they always fell. *(Ossian)*
To fail at all is to fail utterly.
Who does not know how to swim goes to the bottom.

FAIR

Fair and softly goes far.
Fair feathers make fair fowl.
Fair in the cradle, foul in the saddle.
Fair is not fair, but that which pleaseth.
Fair maidens wear no purses.
Fair play is a jewel.
To every bird his nest is fair. *(Italian)*

FAIRY

Farewell, rewards and fairies. *(R. Corbet)*
It is not children only that one feeds with fairy tales. *(Lessing)*

FAITH

Be thou faithful unto death . . . *(New Test., Revelation)*
Faith is the substance of things hoped for . . . *(New Test., Hebr.)*
Faith without works is dead. *(New Test., James)*
Fight the good fight of faith. *(New Test., I Timothy)*
I have kept the faith. *(New Test., II Timothy)*
I know that my redeemer liveth. *(Old Test., Job)*
The just shall live by faith. *(New Test., Romans)*

We walk by faith, not by sight *(New Test., II Corinth.)*
A man should be able to render a reason for the faith that is within him.
A perfect faith lifts us above fear.
Faith is love taking the form of aspiration. *(Channing)*
Faith may be the boast of one too lazy to investigate.
Faith sees by the ears.
Give to faith what belongs to faith.
Love asks faith and faith, firmness.
Men's faiths are wafer-cakes. *(Shakespeare)*
Pin not your faith on another's sleeve.
The way to see by faith is to shut the eye of reason. *(Franklin)*
Where love is there is faith.
Who breaks his faith, no faith is held with him.
You can do very little with faith, but you can do nothing without it. *(S. Butler)*
Faith is a certitude without proofs. *(French)*
It will profit me nothing if I have no faith in it. *(French)*
Knowledge of things divine escapes us through want of faith. *(Greek)*
What faith is there in the faithless? *(Greek)*
Faith has no merit where human reason supplies the proof. *(St. Gregory)*
What is faith unless it is to believe what you do not see. *(St. Augustine)*
Faith is the force of life. *(Tolstoy)*

FALL

Let him that thinketh he standeth take heed lest he fall. *(New Test., I Corinth.)*
He who does not soar high will suffer less by a fall. *(Chinese)*
Better sit still than rise and fall.
Better to go about than to fall into the ditch.
Every slip is not a fall.
Fain would I climb, yet fear I to fall.
Hasty climbers have sudden falls.
He rides sure that never fell.
He falls low that cannot rise again.
He that is down need fear no fall.
He that is fallen cannot help him that is down.
If a man once fall, all will tread on him.
One may sooner fall than rise.
Press not a falling man too far.

Some falls are means the happier to rise. *(Shakespeare)*
The higher standing, the lower fall.
When a tree is falling, everyone cries, "Down with it!"
Who bravely dares must sometimes risk a fall.
Who falls for love of God shall rise a star. *(Jonson)*
Everything that shakes does not fall. *(French)*
One falls to the side to which one leans. *(French)*
If the ox falls, whet your knife. *(Hebrew)*
All things that rise will fall. *(Latin)*
He that lies upon the ground can fall no lower. *(Latin)*
Lofty towers fall with the greatest crash. *(Latin)*
He that falls today may rise tomorrow. *(Spanish)*
He that falls by himself never cries. *(Turkish)*

FALSE

False with one can be false with two.

FALSEHOOD

Falsehood never made a fair hinder end.
O what a goodly outside falsehood hath! *(Shakespeare)*

FAME

Let us now praise famous men. *(Apocrypha)*
All fame is dangerous: good brings envy, bad, shame.
Common fame is a liar.
Contempt of fame begets contempt of virtue.
Fame is a magnifying glass.
Fame is but a hollow echo.
Fame is but an inscription upon a grave.
Fame is but the breath of the people.
Fame is but wind.
Fame is no plant that grows on mortal soil. *(Milton)*
Fame is proof that people are gullible. *(Emerson)*
Fame is the thirst of youth. *(Byron)*
Fame, like man, will grow white as it grows old.
Fame . . . that last infirmity of noble minds. *(Milton)*
Fame . . . The breath of fools, the bait of flattering knaves. *(Granville)*
Fondness for fame is avarice of air. *(Young)*
How partial is the voice of fame! *(Prior)*
She comes unlook'd for, if she comes at all. *(Pope)*
The temple of fame stands upon the grave.

There are many ways to fame.
What is fame compared to happiness?
Fame must be won; honor must not be lost. *(German)*
Fame is as ephemeral as the famous. *(Greek)*
Fame is the perfume of heroic deeds. *(Greek)*
Renown is the mother of virtues. *(Greek)*
True fame is never the gift of chance. *(Greek)*
Fame grows like a tree with hidden life. *(Latin)*
Fame is the shadow of virtue. *(Latin)*
It is a wretched thing to lean on the fame of others. *(Latin)*
Some have the fame and others card the wool. *(Spanish)*

FAMILIARITY
Be thou familiar, but by no means vulgar. *(Shakespeare)*
Give a clown your finger and he'll take your whole hand.
A thing too much seen is little prized. *(French)*
Familiarity breeds contempt. *(Latin)*
Play with an ass and he will whisk his tail in your face. *(Spanish)*

FAMILY
A small family is soon provided for.
God gives us relatives; thank God we can choose our friends. *(A. Mizner)*
He that hath wife and children hath given hostages to fortune. *(Bacon)*
So yourself be good, a fig for your grandfather.
It is a piece of luck to have relatives scarce. *(Greek)*
He that flies from his own family has far to travel. *(Latin)*
All happy families resemble one another; every unhappy family is unhappy in its own way. *(Tolstoy)*

FAMINE
After a famine in the stall, comes a famine in the hall.
All's good in a famine.
More die by food than famine.

FANATIC
A fanatic is one who, having lost sight of his aim, redoubles his effort. *(Santayana)*

FANCY
Fancy flees before the wind.
Fancy is the friend of woe.

Fancy may bolt bran and make you take it for flour.
Fancy may kill or cure.
Fancy surpasses beauty.

FAR

Far folk fare best.

FAREWELL

Fare thee well! and if forever,
Still forever, fare thee well. *(Byron)*
Farewell and be hanged.
So sweetly she bade me adieu,
I thought that she bade me return. *(Shenstone)*
Forever, brother, hail and farewell. [. . . *ave atque vale.*] *(Catullus)*

FARMING

He that tilleth the land shall be satisfied with bread. *(Old Test., Prov.)*
The foot of the farmer manures the field. *(Danish)*
A ploughman on his legs is higher than a lord on his knees.
Farmers fatten most when famine reigns.
He that by the plough would thrive,
Himself must either hold or drive.
He that counts all costs will never put plough in the earth.
. . . make two ears of corn . . . to grow where only one grew before. *(Swift)*
No one hates his job so heartily as a farmer. *(H. L. Mencken)*
None says his garner is full.
Plough deep while sluggards sleep.
'Tis the farmer's care that makes the field bear.
Under water, famine; under snow, bread.
To plow is to pray—to plant is to prophesy . . .
A bad farmer's hedge is full of gaps. *(Gaelic)*
Each man reaps his own farm. *(Latin)*
Let us seek bread with the plough. *(Latin)*
Praise a great estate, but cultivate a small one. *(Latin)*
The master's eye is the best fertilizer. *(Latin)*
The way of cultivation is not easy. *(Latin)*

FASHION

The fashion of this world passeth away. *(New Test., I Corinth.)*
As good be out of the World as out of the Fashion.
Every man wears his belt in his own fashion.

Everyone after his fashion.
Fashion ever is a wayward child.
Fine clothes wear soonest out of fashion.
For fashion's sake, as dogs go to church.
He is only fantastical that is not in fashion. *(Burton)*
If you are not in fashion, you are nobody. *(Chesterfield)*
Leave the Mode to its own vagaries. *(Walpole)*
So many lands, so many fashions.
The fashion wear out more apparel than the man. *(Shakespeare)*
The present fashion is always handsome.
Tailors and writers must mind the fashion.
You cannot be both fashionable and first-rate. *(L. P. Smith)*
Follow the fashion, or quit the world. *(French)*
Men after the modern fashion and asses after the ancient. *(Italian)*
Fashion is more powerful than any tyrant. *(Latin)*

FAST
As fast as a dog will lick a dish.
Fast bind, fast find.
He that runs fast will not run long.
Fast enough is well enough. *(Latin)*

FASTING
He fasts enough who eats with reason.
Surfeit is the father of much fast. *(Shakespeare)*
Whoso will pray, he must fast and be clean,
  And fat his soul and make his body lean. *(Chaucer)*
He fasts enough that has had a bad meal. *(Italian)*

FAT
Jeshurun waxed fat, and kicked. *(Old Test., Deut.)*
A man must take the fat with the lean.
Everyone bastes the fat hog, while the lean one burns.
Fat drops from fat flesh.
Fat, fair and forty.
Fat flesh freezes soon.
Fat paunches make lean pates.
Laugh and be fat.
Little knows the fat sow what the lean thinks.
Nobody loves a fat man.
Oft and little eating makes a fat man.
Who drives fat oxen should himself be fat. *(S. Johnson)*

Fat hens lay few eggs. *(German)*
Fat heads, lean brains. *(Italian)*
A fat belly does not produce a fine sense. *(Latin)*

FATE

Fate laughs at probabilities.
Flee never so fast, you cannot flee your fortune.
He that is born to be hanged shall never be drowned.
I am the master of my fate;
I am the captain of my soul. *(W. E. Henley)*
Men at some time are masters of their fates. *(Shakespeare)*
No flying from fate.
To bear is to conquer our fate.
Will, in us, is over-ruled by fate. *(Marlowe)*
Man blindly works the will of fate. *(German)*
All things are produced by fate. *(Greek)*
Fate leads the willing, drags the unwilling. *(Greek)*
He that is to die by the gallows may dance on the river. *(Italian)*
From no place can you exclude the fates. *(Latin)*
Many have come upon their fate while shunning fate. *(Latin)*
No one is made guilty by fate. *(Latin)*
The fates will find a way. *(Latin)*
Whither the fates lead, virtue will follow. *(Latin)*
No man can make his own hap. *(Scottish)*
She's an old wife that wats her weird. *(Scottish)*
If you're fated to be drowned, you'll drown in a spoonful of water. *(Yiddish)*

FATHER

A wise son maketh a glad father. *(Old Test., Prov.)*
He that honoreth his father shall have a long life. *(Aprocrypha)*
It is not a father's anger but his silence that a son dreads. *(Chinese)*
The father, in praising his son, extols himself. *(Chinese)*
Ask the mother if the child be like the father.
He that loves the tree loves the branch.
It is a wise father that knows his own child.
Like father, like son.
No love to a father's.
No man is responsible for his father . . .
One father can support ten children, but ten children hardly one father.

One father is more than a hundred schoolmasters.
Raw dads make fat lads.
The father to the bough, the son to the plough.
You may thank God that your father was born before you.
A father loves his children in hating their faults. *(French)*
It is a wise child that knows its own father. *(Homer)*
Whom should he bear with if not with his own father? *(Latin)*
A father's blessing cannot be drowned in water nor consumed by fire. *(Russian)*
A father's love for all others is air. *(Spanish)*
He that has his father for judge goes safe to the trial. *(Spanish)*

FAULT

A fault confessed is half redressed.
A fault is sooner found than mended.
A fault once denied is twice committed.
Be to her virtues very kind,
  Be to her faults a little blind. *(Prior)*
Clean your finger before you point at my spots.
Condemn the fault and not the actor of it? *(Shakespeare)*
Everyone puts his fault on the times.
Faultless to a fault. *(Browning)*
Faults are thick where love is thin.
Faults done by night will blush by day.
He is lifeless that is faultless.
He may find fault that cannot mend.
He that commits a fault thinks everyone speaks of it.
In a leopard the spots are not observed.
In every fault there is folly.
Love your enemies, for they tell you your faults.
Men do not support faults which they do not commit.
Men's faults do seldom to themselves appear. *(Shakespeare)*
Mistakes remembered are not faults forgot.
Our faults are not written on our face.
Tell me my faults, and mend your own.
The first faults are theirs that commit them;
  The second theirs that permit them.
The greatest fault is to be conscious of none.
They who seek only for faults, see nothing else.
Those who live in glass houses should not throw stones.
To maintain a fault known is a double fault.

With all thy faults, I love thee still. *(Cowper)*
Happy the man when he has not the defects of his qualities. *(French)*
If we had no faults, we should not take so much pleasure in remarking them in others. *(La Rochefoucauld)*
Only great men may have great faults. *(French)*
The hunchback sees not his own hump, but that of his neighbor. *(French)*
We never confess our faults except through vanity. *(La Rochefoucauld)*
Who commits the fault must drink it. *(French)*
The fault of another is a good teacher. *(German)*
When you would arraign your neighbor's faults, think first of your own. *(Greek)*
Love him who tells you your faults in private. *(Hebrew)*
A man must have his faults. *(Latin)*
He has no fault except that he has no fault. *(Latin)*
He who overlooks a fault, invites the commission of another. *(Latin)*
Let a fault be concealed by its nearness to a virtue. *(Latin)*
No one is born without faults. *(Latin)*
He who wants a mule without fault must walk on foot. *(Spanish)*
The fault is as great as he that commits it. *(Spanish)*
The fault of the ass must not be laid on the pack-saddle. *(Spanish)*
We see only the faults of another. *(Yiddish)*

FAVOR

Favor will as surely perish as life.
Grace will last, favor will blast.
He may receive courtesies that knows how to requite them.
The favor of the great is no inheritance.
To accept a favor from a friend is to confer one.
Never remember the benefits conferred nor forget the favors received. *(Greek)*
A favor to come is better than a hundred received. *(Italian)*
A favor bestowed by a hard man is bread made of stone. *(Latin)*
He has received a favor who has granted one to a deserving person. *(Latin)*
He who does not know how to grant has no right to seek a favor. *(Latin)*
The favor of ignoble men is won only by ignoble means. *(Latin)*
The greater the favor, the greater the obligation. *(Latin)*
Don't ask as a favor what you can take by force. *(Spanish)*

FEAR

Happy is the man that feareth always . . . *(Old Test., Prov.)*
The greater the fear the nearer the danger. *(Danish)*
Early and provident fear is the mother of safety. *(Burke)*
Extreme fear can neither fight nor fly . . . *(Shakespeare)*
Fear always springs from ignorance. *(Emerson)*
Fear God, and your enemies will fear you.
Fear is stronger than love.
Fear is the father of courage and the mother of safety.
Fear is the offspring of ignorance.
Fear is the parent of cruelty.
Fear is the tax which conscience pays to guilt.
Fear keeps the garden better than the gardener.
Fear may force a man to cast beyond the moon.
Fear kills more than disease.
Fear—the beadle of the law.
Foolish fear doubles danger.
He that feareth every bush must not go a-birding.
He that fears every grass must not piss in the meadow.
He that fears you present will hate you absent.
He that is afraid of wounds must not come nigh a battle.
His heart is in his boots.
His heart is in his mouth.
If I quake, what matters it what I quake at.
Keep your fears to yourself but share your courage.
Nothing is so rash as fear.
Nothing is terrible except fear itself. *(Bacon)*
The fearless man is his own salvation.
The thing we fear we bring to pass.
To fear the worst oft cures the worse. *(Shakespeare)*
'Twas fear that first put on arms.
When our actions do not,
  Our fears do make us traitors. *(Shakespeare)*
Wise fear beats care.
Courage is often caused by fear. *(French)*
Fear follows crime and is its punishment. *(Voltaire)*
Fear lends wings. *(French)*
He that fears leaves, let him not go into the wood. *(French)*
Fear in love has no luck. *(German)*
Fear makes lions tame. *(German)*
If you are terrible to many, beware of many. *(Greek)*

He that has been bitten by a serpent is afraid of a rope. *(Hebrew)*
All fearfulness is folly. *(Italian)*
Fear guards the vineyard. *(Italian)*
Even the bravest are frightened by sudden terrors. *(Latin)*
Fear argues ignoble minds. *(Latin)*
Fear is a hindrance to all virtue. *(Latin)*
Fear is not a lasting teacher of duty. *(Latin)*
Fear makes men ready to believe the worst. *(Latin)*
Fear, not clemency, restrains the wicked. *(Latin)*
He must fear many whom many fear. *(Latin)*
If you wish to fear nothing, consider that everything is to be feared. *(Latin)*
In extreme danger fear feels no pity. *(Caesar)*
It is foolish to fear what cannot be avoided. *(Latin)*
It is torture to fear what you cannot overcome. *(Latin)*
It was fear that first made gods in the world. *(Latin)*
Our fears always outnumber our dangers. *(Latin)*
Terror closes the ears of the mind. *(Latin)*
The less there is of fear, the less there is of danger. *(Latin)*
Who causes fear is himself most fearful. *(Latin)*
Who knows how to fear, knows how to go safely. *(Latin)*
Whom they fear they hate. *(Latin)*
Fear him who fears thee, though he be a fly and thou an elephant. *(Sadi) (Persian)*
He who fears a sparrow will never sow millet. *(Russian)*
Never lose honor through fear. *(Spanish)*
Fear is the beginning of wisdom. *(Spanish)*
Fear not tomorrow's mischance. *(Turkish)*

FEAST
Be not made a beggar by banqueting upon borrowing. *(Apocrypha)*
It's good feasting in another's hall. *(Dutch)*
Better fare hard with good men, than feast with bad.
Feasting is the physician's harvest.
Feasting makes no friendship.
Fiddlers, dogs, and flies come to feasts uncalled.
Little difference between a feast and a bellyful.
Small cheer and great welcome makes a merry feast.
The feast is good until the reckoning comes.
There is no great banquet but some fares ill.
After a feast a man scratches his head. *(French)*
Time enough to keep the feast when it comes. *(French)*

Fools make the banquets and wise men enjoy them. *(Italian)*
Feast today makes fast tomorrow. *(Latin)*
A great feast lasts a short while. *(Yiddish)*

FEATHER
Feather by feather birds build nests.
I am a feather before each wind that blows. *(Shakespeare)*
Fine feathers make fine birds. *(French)*

FEBRUARY
All the months of the year curse a fair February.
February doth cut and sheer.
February fill dyke.
February makes a bridge and March breaks it.

FEELING
Feeling hath no fellow.
Seeing is believing, but feeling is naked truth.
If you wish me to weep, you must first feel grief. *(Horace)*
Trust not to thy feeling . . . *(Latin)*

FEET
Dry feet, warm head, bring safe to bed.
You can't dance at two weddings with one pair of feet. *(Yiddish)*

FENCE
No fence against a flail.
No fence against gold.
No fence against ill-fortune.

FETTER
Let the smith himself wear the fetters he forged.
No man loveth his fetters, be they made of gold.
'Tis in vain to kick after you have once put on the fetters.

FICTION
Fiction is not falsehood.
Figs are sweet, but fictions are sweeter.
Make them laugh, make them cry, make them wait. *(Reade)*
Novels are to love as fairy tales to dreams. *(Coleridge)*
The only real people are the people who never existed. *(O. Wilde)*
Where there is leisure for fiction there is little grief. *(S. Johnson)*
Fictions meant to please should be close to the real. *(Horace)*

FIDDLER
In a fiddler's house all are dancers.
Who cannot become a fiddler let him remain a fifer. *(German)*

FIDELITY
Be thou faithful unto the end. *(New Test., Revelation)*
Fidelity ennobles even servitude.
It is better to be faithful than famous.
Who loves me, follows me! *(Francis I) (French)*
Fidelity gained by bribes is overcome by bribes. *(Latin)*
Prosperity asks for fidelity; adversity exacts it. *(Latin)*
The fidelity of barbarians depends on fortune. *(Latin)*

FIELD
Good corn is not reaped from a bad field. *(Danish)*
Fields have eyes and hedges ears.
There is nothing like having the key of the fields. *(French)*

FIG
Fig-tree fuel: much smoke and little fire.
Peel a fig for your friend, a peach for your enemy.

FIGHT
He smote them hip and thigh with great slaughter. *(Old Test., Judges)*
Better come to the latter end of a feast than the beginning of a fray.
Fight dog, fight bear.
That cock won't fight.
There is such a thing as a man being too proud to fight. *(W. Wilson)*
What can alone ennoble fight? A noble cause.
We fight to great disadvantage when we fight with those who have nothing to lose. *(Italian)*
Do not fight against two adversaries. *(Latin)*
The fight is over when the enemy is down. *(Latin)*

FILE
It is a good file that cuts iron without making a noise. *(Italian)*

FIND
Finding is keeping.
He findeth that surely binds.
Nothing seek, nothing find.
Take heed you find not what you do not seek.
He that hides can find. *(French)*

FINGER

All the fingers are not alike.

Do not put your finger in too tight a ring.

Fingers were made before forks and hands before knives.

Fingers are shaped like pegs, so that we may insert them in our ears when we hear evil. *(Hebrew)*

FIRE

You k'n hide de fire, but w'at you gwine do wid de smoke? *(American Negro)*

Behold how great a matter a little fire kindleth. *(New Test., James)*

Kindle not a fire you cannot put out. *(Chinese)*

It is bad to be between two fires. *(Danish)*

The fire cares little whose cloak it burns. *(Danish)*

He that would have fire must bear with smoke. *(Dutch)*

A burnt child dreads the fire.

A fair fire makes a room gay.

Fire and water are good servants, but bad masters.

In the coldest flint there is hot fire.

Pouring oil into the fire is not the way to quench it.

Put not fire to flax.

Small lights are soon blown out; huge fires abound . . . *(Shakespeare)*

The fire which warms us at a distance will burn us when near.

When your neighbor's house is on fire, look to your own.

A scalded cat fears cold water. *(French)*

Fire is half bread. *(French)*

Fire is put out by fire. *(French)*

The fire which seems extinguished often slumbers beneath the ashes. *(French)*

A little fire burns up a great deal of corn. *(Hebrew)*

Fire and flax agree not. *(Italian)*

The same fire purifies gold and consumes straw. *(Italian)*

Who makes a fire of straw has much smoke and nothing else. *(Italian)*

Out of the frying pan into the fire. *(Tertullian)*

The more the fire is covered up, the more it burns. *(Latin)*

The nearer the fire, the hotter. *(Latin)*

There is no smoke without fire. *(Latin)*

Better a wee fire to warm us than a mickle fire to burn us. *(Scottish)*

Don't play with fire. *(Yiddish)*

Fire is a thief. *(Yiddish)*

FIRST

First come, first served.
He that riseth first is first dressed.
The first blow is half the battle.
The first dish is aye best eaten.
The foremost dog catches the hare.
Better first in a village than second in Rome. *(Caesar)*
He who comes first grinds first. *(Spanish)*

FISH

All fish are not caught with flies.
Better are small fish than an empty dish.
Don't teach fishes to swim.
Fish begin to stink at the head.
Fish follow the bait.
It's a silly fish that is caught twice with the same bait.
It is good fish if it were but caught.
Neither fish, nor flesh, nor good red herring.
The fish once caught, new bait will hardly bite. *(Spenser)*
The fish will soon be caught that nibbles at the bait.
The great fish eat up the small.
There are as good fish in the sea as ever came out of it.
All is fish that comes to net. *(French)*
Fish must swim thrice [*i.e. in water, in sauce, in wine*]. *(French)*
We have other fish to fry. *(French)*
Like a fish out of water. *(Latin)*
Every fish is not a sturgeon. *(Russian)*
Where there are no fish, even a crawfish calls himself a fish. *(Russian)*
Big fish are caught in a big river. *(Yiddish)*
The biggest fish has only one head. *(Yiddish)*

FISHING

Who cannot catch fish must catch shrimps. *(Chinese)*
A fishing rod is a stick with a hook at one end and a fool at the other.
Catching fish is not the whole of fishing.
He is a fond fisher that angles for a frog.
Here comes the trout that must be caught with tickling. *(Shakespeare)*
It is good fishing in troubled waters.
Never a fisherman need there be
  If fishes could hear as well as see.
No man is born an Artist nor an Angler. *(Walton)*

The best fishing is in the deepest water.
The end of fishing is not angling, but catching.
The hasty angler loses the fish.
One must lose a minnow to catch a salmon. *(French)*
He is a poor fisherman that will not wet his feet. *(German)*
He who holds the hook is aware in what waters many fish are swimming. *(Latin)*
There's no taking trout with dry breeches. *(Spanish)*

FIST
If you have no hand you can't make a fist. *(Yiddish)*

FIT
All is fine that is fit.
As fit as a pudding for a friar's mouth.
Every shoe fits not every foot.
If the cap fits, wear it.
Set the saddle on the right horse. *(Hebrew)*

FLAG
He changes his flag to conceal his being a pirate.
A banner need not do much thinking. *(French)*
The flag protects the cargo. *(French)*

FLAT
As flat as a flounder.
As flat as a pancake.

FLATTERY
A flatterer's mouth worketh ruin. *(Apocrypha)*
A man that flattereth his neighbor spreadeth a net for his feet. *(Old Test., Prov.)*
Bring no more vain oblations; incense is an abomination unto me. *(Old Test., Isaiah)*
The Lord shall cut off all flattering lips . . . *(Old Test., Psalms)*
A flatterer is a fool who despises me or a knave who wants to cheat me. *(Chinese)*
Better flatter a fool than fight him.
Claw me and I'll claw thee.
Flattery corrupts both the receiver and the giver.
Flatterers haunt not cottages.
Flatterers look like friends as wolves resemble dogs.

Flattery is like Cologne water, to be smelt of, not swallowed.
Flattery is monstrous in a true friend.
Flattery is the turnpike road to Fortune's door.
For flattery is the bellows blows up sin. *(Shakespeare)*
. . . for flattery's the food of fools. *(Swift)*
Flattery sits in the parlor, when plain dealing is kicked out of doors.
He that hath no honey in his pot, let him have it in his mouth.
He that loves to be flattered is worthy o' the flatterer. *(Shakespeare)*
He that rewards flattery begs it.
The coin most current among us is flattery.
The same man cannot be both friend and flatterer.
What flatters a man is that you think him worthy of flattery.
When flatterers meet, the devil goes to dinner.
Every flatterer lives at the expense of the person who listens to him. *(La Fontaine)*
One catches more flies with a spoonful of honey than with twenty casks of vinegar. *(French)*
Flatterers and dogs soil their own masters. *(German)*
Flatterers are cats that lick before and scratch behind. *(German)*
It is easier for men to flatter than to praise. *(German)*
The devil is civil when he is flattered. *(German)*
I cannot be your friend and your flatterer too. *(German)*
A flatterer is a secret enemy. *(Hungarian)*
A flatterer's throat is an open sepulchre. *(Italian)*
Who paints me before, blackens me behind. *(Italian)*
A flatterer's speech is honeyed poison. *(Latin)*
Flattery is the handmaid of the vices. *(Latin)*
How closely flattery resembles friendship! *(Latin)*
The flatteries of a bad man cover treachery. *(Latin)*
Who delight in flattery, pay by a late repentance. *(Latin)*
Your flattery is so much bird lime. *(Latin)*
Daub yourself with honey and you will never want flies. *(Spanish)*
It is not as shameful to steal as to flatter. *(Yiddish)*

FLEA
One flea cannot raise a coverlet. *(Chinese)*
He that lies with dogs riseth with fleas.
That's a valiant flea that dare eat his breakfast on the lip of a lion. *(Shakespeare)*
The flea, though he kill none, does all the harm he can.
Better the wolf eat us than the fleas. *(German)*

The fatter the flea, the leaner the dog. *(German)*
Even a flea can bite. *(Yiddish)*

FLESH

All flesh is grass. *(Old Test., Isaiah)*
The spirit indeed is willing, but the flesh is weak. *(New Test., Matthew)*
Frail as flesh is.
It is a dear collop that is cut out of thy own flesh.
It will not out of the flesh, that is bred in the bone.
The nearer the bone, the sweeter the flesh.
The way of all flesh.
The world, the flesh, and the devil. *(Bk. Com. Prayer)*
All flesh is not venison. *(French)*
No man is free who is a slave to the flesh. *(Latin)*

FLIGHT

The wicked flee when no man pursueth. *(Old Test., Prov.)*
Let us fly and save our bacon. *(Rabelais)*
Who flees the wolf meets with the bear. *(German)*
By flight we often run into our fate. *(Latin)*
He who flees from trial confesses his guilt. *(Latin)*
His heart is in his heels. *(Latin)*
To flee is to triumph. *(Latin)*
To flee and to run are not one. *(Spanish)*

FLIGHTY

Light-heel'd mothers make leaden-heel'd daughters. *(Franklin)*

FLING

After your fling, watch for the sting.

FLINT

In the coldest flint there is hot fire.
The fire in the flint shows not till it is struck.

FLOCK

The flock follow the bell-wether.

FLOWER

Flowers are the pledges of fruit. *(Danish)*
Full many a flower is born to blush unseen . . . *(Gray)*
It is a bad soil where flowers will not grow.

One flower makes no garland.
The bud may have a bitter taste,
  But sweet will be the flower. *(Cowper)*
Painted flowers have no scent. *(French)*
The flower that once has blown forever dies. *(Omar Khayyám)*
Every flower has its perfume. *(Turkish)*

FLY
Dead flies cause the ointment of the apothecary to send forth a stinking savor. *(Old Test., Eccles.)*
Flies come to feasts uninvited.
Flies haunt lean horses.
The fly that feeds on dung is colored thereby.
The fly that playeth too long in the candle, singeth his wings at last.
The fly that sips treacle is lost in the sweets.
To a boiling pot, flies come not.
A fly sat on the chariot wheel and said,
  "What a dust I raise!" *(La Fontaine)*
Hungry flies bite sore. *(German)*
Even a fly has its anger. *(Latin)*
A shut mouth catches no flies. *(Spanish)*

FLYING
Fly, and you will catch the swallow.
He would fain fly, but he wanteth feathers.

FOG
A fog cannot be dispelled with a fan. *(Japanese)*

FOLLOW
Follow the river and you will get to the sea.
Follow the road and you will reach an inn. *(Spanish)*

FOLLY
Folly has the wings of an eagle, but the eyes of an owl. *(Dutch)*
Folly grows without watering.
Folly in youth is sin; in age, it's madness.
Folly is often sick of itself.
Happy the man who knows his follies in his youth.
If folly were grief, every house would weep.
If others had not been foolish, we should be so. *(Blake)*
In folly's cup still laughs the bubble joy. *(Pope)*

It is a great point of wisdom to find out one's own folly.
It is folly to drown on dry land.
It is folly to lay out money in the purchase of reputation.
It is folly to sing twice to a deaf man.
No folly to being in love.
The folly of one man is the fortune of another.
The folly of others is ever most ridiculous to those who are themselves most foolish.
The shortest follies are the best. *(French)*
Who lives without folly is not so wise as he thinks.
(La Rochefoucauld)
Where the old are foolish, the child learns folly. *(German)*
Follies are miscalled the crimes of Fate. *(Homer)*
Folly is a self-chosen misfortune. *(Greek)*
It is well to advise folly, not to punish it. *(Latin)*
It is well to profit by the folly of others. *(Latin)*
The shame is not in having once been foolish, but in not cutting the folly short. *(Horace)*
Wealth excuses folly. *(Latin)*
Folly has more followers than discretion. *(Spanish)*
Whoever falls sick of folly is long in getting cured. *(Spanish)*

FOOD
Better fed than taught.
Better fill a man's belly than his eye.
Good fare lessens care.
Let there be food in the pigeon-house and the pigeons will come to it. *(Spanish)*

FOOL
A fool's soul is ever dancing on the tip of his tongue. *(Arabian)*
The fool who falls into the fire rarely falls out of it. *(Arabian)*
A fool's lips are the snare of his soul. *(Old Test., Prov.)*
A fool's mouth is his destruction. *(Old Test., Prov.)*
A prating fool shall fall. *(Old Test., Prov.)*
A whip for the horse, a bridle for the ass, and a rod for the fool's back. *(Old Test., Prov.)*
Answer a fool according to his folly, lest he be wise in his own conceit.
(Old Test., Prov.)
Answer not a fool according to his folly, lest thou also be like unto him. *(Old Test., Prov.)*

As a dog returneth to his vomit, so a fool returneth to his folly. *(Old Test., Prov.)*

Even a fool when he holdeth his peace is counted wise. *(Old Test., Prov.)*

Fools die for want of wisdom. *(Old Test., Prov.)*

It is better to hear the rebuke of the wise, than . . . the song of fools. *(Old Test., Eccles.)*

Let a bear robbed of her cubs meet a man, rather than a fool in his folly. *(Old Test., Prov.)*

The way of a fool is right in his own eyes. *(Old Test., Prov.)*

The wise man's eyes are in his head; but the fool walketh in darkness. *(Old Test., Eccles.)*

A fool is like other men as long as he is silent. *(Danish)*

Fools build houses and wise men buy them. *(Dutch)*

Thrust not your finger into a fool's mouth. *(Dutch)*

A fool and his money are soon parted.

A fool at forty is a fool indeed.

A fool can dance without a fiddle.

A fool cannot be still.

A fool knows more in his own house than a wise man in another's.

A fool may ask more questions in an hour than a wise man can answer in seven years.

A fool may eke a wise man often guide. *(Chaucer)*

A fool may throw a stone into a well which a hundred wise men cannot pull out.

A fool might be counted wise, if he kept his mouth shut.

A fool must now and then be right by chance.

A fool sees not the same tree that a wise man sees. *(Blake)*

A fool, when he hath spoke, hath done all.

A fool's bolt is soon shot.

A fool's bolt may sometimes hit the mark.

A fool's paradise is a wise man's hell.

A fool's tongue is long enough to cut his own throat. *(Shakespeare)*

A knavish speech sleeps in a foolish ear. *(Shakespeare)*

A rich fool is a wise man's treasurer.

A whip for a fool, and a rod for a school.

An easy fool is a knave's tool.

As the bell clinks so the fool thinks.

Better be a fool than a knave.

By foolish words may men a fool ken.

Every man is a fool sometimes, and none at all times.

Everyone hath a fool in his sleeve.
Fool beckons fool, and dunce awakens dunce.
Fools are made for jests to men of sense.
Fools are wise men in the affairs of women.
Fool is he that deals with fools.
Fools are the game which knaves pursue.
Fools bite one another, but wise men agree together.
Fools cannot hold their tongues. *(Chaucer)*
Fools cut their fingers, but wise men their thumbs.
Fools for arguments use wagers.
Fools have the wit to keep out of the rain.
Fools lade the water, and wise men catch the fish.
Fools make feasts and wise men eat them.
Fools multiply folly.
Fools set stools for wise men to stumble at.
Fools should not see half-done work.
Fools tie knots, and wise men loose them.
Fools will be fools still.
God sendeth fortune to fools.
God hath great need of a fool that plays the fool himself.
He is not a wise man who cannot play the fool on occasion.
He that deals with fools is the fool.
How ill white hairs become a fool . . . *(Shakespeare)*
I would not be in a fool's paradise.
If all fools wore white caps, we should all seem a flock of geese.
If fools went not to market, bad wares would not be sold.
If every fool were to wear a bauble, fuel would be dear.
If every fool wore a crown, we should all be kings.
If wise men play the fool, they do it with a vengeance.
It is better to be a beggar than a fool.
It takes a wise man to be a fool.
He that sends a fool means to follow him.
Men may live fools, but fools they cannot die. *(Young)*
Most fools think they are only ignorant.
Never challenge a fool to do wrong.
No creature smarts so little as a fool. *(Pope)*
No fool like an old fool.
No precepts will profit a fool.
None is a fool always, everyone sometimes.
None is so wise but the fool o'ertakes him.
One fool is enough in a house.
One fool praises another.

Send a fool to market and a fool he'll return.
The dulness of the fool is the whetstone of the wits (*Shakespeare*)
The fool saith, who would have thought it?
The fool shall not enter into heaven, let him be ever so holy. (*Blake*)
The fool wanders, the wise man travels.
The wise man draws more advantage from his enemies, than the fool from his friends. (*Franklin*)
The world is made up of fools and knaves.
There is no art can make a fool wise.
To be a fool born is a disease incurable.
To reprove a fool is but labor lost.
What fools these mortals be! (*Shakespeare*)
Who are a little wise, the best fools be. (*Donne*)
Who at fifty is a fool
Is far too stubborn grown for school.
Who is his own pupil has a fool for a tutor.
Wise men learn by others' harms, fools scarcely by their own.
A fool always finds a bigger fool to admire him. (*French*)
Better be foolish with all than wise by yourself. (*French*)
God alone understands fools. (*French*)
He is a fool who makes his doctor his heir. (*French*)
More fools, more fun. (*French*)
On a fool's beard the barber learns to shave. (*French*)
Since Adam's time, fools have been in the majority. (*French*)
The fool cuts himself with his own knife. (*French*)
To succeed in this world, one must have the appearance of a fool and be wise. (*Montesquieu*)
When the horse has been stolen, the fool shuts the stable. (*French*)
Fools are never uneasy. (*Goethe*)
Fools must not be set on eggs. (*German*)
He is a fool who buys an ox to have cream. (*German*)
If fools ate no bread, corn would be cheap. (*German*)
A fool may sometimes speak to the purpose. (*Greek*)
A prosperous fool is a heavy load. (*Greek*)
Fools grow without watering. (*Italian*)
Who is born a fool is never cured. (*Italian*)
Almost all men are fools. (*Latin*)
No man can play the fool so well as the wise man. (*Latin*)
One fool makes many. (*Latin*)
The treasure of a fool is always in his tongue. (*Latin*)
With fools it is always holiday. (*Latin*)
A fool shoots; God guides the bullet. (*Russian*)

Play the fule weel an ye be wise. *(Scottish)*
He is a great fool who forgets himself to feed another. *(Spanish)*
Unless a fool knows Latin, he is never a great fool. *(Spanish)*
God gave fools mouths not that they might talk, but eat. *(Turkish)*
Speak not of stones to a fool lest he cast them at thy head. *(Turkish)*
A fool says what he knows, and a wise man knows what he says. *(Yiddish)*
A fool who can keep silent is counted among the wise. *(Yiddish)*
Better a slap from a wise man than a kiss from a fool. *(Yiddish)*
Better to lose with a wise man than win with a fool. *(Yiddish)*
Don't fool with a fool. *(Yiddish)*
If God listened to the fool, the world would have another face. *(Yiddish)*
Live a fool, die a fool. *(Yiddish)*
Never show a fool a job half-done. *(Yiddish)*
Rather in hell with a wise man than in paradise with a fool. *(Yiddish)*
When a fool is sent to market, the storekeepers rejoice. *(Yiddish)*

FOOT

Better a bare foot than none.
Right foot first. *(Latin)*
The belly warm, the foot sleepy. *(Spanish)*

FORCE

You may force a man to shut his eyes but you can't make him sleep. *(Danish)*
Clubs are trumps.
Force is no argument.
Force is not a remedy.
Force is of brutes.
Force without foresight is of little avail.
What force cannot effect, fraud shall devise.
Who overcomes by force overcomes but half his foe.
You may lead a horse to water but you can't make him drink.
Force finds a way. *(Latin)*

FOREIGNERS

We are a kind of posterity in respect to them. *(Franklin)*
The more I see of foreigners, the more I love my own. *(French)*

FORESIGHT

He is wise that is ware.

If only our foresight were as good as our hindsight!

He who does not look before finds himself behind. *(French)*

FORGET

A man must *get* a thing before he can *forget* it.

Men are men; the best sometimes forget. *(Shakespeare)*

Seldom seen, soon forgotten.

If I forget thee, O Jerusalem, let my right hand forget her cunning. *(Old Test., Psalms)*

It is sometimes expedient to forget even what you know. *(Latin)*

Let us forget what the earth covers. *(Yiddish)*

FORGIVE

Father, forgive them; for they know not what they do. *(New Test., Luke)*

Forgive us our debts, as we forgive our debtors. *(New Test., Matthew)*

Good to forgive: Best to forget! *(Browning)*

Forgive and forget.

Forgive any, sooner than thyself.

Nobuddy ever fergits where he buried a hatchet. *(Kin Hubbard)*

Only the brave know how to forgive.

The offender never pardons.

They who forgive most shall be most forgiven.

He who forgives readily only invites offense. *(French)*

One pardons in the degree that one loves. *(La Rochefoucauld)*

To understand is to forgive. *(French)*

Forgiveness is better than revenge. *(Greek)*

Know all and you will pardon all. *(Greek)*

To forgive everyone is as much cruelty as to forgive no one. *(Greek)*

To forgive is beautiful. *(Greek)*

FORTUNE

Pitch him into the Nile, and he'll come up with a fish in his mouth. *(Arabian)*

You must have good luck to catch hares with a drum. *(Danish)*

Fortune does not stand waiting at any man's door. *(Dutch)*

A change of fortune hurts a wise man no more than a change of the moon. *(Franklin)*

A good man's fortune may grow out of heels. *(Shakespeare)*

A man's own manners do shape his fortune.

All fortune is to be conquered by bearing it. *(Bacon)*
Call me not fool till Heaven has sent me fortune. *(Shakespeare)*
Fortune ever hath an uncertain end.
Fortune hath in her honey gall. *(Chaucer)*
Fortune makes him a fool whom she makes her darling.
Fortune rules all.
Fortune to one is mother, to another step-mother.
Fortune's friend is mishap's foe.
Give a man luck and throw him into the sea.
Good luck reaches farther than long arms.
Great fortune brings with it great misfortune.
He dances well to whom fortune pipes.
He is a good man whom fortune makes better.
He needs little advice that has fortune on his side.
He that waits upon fortune is never sure of a dinner.
He was born with a caul.
Ill fortune never crushed a man whom good fortune deceived not.
It is better to be born lucky than rich.
Luck for fools and chance for the ugly.
Lucky men need no counsel.
The fortune which nobody sees makes a man unenvied.
The greatest reverses of fortune are most easily borne.
Today a man, tomorrow a mouse.
When fortune favors, none but fools will dally.
Against fortune the carter cracks his whip in vain. *(French)*
Blind fortune pursues blind rashness. *(French)*
Fortune can take from us only what she has given us. *(French)*
Fortune never seems so blind as to those upon whom she has bestowed no favors. *(La Rochefoucauld)*
Greater qualities are needed to bear good fortune than bad. *(French)*
No one is satisfied with his fortune, nor dissatisfied with his intellect. *(French)*
Fortune and misfortune are neighbors. *(German)*
His hens lay eggs with two yolks. *(German)*
It is the fortunate who should praise fortune. *(German)*
Luck is for the few, death for the many. *(German)*
When fortune opens one door, she opens another. *(German)*
Who has luck plays well with bad cards. *(German)*
Every man is the architect of his own fortune. *(Greek)*
Fortune is not on the side of the faint-hearted. *(Greek)*
Fortune, not riches, rules the life of men. *(Greek)*

Fortune knows neither reason or law. *(Greek)*
With a fortunate man all things are fortunate. *(Greek)*
Everything may be borne except good fortune. *(Italian)*
Fortune knocks once at least at every man's gate. *(Italian)*
They make their fortune who are stout and wise. *(Italian)*
To have luck needs little wit. *(Italian)*
A drop of fortune is worth a cask of wisdom. *(Latin)*
A just fortune awaits the deserving. *(Latin)*
Bear good fortune modestly. *(Latin)*
Every man's fortune is molded by his character. *(Latin)*
Fortune and Venus help the bold. *(Latin)*
Fortune can take away riches, but not courage. *(Latin)*
Fortune favors fools. *(Latin)*
Fortune favors the bold. *(Latin)*
Fortune gives too much to many, enough to none. *(Latin)*
Fortune is blind. *(Latin)*
Fortune is gentle to the lowly. *(Latin)*
Fortune is glass; just as it becomes bright, it is broken. *(Latin)*
Fortune molds human affairs as she pleases. *(Latin)*
Fortune turns on her wheel the fate of kings. *(Latin)*
He fell today, I may fall tomorrow. *(Latin)*
He who can bear fortune, can also beware of fortune. *(Latin)*
It is easier to get a favor from fortune than to keep it. *(Latin)*
Not only is Fortune blind herself, but she blinds those whom she favors. *(Latin)*
Seldom are men blessed with good fortune and good sense at the same time. *(Latin)*
The most wretched fortune is safe, for it fears nothing worse. *(Latin)*
We are corrupted by good fortune. *(Latin)*
What fortune has not given, she cannot take away. *(Latin)*
When Fortune flatters, she does it to betray. *(Latin)*
Where God and cruel fortune call, let us follow. *(Latin)*
Fortune turns round like a mill-wheel . . . *(Spanish)*
Good fortune is not known until it is lost. *(Spanish)*
His bread fell into the honey. *(Spanish)*
The brave man carves out his fortune. *(Spanish)*
When fortune knocks, open the door. *(Spanish)*
Where fortune is wanting, diligence is useless. *(Spanish)*
You used to be a baker, though now you wear gloves. *(Spanish)*
A man does not seek his luck: luck seeks its man. *(Turkish)*
Fortune is not far from the brave man's head. *(Turkish)*

The bird of prosperity has lodged in his head. *(Turkish)*
Without luck, it is better not to be born. *(Yiddish)*

FOX

The little foxes, that spoil the vines. *(Old Test., Song of Songs)*
A fox should not be of the jury at a goose's trial.
An old fox is shy of a trap.
An old fox need not be taught tricks.
As long runs the fox as he has feet.
At length the fox is brought to the furrier.
He that will outwit the fox must rise betimes.
If you deal with a fox, think of his tricks.
It is good to follow the old fox.
Old foxes want no tutors.
The fox barks not when he would steal the lamb.
The fox has many tricks, and the cat only one, but that the best of all.
The fox knows much, but more he that catches him.
The fox may grow gray but never good.
The fox preys farthest from home.
The fox smells his own stink first.
The fox's wiles will never enter the lion's head.
Though the fox run, the chicken hath wings.
When the fox is asleep nothing falls into his mouth.
When the fox preacheth, then beware of your geese.
With foxes we must play the fox.
If the lion's skin cannot, the fox's will. *(French)*
If the fox is a butler he will not die of thirst. *(German)*
The fox's death is the hen's life. *(German)*
The fox said the grapes were sour. *(Greek)*
Let every fox take care of his own tail. *(Italian)*
Where there are no dogs the fox is a king. *(Italian)*
An old fox is not easily snared. *(Latin)*
The fox changes his fur but not his habits. *(Latin)*
A fox sleeps but counts hens in his dreams. *(Russian)*
Every fox takes care of his tail. *(Russian)*
The cursed fox thrives the best. *(Spanish)*

FRANCE

France is a meadow that cuts thrice a year.
They order this matter better in France. *(Sterne)*
France is an absolute monarchy, tempered by songs. *(Chamfort)*

FRENCHMAN
Fifty million Frenchmen can't be wrong. *(American)*
Have the Frenchman for thy friend, not for thy neighbor.
The French are wiser than they seem, and the Spaniards seem wiser than they are. *(Bacon)*
When the Frenchman sleeps, the devil rocks him. *(French)*

FREEDOM
Better be a free bird than a captive king. *(Danish)*
Freedom is political power divided into small fragments. *(Hobbes)*
Freedom of speech and religion, from want and fear. *(F. D. Roosevelt)*
Ne'er yet by force was freedom overcome.
Not freedom, but license.
Once the flame of freedom is extinguished, it never lights again.
Restraint from ill is freedom to the wise.
That is not freedom where all command.
That man is free who is protected from injury.
The cause of freedom is the cause of God.
The lovers of freedom will be free.
The sweetest freedom is an honest heart.
The world is as free for a fly as for an eagle.
Those who expect to reap the blessings of freedom, must undergo the fatigue of supporting it. *(Paine)*
To be free is to live under a government by law.
Countries are well cultivated, not as they are fertile, but as they are free. *(Montesquieu)*
He is not free who drags his chain after him. *(French)*
Man is free at the moment he wishes to be. *(Voltaire)*
All are not free who mock their chains. *(German)*
All the arts of pleasure grow when suckled by freedom. *(German)*
Freedom is only in the land of dreams. *(Schiller)*
Only a free soul will never grow old. *(German)*
Who has lost his freedom has nothing else to lose. *(German)*
No bad man is free. *(Greek)*
No man is free who is not master of himself. *(Greek)*
To speak his thought is every freeman's right . . . *(Homer)*
Injurious is the gift that takes away freedom. *(Italian)*

FRIEND
A faithful friend is the medicine of life. *(Apocrypha)*
Faithful are the wounds of a friend; but the kisses of an enemy are deceitful. *(Old Test., Prov.)*

Greater love hath no man than this, that a man lay down his life for his friends. *(New Test., John)*

Iron sharpeneth iron; so a man sharpeneth the countenance of his friend. *(Old Test., Prov.)*

To a friend's house the road is never long. *(Dutch)*

One God, one wife, but many friends. *(Dutch)*

A friend in need is a friend indeed.

A friend in the market is better than money in the chest.

A friend is a person with whom I may be sincere. *(Emerson)*

A friend is long a-getting and soon lost.

A friend is never known till he is needed.

A false friend and a shadow attend only while the sun shines.

A friend is worth all hazards we can run.

A friend should bear his friend's infirmities. *(Shakespeare)*

A friend's frown is better than a foe's smile.

A good friend is my nearest relation.

A good friend never offends.

A judicious friend is better than a zealous.

A man dies as often as he loses his friends. *(Bacon)*

A true friend is forever a friend.

Above our life we love a steadfast friend. *(Marlowe)*

All are not friends that speak us fair.

An old friend is a new house.

As a man is friended, so the law is ended.

As good a foe that hurts not, as a friend that helps not.

Be slow in choosing a friend, slower in changing.

Better be a nettle in the side of your friend than his echo. *(Emerson)*

Better an open enemy than a false friend.

Better new friend than old foe.

Better to abide a friend's anger than a foe's kiss.

Choose thy friends like thy books—few but choice.

Do good to thy friend to keep him, to thy enemy to gain him. *(Franklin)*

Friends agree best at a distance.

Friends are as dangerous as enemies. *(De Quincey)*

Friends are like fiddle-strings—they must not be screwed too tight.

Friends got without desert are lost without cause.

Friends may meet, but mountains never greet.

He is a fair-weather friend.

He is a good friend that doth thee good.

He is a good friend that speaks well of me behind my back.

He is my friend that succoreth me, not he that pitieth me.
He is my friend that grindeth at my mill.
He will never have true friends who is afraid of making enemies.
I will be thy friend but not thy vice's friend.
If you have one true friend, you have more than your share.
It is better to lose a new jest than an old friend.
Life without a friend is death without a witness.
Love your friend, but look to yourself.
My son, keep well thy tongue, and keep thy friend. *(Chaucer)*
No receipt openeth a heart but a true friend.
Old friends are best.
One enemy can do more hurt than ten friends can do good.
Promises may get friends, but performance must keep them.
The best mirror is an old friend.
The only way to have a friend is to be one.
The vanquished have no friends.
The wretched have no friends.
They are rich who have true friends.
Three faithful friends—an old wife, an old dog, and ready money.
A faithful friend is an image of God. *(French)*
Be a friend to yourself and others will befriend you. *(French)*
Change your pleasures, but not your friends. *(Voltaire)*
Fate makes relatives, but choice makes friends. *(French)*
It is more shameful to distrust one's friends than to be deceived by them. *(La Rochefoucauld)*
Nothing is so dangerous as an ignorant friend. *(French)*
Our best friends are the source of our greatest sorrow. *(French)*
The friends of my friends are my friends. *(French)*
Try thy friends ere thou hast need of them. *(French)*
When my friends are one-eyed, I look at their profile. *(Joubert)*
A false friend has honey in his mouth, gall in his heart. *(German)*
A friend? A single soul dwelling in two bodies. *(Greek)*
A friend to all is a friend to none. *(Greek)*
Be more ready to visit a friend in adversity than in prosperity. *(Greek)*
Friends have all things in common. *(Greek)*
If you never tell your secret to a friend, you will never fear him when he becomes your enemy. *(Greek)*
Invite your friend to a feast, but leave your enemy alone. *(Greek)*
Let me have no good thing unknown to a friend. *(Greek)*
We should behave to our friends as we would wish our friends to behave to us. *(Greek)*

Without friends no one would choose to live. *(Greek)*
Friends tie their purse with a cobweb thread. *(Italian)*
From my friends God defend me, from my enemies I can defend myself. *(Italian)*
A friend must not be wounded, even in jest. *(Latin)*
Admonish your friends in private; praise them in public. *(Latin)*
Before you make a friend eat a bushel of salt with him. *(Latin)*
Friends are thieves of time. *(Latin)*
Friends disappear with the dregs from the empty wine casks. *(Latin)*
He does good to himself who does good to his friends. *(Latin)*
Nothing can be purchased which is better than a true friend. *(Latin)*
Prosperity makes friends and adversity tries them. *(Latin)*
Prove thy friend ere thou have need. *(Latin)*
Treat your friend as if he might become an enemy. *(Latin)*
Unless you bear with the faults of a friend, you betray your own. *(Latin)*
When fortune begins to frown, friends will be few. *(Latin)*
When fortune is fickle, the faithful friend is found. *(Latin)*
When there are friends there is wealth. *(Latin)*
He who has a thousand friends has not a friend to spare . . . *(Persian)*
An untried friend is like an uncracked nut. *(Russian)*
When there are two friends to one purse, the one sings, the other weeps. *(Spanish)*
When a friend asks there is no tomorrow. *(Spanish)*
May God not prosper our friends that they forget us. *(Spanish)*
He that trusts a faithless friend has a good witness against him. *(Spanish)*
The friend looks at the head, the enemy at the foot. *(Turkish)*
Make new friends, but don't forget the old ones. *(Yiddish)*

FRIENDSHIP

A broken friendship may be soldered, but will never be sound.
Friendship cannot live with ceremony, nor without civility.
Friendship cannot stand always on one side.
Friendship consists not in saying "What's the best news?"
Friendship is a disinterested commerce between equals. *(Goldsmith)*
Friendship is a sheltering tree.
Friendship is not to be bought at a fair.
Friendship is the gift of the gods . . .
Friendship is to be purchased only by friendship.
Friendship's full of dregs. *(Shakespeare)*

Keep your friendships in repair. *(Emerson)*
Love is only chatter,
Friends are all that matter. *(G. Burgess)*
Most friendship is feigning, most loving mere folly. *(Shakespeare)*
No friendship can survive the gift of gold.
The bird a nest, the spider a web, man friendship. *(Blake)*
To friendship every burden is light.
While the pot boils, friendship blooms.
Friendship is a prodigal, but love is a miser. *(French)*
Friendship is the marriage of the soul. *(French)*
Love and friendship exclude each other. *(French)*
The friendship of the wicked changes to fear, and fear to hate. *(French)*
The less friends one has, the more one feels the value of friendship. *(French)*
Time, which strengthens friendship, weakens love. *(French)*
A lost friendship is an enmity won. *(German)*
Friendship is equality. *(Greek)*
It is better to make one's friendships at home. *(Greek)*
Without confidence there is no friendship. *(Greek)*
Reconciled friendship is a wound ill salved. *(Italian)*
The friendship of the great is fraternity with lions. *(Italian)*
Friendship is but a name. *(Latin)*
Just as yellow gold is tested in the fire, so is friendship to be tested by adversity. *(Ovid)*
The name of friend is common, but faith in friendship is rare. *(Latin)*
The vulgar herd estimate friendship by its advantages. *(Latin)*

FROG

The frog's own croak betrays him.
Where there are no swamps there are no frogs. *(German)*
Though boys throw stones at frogs in sport, the frogs do not die in sport, but in earnest. *(Greek)*
Even a frog would bite if it had teeth. *(Italian)*

FRUIT

The fruit falls not far from the stem. *(Dutch)*
Forbidden fruit is sweetest.
Fruit is gold in the morning; silver in the afternoon, and lead at night.
Fruit out of season, sorrow out of reason.
Fruit ripens not in the shade.
Fruits that blossom first will first be ripe.

He that will have the fruit must climb the tree.
It is only at the tree loaded with fruit that people throw stones.
Like tree, like fruit.
Much bruit, little fruit.
We cannot eat the fruit while the tree is in blossom.
One must not pluck the fruit before it is ripe. *(French)*
Better the fruit lost than the tree. *(German)*
The better the fruit, the more wasps to eat it. *(German)*
There is no worse fruit than that which never ripens. *(Italian)*
Go to a pear-tree for pears—not to an elm. *(Latin)*

FULL
As full as an egg is of meat.
Full vessels give the least sound.

FUNERAL
After a funeral, a feast.
At a funeral we comfort ourselves with the difference betwixt us and the dead.

FUTILITY
It's little good a-watering last year's crop.
To tilt at windmills. *(Cervantes)*

FUTURE
Have no care for the future, and you will sorrow for the present. *(Chinese)*
Heav'n from all creatures hides the Book of Fate. *(Pope)*
After us the deluge. *(French)*
He must be mad who builds upon the future. *(French)*
I never think of the future. It comes soon enough. *(Einstein)*
Let the mind of man be blind as to future destiny. *(Greek)*
No man can tell what the future may bring forth. *(Greek)*
Fear of the future is worse than one's present fortune. *(Latin)*
No one has any right to draw for himself upon the future. *(Latin)*

G

GAIN

Love of gain turns wise men into fools. *(Chinese)*

To make any gain some outlay is necessary. *(Dutch)*

A going foot is aye getting.

Bad gains are truly losses.

Better it is to have more of gain and less honor.

Desire of gain, the basest minds' delight.

Evil-gotten goods are evil spent.

He gains enough that misses an ill turn.

Honor and profit lie not all in one sack.

Light gains make heavy purses.

Lightly come, lightly go.

No one was ever ruined by taking a profit.

No pains, no gains.

Of good ill got, the third heir joyeth not.

Pain is forgotten where gain follows.

Sometimes the best gain is to lose.

Soon gotten, soon spent.

To gain teacheth how to spend.

What I lost in the saltfish, I gained in the red herring.

Whatsoever is somewhere gotten is somewhere lost.

Ill-gotten gain brings loss. *(Greek)*

Ill-gotten gains work evil. *(Greek)*

Evil gain does not bring good luck. *(Latin)*

Ill-gotten gains will be ill spent. *(Latin)*

No man should make a gain of another's ignorance. *(Latin)*

Rather lose honorably than gain basely. *(Latin)*

To gain without another's loss is impossible. *(Latin)*

GALLOWS

What belongs to the gallows does not drown. *(Dutch)*

The gallows takes its own. *(Dutch)*
Two can lie the third to the gallows. *(German)*

GAMBLING

A pack of cards is the devil's prayer-book.
At the game's end we shall see who gains.
Death and the dice level all distinctions.
Fools for arguments use wagers.
Gamesters and racehorses never last long.
Gambling is the child of avarice, but the parent of prodigality.
Gaming is a principle inherent in human nature. *(Burke)*
Gaming is the mother of lies and perjuries.
Hazard is the very mother of lyings. *(Chaucer)*
He that plays his money ought not to value it.
I would cheat my own father at cards.
Keep flax from fire, youth from gaming.
Man is a gaming animal. *(Lamb)*
Nothing stake, nothing draw.
Nothing venture, nothing have.
Nought lay down, nought take up.
The devil goes share in gaming.
The devil is in the dice.
Without danger the game grows cold.
At play, anything may happen. *(French)*
One begins by being a dupe and ends by being a rascal. *(French)*
The game is not worth the candle. *(French)*
Young gambler—old beggar. *(German)*
It is a silly game where nobody wins. *(Italian)*
Lest he should lose, the gambler ceases not to lose. *(Latin)*
The better the gambler, the worse the man. *(Latin)*
The devil invented dicing. *(St. Augustine)*
Gie o'er when the play is gude. *(Scottish)*

GARDEN

God Almighty first planted a garden. (*Bacon*)
The market is the best garden.
There is no ancient gentlemen but gardeners. *(Shakespeare)*
This rule in gardening ne'er forget,
  To sow dry and set wet.
One should cultivate his garden. *(Voltaire)*
As is the garden such is the gardener. *(Hebrew)*
The gardener's feet do no harm to the garden. *(Spanish)*

GARLIC

Garlic makes a man wink, drink and stink.

GARRULITY

A fond old man is as full of words as a woman.

A garrulous tongue entangles all things. *(Latin)*

GENIUS

Genius can breathe freely only in an atmosphere of liberty. *(J. S. Mill)*

Genius is mainly an affair of energy.

Genius is one per cent inspiration and ninety-nine per cent perspiration. *(Edison)*

Genius is nothing but labor and diligence.

Genius is of no country.

Genius is the capacity of evading hard work.

Genius must be born and never can be taught.

Genius rusts for want of use.

Genius without education is like silver in the mine. *(Franklin)*

Great wits are sure to madness near allied. *(Dryden)*

Hunger is the handmaid of genius.

In the republic of mediocrity, genius is dangerous. *(Ingersoll)*

Rules and models destroy genius.

The eagle never lost so much time as when he submitted to learn of the crow. *(Blake)*

When Nature has work to be done, she creates a genius to do it. *(Emerson)*

Doing what is impossible for talent is genius. *(French)*

Genius is patience. *(Buffon)*

Genius is the capacity for taking pains. *(Napoleon)*

Genius is the talent of a man who is dead. *(Goncourt)*

The first and last thing required of genius is the love of truth. *(Goethe)*

The lamp of genius burns more brightly than the lamp of life. *(Schiller)*

Adversity reveals genius, prosperity hides it. *(Horace)*

The memory of genius is immortal. *(Latin)*

The worship of genius never makes a man rich. *(Petronius)*

When genius is punished, its fame is exalted. *(Tacitus)*

GENTLE

A gentle heart is tied with an easy thread.

Gentle is that gentle does.

There is no severity like gentleness.

The gentle ewe is sucked by every lamb. *(Italian)*

Power can do by gentleness what violence fails to accomplish. *(Latin)*
A gentle hand may lead the elephant with a hair. *(Persian)*

GENTLEMAN

A gentleman without an estate is a pudding without suet.
A king can make a nobleman, but only God can make a gentleman.
Gentlemen and rich men are venison in heaven.
Gentility is but ancient riches.
Gentility without ability is worse than plain beggary.
Gentry sent to market will not buy one bushel of corn.
He is gentle that doth gentle deeds. *(Chaucer)*
He was meant for a gentleman, but was spoilt in the making. *(Swift)*
It is almost a definition of a gentleman to say he is one who never inflicts pain. *(Newman)*
It is not the gay coat makes a gentleman.
Manners and money make the gentleman.
Once a gentleman, always a gentleman.
When Adam dolve and Eve span
  Who was then the gentleman? *(John Ball)*
Who would be a gentleman, let him storm a town.
A gentleman who lives ill is a monster in nature. *(Molière)*
The gentleman of honor, ragged sooner than patched. *(Cervantes)*

GERMAN

The German's wit is in his fingers. *(French)*
The Germans want to be governed. *(German)*
We Germans fear God, but nothing else in the world. *(Bismarck)*
Where Germans are, Italians like not to be. [*sic.*] *(Italian)*

GIANT

The awakening of a giant shakes the earth. *(Arabian)*
A giant will starve with what will surfeit a dwarf.
The giant loves the dwarf.
Pigmies placed on the shoulders of giants see more than the giants themselves. *(Latin)*

GIDDY

He that is giddy thinks that the world turns around. *(Shakespeare)*

GIFT

A gift destroyeth the heart. *(Old Test., Eccles.)*
A gift is as a precious stone in the eyes of him that hath it. *(Old Test., Prov.)*

He that hateth gifts shall live. *(Apocrypha)*
The gift blindeth the wise, and perverteth the words of the righteous. *(Old Test., Exodus)*

Secret gifts are openly rewarded. *(Danish)*
A gift blindeth the eyes.
A gift much expected is paid, not given.
A man's gift makes room for him.
A slight gift, small thanks.
A wicked man's gift hath a touch of its master.
Gifts are scorned where givers are despised. *(Dryden)*
Gifts enter everywhere without a wimble.
Gifts make beggars bold.
Great gifts are for great men.
Great gifts are from great men.
He doubles his gift who gives in time.
He that is won with a nut may be lost with an apple.
Look not a gift horse in the mouth.
Nothing costs so much as what is given us.
One gift well given recovers many losses.
Rich gifts wax poor when givers prove unkind. *(Shakespeare)*
The gods themselves cannot recall their gifts.
When the pig's proffered, hold up the pole.
A gift in the hand is better than two promises. *(French)*
Fair is he that comes, but fairer he that brings. *(French)*
A small gift is better than a great promise. *(German)*
Gifts come from above in their own forms. *(German)*
Gifts make the water to run back. *(German)*
Whatever a man has is only a gift. *(German)*
A gift, though small, is welcome. *(Greek)*
Gifts persuade even the gods. *(Greek)*
The gifts of a bad man bring no good with them. *(Greek)*
The gifts of a foe are not gifts. *(Greek)*
Beware of him who makes thee presents. *(Italian)*
What is bought is cheaper than a gift. *(Italian)*
Blessed is he who gets the gift, not he for whom it is meant. *(Latin)*
How blind men are to Heaven's gifts! *(Latin)*
I fear the Greeks and the gifts they bring. *(Vergil)*
Never examine the teeth of a gift-horse. *(Latin)*
The gift derives its value from the rank of the giver. *(Latin)*
A gift is cheap, but love is dear. *(Russian)*

Gifts break rocks. *(Spanish)*
When you're offered a heifer, run with a halter. *(Spanish)*

GILD
If the pills were pleasant, they would not want gilding.

GIRL
Glasses and lasses are brittle ware.
A girl unemployed is thinking of mischief. *(French)*
Dear to the heart of girls is their own beauty. *(Ovid)*
It is no sin to look at a nice girl. *(Russian)*
A girl draws more than a rope. *(Spanish)*
Let every girl attend to her spinning. *(Spanish)*

GIVING
A hand accustomed to take is far from giving. *(Arabian)*
He gives double who gives unasked. *(Arabian)*
Give to the poor, and thou shalt have treasure in heaven. *(New Test., Matthew)*
God loveth a cheerful giver. *(New Test., II Corinth.)*
It is more blessed to give than to receive. *(New Test., Acts)*
The liberal soul shall be made fat. *(Old Test., Prov.)*
The wise man does not lay up treasure. The more he gives the more he has. *(Chinese)*
A little given seasonably excuses a great gift.
Better an apple given than eaten.
Give a loaf and beg a shrive.
Give a thing, and take a thing, to wear the devil's gold ring.
Give and spend, and God will send.
Give every man his due.
Give him an inch and he'll take an ell.
Give him enough rope and he'll hang himself.
Give him the other half egg and burst him.
Give me roast meat and beat me with the spit.
Giving is dead, restoring very sick.
Giving much to the poor doth enrich a man's store.
God loves a cheerful giver.
He gives by halves, who hesitates to give.
He gives twice who gives in a trice.
He that gives his heart will not deny his money.
He that gives me small gifts would have me live.
He that gives to be seen will relieve none in the dark.

He that is long a-giving knows not how to give.
He who gives fair words feeds you with an empty spoon.
Not what we give, but what we share,
  For the gift without the giver is bare. *(J. R. Lowell)*
One must be poor to know the luxury of giving.
Steal the hog, and give the feet for alms.
The generous man pays for nothing so much as for what is given him.
The goods received, the giver is forgot.
The hand that gives, gathers.
The truly generous is the truly wise.
They are free of fruit that want an orchard.
To give and to have doth a wise brain crave.
What we gave, we have; what we spent, we had; what we left, we lost.
Who gives little can give often.
Who gives to all denies all.
Who shuts his hand, hath lost his gold:
  Who opens it, hath it twice told.
He who can give has many a good neighbor. *(French)*
I find nothing so dear as what is given me. *(Montaigne)*
What is called liberality is often merely the vanity of giving. *(La Rochefoucauld)*
To give is the business of the rich. *(Goethe)*
What you give is written in sand; what you take, with an iron hand. *(German)*
Give is a good girl; but Take is bad, and she brings death. *(Greek)*
Things that are truly given must not be taken away. *(Greek)*
Give a clown your finger and he'll take your whole hand. *(Italian)*
Giving is fishing. *(Italian)*
He who gives bread to others' dogs is barked at by his own. *(Italian)*
Be careful to whom you give. *(Latin)*
Bounty has no bottom. *(Latin)*
Giving calls for genius. *(Latin)*
He sends his present with a hook attached. *(Latin)*
I give that you may give. [*Do ut des.*] *(Latin)*
Let your portal be wide to the giver. *(Latin)*
The good that can be given, cannot be removed. *(Latin)*
Whatever I have given I still possess. *(Latin)*
While you look at what is given, look also at the giver. *(Latin)*
Giff-gaff makes gude friends. *(Scottish)*
Sic as ye gie, sic will ye get. *(Scottish)*
Give me a seat and I'll make room to lie down. *(Spanish)*

Giving and keeping require brains. *(Spanish)*
He who gives to the public gives to no one. *(Spanish)*
He who would take must give. *(Spanish)*
It is not much to give the leg to him that gave you the fowl. *(Spanish)*
Not he gives who likes, but who has. *(Spanish)*
People don't give black puddings to one who kills no pigs. *(Spanish)*
To give is honor; to lose is grief. *(Spanish)*
Whoever gives thee a bone would not wish to see thee dead. *(Spanish)*

GLASS
Whose house is of glass must not throw stones at another's.

GLORY
Like madness is the glory of this life. *(Shakespeare)*
Military glory—the attractive rainbow that rises in showers of blood. *(Lincoln)*
Seldom comes Glory till a man be dead.
The desire of glory is the torch of the mind.
The paths of glory lead but to the grave. *(Gray)*
We rise in glory as we sink in pride. *(Young)*
Glory is never where virtue is not. *(French)*
Glory is the recompense of gallant actions. *(French)*
No flowery road leads to glory. *(French)*
The glory of great men should be measured by the means they have used to acquire it. *(La Rochefoucauld)*
When glory comes, memory departs. *(French)*
Glory drags all men captive at the wheel of her glittering car. *(Latin)*
Glory is a mighty spur. *(Latin)*
Glory paid to our ashes comes too late. *(Latin)*
He will have true glory who despises glory. *(Latin)*
If glory comes after death, I am in no hurry. *(Latin)*
The glory of good men is in their conscience and not in the mouths of men. *(Latin)*
Thus passes away the glory of the world.
[*Sic transit gloria mundi.*] *(Latin)*

GLUTTONY
There is death in the pot. *(Old Test., II Kings)*
A belly full of gluttony will never study willingly.
A greedy man God hates.
Gluttony is the sin of England.
He has a hole under his nose that all his money runs into.

He will spend a whole year's rent at one meal's meat.
He will never have enough till his mouth is full of mould.
His eye is bigger than his belly.
I saw few die of hunger; of eating, a hundred thousand.
If it were not for the belly, the back might wear gold.
Surfeit slays more than the sword.
The fool that eats till he is sick, must fast till he is well.
The table robs more than a thief.
They are as sick that surfeit with too much, as they that starve with nothing. *(Shakespeare)*
They have digged their grave with their teeth.
Who hastens a glutton chokes him.
Your belly will never let your back be warm.
Gluttony kills more than the sword. *(French)*
Surfeit has killed more than famine. *(Greek)*
The first in banquets but the last in fight. *(Greek)*
Greediness closed Paradise. *(Pope Innocent III)*
Greediness is rich and shame poor. *(Latin)*
Ingenious is gluttony. *(Latin)*
He has two stomachs—one to eat and one to work.
The mouth has a little hole, but it can swallow house and roof. *(Yiddish)*

GOAT
If the beard were all, the goat might preach. *(Danish)*
An old goat is never more revered for his beard.
Where the goat is tied she must browse. *(French)*
Where the goat leaps, leaps that which sucks her. *(Spanish)*
Be not in haste, O goat, to go to the woods; you'll reach the wolf later. *(Yiddish)*

GOD
There is no God but God. *(The Koran)*
Canst thou by searching find out God? *(Old Test., Job)*
Fear God and keep his commandments. *(Old Test., Eccles.)*
God is love; and he that dwelleth in love dwelleth in God, and God in him. *(New Test., I John)*
God is no respecter of persons. *(New Test., Acts)*
God is our refuge and our strength. *(Old Test., Psalms)*
God is a spirit. *(New Test., John)*
God will provide. *(Old Test., Genesis)*
If God be for us, who can be against us? *(New Test., Romans)*

The Lord is my light and my salvation. *(Old Test., Psalms)*
The fear of the Lord is the beginning of wisdom. *(Old Test., Prov.)*
The Lord reigneth; let the earth rejoice. *(Old Test., Psalms)*
The mercy of the Lord is from everlasting to everlasting. *(Old Test., Psalms)*
Though he slay me, yet will I trust him. *(Old Test., Job)*
Whom the Lord loveth he chasteneth. *(New Test., Hebr.)*
Father and mother are kind, but God is kinder. *(Danish)*
God gives little folk small gifts. *(Danish)*
There is no key to God's counsel chamber. *(Danish)*
God does not pay weekly, but he pays at the end. *(Dutch)*
When it is God's will to plague a man, a mouse can bite him to death. *(Dutch)*
A God all mercy is a God unjust. *(Young)*
Better God than gold.
Every man for himself and God for us all.
Get the spindle ready and God will send the flax.
God arms the harmless.
God comes at last when we think he is farthest off.
God comes to see without a bell.
God comes with leaden feet, but strikes with iron hands.
God complains not, but doth what is fitting.
God gives his wrath by weight, and without weight his mercy.
God helps them who help themselves.
God is a good man.
God is a sure paymaster.
God is no botcher.
God is where he was.
God loves good accounts.
God moves in a mysterious way
His wonders to perform. *(Cowper)*
God never sends mouths but he sends meat.
God sends corn and the devil mars the sack.
God sends men cold according to their cloth.
God strikes with his finger and not with his arm.
Have God and have all.
He is poor that God hates.
He loseth nothing that loseth to God.
In the faces of men and women I see God. *(Whitman)*
Just are the ways of God
And justifiable to men. *(Milton)*

Man doth what he can, and God what he will.
Not God above gets all men's love.
The grace of God is gear enough.
The way to God is by ourselves.
Thou Great First Cause, least understood. *(Pope)*
To be is to live with God. *(Emerson)*
What God will, no frost can kill.
Where there is peace, God is.
Whom God will help nae man can hinder.
Better deal with God than with his saints. *(French)*
God often visits us, but most of the time we are not at home. *(French)*
God puts a good root in the little pig's way. *(French)*
God saves the moon from the wolves. *(French)*
God will know his own. *(French)*
If God did not exist it would be necessary to invent him. *(Voltaire)*
The Eternal Being is for ever if he is at all. *(French)*
The servant of God has a good master. *(Pascal)*
A mighty fortress is our God . . . *(Luther)*
God gives the milk but not the pail. *(German)*
There is a God to punish and avenge. *(German)*
God has many names though he is only one being. *(Greek)*
God is a geometrician. *(Plato)*
God is truth and light his shadow. *(Plato)*
God's mouth knows not to utter falsehood. *(Greek)*
He is to be feared who fears the gods. *(Greek)*
God gives a cursed cow short horns. *(Italian)*
God is everywhere except where he has his delegate. *(Italian)*
God sends nothing but what can be borne. *(Italian)*
When God will not, the saints cannot. *(Italian)*
God is patient because eternal. *(St. Augustine)*
He who has known God reverences him. *(Latin)*
If God be with us, who shall stand against us? *(Latin)*
Man proposes, but God disposes. *(Latin)*
No one against God except God himself. *(Latin)*
To the greater glory of God. [*Motto of Jesuits*] *(Latin)*
We do nothing without the leave of God. *(Latin)*
No threshold without God. *(Russian)*
Everyone in his own house and God in all men's. *(Spanish)*
Everyone is as God made him and very often worse. *(Spanish)*
God gives almonds to some who have no teeth. *(Spanish)*
God helps everyone with what is his own. *(Spanish)*

God is a good worker, but he loves to be helped. *(Spanish)*
God made us and we wonder at it. *(Spanish)*
God who gives the wound gives the salve. *(Spanish)*
God will provide, but a bundle of straw will not be amiss. *(Spanish)*
When God dawns he dawns for all. *(Spanish)*
When God pleases, it rains in fair weather. *(Spanish)*
We are because God is. *(Swedenborg)*
God postpones, he does not overlook. *(Turkish)*
That man is to be feared who fears not God. *(Turkish)*
Don't bargain with God. *(Yiddish)*
Each for himself, God for all. *(Yiddish)*
Give to God what is God's; unto man, what is man's. *(Yiddish)*
God feeds even the worm in the earth. *(Yiddish)*
God tempers the cold to our clothes. *(Yiddish)*
God has given; God has taken away. *(Yiddish)*
God is a father; luck, a step-father. *(Yiddish)*
God is one; what He does, sees none. *(Yiddish)*
God leads a man along the road he would go. *(Yiddish)*
God sends the cure before the plague. *(Yiddish)*
God knows what He does. *(Yiddish)*
God punishes with one hand and blesses with the other. *(Yiddish)*
If God lived on earth, men would break his windows. *(Yiddish)*
If it's God's will, a broomstick can shoot. *(Yiddish)*
Man rides and God holds the reins. *(Yiddish)*
Whom God loves he punishes. *(Yiddish)*

GODS

As flies to wanton boys are we to the gods. *(Shakespeare)*
If we meet no gods, it is because we harbor none. *(Emerson)*
The gods did not send corn only for the rich.
I do not know whether there are gods, but there ought to be. *(Diogenes)*
Let us beware the jealousy of the gods. *(Greek)*
It was fear that first made gods in the world. *(Latin)*
Whom the gods would destroy they first make mad. *(Latin)*
The mills of the gods grind slow but exceeding small. *(Greek)*

GOING

Without going you can get nowhere. *(Chinese)*
Go farther and fare worse.
You must learn to creep before you go.

By dint of going wrong all will come right. *(French)*
One may go a long way after he is tired. *(French)*
Go softly over bad bits of road. *(Italian)*
Who goes not sees not. *(Italian)*
The slower you go the further you be. *(Russian)*

GOLD
Gold hath been the ruin of many. *(Apocrypha)*
Better whole than patched with gold. *(Danish)*
A gold ring does not cure a felon *(wart)*.
A golden dart kills where it pleases.
A golden hammer breaks an iron gate.
A man may buy gold too dear.
All is not gold that glitters.
An ass loaded with gold climbs to the top of the castle.
Chains of gold are stronger than chains of iron.
Gold dust blinds all eyes.
Gold goes in at any gate, except Heaven's.
Gold is a deep-persuading orator.
Gold is a good doctor.
Gold is but muck.
Gold is the devil's fishhook.
Gold maketh an honest man an ill man.
Gold opens all locks.
Gold were as good as twenty orators. *(Shakespeare)*
Gold when present causeth fear; when absent, grief.
He is worth gold that can win it.
Kill not the goose that lays the golden eggs.
O love of gold! thou meanest of amours! *(Young)*
Old women's gold is not ugly.
That is gold which is worth gold.
The balance distinguishes not between gold and lead.
We live by the gold for which other men die. *(Prior)*
What words won't do, gold will.
A man of straw is worth a woman of gold. *(French)*
Even to ugliness gold gives a look of beauty. *(French)*
Gold is proved by touch. *(French)*
Before gold even kings remove their hats. *(German)*
Man must govern, not serve, gold. *(German)*
As the touchstone tries gold, so gold tries men. *(Greek)*
Gold is an unseen tyrant. *(Greek)*

Gold is pale because it has so many thieves plotting against it. *(Greek)*
Man prates, but gold speaks. *(Italian)*
Poison is drunk out of gold cups. *(Latin)*
When a ship sinks, gold weighs down its owners. *(Latin)*
There is no lock if the pick is of gold. *(Spanish)*
Gold shines in the mud. *(Yiddish)*

GOLDEN AGE

The golden age never was the present age.

GOLDEN RULE

Whatsoever ye would that men should do unto you, do ye even so to them. *(New Test., Matthew)*
What is hateful to thyself do not unto thy neighbor. *(Talmud)*

GOOD

Abhor that which is evil; cleave to that which is good. *(New Test., Romans)*
Can any good thing come out of Nazareth? *(New Test., John)*
A man has no more goods than he gets good of.
A man far from his good is near his harm.
Good and quickly seldom meet.
Good enough is never ought.
Good finds good.
Good for the liver may be bad for the spleen.
Good hand, good hire.
Good is good, but better carries it.
Good that comes too late is good as nothing.
Goodly is he that goodly doeth.
He cannot be good that knows not why he is good.
It is an ill wind that blows nobody good.
It is good if it were but caught.
Nothing but is good for something.
One good turn asketh another.
That is my good that does me good.
That is not always good in the maw that is sweet in the mouth.
The good is the enemy of the best.
Well is that well does.
Good comes to better, and better to bad. *(French)*
Good things are hard. *(Greek)*
So good that he is good for nothing. *(Italian)*
Good ware makes quick markets. *(Latin)*

What is good is never plentiful. *(Spanish)*
If you put good in, you can take good out. *(Yiddish)*

GOODNESS
Let us not be weary in well-doing. *(New Test., Galatians)*
True goodness springs from a man's own heart. *(Chinese)*
A good heart is better than all the heads in the world.
Be good and you will be lonesome. *(Mark Twain)*
Be good, sweet maid, and let who can be clever. *(Kingsley)*
Do good by stealth and blush to find it fame. *(Pope)*
Do good if you expect to receive it.
Good and evil are chiefly in the imagination.
Good men are a public good.
Good will should be taken for part payment.
He can never be good that is not obstinate.
He cannot long be good that knows not why he is good.
The evil that men do lives after them;
  The good is oft interred with their bones. *(Shakespeare)*
There is some soul of goodness in things evil. *(Shakespeare)*
The end of good is an evil, and the end of evil is a good.
(La Rochefoucauld)
He that helps the evil hurts the good. *(Greek)*
If you wish to be good, first believe that you are bad. *(Greek)*
Say not that the good are dead. *(Greek)*
The good man makes others good. *(Greek)*
To a good man nothing that happens is evil. *(Greek)*
Evil things are neighbors to good. *(Latin)*
Honest fame awaits the truly good. *(Latin)*
In every good man a god doth dwell. *(Latin)*
Rather be called good than fortunate. *(Latin)*
That which is good makes men good. *(Latin)*
A good man's pedigree is little hunted up. *(Spanish)*

GOOSE
A goose drinks as much as a gander. *(Danish)*
The goose hisses but does not bite. *(Dutch)*
A goose is a goose still, dress it as you will.
All his geese are swans.
Feather by feather the goose is plucked.
Goslings lead the geese to water.
The old goose plays not with foxes.

What is sauce for the goose is sauce for the gander
When the rain raineth and the goose winketh,
  Little wots the gosling what the goose thinketh.
Young is the goose that will not eat oats.
When one goose drinks, all drink. *(German)*
Kill not the goose that lays the golden egg. *(Greek)*

GOSSIP

All that is said in the kitchen should not be heard in the hall.
Gossips and lying go together.
Gossips and frogs drink and talk.
He was scant of news that told his father was hanged.
If you do what you should not, you must hear what you would not.
Gossips fall out and tell each other truths. *(Spanish)*
It is no time to gossip with the dying. *(Turkish)*

GOVERNMENT

An oppressive government is more to be feared than a tiger. *(Chinese)*
Govern yourself and you can govern the world. *(Chinese)*
A government of laws and not of men. *(J. Adams)*
Ill can he rule the great that cannot reach the small. *(Spenser)*
It is error alone which needs support of government. *(Jefferson)*
No man is good enough to govern another without that other's consent. *(Lincoln)*
The whole of government consists in the art of being honest. *(Jefferson)*
The right divine to govern wrong. *(Pope)*
The world is governed too much.
They that govern the most make the least noise.
To govern mankind one must not overrate them. *(Chesterfield)*
A wise man neither suffers himself to be governed, nor attempts to govern others. *(La Bruyère)*
Every country has the government it deserves. *(French)*
Republics end through luxury; monarchies through poverty. *(Montesquieu)*
Command shows the man. *(Greek)*
As the government, so the people. *(Italian)*
A hated government does not endure long. *(Seneca)*
Divide and rule. [*Divide et impera.*] *(Latin)*
With how little wisdom is the world governed! *(Pope Julius III)*
The good governor should have a broken leg and keep at home. *(Cervantes)*

GOWN
That is the best gown that goes up and down the house.

GRACE
Ye have fallen from grace. *(New Test., Galatians)*
Grace will last, beauty will blast.
In space comes grace.
So grace is a gift of God and kind wit a chance.
Grace is to the body what judgment is to the mind. *(La Rochefoucauld)*

GRADUAL
Feather by feather the goose is plucked.
Little by little the cat eateth up the bacon flickle
Step by step the ladder is ascended.

GRAPES
The fathers have eaten sour grapes, and the children's teeth are set on edge. *(Old Test., Ezekiel)*
Winter grapes sour, wedder you kin reach 'em or not. *(American Negro)*
When the fox cannot reach the grapes he says they are not ripe. *(Greek)*

GRASP
Grasp no more than thy hand will hold.

GRASS
Grass grows at last above all graves.
Grass grows not upon the highway.
While the grass grows the horse starves.
Grass does not spring where the grand signor's horse sets his foot. *(Italian)*

GRATITUDE
Do not cut down the tree that gives you shade. *(Arabian)*
In everything give thanks. *(New Test., I Thessal.)*
Gratitude is the music of the heart.
Praise the bridge that carried you over.
Words are but empty thanks.
The gratitude of most men is nothing but a secret hope of receiving greater favors. *(La Rochefoucauld)*
What soon grows old? Gratitude. *(Greek)*
Be not ungrateful to your old friend. *(Hebrew)*

One good turn deserves another. *(Latin)*
Scratch my back and I'll scratch yours. *(Latin)*
Thanks are justly due for boons unbought. *(Latin)*
To the grateful man give more than he asks. *(Latin)*

GRAVE

De graveyard is de cheapes' boardin'-house. *(American Negro)*
Man goeth to his long home. *(Old Test., Eccles.)*
There the wicked cease from troubling; and there the weary be at rest. *(Old Test., Job)*
A piece of churchyard fits everybody.
Earth is the best shelter.
For who's a prince or beggar in the grave? *(Otway)*
Gilded tombs do worms infold. *(Shakespeare)*
In the grave, dust and bones jostle not for the wall.
In the grave there is no work and no device.
Our lives are but our marches to the grave. *(J. Fletcher)*
The grave is the general meeting place.
The grave's a fine and private place,
But none, I think, do there embrace. *(Marvell)*
The more thy years the nearer thy grave.
We shall all lie alike in our grave.
He who lies in the grave is well lodged. *(German)*
Only in the grave is there rest. *(Yiddish)*

GREAT

And seekest thou great things for thyself? seek them not. *(Old Test., Jeremiah)*
Great men are not always wise. *(Old Test., Job)*
Towers are measured by their shadows and great men by their calumniators. *(Chinese)*
Desire of greatness is a godlike sin. *(Dryden)*
Great and good are seldom the same man.
Great birth is a very poor dish at table.
Great bodies move slowly.
Great heights are hazardous to the weak head.
Great hopes make great men.
Great let me call him, for he conquers me. *(Young)*
Great marks are soonest hit.
Great men are oft overthrown by small means.
Great men have great faults.
Great men have more adorers than friends.

Great men will always pay deference to greater. *(Lander)*
Great men's vices are esteemed as virtues.
Great smoke, little roast.
Great weights may hang on small wires.
Great winds blow upon high hills.
Great without small makes a bad wall.
Greatness knows itself. *(Shakespeare)*
He is great who confers the most benefits. *(Emerson)*
It is as easy to be great as to be small. *(Emerson)*
Look high and fall low.
No really great man ever thought himself so. *(Hazlitt)*
Some are born great, some achieve greatness, and some have greatness thrust upon them. *(Shakespeare)*
The favor of the great is no inheritance.
The great put the little on the hook.
The great would have none great, and the little all little.
The greatest men are the simplest.
The top of honor is a slippery place.
There would be no great ones if there were no little ones.
To be great is to be misunderstood. *(Emerson)*
The great are only great because we are on our knees. *(Proudhon)*
The great oak bears small fruit. *(German)*
With great men one must allow five to be an even number. *(German)*
Goodness is not tied to greatness, but greatness to goodness. *(Greek)*
He is great whose faults can be numbered. *(Hebrew)*
Great men's sons seldom do well. *(Latin)*
It is a rough road that leads to the heights of greatness. *(Latin)*

GREEK
When Greek meets Greek, then comes the tug of war.
I fear the Greeks, even when bringing gifts. *(Vergil)*

GREED
Grasp all, lose all.
Greedy folks have long arms.
Greedy is the good-less.
He can hide his meat and seek more.
Greed and the eye can no man fill. *(German)*
The eye is bigger than the mouth. *(Yiddish)*

GRIEF
All griefs with bread are less.

Everyone can master a grief but he that has it. *(Shakespeare)*
Great griefs medicine the less.
Grief is a species of idleness. *(S. Johnson)*
Grief makes one hour ten.
Grief once told brings somewhat back of peace. *(W. Morris)*
Grief should be the instructor of the wise. *(Byron)*
New grief awakens old.
The grief of the head is the grief of griefs.
The only cure for grief is action.
There is a sort of pleasure in indulging grief.
Little griefs make us tender; great ones make us hard. *(Chenier)*
Great souls suffer in silence. *(Schiller)*
Of all the many ills common to all men, the greatest is grief. *(Greek)*
Wherein is life sweet to him who suffers grief? *(Greek)*
Grief is carried off by tears. *(Latin)*
He grieves sincerely who grieves unseen. *(Latin)*
Light griefs can speak; but deeper ones are dumb. *(Latin)*
Suppressed grief suffocates. *(Latin)*
There is no grief which time does not lessen. *(Latin)*
Do not rejoice at my grief, for when mine is old, yours will be new. *(Spanish)*
He that conceals his grief finds no remedy for it. *(Turkish)*

GROOM
Every groom is a king at home.

GROWTH
A growing youth has a wolf in his belly. *(Italian)*
Under his nose it's beginning to sprout; but in his head it hasn't even been sown. *(Russian)*

GUARD
He sets the fox to keep his geese.
Guard yourself against your friends, not your enemies. *(Yiddish)*

GUESS
Some had rather guess at much than take pains to learn a little.
Guessing is missing. *(German)*

GUEST
A constant guest is never welcome.
An unbidden guest knows not where to sit.
Fresh fish and new-come guests smell in three days.

He is an ill guest that never drinks to his host.
Welcome the coming, speed the parting guest.
The unbidden guest is ever a pest. *(German)*
A great guest is always dear to a host. *(Russian)*
An unbidden guest is worse than a Tartar. *(Russian)*
A house filled with guests is eaten up. *(Spanish)*
The guest is not welcome to the guest, but both to the host. *(Turkish)*
Good guests come uninvited. *(Yiddish)*

GUILT
He who flees proves himself guilty. *(Danish)*
A man is held to be innocent until he is proved guilty.
Guilt has very quick ears to an accusation.
Guilt is always jealous.
He that knows no guilt can know no fear.
Men that are greatly guilty are never wise.
Suspicion always haunts the guilty mind. *(Shakespeare)*
The guilty mind needs no accuser.
The guilt and not the scaffold makes the shame. *(French)*
He who is guilty believes all men speak ill of him. *(Italian)*
A mind conscious of guilt is its own accuser. *(Latin)*
Those whom guilt stains it makes equal. *(Latin)*

GULLIBLE
Do you see any green in my eye?
He thinks the moon is made of green cheese.

GUT
The gut has no window. *(Yiddish)*

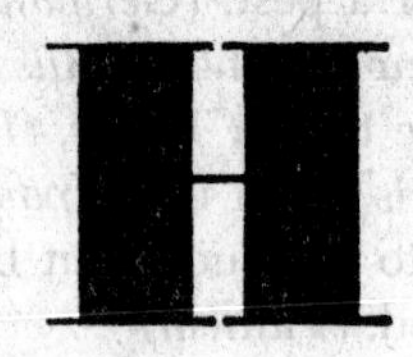

HABIT

Men's natures are alike; it is their habits that carry them far apart. *(Chinese)*

An ounce of habit is worth a pound of intellect.

Habits are first cobwebs, then cables.

Habit is ten times nature.

Habit rules the unreflecting herd. *(Wordsworth)*

How use doth breed a habit in a man! *(Shakespeare)*

It is hard to break a hog of an ill custom.

Nothing so needs reforming as other people's habits. *(Mark Twain)*

The old coachman likes to hear the whip.

'Tis easier to prevent bad habits than to break them.

Habit is second nature. *(Montaigne)*

Man is an animal of habits. *(German)*

The habit is not a trifle. *(Greek)*

A nail is driven out by another nail; habit is overcome by habit. *(Latin)*

Great is the power of habit. *(Latin)*

Habit is stronger than nature. *(Latin)*

Habits, if not resisted, soon become necessity. *(Latin)*

How many unjust things are done from habit! *(Terence)*

Use establishes habit. *(Latin)*

HAIL

Hail brings frost in the tail.

HAIR

The very hairs of your head are numbered. *(New Test., Matthew)*

A bald head is soon shaven.

A curled pate will grow bald.

Long hair, short wit.

Short hair is soon brushed. *(German)*

Hair adds beauty to a good face, and terror to an ugly one. *(Greek)*
It is not white hair that engenders wisdom. *(Greek)*
Even a hair has its own shadow. *(Latin)*
Ugly is a field without grass, a plant without leaves, or a head without hair. *(Ovid)*

HALF
Half a loaf is better than no bread.
Never do things by halves.
The half is more than the whole. *(Greek)*

HAMMER
You must be either hammer or anvil. *(French)*

HAND
Kiss the hand which you cannot bite. *(Arabian)*
His hand will be against every man, and every man's hand against him. *(Old Test., Genesis)*
The voice is Jacob's voice, but the hands are the hands of Esau. *(Old Test., Genesis)*
Put your hand quickly to your hat and slowly to your purse. *(Danish)*
A clean glove often hides a dirty hand.
A clean hand wants no washing.
Hands off and fair play.
Hands were made for honest labor,
Not to plunder or to steal. *(Watts)*
Help, hands, for I have no lands.
It is a bad hand that refuses to guard the head.
Let not your right hand know what the left is doing.
Many hands make light work.
Nothing enters into a closed hand.
Put not thy hand between the bark and the tree.
The gods hear men's hands before their lips.
The hand of little employment hath the daintier sense. *(Shakespeare)*
The wise hand doth not all that the foolish mouth speaks.
Worse than a bloody hand is a hard heart. *(Shelley)*
Open hand makes open hand. *(German)*
One hand washes another, and both the face. *(Greek)*
Let your left hand turn away what your right attracts. *(Hebrew)*
The right hand is slave to the left. *(Italian)*
God looks with favor at pure, not full, hands. *(Latin)*

The same hand that makes the sign of the cross, sharpens the knife. *(Russian)*
Hand play, churl's play. *(Spanish)*
White hands are no offense. *(Spanish)*
No one cuts the hand that gives. *(Turkish)*
Two hands are for the defense of one head. *(Turkish)*

HANDSOME

Handsome is that handsome does.
The handsomest flower is not the sweetest.
A handsome shoe often pinches the foot. *(French)*
Handsome is not what is handsome, but what pleases. *(Yiddish)*

HANGING

Hang the young thief, and the old one will not steal. *(Danish)*
A halter made of silk is a halter still.
A man is never undone till he be hanged. *(Shakespeare)*
All are not hanged that are condemned.
As good be hanged for an old sheep as for a young lamb.
Hang a dog on a crab-tree and he'll never love verjuice.
Hanging and wiving go by destiny.
Hanging is the worst use a man can be put to.
He rises over-early that is hanged ere noon.
He that's born to be hanged shall never be drowned.
No haste to hang true men.
There are more ways to kill a dog than by hanging.
We must all hang together or we shall all hang separately. *(Franklin)*
You'll dance at the end of a rope without teaching.
Give him enough rope and he'll hang himself. *(French)*
Who hangs himself in the chimney should not complain of smoke. *(German)*
He came soon enough who was hanged by candle light. *(Spanish)*
Name not a rope in the house of him that was hanged. *(Spanish)*
If I hang by the head, I hang by the feet too. *(Yiddish)*

HAPPEN

Everything happens for the best.
What happens to one may happen to another.
Everybody is wise after the thing has happened. *(French)*
What does not happen in a year may happen in a moment. *(Spanish)*

HAPPINESS

He is happy who knows his good fortune. *(Chinese)*

Better be happy than wise.

Happiness is a habit to be cultivated.

Happiness is a way-station between too little and too much.

Happiness is but a name. *(Burns)*

Happy is he that is happy in his children.

Happy man, happy dole.

He is happy that knoweth not himself happy.

How bitter a thing it is to look into happiness through another man's eyes! *(Shakespeare)*

I were but little happy if I could say how much.

Man is not born for happiness.

Man is the artificer of his own happiness. *(Thoreau)*

No happiness without holiness.

No one can be perfectly happy till all are happy. *(H. Spencer)*

Oh, make us happy and you make us good. *(Browning)*

That action is best which procures the greatest happiness of the greatest numbers. *(Hutcheson)*

The days that make us happy make us wise. *(Masefield)*

'Tis not good to be happy too young.

We have no more right to consume happiness without producing it than to consume wealth without producing it. *(G. B. Shaw)*

We ne'er can be made happy by compulsion. *(Coleridge)*

Call no man happy till he dies. *(French)*

Happiness does away with ugliness. *(French)*

Happiness is made to be shared. *(French)*

One is never as happy or as unhappy as he thinks. *(La Rochefoucauld)*

The will of a man is his happiness. *(Schiller)*

A man's happiness is to do a man's true work. *(Greek)*

Only at the end of a man's prosperous life dare we pronounce him happy. *(Greek)*

A happy life consists in tranquility of mind. *(Latin)*

Happiness invites envy. *(Latin)*

He is not happy who does not think himself so. *(Latin)*

Nature gives all the chance for happiness, knew they but how to use it. *(Latin)*

HARD

Hard with hard makes not the stone wall. *(Latin)*

HARE

Hares are not caught with drums. *(Dutch)*
He who would have a hare for breakfast, must hunt overnight.
Lame hares are ill to help.
The hare may pluck the dead lion by the beard.
One catches the hare and another eats it. *(German)*
Who hunts two hares together catches neither. *(German)*
Running hares do not need the spur. *(Italian)*
First catch your hare. *(Latin)*
The hound pursues the hare; the hare pursues freedom. *(Russian)*

HARM

Harm watch, harm catch.
It costs more to do ill than to do well.
When the harm is done, it is useless to unstring the bow. *(French)*

HARVEST

He that regardeth the wind shall not sow and he that regardeth the clouds shall not reap. *(Old Test., Eccles.)*
He that sleeps in harvest is a son that causeth shame. *(Old Test., Prov.)*
In the morning sow thy seed, and in the evening withhold not thine hand. *(Old Test., Eccles.)*
. . . reaping where thou hast not sown, and gathering where thou hast not strewed. *(New Test., Matthew)*
The harvest truly is plenteous, but the laborers are few. *(New Test., Matthew)*
Good harvests make men prodigal, bad ones provident.
Harvest comes not every day, though it comes every year.
Harvest follows seed-time.
Harvest will come, and then every farmer's rich.
He that hath a good harvest may be content with some thistles.
When corn is ripe, 'tis time to reap.
You mustn't spit on the harvest, as Papa Noah said. *(French)*
Live within your harvest. *(Latin)*
Who eat their corn while yet 'tis green,
At the true harvest can but glean. *(Sadi) (Persian)*

HASTE

Haste is of the devil. *(Arabian)*
Man is created of hastiness. *(The Koran)*
Haste is not speed. *(Dutch)*
A hasty man never wants woe.

A prudent haste is wisdom's leisure.
Do in haste and repent at leisure.
Fools haste to no speed.
Good and quickly seldom meet.
Haste and wisdom are things far odd.
Haste comes not alone.
Haste makes waste.
Haste trips up its own heels.
Hasty climbers have sudden falls.
Hasty gamesters oversee.
Hasty people will never make good midwives.
He hasteth well that wisely can abide.
He that is hasty fishes in an empty pond.
He tires betimes that spurs too fast betimes. *(Shakespeare)*
Let us leave hurry to slaves. *(Emerson)*
Nothing is more vulgar than haste. *(Emerson)*
Stay a while that we may make an end the sooner.
The more haste, the worse speed.
Though I am always in haste, I am never in a hurry. *(J. Wesley)*
Too swift arrives as tardy as too slow. *(Shakespeare)*
With eager feeding food will choke the feeder.
Too great haste leads us to error. *(French)*
Haste comes late in the end. *(German)*
Nothing in haste but catching fleas. *(German)*
Haste is ever the parent of failure. *(Greek)*
Haste is slow. *(Latin)*
He hastens to repentance who hastily judges. *(Latin)*
Make haste slowly. [*Festina lente.*] *(Latin)*
Haste manages all things badly. *(Latin)*
Nothing can be done at once hastily and prudently. *(Latin)*
The hasty bitch brings forth blind whelps. *(Latin)*
Unless we hasten, we shall be left behind. *(Latin)*
Who pours water hastily into a bottle spills more than goes in. *(Spanish)*
Nothing good ever comes from haste. *(Yiddish)*

HAT
Pull down thy hat on the windy side.

HATE
Hatred stirreth up strife: but love covereth all sins. *(Old Test., Prov.)*
Cherish those hearts that hate thee. *(Shakespeare)*

Folks never understand the folks they hate. *(J. R. Lowell)*
Hate and mistrust are the children of blindness.
Hate knows no age but death.
Hate not at the first harm.
Hating people is like burning down your own house to get rid of a rat. *(H. E. Fosdick)*
Hatreds are the cinders of affection.
Hatred is blind, as well as love.
Hatred is self-punishment.
Hatred is the coward's revenge for being intimidated. *(G. B. Shaw)*
He could eat me without salt.
He could eat my heart with garlic.
In time we hate that which we often fear. *(Shakespeare)*
It does not matter what a man hates provided he hates something. *(Butler)*
Severity breeds fear; roughness, hatred.
There are no eyes so sharp as the eyes of hatred.
A true man hates no one. *(French)*
He who is hated by all cannot expect to live long. *(French)*
Violent hatred sinks us below those we hate. *(French)*
Hatred renewed is worse than at first. *(Italian)*
Hatred is a settled anger. *(Latin)*
Hatred openly proclaimed loses its chance for vengeance. *(Latin)*
Let them hate me so long as they fear me. *(Latin)*
Press not thy hatred too far. *(Latin)*
The malevolent have hidden teeth. *(Latin)*
We hate whom we have injured. *(Latin)*
Whom men fear they hate, and whom they hate they wish dead. *(Latin)*

HAVE

Better have than hear of.
"Had I a fish" is good without mustard.
If you have not what you like, you must like what you have. *(French)*
Who has not, cannot. *(French)*
Who has, is. *(Italian)*
There are but two lineages in the world, Have-much and Have-little. *(Cervantes)*

HAWK

Hawks will not pick hawks' eyes out.
Pheasants are fools if they invite the hawk to dinner.

The first point of hawking is hold fast.
With empty hands no man should hawks allure.
The hawk flies high but not above the sun. *(German)*
The hawk ever lives in battle. *(Latin)*

HAY
Make hay while the sun shines.

HEAD
All heads are not sense boxes.
Be not a baker if your head be of butter.
Be sure that your head be not higher than your hat.
Better be the head of an ass than the tail of a horse.
Better be the head of a dog than the tail of a lion.
Better be the head of a pike than the tail of a sturgeon.
Cover your head by day as much as you will, by night as much as you can.
He that hath a head of wax must not walk in the sun.
No man's head aches while he comforts another.
One good head is better than a thousand strong hands.
Scabby heads love not the comb.
So many heads, so many wits.
He that has no head needs no hat. *(French)*
A good head is rarely set on a fat belly. *(German)*
The head is only a funnel for the stomach. *(German)*
Two heads are better than one. *(Greek)*
He that has a head of glass must not throw stones at another. *(Italian)*
He who has a head will not want for a hat. *(Italian)*
A great head has great cares. *(Russian)*
When the head aches, all the body is out of tune. *(Spanish)*
A big head has a big ache. *(Turkish)*
If you have nothing in your head, you should have something in your feet. *(Yiddish)*

HEAL
A man is not so soon healed as hurt.

HEALTH
A cool head and warm feet live long.
A healthy body is the guest-chamber of the soul; a sick, its prison. *(Bacon)*
After dinner sit a while; after supper walk a mile.

All health is better than wealth.
Clothe warm, eat little, drink well, so shalt thou live.
Diet cures more than doctors.
Early to bed and early to rise,
Makes a man healthy, wealthy, and wise. *(Franklin)*
Good wife and health is man's best wealth.
He that goes to bed thirsty rises healthy.
He that liveth by physic liveth miserably.
He that never was sick dies the first.
He who hath good health is young.
Head and feet keep warm, the rest will take no harm.
Health and cheerfulness beget each other.
Health and money go far.
Health and wealth create beauty.
Health is not valued till sickness comes.
Health is the first muse, and sleep is the condition to produce it. *(Emerson)*
It is better to lose health like a spendthrift than to waste it like a miser. *(Stevenson)*
Joy and Temperance and Repose
Slam the door in the doctor's nose. *(Longfellow)*
Nature, time, and patience are the three great physicians.
The best doctors in the world are Doctor Diet, Doctor Quiet, and Doctor Merryman.
The healthy know not of their health, but only the sick.
Wash your hands often, your feet seldom, your head never.
He dies every day who lives a lingering life. *(French)*
He that wants health wants everything. *(French)*
It is a grievous illness to preserve one's health by a regimen too strict. *(French)*
Rise at five, dine at nine; sup at five, to bed at nine. *(French)*
When you are well keep as you are. *(French)*
Study sickness while you are well. *(German)*
Guard the health both of body and of soul. *(Greek)*
Health without money is half a malady. *(Italian)*
A sound mind in a sound body. *(Latin)*
Before supper walk a little, after supper do the same. *(Latin)*
Good health and good sense are two great blessings. *(Latin)*
He destroys his health by laboring to preserve it. *(Vergil)*
Better lose a supper than have a hundred doctors. *(Spanish)*

He that would be healthy must wear his winter clothes in summer. *(Spanish)*

To the well man every day is a feast. *(Turkish)*

HEAR

From hearing comes wisdom, from speaking, repentance.
He that will not hear must feel.
Hear twice before you speak once.
Hear and be just. *(Latin)*
Hear both sides. *(Latin)*
Hear first and speak afterwards. *(Spanish)*

HEART

He that is of merry heart hath a continual feast. *(Old Test., Prov.)*
Out of the abundance of the heart the mouth speaketh. *(New Test., Matthew)*
The heart is deceitful above all things, and desperately wicked. *(Old Test., Jeremiah)*
The heart knoweth its own bitterness. *(Old Test., Prov.)*
Where your treasure is, there will your heart be also. *(New Test., Luke)*
A bushel of hearts is not worth one grain of rice. *(Chinese)*
The heart of the wise should reflect all objects, without being sullied by any. *(Confucius)*
When there is room in the heart there is room in the house. *(Danish)*
The heart does not lie. *(Dutch)*
A gentle heart is tied with an easy thread.
A good heart cannot lie.
A good heart conquers ill fortune.
A good heart is better than all the heads in the world.
Every heart hath its own ache.
He wears his heart on his sleeve.
Hearts alone buy hearts.
Hearts may agree though heads differ.
If wrong our hearts, our heads are right in vain. *(Young)*
It is a poor heart that never rejoices.
Kind hearts are more than coronets. *(Kingsley)*
Kind hearts are soonest wronged.
Knit your hearts with an unslipping knot. *(Shakespeare)*
More strength in a true heart than in a walled city.
No sky is heavy if the heart be light.
That which cometh from the heart will go to the heart.
The faithless heart betrays the head unsound.

The heart governs the understanding.
The heart is but little, yet great things cannot fill it.
The heart of a man is the place the Devil's in.
The joy of the heart colors the face.
The same heart beats in every human breast.
The selfish heart deserves the pain it feels.
There are strings in the human heart which had better not be vibrated. *(Dickens)*
What stronger breastplate than a heart untainted! *(Shakespeare)*
What the heart did think, the tongue would clink.
When the heart is on fire, some sparks fly out of the mouth.
Where hearts are true, few words will do.
Where the mind is past hope, the heart is past shame.
Everyone speaks well of his heart, but no one dares speak ill of his head. *(La Rochefoucauld)*
The head is always the dupe of the heart. *(La Rochefoucauld)*
The heart has reasons which reason does not know. *(Pascal)*
The heart must either become hardened or break. *(French)*
The mouth obeys poorly when the heart murmurs. *(Voltaire)*
With most people the heart grows old with the body. *(French)*
A better heart makes a stronger arm. *(German)*
A wounded heart is hard to cure. *(Goethe)*
Cold hand, warm heart. *(German)*
Fire in the heart sends smoke into the head. *(German)*
Only the heart without a stain knows perfect ease. *(German)*
When the heart dares to speak, it needs no preparation. *(Lessing)*
A generous heart repairs a slanderous tongue. *(Homer)*
Eat not thy heart. *(Greek)*
The heart is the hidden treasure of man. *(Hebrew)*
The heart of the fool is in his mouth, but the mouth of the wise man is in his heart. *(Hebrew)*
A happy heart is better than a full purse. *(Italian)*
Where there is least heart there is most tongue. *(Italian)*
A good heart helps in misfortune. *(Latin)*
My heart is not made of horn. *(Latin)*
Hearts have as many fashions as the world has shapes. *(Ovid)*
A determined heart will not be counselled. *(Spanish)*
A good heart breaks bad fortune. *(Spanish)*
The heart's testimony is stronger than a thousand witnesses. *(Turkish)*
When the heart is full, the eyes overflow. *(Yiddish)*
You can look in the eye, but not in the heart. *(Yiddish)*

HEAVEN

In my father's house are many mansions. *(New Test., John)*

He who offends against Heaven has none to whom he can pray. *(Confucius)*

Heaven means to be one with God. *(Confucius)*

No one can know the height of heaven without climbing mountains. *(Chinese)*

The net of Heaven has large meshes and yet nothing escapes it. *(Lao Tsze)*

The road to heaven is equally short wherever we die. *(Danish)*

Men go laughing to heaven. *(Dutch)*

All this, and Heaven too! *(P. Henry)*

All places are distant from heaven alike.

Better go to heaven in rags than to hell in embroidery.

Earth has no sorrow that Heaven cannot heal.

Hard must he wink that shuts his eyes from heaven.

He that would conquer heaven must fight.

He will never get to heaven that desires to go thither alone.

Heaven helps those who help themselves.

Heaven is a cheap purchase whatever it cost.

Heaven is far, the world is nigh.

Heaven is the widow's champion and defense. *(Shakespeare)*

Heaven lies about us in our infancy. *(Wordsworth)*

Heaven still guards the right.

Heaven wills our happiness, allows our doom. *(Young)*

Heaven without good society cannot be heaven.

Heaven's never deaf but when man's heart is dumb. *(Quarles)*

No man can resolve himself into heaven. *(D. L. Moody)*

No man must go to heaven who hath not sent his heart thither before.

Our heart is in heaven, our home is not here. *(Heber)*

There is more than one way to Heaven.

There's no going to heaven in a sedan.

We are as near to Heaven by sea as by land. *(Sir H. Gilbert)*

It is harder work getting to hell than to heaven. *(German)*

Heaven protects the just. *(Greek)*

Whatever heaven ordains is best. *(Greek)*

The sword of heaven is not in haste to smite,
  Nor yet doth linger. *(Dante)*

Great is the idleness which prevails in heaven. *(Juvenal)*

Heaven always favors good desires. *(Spanish)*

Heaven is mine if God says amen. *(Spanish)*

Heaven is doing good from good will. *(Swedenborg)*
Even the hen, when it drinks water, looks toward heaven. *(Turkish)*

HEAVY

Every horse thinks his pack heaviest.

HEDGE

A low hedge is easily leaped over.

HEEL

One pair of heels is often worth two pairs of hands.

HEIR

The grief of the heir is only masked laughter. *(Latin)*

HELEN OF TROY

Was this the face that launch'd a thousand ships,
  And burnt the topless towers of Ilium? *(Marlowe)*

HELL

Hell is a circle about the unbelieving. *(The Koran)*
For ill do well, then fear no hell.
From Hell, Hull, and Halifax, good Lord, deliver us.
Hell and Chancery are always open.
Hell hath no fury like a woman scorned.
Hell is the wrath of God—His hate of sin.
No hell will frighten men away from sin.
The primrose path of dalliance. *(Shakespeare)*
The way to Hell's a seeming Heav'n. *(Quarles)*
There is nobody will go to hell for company.
They that be in hell think there's no other heaven.
A single path leads to the house of Hades. *(Aeschylus)*
Not even Hell can lay hands on the invincible. *(Greek)*
One Hades receives all mortals alike. *(Greek)*
The road to Hell is easy to travel. *(Greek)*
He who is in hell knows not what heaven is. *(Italian)*
Hell is paved with good intentions. *(Italian)*
The descent to hell is easy. *(Vergil)*
In hell there is no retention. *(Cervantes)*

HELP

I looked up, and there was none to help. *(Old Test., Isaiah)*
Vain is the help of man. *(Old Test., Psalms)*

All is not at hand that helps.
Every little helps.
God helps them that help themselves.
Help the lame dog over the stile.
Slow help is no help.
What is past my help is past my care.
Everything helps, quoth the wren, when she pissed into the sea. *(French)*
He who greases his wheels helps his oxen. *(Italian)*
Even the just have need of help. *(Italian)*
There is no helping him who will not be advised. *(Italian)*
It is a kindly act to help the fallen. *(Latin)*
One thing asks the help of another. *(Latin)*
A grain does not fill a sack but it helps its fellow. *(Spanish)*
He who helps everybody helps nobody. *(Spanish)*
Help is good everywhere except at one's dinner. *(Yiddish)*
If you can't help your friend with money, help him at least with a sigh. *(Yiddish)*

HEN
Black hens lay white eggs. *(Dutch)*
A setting hen never grows fat.
It's a bad hen that eats at your house and lays at another's. *(Spanish)*

HEREDITY
He that comes of a hen must scrape. *(Italian)*

HERESY
Better heresy of doctrine than heresy of heart. *(Whittier)*
Heresy is the school of pride.

HERMIT
The hermit thinks the sun shines nowhere but in his cell.

HERO
Every hero becomes a bore at last. *(Emerson)*
Hero-worship is strongest where there is least regard for human freedom. *(Spencer)*
It is chance chiefly that makes heroes.
One brave deed makes no hero.
Society is founded on hero-worship. *(Carlyle)*
The race of heroes pass the lamp from hand to hand.

To be conquered by a hero is an honor.
To believe in the heroic makes heroes.
What a hero one can be without moving a finger! *(Thoreau)*
No man is a hero to his valet. *(French)*
There are heroes in evil as well as in good. *(French)*
A man must be a hero to understand a hero. *(Goethe)*
Heroes are bred in lands where livelihood comes hard. *(Greek)*
One brave hero fans another's fire. *(Homer)*
A hero is only known in time of misfortune. *(Hebrew)*
The hero is known on the battle-field. *(Turkish)*

HERRING
Every herring must hang by its own gill.

HESITATE
He that counts all pins in the plough, will never yoke her.
He that forecasts all perils will never sail the sea.
The woman who hesitates is lost.

HIDE
He that hides can find.

HIGH
High places have their precipices.
High regions are never without storms.
The higher the plum-tree the riper the plum.
The highest branch is not the safest roost.
The highest tree hath the greatest fall.
What is too high, that let fly.
High houses are mostly empty in the upper storey. *(German)*

HILL
The higher the hill the lower the grass.
There is no hill without a valley.

HISTORY
History is lies agreed upon.
History repeats itself.
While we read history we make history.
Happy the people whose annals are tiresome. *(Montesquieu)*
Sin writes histories, goodness is silent. *(Goethe)*
History is Philosophy learned from examples. *(Greek)*
Happy is the nation without a history. *(Beccaria)*

HOBBY

Every man hath his hobby-horse.

HOG

A sow may find an acorn as well as a hog. *(Danish)*
The fat hog knows not what the hungry hog suffers. *(Dutch)*
A hog in armor is but a hog.
A pretty pig makes an ugly hog.
Better my hog-dirty home than no hog at all.
Every hog to his trough.
Everyone bastes the fat hog while the lean one burns.
It is ill to drive black hogs in the dark.
The hog is never good but when he is in the dish.
The whole hog or none.
What can you expect from a hog but a grunt?
A hog prefers bran to roses. *(French)*
The worst hog gets the best pear. *(Italian)*
A measly hog infects the whole sty. *(Spanish)*
Every hog has its Martinmas. *(Spanish)*
He who does not kill hogs will not get black puddings. *(Spanish)*

HOLE

The hole calls the thief.

HOLIDAY

A perpetual holiday is a good working definition of hell. *(G. B. Shaw)*
'Tis not a holiday that's not kept holy.

HOLY

A holy habit cleanseth not a foul soul.

HOME

Be not as a lion in thy house, nor frantic among thy servants. *(Apocrypha)*
Eat ye every man of his own vine . . . *(Old Test., II Kings)*
He that is far from home is near to harm. *(Danish)*
A little house well fill'd, a little land well till'd, and a little wife well will'd . . .
Be it ever so humble, there's no place like home. *(Payne)*
Dry bread at home is better than roast meat abroad.
East or west, home is best.
He that lives always at home, sees nothing but home.

Home is home, though it be never so homely.
Home-keeping youths have ever homely wits. *(Shakespeare)*
Pleasant are one's own brands.
Some people see no good near home.
To be happy at home is the ultimate result of all ambition. *(S. Johnson)*
A man without a home is a bird without a nest. *(French)*
Every cock crows on his own dunghill. *(French)*
Where the nest and eggs are, the birds are near. *(French)*
Home is where I hang my hat.
Who is happy should bide at home . . . *(Greek)*
Home is where the heart is. *(Latin)*
Our own home surpasses every other. *(Latin)*
Every cricket knows its own hearth. *(Russian)*
In my own house I am king. *(Spanish)*
The reek of my own house is better than the fire of another. *(Spanish)*
Whom God loves, his house is sweet to him. *(Spanish)*
He that has no rest at home is in the world's hell. *(Turkish)*

HOMER

Seven cities warred for Homer, being dead,
Who, living, had no roof to shroud his head.
The song is divine, but divine Homer wrote it down. *(Greek)*
Envy belittles the genius even of the great Homer. *(Latin)*
I, too, am indignant when the worthy Homer nods. *(Horace)*

HONESTY

An honest man does not make himself a dog for the sake of a bone. *(Danish)*
An honest man is not the worse because a dog barks at him. *(Danish)*
An honest man is a citizen of the world.
An honest man's the noblest work of God. *(Pope)*
An honest look covereth many faults.
An honest man's word is his bond.
An ill-won penny will cast down a pound.
As honest a man as ever broke bread.
As honest a man as ever trod on neat's leather.
He is wise that is honest.
He that loses his honesty has nothing else to lose.
He that resolves to deal with none but honest men must leave off dealing.
Honest men and knaves may possibly wear the same cloth.

Honest men fear neither the light nor the dark.
Honesty is a fine jewel, but much out of fashion.
Honesty is ill to thrive by.
Honesty is no pride.
Honesty is the best policy.
Honesty may be dear bought, but can never be an ill pennyworth.
No legacy so rich as honesty. *(Shakespeare)*
Plain dealing is a jewel.
The honester the man, the worse the luck.
The measure of life is not length, but honesty.
To be honest, as this world goes, is to be one man picked out of ten thousand. *(Shakespeare)*
Too much honesty did never man harm.
You may measure every man's honesty by your own.
A clean mouth and an honest hand . . . *(German)*
Honesty lasts longest. *(German)*
Integrity is better than charity. *(Greek)*
Clean hands are better than full ones. *(Latin)*
Honesty is praised and starves. *(Juvenal)*
It is annoying to be honest to no purpose. *(Ovid)*
Never too late to tread the path of honesty. *(Latin)*
They are all honest men, but my cloak is not to be found. *(Spanish)*

HONEY

Much honey cloys the maw. *(Old Test., Prov.)*
He who would gather honey must bear the sting of the bees. *(Dutch)*
A drop of honey catches more flies than a barrel of vinegar.
Dear bought is the honey that is licked from the horn.
Honey is sweet, but the bee stings.
When you taste honey, remember gall.
Honey in the mouth saves the purse. *(Italian)*
Make yourself all honey, and the flies will devour you. *(Italian)*
Where there is honey there are bees. *(Latin)*
Honey is not for the ass's mouth. *(Spanish)*

HONOR

Before honor is humility. *(Old Test., Prov.)*
Honor is not seemly for a fool. *(Old Test., Prov.)*
Honor thy father and thy mother. *(Old Test., Exodus)*
Honor the tree that gives you shelter. *(Danish)*
Where the law lacks, honor should eke it out. *(Danish)*

He that desires honors, is not worthy of honor.
He that hath no honor hath no sorrow.
Honor and ease are seldom bedfellows.
Honor and profit lie not in one sack.
Honor buys no beef in the market.
Honors and great employments are great burthens.
Honor and shame from no condition rise . . . *(Pope)*
Honor's but a word to swear by . . .
Honor's but an empty bubble. *(Dryden)*
Honor is the very breath in our nostrils.
Honor should be concerned in honor's cause.
Honor shows the man.
Honor sits smiling at the sale of truth. *(Shelley)*
Honor was but ancient riches.
Honor without profit is a ring on the finger.
Honors never fail to purchase silence.
Honors nourish art.
I am myself the guardian of my honor.
If I lose mine honor, I lose myself. *(Shakespeare)*
It is a worthier thing to deserve honor than to possess it.
Nobody can acquire honor by doing what is wrong.
Take honor from me and my life is done. *(Shakespeare)*
The best dog leaps the stile first.
The fewer men, the greater share of honor.
The louder he talked of his honor, the faster we counted our spoons. *(Emerson)*
There is honor among thieves.
To those whose god is honor, disgrace alone is sin.
When faith is lost, when honor dies,
The man is dead! *(Whittier)*
All is lost save honor. *(Francis I)*
An honor won is surety for more. *(French)*
Let us do what honor demands. *(French)*
Where honor binds me, I must satisfy it. *(French)*
Without money honor is nothing but a malady. *(Racine)*
The king may give the honor, but you must make yourself honorable. *(German)*
Where there is no shame, there is no honor. *(German)*
Among men of honor a word is a bond. *(Italian)*
It is no honor for an eagle to vanquish a dove. *(Italian)*
Honors change manners. *(Latin)*

What is honorable is fitting and what is fitting is honorable. *(Latin)*
What is most honorable is also safest. *(Latin)*
Who loses honor can lose nothing else. *(Latin)*
The post of honor is the post of danger. *(Latin)*
Honor is on his tongue and ice under it. *(Russian)*
Don't run after honors, and they will come to you of themselves. *(Yiddish)*
Run away from dishonor, and don't run after honors. *(Yiddish)*
Take your public honors, but stay at home. *(Yiddish)*

HOOK
A hook is well lost to catch a salmon.
The hook without bait catches no fish. *(German)*

HOPE
Hope deferred maketh the heart sick. *(Old Test., Prov.)*
Hope maketh not ashamed. *(New Test., Romans)*
Hope to the end. *(New Test., I Peter)*
Who against hope believed in hope. *(New Test., Romans)*
Hope is the poor man's income. *(Danish)*
A good hope is better than a bad possession.
As long as there is life there is hope.
Great hopes make great men.
He hopes to eat of the goose that shall graze on your grave.
He that hopes no good fears no ill.
He that lives in hope dances without a fiddle.
He that wants hope is the poorest man alive.
He who lives on hope makes a thin belly.
Hope is a good breakfast but a bad supper.
Hope is as cheap as despair.
Hope is generally a wrong guide, but good company by the way. *(Halifax)*
Hope is grief's best music.
Hope is the parent of faith.
Hope is the poor man's bread.
Hope is worth any money.
Hope never leaves a wretched man that seeks her.
Hope often deludes the foolish man.
Hope springs eternal in the human breast. *(Pope)*
Hope well and have well.
Hopers go to hell.

If it were not for hope, the heart would break.
In all the wedding cake, hope is the sweetest plum.
Long hope is the fainting of the soul.
Never quit certainty for hope.
None so well but he hopes to be better.
Take hope from man and you make him a beast.
The gods are kind, and hope to men they give. *(W. Morris)*
The heart bowed down by weight of woe
  To weakest hope will cling. *(Bunn)*
The miserable have no medicine
  But only hope. *(Shakespeare)*
When our hopes break, let our patience hold.
When there is no hope, there can be no endeavor.
Who lives by hope will die of hunger.
Hope deceives, enjoyment undeceives. *(French)*
Hope makes the fool rich. *(German)*
Hope is a waking dream. *(Greek)*
Hope stays with those who have nothing else. *(Greek)*
It is hope which maintains most men. *(Greek)*
There is hope for the living but none for the dead. *(Greek)*
All hope abandon, ye who enter here. *(Dante)*
He gains much who loses a vain hope. *(Italian)*
A man may hope for anything while he has life. *(Latin)*
Cease to hope and you will cease to fear. *(Latin)*
Do not hope without despair, nor despair without hope. *(Latin)*
I do not buy hope with money. *(Latin)*
It is hope which makes even the fettered miner live. *(Ovid)*
Let the fearful be allowed to hope. *(Latin)*
Many a hopeful man has hope beguiled. *(Latin)*
Put aside trifling hopes. *(Horace)*
The hope of life returns with the sun. *(Latin)*
While there is life there is hope. *(Latin)*
Better a good hope than a bad holding. *(Spanish)*

HORSE

In a wind horses and cows do not agree. *(Chinese)*
Judge not the horse by his saddle. *(Chinese)*
A borrowed horse and your own spurs make short miles. *(Danish)*
A hard bit does not make the better horse. *(Danish)*
Better a poor horse than an empty stall. *(Danish)*
When the manger is empty the horses fight. *(Danish)*

A good horse is worth his fodder. *(Dutch)*
A galled horse will not endure the comb.
A good horse oft needs a good spur.
A good horse should be seldom spurred.
A horse! a horse! my kingdom for a horse! *(Shakespeare)*
A horse stumbles that has four legs.
A horse that will not carry a saddle must have no oats.
A kick from a mare never hurts a horse.
A short horse is soon curried.
All lay the load on the willing horse.
As good horses draw in carts, as coaches.
Better a lean jade than an empty halter.
Do not spur a free horse.
Good horses make short miles.
He is a gentle horse that never cast his rider.
He is free of horse that never had one.
If you ride a horse, sit close and tight,
  If you ride a man, sit easy and light. *(Franklin)*
It is a good horse that never stumbles.
It is the bridle and spur that makes a good horse.
Lay the saddle on the right horse.
Let a horse drink when he will, not what he will.
One thing thinketh the horse and another he that saddles him.
Spur not an unbroken horse.
The best thing for the inside of a man is the outside of a horse.
The blind horse is fittest for the mill.
The gray mare is the better horse.
The horse next the mill carries all the grist.
The old horse may die waiting for new grass.
There is no good horse of a bad color.
When the steed is stolen, shut the stable door.
Who may water the horse may drink himself.
You may lead a horse to water, but you can't make him drink.
An old horse for a young soldier. *(French)*
Better ride a lame horse than go afoot. *(German)*
A good horse never lacks a saddle. *(Italian)*
A horse grown fat kicks. *(Italian)*
A lean horse does not kick. *(Italian)*
A runaway horse punishes himself. *(Italian)*
Never spur a willing horse. *(Italian)*
The horse that draws best is most whipped. *(Italian)*

The ear of a bridled horse is in his mouth. *(Latin)*
Trust not the horse, ye Trojans. *(Vergil)*
One whip is enough for a good horse, for a bad one not a thousand. *(Russian)*
Who buys a horse buys care. *(Spanish)*
Ride not a free horse to death. *(Spanish)*
The best feed of a horse is his master's eye. *(Spanish)*
A horse is his who mounts it. *(French)*
The wagon rests in winter, the sleigh in summer, the horse never. *(Yiddish)*
Whip the horse with oats, not with a whip. *(Yiddish)*

HOSPITALITY

Be not forgetful to entertain strangers: for thereby some have entertained angels unawares. *(New Test., Hebrews)*
A woeful hostess brooks not merry guests. *(Shakespeare)*
Fish and guests in three days are stale.
Open the door but shut not up the countenance.
Welcome the coming, speed the parting guest. *(Pope)*
The first day a man is a guest, the second a burden, the third a pest. *(French)*
It is more disgraceful to turn out a guest than not to admit him. *(Latin)*

HOUR

An hour in the morning before breakfast is worth two all the rest of the day.
An hour of pain is as long as a day of pleasure.
It chanceth in an hour what comes not in seven years.
Pleasure and action make the hours seem short. *(Shakespeare)*
The darkest hour is just before the dawn.
For the unhappy how slowly pass the hours! *(French)*
Hours were made for man, and not man for the hours. *(Rabelais)*
All our sweetest hours fly fastest. *(Latin)*
The hour which gives us life begins to take it away. *(Latin)*

HOUSE

How can one pole build a great house? *(Chinese)*
A house divided against itself cannot stand.
A house ready made, but a wife to make.
A man's house is his castle.
Better an empty house than an ill tenant.

Better one's house to be too little one day, than too big all the year after.
Choose not a house near an inn or in a corner.
Fools build houses, and wise men live in them.
He that has a house to put 's head in has a good head-piece. *(Shakespeare)*
He that hath no house must lie in a yard.
He that in a neat house will dwell,
Must priest and pigeon thence expel.
Houses go mad when women gad.
Make not the door wider than the house.
Set not your house on fire to be revenged of the moon.
The house shows the owner.
Half a house is half a hell. *(German)*
In old houses many mice, in old furs many lice. *(German)*
A house built on the highway is either too high or too low. *(Italian)*
He burns his house to frighten the rats and warm himself. *(Spanish)*
In my own house I am king. *(Spanish)*
A wee house has a wide throat. *(Scottish)*

HOUSEKEEPER

Everything is of use to a housekeeper.
Fat housekeepers make lean executors.
The fingers of the housewife do more than a yoke of oxen. *(German)*
The day I did not sweep my house, unexpected visitors came. *(Spanish)*

HOWL

One must howl with the wolves.

HUMILITY

Whosoever exalteth himself shall be abased; and he that humbleth himself shall be exalted. *(New Test., Luke)*
Whosoever shall smite thee on the right cheek, turn to him the other also. *(New Test., Matthew)*
He that is humble, ever shall have God to be his guide. *(Bunyan)*
Humble hearts have humble desires.
Nearest the throne itself must be
The footstool of humility. *(Montgomery)*
The boughs that bear most hang lowest.
The lowly heart doth win the love of all.
There is no true holiness without humility.
Make yourself a lamb, and the wolf will eat you. *(French)*

There is no humiliation for humility. *(French)*
Rather to bow than break is profitable;
  Humility is a thing commendable. *(French)*
The humble suffer from the folly of the great. *(La Fontaine)*
Too much humility is pride. *(German)*
Humility often gains more than pride. *(Italian)*
Humble things become the humble. *(Latin)*
Humble thyself in all things. *(Thomas a Kempis)*
Make way for your betters. *(Latin)*
The humble are in danger when the powerful disagree. *(Latin)*

HUNCHBACK
The hunchback does not see his own hump, but sees his companion's.
The hunchback must carry his hump. *(Yiddish)*

HUMOR
Everything is funny as long as it happens to somebody else.
Humor is gravity concealed behind a jest.
A sense of humor is the only thing that keeps intelligent people from
  hanging themselves. *(Voltaire)*

HUNGER
Blind horse knows when de trough is empty. *(American Negro)*
A hungry dog does not fear the stick.
A hungry kite sees a dead horse afar off.
A hungry man is an angry man.
A hungry man smells meat afar off.
All's good in a famine.
Every one of us would kill rather than not have beef. *(S. Johnson)*
Famine ends famine.
Hard fare makes hungry bellies.
He that's full takes no care of him that's fasting.
Hunger and cold deliver a man up to his enemy.
Hunger breaks stone walls.
Hunger fetches the wolf out of the woods.
Hunger finds no fault with the cook.
Hunger is good kitchen meat.
Hunger is not dainty.
Hunger is sharper than the sword.
Hunger knows no friend.
Hunger makes hard beans sweet.
Hungry dogs will eat dirty puddings.

Hungry flies bite sore.
Hungry men think the cook lazy.
Hungry roosters don't cackle when they find a worm.
Nothing comes amiss to a hungry stomach.
The stomach sets us to work.
They that die by famine die by inches.
To the hungry no bread is bad.
A hungry horse makes a clean manger. *(French)*
A man who wants bread is ready for anything. *(French)*
Hunger is a bad adviser. *(French)*
Hunger is violent, and will be fed. *(Greek)*
A hungry ass eats any straw. *(Italian)*
Hunger changes beans into almonds. *(Italian)*
The full belly does not believe in hunger. *(Italian)*
Hungry bellies have no ears. *(Cato)*
Hunger sweetens beans. *(Latin)*
The hungry stomach despises not common food. *(Latin)*
The hungry sigh; the sated belch. *(Russian)*
The open mouth never remains hungry. *(Russian)*
Hunger is hard in a hale maw. *(Scottish)*
A hungry man discovers more than a hundred lawyers. *(Spanish)*
Hunger is the best sauce in the world. *(Spanish)*
When a Jew is hungry, he sings; a peasant, beats his wife. *(Yiddish)*

HUNTING
He who hunts with cats will catch mice. *(Danish)*
Detested sport,
  That owes its pleasures to another's pain. *(Cowper)*
Don't think to hunt two hares with one dog.
Hounds and horses devour their masters.
All are not hunters that blow the horn. *(French)*
One cannot hunt eels and hares at the same time. *(German)*

HUSBAND
Husbands, love your wives, and be not bitter against them.
(New Test., Coloss.)
The more a husband loves his wife, the more he increases her whims.
(Chinese)
The more a wife loves her husband, the more she corrects his faults.
(Chinese)
When the husband earn well, the wife spends well. *(Dutch)*

A good husband makes a good wife.
A good wife makes a good husband.
A happy couple: the husband deaf, the wife blind.
A husband's wrath spoils the best broth.
Emperors are only husbands in wives' eyes. *(Byron)*
Feed the brute!
Husbands are in heaven whose wives scold not.
In the husband wisdom, in the wife gentleness.
Sorrow for the husband dead is like a pain in the elbow, short and sharp.
The calmest husbands make the stormiest wives.
The married man must turn his staff into a stake.
We wedded men live in sorrow and care. *(Chaucer)*
When the husband dies, the neighbors learn how many children he has.
Serve your husband as your master, and beware of him as a traitor. *(Montaigne)*
Better a husband without love than a jealous husband. *(Italian)*
The husband is the last to know the dishonor of his house. *(Latin)*
A husband's cuffs leave no mark. *(Russian)*
A husband with one eye rather than one son. *(Spanish)*
Let it be a husband though it be but a log. *(Spanish)*
To know the husband, observe the face of the wife. *(Spanish)*

HYPOCRITE

A mouth that prays, and a hand that kills. *(Arabian)*
Woe unto you, scribes and Pharisees, hypocrites! for ye are like unto whited sepulchres . . . *(New Test., Matthew)*
Ye blind guides, which strain at a gnat, and swallow a camel. *(New Test., Matthew)*
Beware of the man of two faces. *(Dutch)*
A saint abroad, and a devil at home.
A sheep without, a wolf within.
Built God a church, and laughed his word to scorn. *(Cowper)*
Carrion crows bewail the dead sheep, and then eat them.
Fair without, foul within.
He carries fire in one hand and water in the other.
He looks one way and rows another.
He that speaks me fair and loves me not, I'll speak him fair and trust him not.
I want that glib and oily art
To speak and purpose not. *(Shakespeare)*

Never carry two faces under one hood.
No man is a hypocrite in his pleasures. *(S. Johnson)*
O what may a man within him hide,
  Though angel on the outward side! *(Shakespeare)*
The cross on his breast and the devil in his heart.
The devil can cite Scripture for his purpose. *(Shakespeare)*
Who point, like finger-posts, the way
  They never go. *(T. Moore)*
A honeyed tongue with a heart of gall. *(French)*
Hypocrisy is a homage which vice pays to virtue. *(La Rochefoucauld)*
I hate a bad man saying what is good. *(Greek)*
Those who daub both sides of the wall. *(Latin)*
A holy face and a cat's claws. *(Spanish)*
To fawn with the tail and bite with the mouth. *(Spanish)*

ICE

Trust not one night's ice.

When it cracks, it bears; when it bends, it breaks.

IDEA

A nice man is a man of nasty ideas. *(Swift)*

Early ideas are not usually true ideas.

God screens us evermore from premature ideas. *(Emerson)*

Wise men possess ideas; most of us are possessed by them.

Everyone knows it, but the idea has not occurred to everyone.

IDEAL

Our ideals are our better selves.

IDLENESS

An idle person is the devil's playfellow. *(Arabian)*

Drowsiness shall clothe a man with rags. *(Old Test., Prov.)*

Go to the ant, thou sluggard; consider her ways, and be wise. *(Old Test., Prov.)*

The slothful man saith, There is a lion in the way. *(Old Test., Prov.)*

Woe to the idle shepherd that leaveth the flock. *(Old Test., Habak.)*

He who does nothing but sit and eat, will wear away a mountain of wealth. *(Chinese)*

All things are easy to industry; all things difficult to sloth.

An idle brain is the devil's shop.

An idle head is a box for the wind.

An idle person tempts the devil to tempt him.

An idle youth, a needy age.

As good be an addled egg as an idle bird.

As idle as a painted ship
Upon a painted ocean. *(Coleridge)*

Be not idle, and you shall not be longing.
Doing nothing is doing ill.
Expect poison from the standing water. *(Blake)*
For Satan finds some mischief still
  For idle hands to do. *(Watts)*
God loves an idle rainbow,
  No less than the laboring sea. *(Hodgson)*
He is idle that might be better employed.
Idle dogs worry sheep.
Idle folk have the least leisure.
Idle folk have the most labor.
Idleness is the appendix to nobility.
Idleness is emptiness.
Idleness is the canker of the mind.
Idleness is the key of beggary.
Idleness is the mother of poverty.
Idleness is the nurse of vices.
Idleness is the root of all mischief.
Idleness makes the wit rust.
Idleness overthrows all.
If the devil find a man idle, he'll set him to work.
If you are idle, be not solitary; if you are solitary, be not idle.
It is well to lie fallow for a while.
Laziness travels so slowly that poverty soon overtakes him.
Many faint with toil,
  That few may know the cares and woes of sloth. *(Shelley)*
Mother of vices, called Idleness.
Of idleness comes no goodness.
Pastime, like wine, is poison in the morning.
Sloth brings in all woe.
Sloth is a foe unto all virtuous deeds.
Sloth is the devil's pillow.
Sloth must breed a scab.
Sluggish idleness, the nurse of sin.
The insupportable labor of doing nothing.
The lazy man gets round the sun
  As quickly as the busy one.
To do nothing is in every man's power. *(S. Johnson)*
To do nothing is the way to be nothing.
Trouble springs from idleness, and grievous toil from needless ease.
(Franklin)

We would all be idle if we could.
You'll soon learn to shape idle a coat.
Indolence is the sleep of the mind. *(French)*
It is only idle people who can find time for everything. *(French)*
We have more idleness of mind than of body. *(French)*
Idleness has poverty for wages. *(German)*
Idleness makes the fullest purse empty. *(German)*
Idleness cannot support even the frugal life. *(Greek)*
An indolent man draws his breath but does not live. *(Latin)*
Idleness is ever the root of indecision. *(Latin)*
Idleness is the sepulchre of a living man. *(Latin)*
Idleness wastes the sluggish body, as water is corrupted unless it moves. *(Ovid)*
It is better to do nothing, than to be doing of nothing. *(Latin)*
No deity assists the idle. *(Latin)*
No one has become immortal by sloth. *(Latin)*
That shameful Siren, sloth, is ever to be avoided. *(Horace)*
The indolent but delightful condition of doing nothing.
(Pliny—cf. Italian: Dolce far niente.)
The idle mind knows not what it wants. *(Latin)*
They do nothing laboriously. *(Latin)*
We excuse our sloth under pretext of difficulty. *(Latin)*
Idle bairns are the devil's work-houses. *(Scottish)*

IDOLATRY
An idiot holds his bauble for a god. *(Shakespeare)*
He who slays a king or dies for him are alike idolaters. *(G. B. Shaw)*

"IF"
"Had I a fish" is good without butter.
If "if's" and "an's" were pots and pans,
There'd be no trade for tinkers.
"If" is the only peacemaker. *(Shakespeare)*
If my aunt had been a man, she'd have been my uncle.
If the sky falls we shall catch larks.
With the help of an "if," you might put Paris in a bottle. *(French)*

IGNORANCE
Be not ignorant of anything in great matter or small. *(Apocrypha)*
The man who does not learn is dark, like one walking in the night.
(Chinese)
A man without knowledge is like one that is dead.

Being ignorant is not so much a shame, as being unwilling to learn.
Better unfed than untaught.
Had I wist comes too late.
He cannot say B to a battledore.
He doesn't know A from a bull's foot.
He that knows nothing, doubts nothing.
He that knows little often repeats it.
He who knows nothing is confident of everything.
Ignorance is a voluntary misfortune.
Ignorance is the dominion of absurdity.
Ignorance is the mother of admiration.
Ignorance is the mother of devotion.
Ignorance is the mother of impudence.
Ignorance never settles a question.
It is better to know nothing than to know what ain't so. *(Josh Billings)*
O thou monster, Ignorance, how deformed dost thou look!
(Shakespeare)
Our lives are shortened by our ignorance.
The ignorant hath an eagle's wings and an owl's eyes.
The tragedy of ignorance is its complacency.
There is no darkness but ignorance. *(Shakespeare)*
There is no slavery but ignorance. *(Ingersoll)*
To be ignorant of one's ignorance is the malady of ignorance.
Where ignorance is bliss,
'Tis folly to be wise. *(Gray)*
Better unborn than untaught. *(Plato)*
Ignorance of one's misfortunes is clear gain. *(Greek)*
Ignorance and conceit go hand in hand. *(Hebrew)*
"Had I known" was a fool. *(Latin)*
I am not ashamed to confess that I am ignorant of what I do not know. *(Cicero)*
Ignorance is a feeble remedy for our ills. *(Latin)*
It is well to be ignorant of many things. *(Latin)*
The ignorant arise and seize Heaven itself. *(St. Augustine)*
What darkness of mind there is in mortal minds! *(Ovid)*
Whatever is unknown is magnified. *(Latin)*

ILL
He that does ill hates the light.
He who hath done ill once will do it again.
Ill doers are ill thinkers.

One ill causes another.
'Tis a good ill that comes alone.
Ill is the eve of well. *(Italian)*

ILL-GOTTEN
Ill-got, ill-spent.
Ill-gotten goods never prosper. *(German)*
Come with the wind, gone with the water. *(Latin)*

ILLEGITIMATE
Born on the wrong side of the blanket.

ILLNESS
Better wear out shoes than sheets.
Every ill man hath his ill day.

IMAGINATION
Imagination is a poor substitute for experience. *(H. Ellis)*
Imagination wanders far afield.
The great instrument of moral good is the imagination. *(Shelley)*
The lunatic, the lover, and the poet,
  Are of imagination all compact. *(Shakespeare)*
Imagination is the eye of the soul. *(Joubert)*
Imagination is more important than knowledge. *(Einstein)*

IMITATION
Easy to look at, difficult to imitate. *(Chinese)*
One dog looks at something, and a hundred dogs at him. *(Chinese)*
He that lives next door to a cripple will learn to halt.
Imitation is the sincerest of flattery.
Imitation is suicide. *(Emerson)*
No man was ever great by imitation. *(S. Johnson)*
There is a difference between imitation and counterfeiting.
As the old birds sing, the young birds twitter. *(German)*
Man is an imitative creature. *(German)*
A needy man is lost when he wishes to imitate a powerful man. *(Latin)*
By looking at squinting people you learn to squint. *(Latin)*
The grape gains its purple tinge by looking at another grape. *(Latin)*

IMMODERATION
He that forsakes measure, measure forsakes him.

IMMORTALITY

For this corruptible must put on incorruption and this mortal must put on immortality. *(New Test., I Corinth.)*

God created man to be immortal. *(Apocrypha)*

If a man die, shall he live again? *(Old Test., Job)*

My flesh shall rest in hope. *(New Test., Acts)*

All men desire to be immortal.

Belief in the future life is the appetite of reason. *(Landor)*

Dust thou art, to dust returnest,
Was not spoken of the soul. *(Longfellow)*

Earth to earth, ashes to ashes, dust to dust, in sure and certain hope of the resurrection. *(Bk. Com. Prayer)*

He hath not lived that lives not after death.

He sins against this life who slights the next. *(Young)*

I swear I think there is nothing but immortality. *(Whitman)*

Immortality is the glorious discovery of Christianity. *(Channing)*

Men are immortal till their work is done.

The universe is a stairway leading nowhere unless man is immortal.

There is nothing strictly immortal but immortality. *(Sir T. Browne)*

To desire immortality is to desire the eternal perpetuation of a great mistake. *(Schopenhauer)*

IMPARTIALITY

Hear the other side. *(Latin)*

IMPATIENCE

He that would have a cake out of the wheat must tarry the grinding. *(Shakespeare)*

IMPOSSIBLE

A toad propping a bed-post firmly. *(Chinese)*

One foot cannot stand on two boats. *(Chinese)*

You cannot clap with one hand. *(Chinese)*

A wise man never attempts impossibilities.

Hope not for impossibles.

Impossibilities recede as experience advances.

Nothing is impossible to a willing heart.

One cannot be in two places at once.

The inverted pyramid can never stand.

To believe a business impossible is the way to make it so.

You can't have your cake and eat it too.

You can't make a silk purse out of a sow's ear.

You can't sell the cow and have the milk too.
"Impossible" . . . That is not French. *(Napoleon)*
It is always the impossible that happens. *(French)*
It is a disease of the soul to be enamored of the impossible. *(Greek)*
You cannot make a crab walk straight. *(Greek)*
You cannot drink and whistle at the same time. *(Italian)*
It is certain, because it is impossible. *(Tertullian)*
There is no obligation to attempt the impossible. *(Latin)*
Only he who attempts the absurd is capable of achieving the impossible. *(Unamuno)*
Not even a thousand men in armor can strip a naked man. *(Turkish)*

IMPULSE
Impulse manages all things badly. *(Latin)*
What is now reason was formerly impulse. *(Latin)*

INCONSISTENCY
Blind guides which strain at a gnat and swallow a camel. *(New Test., Matthew)*
To see the mote in another's eye and not the beam in your own. *(New Test., Matthew)*
He leaps into a deep river to avoid a shallow brook.
To jump out of the frying pan into the fire.
To jump into the water for fear of the rain. *(French)*
He runs from the bear to fall in with the wolves. *(Russian)*

INCONVENIENCE
Better a mischief than an inconvenience.

INDECISION
How long halt ye between two opinions? *(Old Test., I Kings)*
No man, having put his hand to the plow, and looking back, is fit for the kingdom of God. *(New Test., Luke)*
I am at war 'twixt will and will not. *(Shakespeare)*
He who considers too much will perform little. *(German)*
The gods hate those who hesitate. *(Greek)*
In indecision itself grief is present. *(Latin)*
Through indecision opportunity is often lost. *(Latin)*
While we consider when to begin, it becomes too late. *(Latin)*

INDEPENDENCE
A ploughman on his legs is higher than a gentleman on his knees.
He travels the fastest who travels alone. *(Kipling)*

I care for nobody, no, not I,
  And nobody cares for me.
I would rather sit on a pumpkin and have it all to myself than be crowded on a velvet cushion. *(Thoreau)*
Let every vat stand upon its own bottom.
Paddle your own canoe.
So live that you can look any man in the eye and tell him to go to hell.
Independence, like honor, is a rocky island without a beach. *(Napoleon)*
Follow your own bent, no matter what people say. *(German)*
Let each man have the wit to go his own way. *(Latin)*
The strongest man in the world is he who stands most alone. *(Ibsen)*
A little in your own pocket is better than much in another's purse. *(Spanish)*
Every man for himself, and God for us all. *(Spanish)*

INDIFFERENCE
Thou art neither hot nor cold. *(New Test., Revelation)*
Come and welcome; go by, and no quarrel.
What turn the matter takes,
  I deem it all but ducks and drakes.
The moon does not heed the barking of dogs. *(Latin)*

INDUSTRY
A diligent spinner has a large shift.
At the working man's house hunger looks in, but dares not enter.
Elbow grease gives the best polish.
God gives all things to industry.
I will keep no more cats than will catch mice.
If the brain sows not corn, it plants thistles.
Industry is a loadstone to draw all good things.
Industry is fortune's right hand, and frugality her left.
Industry need not wish.
Industry pays debts.
Plough deep while sluggards sleep,
  And you shall have corn to sell and keep.
Put your shoulder to the wheel.
The dog that trots about finds a bone.
The sleeping fox catches no poultry.
The used key is always bright.
Where bees are there is honey.
All things are won by industry. *(Greek)*

The cat would eat fish and would not wet her feet. *(Latin)*
Diligence is the mother of good fortune. *(Spanish)*
Pray to God and ply the hammer. *(Spanish)*
To be busy at something is a modest maid's holiday. *(Spanish)*

INFECTION
One scabbed sheep will taint a whole flock.

INFLUENCE
A cock has great influence on his own dunghill. *(Latin)*
Each man, in corrupting others, corrupts himself. *(Latin)*

INGRATITUDE
A thankless man never does a thankful deed. *(Danish)*
He hath brought up a bird to peck out his own eyes.
Hell is full of the ungrateful.
How sharper than a serpent's tooth it is
  To have a thankless child! *(Shakespeare)*
I taught you to swim, and now you'd drown me.
Ingratitude is a weed of every clime.
Past services are soon forgotten.
Save a thief from the gallows, and he will cut your throat.
The axe goes to the wood from which it borrowed its helve.
Ingratitude is the mother of every vice. *(French)*
One finds few ingrates as long as he is capable of bestowing favors. *(La Rochefoucauld)*
Unhang one that is hanged, and he will hang you. *(French)*
They whom I benefit injure me most. *(Sappho)*
An ungrateful man is a tub full of holes. *(Latin)*
Earth produces nothing worse than an ungrateful man. *(Latin)*
You love a nothing when you love an ingrate. *(Latin)*
Eaten bread is soon forgotten. *(Spanish)*
Ingratitude is the daughter of pride. *(Spanish)*
The wicked are always ungrateful. *(Spanish)*

INHERITANCE
He goes long barefoot that waits for dead men's shoes.
He pulls with a long rope that waits for another's death.
Let an ill man lie in thy straw, and he looks to be thy heir.
The fork is commonly the rake's heir.
Many heirs make small portions. *(German)*
The next heir is always suspected and hated. *(Latin)*

The tears of an heir are laughter under a mask. *(Latin)*
He comes for the inheritance, and has to pay the funeral expenses. *(Yiddish)*

INJURY

He that does you an ill turn will never forgive you.
He that injures one threatens a hundred.
It costs more to revenge injuries than to bear them.
Write injuries in dust, benefits in marble. *(French)*
A worthy man forgets past injuries. *(Greek)*
The injuries we do and those we suffer are seldom weighed in the same scale. *(Greek)*
How bitter it is when you have sown benefits to reap injuries! *(Latin)*
It is better to receive than to do an injury. *(Latin)*
It is the mark of a good man not to know how to do an injury. *(Latin)*
No one is injured except by himself. *(Latin)*
The remedy for injuries is to forget them. *(Latin)*
Whom they have injured they also hate. *(Latin)*

INJUSTICE

Injustice in the end produces independence. *(Voltaire)*
To do injustice is more disgraceful than to suffer it. *(Plato)*

INN

A handsome hostess makes a dear reckoning.
He goes not out of his way that goes to a good inn.
Let the world wag, and take mine ease in mine inn.
Whosoever reckoneth without his host, he reckoneth twice.
A foolish innkeeper! He has brandy and he sells it. *(Yiddish)*

INNOCENCE

Innocence is its own defense.
Innocence is no protection.
Innocence itself hath need of a mask.
The innocent are gay.
What is that which innocence dare not?
We become innocent when we are unfortunate. *(French)*
True innocence is ashamed of nothing. *(Russian)*
A mind conscious of innocence laughs at the lies of rumor. *(Latin)*

INQUISITIVE

He that pries into every cloud may be stricken with a thunderbolt.
He who peeps through a hole may see what will vex him.

INSIGNIFICANT

The smallest insect may cause death by its bite. *(Chinese)*

A feather shows the way the wind blows.

The least and weakest man can do some harm.

A spark may consume a city. *(Hungarian)*

INSOLENCE

Insolence is pride with her mask pulled off.

The insolent are never without wounds. *(Turkish)*

INSPIRATION

Ninety per cent of inspiration is perspiration.

Inspiration cannot be commanded. *(French)*

INSTINCT

By a divine instinct men's minds mistrust ensuing dangers. *(Shakespeare)*

Instinct is untaught ability.

We heed no instincts but our own. *(French)*

It is the instinct of understanding to contradict reason. *(German)*

INSULT

An injury is much sooner forgiven than an insult.

Insults are like bad coins; we cannot help their being offered, but we need not take them.

The way to procure insults is to submit to them.

He who allows himself to be insulted deserves to be. *(French)*

If you speak insults, you shall also hear them. *(Latin)*

It is often better to see an insult than to avenge it. *(Latin)*

To add insult to injury. *(Latin)*

INTELLIGENCE

To perceive things in the germ is intelligence. *(Lao-Tsze)*

All things are slaves to intelligence. *(Greek)*

INTENTION

Stain not fair acts with foul intentions. *(Sir T. Browne)*

Hell is paved with good intentions. *(French)*

Good intentions are solaces in misfortune. *(Latin)*

INVALID

An invalid lives on his ailments. *(Yiddish)*

INVENTION

God hath made man upright; but they have sought out many inventions. *(Old Test., Eccles.)*

Invention breeds invention.

If it is not true, it is very well invented. *(Italian)*

Nothing is invented and perfected at the same time. *(Latin)*

INVITATION

He who comes uncalled, sits unserved.

Small invitation will serve a beggar.

INVOLVED

In for a penny, in for a pound.

IRISH

A servile race in folly nursed,
 Who truckle most when treated worst. *(Swift)*

An Irishman never speaks well of another Irishman.

IRON

Iron sharpeneth iron. *(Old Test., Prov.)*

Iron long fired becomes steel. *(Chinese)*

He is teaching iron to swim.

Many irons in the fire, part must cool.

We must beat the iron while it is hot.

The iron entered into his soul. *(Latin)*

ITALY

Italy is a paradise for horses, hell for women . . . *(Burton)*

The Italians are wise before the deed . . .

All Italians are plunderers. *(Napoleon)*

Italy is only a geographical expression. *(Metternich)*

JACK

Every Jack must have his Jill.
Jack of all trades is master of none.

JEALOUSY

Jealousy is cruel as the grave. *(Old Test., Song of Songs)*
A jealous woman believes everything her passion suggests.
A lewd bachelor makes a jealous husband.
It is the green-eyed monster which doth mock the meat it feeds on. *(Shakespeare)*
Jealousy shuts one door and opens two.
Love, being jealous, makes a good eye look asquint.
Trifles light as air are to the jealous confirmations strong as proof of Holy Writ. *(Shakespeare)*
Where there is love, there is jealousy.
Jealousy is nourished by doubt. *(French)*
Jealousy is a pain which seeks what causes pain. *(German)*
Jealousy is inborn in women's hearts. *(Greek)*
A loving man, a jealous woman. *(Italian)*
A jealous woman sets the whole house afire. *(Latin)*
Love is never without jealousy. *(Latin)*

JEST

It is not good jesting with God, Death, or the Devil. *(Arabian)*
A jest breaks no bones.
A jest is as good lost as found.
A joke's a very serious thing.
A joke never gains over an enemy, but often loses a friend.
Jest with an ass, and he will flap you in the face with his tail.
Jest not with the two-edged sword of God's word.
Jesters do oft prove prophets.

Jesting lies bring serious sorrows.
Many a true word is spoken in jest.
The truest jests sound worse in guilty ears.
The wise make jests and fools repeat them.
The worst jests are those which are true. *(French)*
A jest loses its point when the jester laughs himself. *(German)*
When the demand is a jest, the fittest answer is a scoff. *(Greek)*
Drop the jest when it is most amusing. *(Italian)*
A jest that comes too near the truth leaves a sting behind. *(Latin)*
Better lose a jest than a friend. *(Latin)*
All in the way of a joke the wolf goes to the ass. *(Spanish)*
Jesting costs money. *(Spanish)*
Jests that give pain are no jests. *(Spanish)*
A jest is half a truth. *(Yiddish)*

JEW
A Christianized Jew and a reconciled foe are not to be trusted. *(Russian)*

No Jew is a fool, no hare lazy. *(Spanish)*
All the Jew has is money to lose, and time to be sick. *(Yiddish)*
Even Moses couldn't get along with the Jews. *(Yiddish)*
No misfortune avoids a Jew. *(Yiddish)*

JOY
Weeping may endure for a night, but joy cometh in the morning. *(Old Test., Psalms)*
Joy is like the ague; one good day between two bad ones. *(Danish)*
A joyous evening often leads to a sorrowful morning. *(Dutch)*
A joy that's shared is a joy made double.
Every inch of joy has an ell of annoy.
Forever the latter end of joy is woe. *(Chaucer)*
Sorrows remembered sweeten present joy.
Sweets with sweets war not, joy delights in joy. *(Shakespeare)*
There's not a joy the world can give like that it takes away. *(Byron)*
Who bathes in worldly joys, swims in a world of fears.
Great joys weep, great sorrows laugh. *(French)*
Brief is sorrow, and endless is joy. *(Schiller)*
After sorrow, joy. *(Latin)*
It is heaven's will for sorrow to follow joy. *(Latin)*
Joy surfeited turns to sorrow. *(Latin)*
Joys do not abide, but take wing and fly away. *(Latin)*

JUDGE

Judge not, that ye be not judged. *(New Test., Matthew)*
Do not judge of the ship from the land.
Forbear to judge, for we are sinners all.
He who will have no judge but himself condemns himself.
Never judge by appearances.
Thieves for their robbery have authority
  When judges steal themselves. *(Shakespeare)*
When a judge puts on his robe, he puts off his relations to any.
You cannot judge of the wine by the barrel.
He who is a judge between two friends loses one of them. *(French)*
Judge not the tree by its bark. *(French)*
The duty of the judge is to administer justice, but his practice is to delay it. *(French)*
He hears but half who hears one side only. *(Greek)*
Well to judge depends on well to hear. *(Italian)*
A corrupt judge weighs truth badly. *(Latin)*
Hear the other side. *(Latin)*
Men judge the affairs of others better than their own. *(Latin)*
No one should be a judge in his own cause. *(Latin)*
That money is well lost which the guilty man gives to the judge. *(Latin)*
The judge is condemned when the guilty is acquitted. *(Latin)*
The law is loosened when the judge grows tender-hearted. *(Latin)*
The magistrate is a speaking law, but the law is a silent magistrate. *(Latin)*
The upright judge condemns the crime, but does not hate the criminal. *(Latin)*
He who has his father for the judge, goes into court with an easy mind. *(Spanish)*

JUDGMENT

Many complain of their memory, but few of their judgment.
Men's judgments sway on the side that fortune leans.
None judge so wrong as those who think amiss. *(Pope)*
They have right to censure that have a heart to help.
'Tis with our judgments as our watches, none
  Go just alike, yet each believes his own. *(Pope)*
Who reproves the lame must go upright.
Whoso giveth hasty judgment
  Must be the first that shall repent.
All wholesale judgments are imperfect. *(French)*

Of judgment everyone has a stock on hand for sale. *(Italian)*
Haste in judgment is criminal. *(Latin)*
The judgment of man is fallible. *(Latin)*
To him of good judgment, the sound of a gnat suffices. *(Turkish)*

JUNE
A dripping June brings all things in tune.
Calm weather in June sets corn in tune.

JURY
A fox should not be of the jury at a goose's trial.
A man should be tried by a jury of his peers.

JUSTICE
One hour in doing justice is worth a hundred in prayer. *(Arabian)*
The memory of the just is blessed . . . *(Old Test., Prov.)*
The path of the just is as the shining light . . . *(Old Test., Prov.)*
As crimes do grow, justice should rouse herself.
Be just before you are generous.
Delay of justice is injustice.
He that buyeth magistracy must sell justice.
He that is void of fear, must soon be just.
Justice is a virtue to be shared by all.
Justice is blind.
Justice without wisdom is impossible.
Live and let live is the rule of common justice.
Sparing justice feeds iniquity. *(Shakespeare)*
The extremity of justice is injustice.
There's no god dare wrong a worm. *(Emerson)*
Though justice has leaden feet, it has leaden hands.
Where justice reigns, 'tis freedom to obey.
Justice is truth in action. *(Joubert)*
To everyone his own, is but justice. *(French)*
We love justice greatly, and just men but little. *(French)*
Justice has a waxen nose. *(German)*
Any time is the proper time for justice. *(Greek)*
Every place is safe to him who lives in justice. *(Greek)*
If all men were just, there would be no need of valor. *(Greek)*
Justice, even if slow, is sure. *(Greek)*
As soon as Justice returns, the golden age returns. *(Vergil)*
He who spares the bad seeks to corrupt the good. *(Latin)*
Justice again our guide. [*Astrea redux.*] *(Latin)*

Justice shines by its own light. *(Latin)*
Let justice be done, though the heavens fall. *(Latin)*
Pardon one offense and you encourage many. *(Latin)*
The just hand is a precious ointment. *(Latin)*
There should be no sword in the hand of justice. *(Latin)*
You are guilty of a crime when you do not punish crime. *(Latin)*
Justice is half religion. *(Turkish)*

KEEP
Keep your breath to cool your porridge.
Keep a thing seven years and you'll find use for it. *(Gaelic)*
Never give the wolf the wether to keep. *(Latin)*

KEEPER
Kings and bears oft worry their keepers.
Who shall keep the keepers? *(Latin)*
Am I my brother's keeper? *(Old Test., Genesis)*

KEY
All the keys hang not at one man's girdle.
Not every key fits every lock.
The key that is used grows bright. *(German)*
A golden key opens all doors. *(Yiddish)*

KICK
I should kick, being kick'd. *(Shakespeare)*

KIN
A little more than kin and less than kind. *(Shakespeare)*
A man cannot bear all his kin on his back.

KINDNESS
Kindness is more binding than a loan. *(Chinese)*
A forced kindness deserves no thanks.
A kind heart loseth naught at last.
Kindness is the sunshine in which virtue grows.
Kindness, nobler ever than revenge.
One kindness is the price of another.
The greater the kindred, the less the kindness.
The heart benevolent and kind
  The most resembles God. *(Burns)*

To kill a wife with kindness.
Who does a kindness is not therefore kind.
With kindness, lo, the ape doth kill the whelp.
With the sweet milk of human kindness bless'd.
Kindness consists in loving people more than they deserve. *(Joubert)*
Nothing grows old sooner than a kindness. *(French)*
Kindness breaks no bones. *(German)*
Kindness is ever the begetter of kindness. *(Greek)*
Kindness to the good is a better investment than kindness to the rich. *(Latin)*
Nothing is so popular as kindness. *(Latin)*
Persistent kindness conquers the ill-disposed. *(Latin)*
A word of kindness is better than a fat pie. *(Russian)*

KING
Honor the king. *(New Test., I Peter)*
A good king is a public servant.
A king promises, but observes only when he pleases.
A king's a king, do Fortune what she can.
A king's favor is no inheritance.
A king's word should be a king's bond.
A king of shreds and patches. *(Shakespeare)*
Authority forgets a dying king. *(Tennyson)*
Every law is broken to become a king.
He is the fountain of honor. *(Bacon)*
He that eats the king's goose shall be choked with his feathers.
He that is hated of his subjects cannot be counted a king.
If the king is in the palace, nobody looks at the walls.
Kings climb to eminence over men's graves.
Kings have long ears.
Kings' misdeeds cannot be hid in clay. *(Shakespeare)*
Kings that made laws first broke them.
Kings will be tyrants from policy, when subjects are rebels from principle. *(Burke)*
Many eyes are upon the king.
Monarchs seldom sigh in vain.
Never king dropped out of the clouds.
Royalty is but a feather in a man's cap. *(Cromwell)*
Scratch a king and find a fool. *(D. Parker)*
The fortune which made you a king, forbade you to have a friend. *("Junius")*

The greatest king must at last go to bed with a shovel
The king can do no wrong.
The king is a name of dignity and office, not of person. *(Milton)*
The king never dies.
The king who fights his people fights himself. *(Tennyson)*
The king's cheese goes three parts away in parings.
The king's word is more than another man's oath.
The right divine of kings to govern wrong. *(Pope)*
The royal crown cures not the headache.
The trappings of monarchy would set up an ordinary republic. *(S. Johnson)*
There's such divinity doth hedge a king . . . *(Shakespeare)*
Vainest of all things is the gratitude of kings.
Whoever is king is also the father of his country.
A dead king is not a man less. *(French)*
The first king was a successful soldier. *(Voltaire)*
The king is dead. Long live the king! *(French)*
The virtue of kings consists in justice. *(French)*
'Tis clemency that is the surest mark by which the world may know a true monarch. *(Corneille)*
When kings are building, draymen have something to do. *(German)*
Deceived for once, I trust not kings again. *(Homer)*
Dreadful is the wrath of kings. *(Homer)*
Nothing becomes a king so much as justice. *(Greek)*
The subjects' love is the king's best guard. *(Italian)*
A king is he who has no fear, and desires naught. *(Latin)*
Every monarch is subject to a mightier one. *(Latin)*
Kings go mad, and the people suffer for it. *(Latin)*
Kings have long hands. *(Latin)*
On alien soil, kingship stands not sure. *(Seneca)*
Stolen scepters are held in anxious hands. *(Seneca)*
The halls of kings: full of men, void of friends. *(Latin)*
The king reigns but does not govern. *(Polish)*
The king's leavings are better than my lord's bounty. *(Spanish)*

KISS

The kisses of an enemy are deceitful. *(Old Test., Prov.)*
A kiss of the mouth often touches not the heart.
A lisping lass is good to kiss.
After kissing comes more kindness.
Do not make me kiss, and you will not make me sin.

He is a fool that kisses the maid when he may kiss the mistress.
Kiss the place to make it well.
Kiss till the cows come home.
Kisses and favors are sweet things,
But those have thorns and these have stings. *(Herrick)*
Kissing don't last: cookery do.
Kissing goes by favor.
Kissing is nigh cousin unto the foul deed.
Many kiss the hand they wish cut off.
Never a lip that can't be kissed into smiles.
Oh, fie, Miss, you must not kiss and tell. *(Congreve)*
She had rather kiss than spin.
She that will kiss will do worse.
Stolen kisses are sweetest.
Wanton kisses are keys of sin.
Woman that crys hush bids kiss.
You must kiss the rod.
Many kiss the child for love of the nurse. *(Latin)*
The hawk kissed the hen—up to the last feather. *(Russian)*
Gin a body kiss a body,
Need a body cry? *(Scottish)*
A kiss for the child is as good as a kiss for its mother. *(Yiddish)*
Don't kiss a homely maid—she'll brag about it. *(Yiddish)*

KITCHEN
A fat kitchen makes a lean will.
A little kitchen makes a large house.
Silk and velvet put out the kitchen fire. *(German)*
Who hangs around the kitchen smells of smoke. *(Italian)*

KITE
If the frog and mouse quarrel, the kite will see them agreed.
The kite's malady: its wing broken and its beak sound. *(French)*

KNAVE
A crafty knave needs no broker.
An old knave is no babe.
Better be a fool than a knave.
Clever men are the tools for knaves.
'Gainst thieves and knaves men shut their gate. *(Shakespeare)*
Knavery's plain face is never seen till used. *(Shakespeare)*
Knaves and fools divide the world.

Once a knave and ever a knave.
The fox condemns the trap, not himself. *(Blake)*
When knaves fall out, true men come by their own.
One knave is usher to another. *(Greek)*
Successful knaves are insufferable. *(Greek)*

KNIFE
One knife whets another.
One knife keeps another in its sheath. *(Italian)*
The knife cuts not the hand of gold. *(Turkish)*

KNOWLEDGE
A man of knowledge increaseth strength. *(Old Test., Prov.)*
He that increaseth knowledge increaseth sorrow. *(Old Test., Eccles.)*
Knowledge puffeth up, but charity edifieth. *(New Test., I Corinth.)*
Profess not the knowledge thou hast not. *(Old Test., Prov.)*
The fear of the Lord is the beginning of knowledge. *(Old Test., Prov.)*
To know one's ignorance is the best part of knowledge. *(Chinese)*
A little knowledge is a dangerous thing. *(Pope)*
A man is but what he knoweth. *(Bacon)*
A man without knowledge is as one that is dead.
An investment in knowledge pays the best interest. *(Franklin)*
He that knows little often repeats it.
Knowledge is the wing wherewith we fly to heaven. *(Shakespeare)*
It is better not to know so much than to know many things that ain't so. *(J. Billings)*
Knowledge and timber shouldn't be used till they are seasoned.
Knowledge comes, but wisdom lingers. *(Tennyson)*
Knowledge in youth is wisdom in age.
Knowledge is a treasure, but practice is the key to it.
Knowledge is folly except grace guide it.
Knowledge is power.
Knowledge is the action of the soul.
Knowledge is the only elegance. *(Emerson)*
No man is the wiser for his learning.
The desire for knowledge increases with its acquisition.
The greatest clerks be not the wisest men. *(Chaucer)*
They know enough who know how to learn.
Those who really thirst for knowledge always get it.
It is better to know something about everything than all about one thing. *(Pascal)*

Knowledge finds its price. *(French)*
He who knows has many cares. *(German)*
Know thyself. *(Greek)*
Only one good: knowledge; only one evil: ignorance. *(Greek)*
He knows enough that knows how to hold his peace. *(Italian)*
He who knows nothing never doubts. *(Italian)*
To know everything is to know nothing. *(Italian)*
Who knows most believes least. *(Italian)*
Who knows most forgives most. *(Italian)*
A learned man has always riches in himself. *(Latin)*
All wish to know, but none to pay the fee. *(Latin)*
Better ignorance than half-knowledge. *(Latin)*
It is not permitted us to know all. *(Latin)*
To know is not to know, unless someone else knows that I know.
Let him who knows how ring the bells. *(Spanish)*
He who would know all, grows old soon. *(Yiddish)*

LABOR

Come unto me, all ye that labor and are heavy laden. *(New Test., Matthew)*

I have bestowed upon you labor in vain. *(New Test., Galat.)*

In all labor there is profit. *(Old Test., Prov.)*

Man is born unto labor. *(Old Test., Job)*

The laborer is worthy of his hire. *(New Test., Luke)*

The sleep of a laboring man is sweet. *(Old Test., Eccles.)*

What profit hath a man of all the labor which he taketh under the sun? *(Old Test., Eccles.)*

Be the first in the field and the last to the couch. *(Chinese)*

A carpenter is known by his chips.

A little labor, much health.

A man of many trades begs his bread on Sundays.

A ploughman on his legs is higher than a gentleman on his knees.

A toiling dog comes halting home.

Bodily labor earns not much.

Change of toil is toil's sufficient cure.

Handle your tools without mittens.

He that hath a trade hath an estate. *(Franklin)*

He that labors and thrives spins gold.

Honest labor bears a lovely face.

Honor lies in honest toil.

Labor as long lived; pray as ever dying.

Labor for labor's sake is against nature. *(Locke)*

Labor is but refreshment from repose.

Labor is the law of happiness.

Labor is the handmaid of religion.

Labor warms, sloth harms.

Laboring men count the clock oftenest.

Many faint with toil,
  That few may know the cares and woes of sloth. *(Shelley)*
The labor we delight in physics pain. *(Shakespeare)*
The laboring people are poor because they are numerous.
Toil is the law of life and its best fruit.
Each one to his own trade. *(French)*
Labor is often the father of pleasure. *(French)*
A good laborer is better than a bad priest. *(German)*
Sweet is the memory of past labor. *(Greek)*
The gods will sell us all good things at the price of labor. *(Greek)*
To him that toils God owes glory. *(Greek)*
Toil is the sire of fame. *(Greek)*
Virtue proceeds through toils. *(Greek)*
If I had not lifted up the stone, you had not found the jewel. *(Hebrew)*
God walks among the pots and pipkins. *(Latin)*
He who would eat the kernel must crack the shell. *(Latin)*
It is not the part of a man to fear sweat. *(Latin)*
Labor conquers everything. *(Latin)*
Life grants no boon to man without much toil. *(Latin)*
O sweet solace of labor! *(Latin)*
To labor is to pray. *(Latin)*
Why seekest thou rest, since thou art born to labor? *(Latin)*
Who does not teach his child a trade brings him up to steal. *(Persian)*
Life is in labor. *(Russian)*

LADY

Ladies, by all the laws of war, are privileged. *(Shakespeare)*
Ladies are whitest in a blackamoor's land.
You a lady, I a lady, who shall drive the hogs a-field? *(Spanish)*

LAMB

A lamb in the house, and a lion in the field.
The ewe that will not hear her lamb when it baes will never answer
  a calf when it bleats. *(Shakespeare)*
Make yourself a lamb and the wolves will eat you. *(French)*

LAME

A lame traveler should get out betimes.
The lame returns sooner than the staggerer.
We must wait for the lame man. *(French)*

LAMP

If you would have your lamp burn, you must pour oil into it. *(German)*

LAND

Good land, evil way.
Estate in two parishes is bread in two wallets.
Land was never lost for want of an heir.
Who buys land buys war. *(Italian)*
The land a man knows is his mother. *(Spanish)*

LANE

It is a long lane that has no turning.

LANGUAGE

Custom is the most certain mistress of language. *(Jonson)*
Language was the immediate gift of God. *(N. Webster)*
Language is fossil poetry. *(Emerson)*
Language is the dress of thought. *(S. Johnson)*
Languages are the pedigrees of nations. *(S. Johnson)*
Speak that I may see thee.
That is not good language that all understand not.
The knowledge of the ancient languages is mainly a luxury. *(J. Bright)*
He who is ignorant of foreign languages knows not his own. *(Goethe)*

LARGE

As large as life.

LARK

He thinks that roasted larks will fall into his mouth.
Merry larks are ploughmen's clocks.
The busy lark, the messenger of day. *(Chaucer)*
To rise with the lark, and go to bed with the lamb.

LASS

Glasses and lasses are brittle ware.
He that loves glass without G,
  Take away L and that's he.
Put on your glasses and you'll say goodbye to the lasses.

LAST

He that cometh last to pot is soonest wroth.
Last but not least.
Last makes fast.
The last drop makes the cup run over.
The last feather breaks the camel's back.

For the last comer the bones. *(French)*
The last one must shut the door. *(Italian)*
It's the last one whom the dogs attack. *(Yiddish)*

LATE

It is too late to cover the well when the child is drowned. *(Danish)*
Better late than never, but better never late.
It is no time to stoop when the head is off.
You came a day after the fair.
It is too late for the bird to scream when it is caught. *(French)*
It is too late to lock the stable door when the steed is stolen. *(French)*
Who rises late must trot all day. *(French)*
A little too late, much too late. *(German)*
It is too late to come with the water when the house is burned down. *(Italian)*
The late comer is ill lodged. *(Italian)*
When the head is broken the helmet is put on. *(Italian)*
Better late than never. *(Latin)*
He who comes late must eat what is left. *(Yiddish)*

LAUGH

As the crackling of thorns under a pot, so is the laughter of a fool. *(Old Test., Eccles.)*
Even in laughter the heart is sorrowful; and the end of mirth is heaviness. *(Old Test., Prov.)*
A maid that laughs is half taken.
A fool laughs when others laugh.
A good laugh is sunshine in a house.
And if I laugh at any mortal thing,
'Tis that I may not weep. *(Byron)*
And the loud laugh that spoke the vacant mind. *(Goldsmith)*
Better the last smile than the first laugh.
He is not laughed at that laughs at himself first.
He laughed in his sleeve.
He laugheth that winneth.
He laughs best that laughs last.
He that laughs at his own jest mars the mirth of it.
He who laugheth too much has the nature of a fool.
I'll laugh and be fat, for care killed a cat.
Laugh, and the world laughs with you,
Weep, and you weep alone. *(E. W. Wilcox)*
Laughter is the hiccup of a fool.

Learn weeping and then thou shalt laugh gaining.
Let us not be laughing-stocks to other men's humors. *(Shakespeare)*
Our sincerest laughter
With some pain is fraught. *(Shelley)*
She can laugh and cry both in a wind.
The giggler is a milk-maid.
The laughter of man is the contentment of God.
The vulgar often laugh but never smile. *(Chesterfield)*
He who laughs on Friday will weep on Saturday. *(French)*
That day is lost on which one has not laughed. *(French)*
We must laugh before we are happy, lest we die before we laugh at all. *(French)*
He who tickles himself may laugh when he pleases. *(German)*
Men show their characters in what they think laughable. *(Goethe)*
No one is sadder than he who laughs too much *(German)*
Ill-timed laughter is a dangerous evil. *(Greek)*
The fool will laugh though there be nothing to laugh at. *(Greek)*
The gods have not granted to mortals laughter without tears. *(Greek)*
Laughter makes good blood. *(Italian)*
All things are cause for either laughter or weeping. *(Latin)*
He chastises manners with a laugh. *(Latin)*
Laugh, if you are wise. *(Latin)*
The price of a laugh is too high, if it is raised at the expense of propriety. *(Latin)*
To condemn by a cutting laugh comes readily to all. *(Latin)*
What is viler than to be laughed at? *(Latin)*
He who loves to laugh has teeth that are white. *(Russian)*
Let people laugh, as long as I am warm. *(Spanish)*
Laughter comes of itself; so does weeping. *(Yiddish)*
When you laugh, all see; when you weep, no one. *(Yiddish)*

LAW

The letter killeth, but the spirit giveth life. *(New Test., II Corinth.)*
To violate the law is the same crime in the emperor as in the subject. *(Chinese)*
God help the sheep when the wolf is judge. *(Danish)*
A friend in court is worth a penny in a man's purse.
A pennyweight of love is worth a pound of law.
A precedent embalms a principle.
A rich knave is a libel on the law.
A rotten case abides no handling. *(Shakespeare)*
Agree, for the law is costly.

Bad laws are the worst sort of tyranny.
Better live where nothing is lawful, than where all things are lawful.
Fear the beadle of the law.
Hard cases make bad law.
He that goes to law holds a wolf by the ears.
He that loves law will get his fill of it.
I know no method to secure the repeal of bad laws so effective as their stringent execution. *(U. S. Grant)*
Ill manners produce good laws.
In a thousand pounds of law there's not an ounce of love.
Law cannot persuade where it cannot punish.
Law governs man and reason the law.
Law is a bottomless pit.
Law is a pickpurse.
Law is whatever is boldly asserted and plausibly maintained. *(A. Burr)*
Lawmakers should not be lawbreakers.
Laws are not masters but servants.
Laws grind the poor and rich men rule the law.
Laws, like houses, lean on one another.
Laws are like cobwebs which catch small flies, but let wasps and hornets break through. *(Swift)*
Laws too gentle are seldom obeyed; too severe, seldom executed. *(Franklin)*
Laws were made to be broken.
Lawsuits consume time, money, rest, and friends.
Magna Charta is such a fellow that he will have no sovereign. *(Coke)*
Many lords, many laws.
Much law but little justice.
New lords, new laws.
No man e'er felt the halter draw,
With good opinion of the law. *(Trumbull)*
One precedent creates another.
Petty laws breed great crimes.
Possession is nine points of the law.
Possession is eleven points of the law and there are but twelve.
Reason is the life of the law. *(Coke)*
Show me the man, and I'll show you the law.
So many laws argue so many sins. *(Milton)*
That which is a law today is none tomorrow.
The best use of good laws is to teach men to trample bad laws under their feet. *(W. Phillips)*

The brain may devise laws for the blood, but a hot temper leaps o'er a cold decree. *(Shakespeare)*
The law blushes when children correct their parents.
The law groweth of sin, and doth punish it.
The law is ended as a man is friended.
The law is for the protection of the weak more than the strong.
The law is not the same at morning and at night.
The worst of law is that one suit brings twenty.
There is no worse torture than the torture of laws. *(Bacon)*
Unnecessary laws are not good laws.
Where law can do no right,
Let it be lawful that law bar no wrong. *(Shakespeare)*
When men are pure, laws are useless; when men are corrupt, laws are broken.
Where law ends, there tyranny begins.
Who breaks no law is subject to no king.
Whoso loves law dies either mad or poor.
Better have no laws at all than in prodigious numbers. *(Montaigne)*
Laws are useful to those who have; vexatious to those who have not. *(French)*
Laws have wax noses. *(French)*
Lawsuits are gulfs. *(French)*
The atrocity of a law prevents its execution. *(French)*
The clatter of arms drowns the voice of the law. *(Montaigne)*
The law often allows what honor forbids. *(French)*
A lawsuit is civil war. *(German)*
By lawsuits no one has become rich. *(German)*
He who goes to law for a sheep loses his cow. *(German)*
Judges should have two ears, both alike. *(German)*
There is no law without a loophole for him who can find it. *(German)*
All things by law. *(Greek)*
Draco made his laws not with ink, but with blood. *(Greek)*
Law is the tyrant of mankind. *(Greek)*
Laws are not made for the good. *(Greek)*
The man who does no wrong needs no law. *(Greek)*
A lean compromise is better than a fat lawsuit. *(Italian)*
All things obey fixed laws. *(Latin)*
Arms and laws do not flourish together. *(Latin)*
Extreme law, extreme injustice. *(Latin)*
Go not to law because the musician keeps false time with his foot. *(Latin)*

Ignorance of the law excuses no one. *(Latin)*
Law is founded not on theory but on nature. *(Latin)*
Law is the safest helmet. *(Latin)*
Laws are dumb in the midst of arms. *(Latin)*
Laws were made that the stronger might not in all things have his way. *(Latin)*
Of what use laws nullified by immorality? *(Latin)*
Safer not to accuse a bad man than to acquit him. *(Latin)*
So many lands, so many laws. *(Latin)*
The laws obey custom. *(Latin)*
The more laws, the more offenders. *(Latin)*
The prince is not above the laws. *(Latin)*
The safety of the people is the highest law. *(Latin)*
The verdict acquits the raven, but condemns the dove. *(Latin)*
We are lost by what is lawful. *(Latin)*
Fear not the law, but the judge. *(Russian)*
The nobleman is always in the right when the peasant sues. *(Russian)*
Truth is straight but judges are crooked. *(Russian)*
Where is there any book of the law so clear to each man as that written in his heart? *(Tolstoy)*
He goes safely to trial whose father is the judge. *(Spanish)*
Laws go as kings like. *(Spanish)*
If the judge be your accuser, may God be your help. *(Turkish)*

LAWYER

Woe unto you, lawyers! for ye have stolen away the key of knowledge. *(New Test., Matthew)*
"Virtue in the middle," said the Devil, when he sat down between two lawyers. *(Danish)*
A good lawyer, an evil neighbor.
As well open an oyster without a knife, as a lawyer's mouth without a fee.
Fair and softly, as lawyers go to heaven.
Few lawyers die well, few physicians live well.
He that is his own lawyer has a fool for his client.
I know you lawyers can with ease
Twist words and meanings as you please. *(Gay)*
If the laws could speak, they would first complain of lawyers.
Lawyers are more ready to get a man into trouble than out of it.
Lawyers' gowns are lined with the wilfulness of their clients.
If there were no bad people there would be no good lawyers.

Necessity has no law; I know some attorneys of the same. *(Franklin)*
Three Philadelphia lawyers are a match for the devil.
Lawyers' houses are built on the heads of fools. *(French)*
One may steal nothing but a lawyer's purse. *(French)*
The lawyer's pouch is a mouth of hell. *(French)*
Until hell is full no lawyer will be saved. *(French)*
A lawyer and a cart-wheel must be greased. *(German)*
The good have no need of an advocate. *(Greek)*
A lawyer never goes to law himself. *(Italian)*
A peasant between two lawyers is like a fish between two cats. *(Spanish)*

LAZY
A lazy boy and a warm bed are difficult to part. *(Danish)*
A lazy ox is better for the goad.
A lazy sheep thinks its wool heavy.
A lazy youth, a lousy age.
As lazy as the dog that leaned against a wall to bark.
Come day, go day, God send Sunday.
Laziness travels so slowly that Poverty soon overtakes him. *(Franklin)*
Lazy folks take the most pains.
The sleeping fox catches no poultry.
It cost the devil little trouble to catch a lazy man. *(German)*
He's willing to swallow but too lazy to chew. *(Russian)*
To the lazy every day is a holiday. *(Turkish)*
A lazy man should be sent for the Angel of Death. *(Yiddish)*

LEADER
He that rides behind another must not think to guide.
If two men ride on a horse, one must ride behind.
The foremost dog catches the hare.
Whoever is foremost leads the herd. *(German)*

LEAK
A small leak will sink a ship.

LEAN
As lean as a rake.
You must take the lean with the fat.

LEAP
A great leap gives a great shake.

Look before you leap.
One must step back to make a better leap. *(French)*

LEARN
As the old cock crows, so crows the young.
Learn not and know not.
Learn of the mole to plough, the worm to weave. *(Pope)*
Live and learn.
Better learn late than never. *(Greek)*
Find time to be learning somewhat good. *(Greek)*
Still I am learning. [*Ancora imparo.*] (*Michelangelo*)
It is lawful to learn even from an enemy. *(Latin)*
Learn young, learn fair; learn auld, learn mair. *(Scottish)*
It is well to live that one may learn. *(Spanish)*
He learns to shave on another's beard. *(Yiddish)*

LEARNING
Much learning doth make thee mad. *(New Test., Acts)*
Learning without thought is labor lost; thought without learning is dangerous. *(Chinese)*
High-larnt nigger ain't much use at de log-rollin'. *(American Negro)*
A learned blockhead is a greater blockhead than an ignorant one. *(Franklin)*
A man becomes learned by asking questions.
He that lives well is learned enough.
I pity unlearned gentlemen on a rainy day. *(Falkland)*
Learned men are cisterns of knowledge, not the fountain-heads.
Learning was ne'er entailed from father to son.
Learning is the eye of the mind.
Learning makes the wise wiser, and the fool more foolish.
Learning teacheth more in one year than experience in twenty. *(Ascham)*
Much learning shows how little mortals know.
Swallow your learning in the morning; digest it in the evening.
The world would perish were all men learned.
Of what use is learning without understanding? *(French)*
If you love learning you shall be learned. *(Greek)*
There is no royal road to learning. *(Euclid)*
A learned man has always wealth in himself. *(Latin)*
A single day among the learned lasts longer than the longest life of the ignorant. *(Seneca)*

How many perish in the earth through vain learning! *(Thomas à Kempis)*

It takes ten pounds of common-sense to carry one pound of learning. *(Persian)*

LEAVE

Leave off while the play is good.

It is better to leave than to lack.

LEG

Lose a leg rather than life.

LEISURE

A life of leisure and a life of laziness are two things.

Employ thy time well if thou meanest to gain leisure.

He enjoys true leisure who has time to improve his soul's estate. *(Thoreau)*

Idle folk have the least leisure.

Leisure is the mother of Philosophy. *(Hobbes)*

Leisure is the reward of labor.

Leisure is the time for doing something useful.

Leisure is the best of all possessions. *(Greek)*

He was never less at leisure than when at leisure. *(Latin)*

Leisure nourishes the body and the mind. *(Latin)*

Leisure with dignity. [*Otium cum dignitate.*] *(Latin)*

Leisure without study is death. *(Latin)*

You will soon break the bow if you keep it always stretched. *(Latin)*

LEND

A good man sheweth favor, and lendeth. *(Old Test., Psalms)*

Lend to one who will not repay, and you will provoke his dislike. *(Chinese)*

Great spenders are bad lenders.

It is better to give one shilling than to lend a pound.

Lend only what you can afford to lose.

Lend to an enemy, and you'll gain him; to a friend, and you'll lose him.

Seldom comes a loan laughing home.

What we spent we had; what we gave we have; what we lent we lost.

The ant is not given to lending. *(French)*

He who lends to the poor gets his interest from God. *(German)*

A loan though old is no gift. *(Hungarian)*

Who lends loses double. *(Italian)*
What you lend is lost. *(Latin)*
He who has but one coat cannot lend it. *(Spanish)*
Lend to your friend and ask payment of your enemy. *(Spanish)*
You buy yourself an enemy when you lend a man money. *(Yiddish)*

LENITY
Too much lenity makes robbers bold. *(Shakespeare)*

LETTER
As keys do open chests, so letters open breasts.
Never read over your old letters. *(Maupassant)*
A letter does not blush. *(Latin)*
The written letter remains. *(Latin)*

LIAR
I said in my haste, all men are liars. *(Old Test., Psalms)*
Liars begin by imposing on others, and end by deceiving themselves. *(Bacon)*
Liar, lick dish.
None speaks false where there is none to hear.
Old men and far travelers may lie by authority.
The greater the fool, the greater the liar.
Show me a liar, and I'll show you a thief. *(French)*
A liar is not believed even when he speaks the truth. *(Hebrew)*
A liar is sooner caught than a cripple. *(Italian)*
Liars are always most disposed to swear. *(Italian)*
A liar needs a good memory. *(Latin)*
A liar believes no one. *(Yiddish)*
A liar in youth—a thief in old age. *(Yiddish)*
A liar is like a deaf-mute—both do not tell the truth. *(Yiddish)*

LIBEL
The greater the truth, the greater the libel.

LIBERTY
Proclaim liberty throughout the land unto all the inhabitants thereof. *(Old Test., Levit.)*
Where the Spirit of the Lord is, there is liberty. *(New Test., II Corinth.)*
A bean in liberty is better than a comfit in prison.
A crust of bread and liberty.
Eternal vigilance is the price of liberty. *(W. Phillips)*

God grants liberty only to those who love it.
Lean liberty is better than fat slavery.
Liberty is not license.
Liberty is the breath of progress.
Liberty is . . . the choice of working or starving. *(S. Johnson)*
Liberty, when it begins to take root, is a plant of rapid growth. *(Washington)*
The God who gave us life, gave us liberty at the same time. *(Jefferson)*
Where liberty dwells, there is my country. *(Franklin)*
It is not good to have too much liberty. *(Pascal)*
O liberty, what crimes are committed in thy name! *(Mme. Roland)*
The tree of liberty grows only when watered by the blood of tyrants. *(Barère)*
Liberty is given by nature even to mute animals. *(Latin)*
O sweet name of liberty! *(Latin)*
What in some is called liberty, in others is called license. *(Latin)*

LIBRARY
Burn the libraries, for their value is in this book [*i.e., the Koran*]. *(Caliph Omar)*
A great library is the diary of the human race.
My library was dukedom enough. *(Shakespeare)*
The true university of these days is a collection of books. *(Carlyle)*
Food for the soul. [*Inscription on library*] *(Latin)*

LIE
He shall not prosper who deviseth lies. *(Koran)*
Lying lips are an abomination unto the Lord. *(Old Test., Prov.)*
Who knows to lie, knows neither to love nor respect his parents. *(Chinese)*
If lies were Latin, there would be many learned men. *(Danish)*
A blister will rise upon one's tongue that tells a lie.
A lie is a coward's way of getting out of trouble.
A lie stands on one leg, truth on two.
All is not Gospel that thou dost speak.
Ask me no questions and I'll tell you no fibs. *(Goldsmith)*
Better speak rudely, than lie correctly.
Children and fools cannot lie.
Equivocation is half-way to lying, as lying the whole way to hell. *(Wm. Penn)*
Falsehood is the product of all climes.

Falsehood has a perennial spring.
Figures won't lie, but liars will figure. *(C. H. Grosvenor)*
Half the truth is often a great lie.
He that hears much hears many lies.
He that trusts a lie, shall perish in truth.
I give him joy that's awkward at a lie.
It is better to be lied about than to lie.
Men were born to lie, and women to believe them.
One of the striking differences between a cat and a lie is that a cat has only nine lives. *(Mark Twain)*
Sin has many tools, but a lie is a handle which fits them all. *(O. W. Holmes)*
The cruelest lies are often told in silence.
The man who can't tell a lie often thinks he is the best judge of one. *(Mark Twain)*
The mouth that lies slays the soul.
Though a lie be well drest, it is ever overcome.
A lie never grows old. *(Greek)*
Never tell a lie. *(Greek)*
He who says nothing never lies. *(Italian)*
Lies have short legs. *(Italian)*
Though a lie be swift, truth overtakes it. *(Italian)*
A good portion of speaking well consists in knowing how to lie. *(Latin)*
A lie grows in size as it is repeated. *(Latin)*
One lie treads on the heels of another. *(Latin)*
There is no lie so reckless as to be without some proof. *(Latin)*
From long journeys long lies. *(Spanish)*
The deaf man heard the dumb man tell that the blind man saw the lame man run. *(Yiddish)*
You can get far with a lie, but not come back. *(Yiddish)*

LIFE

Life is short and full of blisters. *(American Negro)*
Men are sleeping, and when they die, they wake. *(Koran)*
A living dog is better than a dead lion. *(Old Test., Prov.)*
As for man, his days are as grass . . . *(Old Test., Psalms)*
I would not live alway: for my days are vanity. *(Old Test., Job)*
It is good for us to be here. *(New Test., Matthew)*
Man's life on earth is a warfare. *(Old Test., Job)*
The days of our years are three-score years and ten. *(Old Test., Prov.)*
To live is Christ, and to die is gain. *(New Test., Philippians)*

Every man's life is a fairy-tale written by God's fingers.
(H. C. Anderson)

A long life hath long miseries.
A long life may not be good enough, but a good life is long enough.
A merry life and a short.
An ill life, an ill end.
Anything for a quiet life.
As a man lives, so shall he die;
As a tree falls, so shall it lie.
Everything would fain live.
He lives in fame who dies in virtue's cause. *(Shakespeare)*
He lives long that lives well.
He that begins to live begins to die.
He that lives a knave will hardly die an honest man.
He that lives longest lives but a little while.
I count life just a stuff
To try the soul's strength on. *(Browning)*
I live, and lords do no more.
I wept when I was born, and every day shows why.
It is not how long, but how well we live.
Learn that the present hour alone is man's.
Let all live as they would die.
Life is a bumper filled by fate.
Life is a fatal and contagious complaint.
Life is a jest, and all things show it:
I thought so once, but now I know it. *(Gay)*
Life's a long headache in a noisy street. *(Masefield)*
Life is a long lesson in humility. *(Barrie)*
Life is a loom, weaving illusion.
Life is a pill which none of us can swallow without gilding.
Life is a pure flame and we live by an invisible sun within us.
(Sir T. Browne)

Life is a school of probability. *(Bagehot)*
Life is a shuttle. *(Shakespeare)*
Life is a span.
Life is a very funny proposition after all. *(G. M. Cohan)*
Life is a voyage that's homeward bound. *(Melville)*
Life is an empty dream.
Life is as tedious as a twice told tale. *(Shakespeare)*
Life is but thought. *(Coleridge)*
Life is just one damned thing after another.

Life is made up of little things.
Life is not all beer and skittles.
Life is one long process of getting tired. *(S. Butler)*
Life is short and time is swift.
Life is too short for mean anxieties.
Life is not measured by the time we live.
Life is real! Life is earnest!
  And the grave is not its goal. *(Longfellow)*
Life is the art of drawing conclusions from insufficient premises. *(S. Butler)*
Life is the co-ordination of actions. *(Spencer)*
Life, like a dome of many-colored glass,
  Stains the white radiance of Eternity. *(Shelley)*
Life, like poverty, makes strange bedfellows.
Life will always remain a gamble.
Live and let live.
Live not for time, but eternity.
Make the most of life you may.
Nothing can exceed the vanity of our existence but the folly of our pursuits. *(Goldsmith)*
O Life! thou art a galling load,
  Along a rough, a weary road. *(Burns)*
Plain living and high thinking . . . *(Wordsworth)*
Such a life, such a death.
The business of life is to go forward.
The life of man is a winter's day and a winter's way.
The life of man, solitary, poor, nasty, brutish, and short. *(Hobbes)*
The principal business of life is to enjoy it.
The secret of life is not to do what you like, but to like what you do.
The weariness, the fever, and the fret
  Here, where men sit and hear each other groan. *(Keats)*
The web of our life is of mingled yarn, good and ill together. *(Shakespeare)*
They do not live but linger.
This life is but a thoroughfare full of woe,
  And we but pilgrims passing to and fro. *(Chaucer)*
This life is but an inn, and we the passengers.
To him that lives well every form of life is good. *(S. Johnson)*
We live and die,
  But which is best, you know no more than I. *(Byron)*
We must not look for a golden life in an iron age.

Whilst I yet live, let me not live in vain.
A man cannot live on air. *(French)*
Draw the curtain, the farce is played out. *(Rabelais)*
Life is a fortress unknown to all of us. *(French)*
Life is a kind of sleep: old men sleep longest. *(French)*
Most men employ the earlier part of life to make the other part miserable. *(French)*
My business and my art is to live. *(Montaigne)*
One half of the world knows not how the other half lives. *(Rabelais)*
That long and cruel malady called life. *(French)*
Who lives will see. *(French)*
A bad life, a bad end. *(German)*
A useless life is an early death. *(Goethe)*
Live and let live. *(German)*
As leaves on the trees is the life of man. *(Homer)*
Choose the best life, habit will make it pleasant. *(Greek)*
Life holds more disappointment than satisfaction. *(Greek)*
Life is a battle. *(Greek)*
Life is a perilous voyage. *(Greek)*
Life is a stage, so learn to play your part. *(Greek)*
Life is not to be bought with heaps of gold. *(Homer)*
Life is short and art is long. *(Greek)*
Life is short to the fortunate, long to the unfortunate. *(Greek)*
Life is sweet. *(Greek)*
Live today, forget the past. *(Greek)*
Look at the end of life. *(Greek)*
Not life itself, but living ill, is evil. *(Greek)*
The life of man is the plaything of Fortune. *(Greek)*
They live ill who are always beginning to live. *(Greek)*
Today let me live well; none knows what may be tomorrow. *(Greek)*
We live, not as we wish, but as we can. *(Greek)*
Life is but a dewdrop on the lotus leaf. *(Tagore)*
There is more to life than increasing its speed. *(Gandhi)*
Good or bad, we must all live. *(Italian)*
He is master of another's life who slights his own. *(Italian)*
Live and learn. *(Italian)*
Quick with the quick, and dead with the dead. *(Italian)*
A short life is long enough for living well. *(Latin)*
As long as you live, keep learning how to live. *(Latin)*
He is not worthy of life that causes not life in another. *(Latin)*
He who lives for no one does not necessarily live for himself. *(Latin)*

It is a misery to be born, a pain to live, a trouble to die. *(St. Bernard)*
Let us live then and be glad,
 While young life's before us. [*Gaudeamus, igitur* . . .] *(Latin)*
Life is given us to be used. *(Latin)*
Life is long if it is full. *(Latin)*
Life is nearer every day to death. *(Latin)*
Live as if you were to die tomorrow. *(Latin)*
Live righteously; you shall die righteously. *(Latin)*
Live not to eat but eat to live. *(Latin)*
Live your own life, for you will die your own death. *(Latin)*
Man has been lent, not given, to life. *(Latin)*
Nature has given man no better than shortness of life. *(Latin)*
No one has died miserably who has lived well. *(Latin)*
Oh, life, how long to the wretched, how short to the happy! *(Latin)*
The hour which gives us life begins to take it away. *(Latin)*
They live ill who think they will live forever. *(Latin)*
To live at ease is not to live. *(Latin)*
Tomorrow you will live? Today itself is too late; the wise lived yesterday. *(Martial)*
We are always beginning to live, but are never living. *(Latin)*
We break up life into little bits and fritter them away. *(Latin)*
Life can only be understood backwards; but it must be lived forwards. *(Kierkegaard)*
A living mouse is better than a dead lion. *(Russian)*
He does not live more who lives longer. *(Russian)*
Be happy while ye'er leevin,
 For ye'er a lang time deid. *(Scottish)*
There is ay life for a living man. *(Scottish)*
He who lives a long life must pass through much evil. *(Spanish)*
Let us make hay while the sun shines. *(Spanish)*
The dead to the grave and the living to the loaf. *(Spanish)*
Until death, it is all life. *(Spanish)*
A man should live only so long as he can support himself. *(Yiddish)*
As you live on, you live to see everything. *(Yiddish)*
It is easy to live—hard to die. *(Yiddish)*
One wants to live and cannot; another can and will not. *(Yiddish)*
The worst life is better than the best death. *(Yiddish)*

LIGHT

A lamp unto my feet, and a light unto my path. *(Old Test., Psalms)*
And God said, Let there be light: and there was light. *(Old Test., Genesis)*

And the light shineth in darkness, and the darkness comprehended it not. *(New Test., John)*
I am the light of the world. *(New Test., John)*
Light is sown for the righteous. *(Old Test., Psalms)*
The shining light, that shineth more and more unto the perfect day. *(Old Test., Prov.)*
The true light, which lighteth every man that cometh into the world. *(New Test., John)*
Truly the light is sweet, and a pleasant thing it is for the eyes to behold the sun. *(Old Test., Eccles.)*
Walk while ye have the light, lest darkness come upon you. *(New Test., John)*

Every light has its shadow.
Hail, holy light, offspring of Heav'n firstborn. *(Milton)*
Hide not your light under a bushel.
It is as good to be in the dark as without light.
Lead, Kindly Light, amid the encircling gloom. *(Newman)*
Light—God's eldest daughter.
Light seeking light doth light of light beguile. *(Shakespeare)*
The light is naught for sore eyes.
The thing to do is to supply light and not heat.
The two noblest things which are sweetness and light. *(Swift)*
The more light a torch gives the shorter it lasts.
Every light is not the sun. *(French)*
More light! *(Goethe's last words.)*
Where there is much light, the shadows are deepest. *(German)*
Dry light is ever the best. *(Greek)*

LIGHTLY
Lightly come, lightly go.

LIGHTNING
Lightning strikes not twice in the same place.
When you can use the lightning it is better than cannon. *(Napoleon)*
It is vain to look for a defense against lightning. *(Latin)*

LIKE
As is the mother, so is her daughter. *(Old Test., Ezekiel)*
Like pot, like cover. *(Dutch)*
As like as an apple to an oyster.
As like in taste as chalk and cheese.
Let beggar match with beggar.

Like cow, like calf.
Like cures like.
Like draws to like.
Like loves like.
Like people, like priest.
Like to like.
Owl to owl—crow to crow.
As like as one pea to another. *(French)*
If you have known one, you have known them all. *(Latin)*
Like father, like son. *(Latin)*
Like master, like man. *(Latin)*
Like lip, like lettuce. *(Latin)*
Every sheep with its like. *(Spanish)*

LILY

Consider the lilies of the field . . . they toil not, neither do they spin . . . *(New Test., Matthew)*
Lilies are whitest in a blackamoor's hand.
Lilies that fester smell far worse than weeds. *(Shakespeare)*
White as any lily flower.

LINEN

Linen oft to water, soon to tatter.

LINK

If a link is broken, the whole chain breaks. *(Yiddish)*

LION

Even hares pull a lion by the beard when he is dead. *(Danish)*
A lion among sheep and a sheep among lions.
Destroy the lion while he is yet but a whelp.
If the lion was advised by the fox he would be cunning.
It is not good to wake a sleeping lion.
Lions make leopards tame. *(Shakespeare)*
The lion is not so fierce as they paint him.
The lion's skin is never cheap.
'Tis better playing with a lion's whelp
Than with an old one dying. *(Shakespeare)*
Who nourisheth a lion must obey him.
What weapons has a lion but himself? *(Keats)*
Even a lion must defend himself against the flies. *(German)*
It is an ill office to file the teeth of a lion. *(German)*

A lion may be beholden to a mouse. *(Greek)*
One, but that one a lion. *(Greek)*
Be the tail of a lion rather than the head of a fox. *(Hebrew)*
The lion is known by his claws. *(Italian)*
An old lion is better than a young ass. *(Latin)*
Do not pluck the beard of a dead lion. *(Latin)*

LIP

Lips are no part of the head: only a door for the mouth.
Lips, however rosy, must be fed.
The lips that touch liquor must never touch mine.

LISTEN

A pair of good ears will drain dry a hundred tongues.
Give us grace to listen well. *(Keble)*
It takes a great man to be a good listener.
Listeners seldom hear good of themselves.
He who listens at doors hears much more than he desires. *(French)*
He listens to good purpose who takes note. *(Italian)*
Take care what you say before a wall. *(Persian)*
To a good listener, a few words. *(Spanish)*

LITERATURE

Literature is a bad crutch, but a good walking-stick. *(Lamb)*

LITTLE

A little house well fill'd, a little land well till'd, and a little wife well will'd . . .
A little pot is soon hot.
A little stream drives a light mill.
A little wind kindles, much puts out the fire.
Little dogs start the hare, the great get her.
Little said is soonest mended.
Little strokes fell great oaks.
Of a little take a little and leave a little.
Use the little to get the big.
A little pack serves a little peddler. *(French)*
Little and often fills the purse. *(German)*
A little stone may upset a large cart. *(Italian)*
Little drops produce a shower. *(Latin)*
Many a little makes a mickle. *(Scottish)*

LOAD

It takes little effort to watch a man carry a load. *(Chinese)*

LOCK

No lock will hold against the power of gold.
No lock avails against a hatchet. *(French)*
A lock is made only for the honest man; the thief will break it. *(Yiddish)*

LONDON

He was born within the sound of Bow bells.
Like a Londoner, ask as much more as you will take.
London Bridge was made for wise men to go over and fools to go under.
London is a roost for every bird.

LONELINESS

The four corners of the room are the guests of the lonely man. *(Russian)*
The lonely man is at home everywhere. *(Russian)*

LONG

As long as a Welsh pedigree.
Long-looked-for comes at last.
Longer than a day without bread. *(Italian)*

LONGING

Better go away longing than loathing.

LOOK

A cat may look at a king.
A pitiful look asks enough.
A valiant man's look is more than a coward's sword.
Look before you leap.
Look high and fall low.
Look not for musk in a dog's kennel.
Lookers-on see more than the players.
One must not hang a man by his looks.
The proof of the pudding is in the eating, not in its looks.

LORD

A man is not a lord because he feeds off fine dishes.
The shadow of a lord is a cap for a fool. *(Italian)*

LOSE

Better lose the anchor than the whole ship. *(Dutch)*
What is lost in the fire must be sought in the ashes. *(Dutch)*
Better a little loss than a long sorrow.
Fear not the loss of the bell more than the loss of the steeple.
Give losers leave to speak.
He loseth indeed that loseth at last.
He loseth nothing that loseth not God.
I have lost all and found myself.
Little losses amaze, great tame.
Look for your money where you lost it.
Lose a leg rather than life.
Losers seekers, finders keepers.
Loss embraceth shame.
Loss is no shame.
No man can lose what he never had.
Praising what is lost makes the remembrance dear. *(Shakespeare)*
The cheerful loser is a winner.
The losing horse blames the saddle.
You may lose a fly to catch a trout.
After one loss come many. *(French)*
He has not lost all who has one cast left. *(French)*
If you have not lost a thing, you have it. *(Greek)*
Better lose the saddle than the horse. *(Italian)*
The loss which is unknown is no loss at all. *(Latin)*
A little loss frightens, a great one tames. *(Spanish)*
Let us not throw the rope after the bucket. *(Spanish)*
Losers are always in the wrong. *(Spanish)*
Where you lost your cloak, seek it. *(Spanish)*
We do not know what is good until we have lost it. *(Spanish)*
If you've nothing to lose, you can try everything. *(Yiddish)*

LOUSE

A louse is a beggar's companion.
Better a louse in the pot than no flesh at all.

LOVE

Love can make any place agreeable. *(Arabian)*
Better a dinner of herbs where love is, than a stalled ox and hatred therewith. *(Old Test., Prov.)*
Love is strong as death. *(Old Test., Song of Songs)*

Love is the fulfilling of the law. *(New Test., Romans)*
Many waters cannot quench love, neither can the floods drown it. *(Old Test., Song of Songs)*
There is no fear in love; but perfect love casteth out fear. *(New Test., I John)*
Thy love to me was wonderful, passing the love of women. *(Old Test., II Samuel)*
To be carnally minded is death. *(New Test., Romans)*
A man has a choice to begin love, but not to end it.
A penny-weight of love is worth a pound of law.
Absence sharpens love, presence strengthens it.
All for Love, and the World Well Lost. [*Title*]
All is fair in love and war.
All mankind love a lover.
An oyster may be crossed in love. *(Sheridan)*
As good love comes as goes.
As love knoweth no laws, so it regardeth no conditions.
Calf love, half love; old love, cold love.
Come blows, love goes.
Dry bread is better with love than a fat capon with fear.
Every man as he loveth, quoth the good man when he kissed the cow.
Hasty love is soon hot and soon cold.
Hatreds are the cinders of affection.
He loves bacon well that licks the swine-sty door.
He loves me for little that hates me for nought.
He that hath love in his breast hath spurs in his sides.
Hope is a lover's staff.
Hot love, hasty vengeance.
Hot love soon cold.
How wise are they that are but fools in love!
If Jack's in love, he's no judge of Jill's beauty.
If you hate a man, eat his bread; if you love him, do the same.
If you would be loved, love and be lovable.
In love there is no lack.
In love's wars, he who flieth is conqueror.
It is best to be off with the old love
  Before you go on with the new.
It is good to love the unknown.
Lad's love, a busk of broom,
  Hot awhile and soon done.
Labor is light where love doth pay.

Love and ambition admit no fellowship.
Love and lordship like fellowship.
Love and pride stock Bedlam.
Love and sorrow twins were born on a shining showery morn.
Love asks faith, and faith firmness.
Love built on beauty, soon as beauty dies.
Love can beauties spy
  In what seem faults to every common eye. *(Gay)*
Love can find a way.
Love cannot be compelled.
Love ceases to be a pleasure when it ceases to be a secret.
Love comes in at the window and goes out at the door.
Love finds an altar for forbidden fires. *(Pope)*
Love for love is evenest bought.
Love gains the shrine when pity opens the door.
Love has a tide.
Love in extremes can never long endure.
Love's a malady without a cure.
Love is a smoke raised with the fume of sighs. *(Shakespeare)*
Love is a talkative passion.
Love is a thing aye full of busy dread. *(Chaucer)*
Love is above King or Kaiser, lord or laws.
Love is blind all day and may not see. *(Chaucer)*
Love is blind, and lovers cannot see
  The pretty follies that themselves commit. *(Shakespeare)*
Love is he that alle thing may bind. *(Chaucer)*
Love is like linen, often changed, the sweeter.
Love is like the measles—all the worse when it comes late in life. *(Jerrold)*
Love is love for evermore.
Love is love's reward.
Love is master where he will.
Love is more than great richesse. *(Lydgate)*
Love is never paid but with pure love.
Love is the blossom where there blows
  Everything that lives or grows.
Love is the business of the idle, but the idleness of the busy. *(Bulwer-Lytton)*
Love is the lodestone of love.
Love is the noblest frailty of the mind.
Love is the salt of life.

Love is too young to know what conscience is . . . *(Shakespeare)*
Love is wiser than ambition.
Love is without law.
Love is without reason.
Love keeps his revels where there are but twain. *(Shakespeare)*
Love keeps the cold out better than a cloak.
Love knows no mean or measure.
Love lasteth as long as the money endureth.
Love Laughs at Locksmiths. [*Title*]
Love lives in cottages as well as in courts.
Love looks for love again.
Love makes a good eye squint.
Love maketh a wit of a fool.
Love me, and the world is mine.
Love me little, love me long.
Love me, love my dog.
Love needs no teaching.
Love of lads and fire of chips is soon in and soon out.
Love rules his kingdom without a sword.
Love sees no faults.
Love will creep where it cannot go.
Love will find out the way.
Love will not be drawn, but must be led.
Love's law is out of rule.
Lovers live by love as larks live by leeks.
Loving comes by looking.
Man's love is of man's life a thing apart,
'Tis woman's whole existence. *(Byron)*
Men have died from time to time, and worms have eaten them, but not for love. *(Shakespeare)*
Never was owl more blind than a lover.
No herb will cure love.
No love is foul, nor prison fair.
Nobody wants to kiss when they are hungry.
Old love is little worth when new is more preferred. *(Spenser)*
Of all the paths that lead to a woman's love
Pity's the straightest. *(Beaumont and Fletcher)*
Pains of love be sweeter far
Than all other pleasures are. *(Dryden)*
Peril proves who dearly loves.
Pity is but one remove from love.

Pity swells the tide of love.
Rather let me love than be in love. *(Overbury)*
Sad are the effects of love and pease porridge.
Shall I, wasting in despair,
  Die because a woman's fair? *(Wither)*
She deceiving, I believing,
  What can lovers wish for more? *(Sedley)*
She loves enough that does not hate.
She who has never loved has never lived.
Show thy love to win love.
Speak low, if you speak love. *(Shakespeare)*
Talking of love is making it.
The course of true love did never run smooth. *(Shakespeare)*
. . . the lover,
  Sighing like furnace, with a woeful ballad
  Made to his mistress' eyebrow. *(Shakespeare)*
The difference is wide that the sheets will not decide.
The falling out of lovers is the renewal of love.
The magic of first love is our ignorance that it can ever end. *(D'Israeli)*
The man that loves and laughs must sure do well.
The only present love demands is love.
The sight of lovers feedeth those in love. *(Shakespeare)*
The sweets of love are mixed with tears.
There's beggary in the love that can be reckoned. *(Shakespeare)*
There is no hiding from lovers' eyes.
There lives within the very flame of love
  A kind of wick or snuff that will abate it. *(Shakespeare)*
They do not love that do not show their love.
They love indeed who quake to say they love.
They love too much that die for love.
'Tis better to have loved and lost
  Than never to have loved at all. *(Tennyson)*
'Tis impossible to love and be wise.
To love her is a liberal education.
To love is to believe, to hope, to know. *(Waller)*
Under the blanket the black one is as good as the white.
Until I truly loved, I was alone.
When the wolf comes in at the door, love flies out at the window.
Where love is, there's no lack.
Who ever lov'd, that lov'd not at first sight? *(Marlowe)*
Whom we love best, to them we can say least.

Whoso loves believes the impossible.
With all thy faults, I love thee still. *(Cowper)*
But one always returns to his first love. *(French)*
By beating love decays. *(French)*
Change everything except your loves. *(Voltaire)*
Delicacy is to love what grace is to beauty. *(French)*
Good-day spectacles, farewell girls. *(French)*
In their first passions, women love the lover, and in the others they love love. *(La Rochefoucauld)*
It's love that makes the world go 'round. *(French)*
It is not reason that governs love. *(French)*
Love begins with love. *(French)*
Love does much, money everything. *(French)*
Love does not depend upon our will. *(French)*
Love is an egoism of two. *(French)*
Love is stronger than death. *(French)*
Love is the touchstone of virtue. *(French)*
Love makes the time pass. Time makes love pass. *(French)*
Love never dies of starvation, but often of indigestion. *(French)*
Love often gets the better of reason. *(French)*
Love, smoke, and a cough cannot be hid. *(French)*
Love teaches asses to dance. *(French)*
One's sweetheart is never ugly. *(French)*
The only victory over love is flight. *(Napoleon)*
The woman we love will always be in the right. *(French)*
There are many who would never have been in love, if they had never heard love spoken of. *(La Rochefoucauld)*
There is no such thing as eternal love. *(French)*
True love is the ripe fruit of a lifetime. *(Lamartine)*
To love is to choose. *(French)*
When love is satisfied all charm is gone. *(French)*
When we love, it is the heart that judges. *(French)*
A fence between makes love more keen. *(German)*
If I love you, what business is that of yours? *(Goethe)*
Love knows hidden paths. *(German)*
Love lessens woman's delicacy and increases man's. *(Richter)*
Love's anger is fuel to love. *(German)*
We learn only from those we love. *(Goethe)*
A lovers' quarrel is short-lived. *(Greek)*
He is not a lover who does not love forever. *(Greek)*
Let no man think he is loved by any when he loves none. *(Greek)*

Love is an appetite of generation by the mediation of beauty. *(Socrates)*
Love, resistless in battle. *(Greek)*
Lovers derive their pleasures from their misfortunes. *(Greek)*
Lovers' oaths enter not the ears of the gods. *(Greek)*
Who love too much, hate in the same extreme. *(Greek)*
Knowledge and love together agree not. *(Italian)*
Love is an excuse for its own faults. *(Italian)*
Love is blind, but sees afar. *(Italian)*
Lust is the oldest lion of them all. *(Italian)*
To be able to say how much you love is to love but little. *(Italian)*
Where love is, there the eye is. *(Italian)*
Who has no children does not know what love is. *(Petrarch)*
A woman either loves or hates; there is no third course. *(Latin)*
All love is vanquished by a succeeding love. *(Latin)*
Everyone is blind when maddened by love. *(Latin)*
For what may we lovers not hope? *(Vergil)*
Habit causes love. *(Latin)*
He who falls in love meets a worse fate than he who leaps from a rock. *(Latin)*
He who says overmuch "I love not," is in love. *(Latin)*
How wretched is the man who loves! *(Latin)*
In love, pain and pleasure are at strife. *(Latin)*
Insidious love glides into defenseless breasts. *(Latin)*
Let every lover be pale; that is the color that suits him. *(Latin)*
Listlessness and silence denote the lover. *(Latin)*
Love abounds in honey and poison. *(Latin)*
Love begets love. *(Latin)*
Love is the same in everyone. *(Latin)*
Love conquers all; let us too yield to love. *(Vergil)*
Love is a credulous thing. *(Latin)*
Love is a kind of warfare. *(Latin)*
Love is faithless. *(Latin)*
Love must be fostered with soft words. *(Latin)*
Lover, lunatic. *(Latin)*
Lovers remember all things. *(Latin)*
O happy race of men, if love, which rules heaven, rule your mind! *(Boëthius)*
Only a wise man knows how to love. *(Latin)*
Plenty destroys passion. *(Latin)*
Spice a dish with love, and it pleases every palate. *(Latin)*
Take away Leisure, and Cupid's bow is broken. *(Ovid)*

The falling out of lovers is the renewal of love. *(Latin)*
The less my hope the hotter my love. *(Latin)*
The lover's soul dwells in the body of another. *(Latin)*
The man who loves is easy of belief. *(Latin)*
There are as many pangs in love as shells upon the shore. *(Latin)*
There is love for none except him whom fortune favors. *(Latin)*
There is no living in love without suffering. *(Latin)*
'Tis unseemly for the old man to love. *(Latin)*
To love and be wise is scarcely given to a god. *(Latin)*
Two souls in one, two hearts into one heart. *(Latin)*
Venus lends deaf ears to love's deceits. *(Latin)*
Whatsoever love commands, it is not safe to despise. *(Latin)*
Who can deceive a lover? *(Latin)*
Who can give law to lovers? *(Latin)*
Without bread and wine Venus will starve. *(Latin)*
You must anger a lover if you wish him to love. *(Latin)*
One can't choose when one is going to love. *(Norwegian)*
But I in love was mute and still. *(Pushkin)*
Fanned fires and forced love ne'er did weel. *(Scottish)*
Love is of sae mickle might,
  That it all paines makis light. *(Barbour)*
Slighted love is sair to bide. *(Scottish)*
The wisest man the warl' e'er saw,
  He dearly lov'd the lasses, O. *(Burns)*
He loves thee well who makes thee weep. *(Spanish)*
Love is the child of illusion, and the parent of disillusion. *(Unamuno)*
Love kills happiness, happiness kills love. *(Spanish)*
If you are in love fly to the mountain. *(Turkish)*

LOW
If you make yourself low, people will tread on your head. *(Yiddish)*

LOYALTY
Loyalty is the holiest good in the human heart. *(Latin)*

LUCK
Bad luck often brings good luck.
Give me hap and cast me in the sea.
Good luck comes by cuffing.
Good luck never comes too late.
Good luck reaches farther than long arms.
He was born with a caul.

He was born with a silver spoon in his mouth.
Ill luck is worse than found money.
It is better to be lucky than wise.
Luck for fools and chance for the ugly.
Lucky at cards, unlucky in love.
Lucky men need no counsel.
Some run half-way to meet ill luck.
The more the knave, the better luck.
He that has ill luck gets usage. *(French)*
My right eye itches, some good luck is near. *(Greek)*
Ill luck comes by pounds and goes away by ounces. *(Italian)*
A lucky man is rarer than a white crow. *(Latin)*
Against a lucky man even a god has little power. *(Latin)*
The gods delight in odd numbers. *(Latin)*
When good luck comes to thee, take it in. *(Spanish)*
When ill luck falls asleep, let nobody wake her. *(Spanish)*
For luck one does not need wisdom. *(Yiddish)*
If luck comes to you, offer him a chair. *(Yiddish)*
If luck is your way, your ox calves. *(Yiddish)*
It is better not to be born at all than to be born luckless. *(Yiddish)*
It is better that luck seek the man than man seek luck. *(Yiddish)*
Luck alone does not help a man, if the man does not help along. *(Yiddish)*

LUXURY

A rich man's superfluities are often a poor man's redemption.
Give us the luxuries of life, and we will dispense with its necessities. *(Motley)*
The dainties of the great are the tears of the poor.
The luxurious want many things, the covetous all things.
Those who never had a cushion don't miss it.
Too much plenty makes mouth dainty.
Luxury is like a wild beast, first made fiercer with tying, and then let loose. *(Montaigne)*
The superfluous—a very necessary thing. *(Voltaire)*
It is the superfluous things for which men sweat. *(Latin)*
Superfluities do not hurt. *(Latin)*

MACHINERY

The mystery of mysteries is to view machines making machines. *(D'Israeli)*

Things are in the saddle and ride mankind. *(Emerson)*

Machinery has greatly increased the number of well-to-do idlers. *(Marx)*

MADNESS

The different sorts of madness are innumerable. *(Arabian)*

A mad beast must have a sober driver.

A mad bull is not to be tied up with a pack thread.

A man of gladness seldom falls into madness.

As mad as a March hare.

Every man is mad on some point.

Fetter strong madness in a silken thread. *(Shakespeare)*

Have you not maggots in your brain?

Madness in great ones must not unwatched go. *(Shakespeare)*

Sanity is madness put to a good use.

The mad dog bites his master.

Though this be madness, yet there is method in it. *(Shakespeare)*

To lose your mind you must have a mind to lose.

You'll never be mad, you are of so many minds.

Whom the gods would destroy they first make mad. *(Greek)*

Every madman thinks all other men mad. *(Latin)*

We are all mad at some time or other. *(Latin)*

Who then is sane? He who is not a fool. *(Latin)*

With the mad it is necessary to be mad. *(Latin)*

MAHOMET

If the mountain will not come to Mahomet, Mahomet must go to the mountain. *(Bacon)*

MAGISTRATE

Magistrates are to obey as well as execute laws.

MAID

Judge a maid at the kneading trough and not in a dance. *(Danish)*
A maid and a virgin are not all one.
A maid often seen, a gown often worn,
  Are disesteemed and held in scorn.
A maid hath no tongue but thought. *(Shakespeare)*
A maid should be seen but not heard.
A maid that giveth yieldeth.
A maid that laughs is half taken.
All are not maidens that wear fair hair.
Every maid is undone.
Maids' nays are nothing; they are shy
  But do desire what they deny. *(Herrick)*
Maidens must be mild and meek,
  Swift to hear and slow to speak.
Maidens should be mim till they're married.
Poor maids have more lovers than husbands.
She who scorns a man must die a maid.
When maidens sue, men give like gods. *(Shakespeare)*
When the maid leaves the door open, the cat's in fault.
While the tall maid is stooping, the little one hath swept the house.
Women, dying maids, lead apes in hell.
He must have keen eyes that would know a maid at sight. *(German)*
Glass and a maid are ever in danger. *(Italian)*
To win the mistress, first bribe the maid. *(Latin)*
A maiden's heart is a dark forest. *(Russian)*
The virtuous maid and the broken leg must stay at home. *(Spanish)*
If a maid marries an old man, she becomes a young widow. *(Yiddish)*
Marry off a maid, or she'll marry herself off. *(Yiddish)*

MAJORITY

A majority is always the best repartee. (*D'Israeli*)
One, on God's side, is a majority. (*W. Phillips*)
The opinion of the majority is not the final proof of what is right. *(Schiller)*
The majority never has right on its side. *(Ibsen)*

MAKE

He that makes one basket can make a hundred.
Make or mar.

You can't make an omelet without breaking some eggs. *(French)*
What man has made, man can destroy. *(German)*

MALICE

Malice bears down truth. *(Shakespeare)*
Malice drinketh up the greatest part of its own poison.
Malice hath a strong memory.
Malice never spoke well.
Malice seldom wants a mark to shoot at.
The malice of a witty thing is the barb that makes it stick.
He who digs out malicious talk disturbs his own peace. *(Latin)*
Malice feeds on the living. *(Latin)*
Malice is cunning. *(Latin)*
Malice is blind. *(Latin)*
Malice tells what it sees, but not the causes. *(Latin)*
The malevolent have hidden teeth. *(Latin)*
The malice of one man quickly becomes the ill word of all. *(Latin)*

MAMMON

Ye cannot serve God and Mammon. *(New Test., Matthew)*

MAN

A spectacle unto the earth, and to angels. *(New Test., I Corinth.)*
He hath made the small and the great, and careth for all alike. *(Apocrypha)*
I am fearfully and wonderfully made. *(Old Test., Psalms)*
Male and female created he them. *(Old Test., Genesis)*
Man being in honor abideth not: he is like the beasts that perish. *(Old Test., Psalms)*
Man is born to trouble as the sparks fly upward. *(Old Test., Prov.)*
Man that is born of woman is of few days, and full of trouble. *(Old Test., Job)*
The first man is of the earth, earthy. *(New Test., I Corinth.)*
Thou hast made him a little lower than the angels. *(Old Test., Psalms)*
Men and beasts are all alike. *(Chinese)*
What the superior man seeks is in himself: what the small man seeks is in others. *(Confucius)*
He is a man who acts like a man. *(Danish)*
A man is not known till he comes to honor. *(Dutch)*
A man can do no more than he can.
A man cannot live by the air.
A man far from his good is near his harm.

A man has his hour, and a dog his day.
A man is a lion in his own cause.
A man is a man though he have but a hose on his head.
A man is as good as he has to be; a woman as bad as she dares.
A man is valued according to his own estimate of himself.
A man of words and not of deeds
  Is like a garden full of weeds.
A nice man is a man of nasty ideas. *(Swift)*
All men are bad, and in their badness reign. *(Shakespeare)*
All sorts and conditions of men. *(Bk. Com. Prayer)*
Every man is an impossibility until he is born. *(Emerson)*
God made him, and therefore let him pass for a man. *(Shakespeare)*
Good men and bad men are each less so than they seem.
He will be a man before his mother.
I am as bad as the worst, but thank God I am as good as the best. *(Whitman)*
Man, an animal that makes bargains. *(Adam Smith)*
Man is a beast when shame stands off from him. *(Swinburne)*
Man is a gaming animal. *(Lamb)*
Man is a machine into which we put food and produce thought.
Man is a name of honor for a king.
Man is a noble animal, splendid in ashes, and pompous in the grave. *(Sir T. Browne)*
Man is a substance clad in shadows.
Man is a toad-eating animal.
Man is a tool-making animal.
Man is an animal that cooks his victuals.
Man is fire and woman tow; the devil comes and sets them in a blaze.
Man is Heaven's masterpiece.
Man is Nature's sole mistake.
Man is the bad child of the universe.
Man is the miracle in nature.
Man is the only animal that blushes. Or needs to. *(Mark Twain)*
Man is the only animal that spits.
Man is to man, the sorest, surest ill. *(Young)*
Mankind are earthen jugs with spirits in them. *(Hawthorne)*
Mankind, when left to themselves, are unfit for their own government. *(Washington)*
Men are blind in their own cause.
Men are but children of a larger growth. *(Dryden)*
Men are not angels.

Men have marble, women waxen, minds. *(Shakespeare)*
Men talk wisely but live foolishly.
Men work and think, but women feel.
Modes and customs vary, but human nature is the same. *(Chesterfield)*
Nature revolves, but man advances. *(Young)*
No greater shame to man than inhumanity. *(Spenser)*
No man is born wise or learned.
O the difference of man and man! *(Shakespeare)*
The greatest enemy to man is man.
The only laughing animal is man.
The proper study of mankind is Man. *(Pope)*
There's not so bad a Jill
  But there's as bad a Will.
Though every prospect pleases,
  And only man is vile. *(Heber)*
What then is man? The smallest part of nothing. *(Young)*
Where soil is, men grow,
  Whether to weeds or flowers. *(Keats)*
Women commend a modest man but like him not.
Yes, all men are dust, but some are gold-dust.
You are not wood, you are not stones, but men. *(Shakespeare)*
It is more necessary to study men than books. *(French)*
Man is but a reed, the weakest in nature, but he is a thinking reed. *(Pascal)*
Man is Creation's masterpiece. But who says so?—Man. *(French)*
Man proposes and God disposes. *(French)*
Men make laws, women make manners. *(French)*
Man has a wild beast within him. *(German)*
I teach you the Superman. Man is something which shall be surpassed. *(Nietzsche)*
Man is a rope connecting animal and superman. *(Nietzsche)*
Man—the aristocrat among the animals. *(Heine)*
Only he fears men, who does not avoid them. *(Goethe)*
The noble man is only God's image. *(German)*
For men on earth 'tis best never to be born at all . . . *(Homer)*
I am seeking a man. *(Diogenes)*
Man is a bubble. *(Greek)*
Man is a little soul carrying around a corpse. *(Greek)*
Man is but breath and shadow. *(Epictetus)*
Man is the measure of all things. *(Protagoras)*
Man is the plumeless genus of bipeds. *(Plato)*

Man to man is a god. *(Greek)*
Man was made by the gods for them to try and play withal. *(Greek)*
Most men are bad. *(Greek)*
Nothing in life is certain for men, children of a day. *(Greek)*
The fool of fate—man. *(Greek)*
The lot of man: to suffer and to die. *(Greek)*
Forget not that you are a man. *(Latin)*
It is not fit that men should be compared with gods. *(Latin)*
Man is a reasoning animal. *(Latin)*
Man is dearer to the gods than he is to himself. *(Latin)*
Man is to man a wolf. *(Latin)*
Nothing is more wretched or more proud than man. *(Latin)*
O how contemptible a thing is man unless he can raise himself above humanity. *(Seneca)*
We are dust and shadow. *(Horace)*
What dwarfs men are! *(Latin)*
Even though he's a pig, he's still a man. *(Russian)*
Man carries his superiority inside, animals theirs outside. *(Russian)*
A man's a man for a' that. *(Burns)*
Man's inhumanity to man
  Makes countless thousands mourn. *(Burns)*
A handsome man is not quite poor. *(Spanish)*
A man cannot both ring the bell and walk in the procession. *(Spanish)*
A man is the child of his works. *(Spanish)*
Every man is as God made him—and often worse. *(Spanish)*
A man is one who is faithful to his word. *(Spanish)*
Man is what he is, not what he was. *(Spanish)*

MANNERS
"After you" is good manners.
Do on the hill what you would do in the hall.
Everyone think himself well-bred.
Gentle blood will gentle manners breed. *(Spenser)*
Good breeding consist in concealing how much we think of ourselves and how little we think of the other person. *(Mark Twain)*
Good breeding is the blossom of good sense.
Good manners are made up of petty sacrifices.
He that hath more manners than he ought,
  Is more a fool than he is thought.
Manners before morals. *(O. Wilde)*
Manners makyth man.

Meat is much, but manners are more.
The manners of all nations are equally bad.
Unmannerly a little is better than troublesome a great deal.
Other times, other manners. *(French)*
The society of good women is the foundation of good manners. *(Goethe)*
Don't shake hands too eagerly. *(Greek)*
Evil communications corrupt good manners. *(Menander)*
Degenerate manners grow apace. *(Latin)*
Everyone's manners make his fortune. *(Latin)*
Suit your manners to the man. *(Latin)*
Things which are unbecoming are unsafe. *(Latin)*
What times! What manners! *(Cicero)*
As are the times, so are the manners. *(Spanish)*
Office changes manners. *(Spanish)*

MARCH

March comes in like a lion and goes out like a lamb.
A load of March dust is worth a ducat. *(German)*

MARKET

Forsake not the market for the toll.
No grass grows in the market-place.
The market is the best garden.
You must sell as markets go.
No one has a good market for bad goods. *(French)*
Three women and a goose make a market. *(German)*
He loses his market who has nothing to sell. *(Spanish)*

MARRIAGE

And they two shall be one flesh. *(New Test., Matthew)*
Bone of my bones, and flesh of my flesh. *(Old Test., Genesis)*
It is better to marry than to burn. *(New Test., I Corinth.)*
It is not good that man should be alone. *(Old Test., Genesis)*
Marriage is honorable in all. *(New Test., Hebrews)*
Therefore shall a man leave his father and mother, and shall cleave unto his wife. *(Old Test., Genesis)*
What therefore God hath joined together, let not man put asunder. *(New Test., Matthew)*
To marry once is a duty, twice a folly, thrice is madness. *(Dutch)*
A man may weep upon his wedding day. *(Shakespeare)*
A man without a wife is but half a man.

A married man turns his staff into a stake.
A poor wedding is a prologue to misery.
A young man married is a young man marr'd. *(Shakespeare)*
Advice to those about to marry—Don't. *("Punch" 1845)*
Age and wedlock tame man and beast.
As your wedding ring wears, you'll wear off your cares.
Before you marry, be sure of a house wherein to tarry.
Better be half hanged than ill wed.
Better an old man's darling than a young man's warling.
Better to sit up all night than to go to bed with a dragon.
Doänt thou marry for munny, but goä wheer munny is! *(Tennyson)*
Down to Gehenna or up to the Throne,
He travels the fastest who travels alone. *(Kipling)*
Every woman should marry, and no man. *(Disraeli)*
First thrive and then wive.
For it ne sits not unto fresh May
Forto be coupled to cold January. *(Lydgate)*
Hanging and wiving go by destiny.
Hasty marriage seldom proveth well.
He has a great fancy to marriage that goes to the devil for a wife.
He that is needy when he is married shall be rich when he is buried.
He that marries ere he be wise, will die ere he thrive.
He that marries for money, earns it.
He that marries for wealth, sells his liberty.
He that marries late, marries ill.
In marriage cheat who can.
In marriage the husband should have two eyes, and the wife but one.
It is commonly a weak man who marries for love. *(S. Johnson)*
It is good to marry late or never.
It is hard to wive and thrive both in a year.
It is not marriage that fails; it is people that fail.
Keep thy eyes wide open before marriage, and half shut afterwards. *(Franklin)*
Like blood, like goods, and like age,
Make the happiest marriage.
Many a good hanging prevents a bad marriage.
Marriage halves our griefs, doubles our joys, and quadruples our expenses.
Marriage has many pains, but celibacy has no pleasures. *(S. Johnson)*
Marriage is a lottery.
Marriage is honorable, but housekeeping's a shrew.

Marriage is nothing but a civil contract. *(Selden)*
Marriage leapeth up upon the saddle, and repentance upon the crupper.
Marriages are made in heaven.
Marry a wife of thine own degree.
Marry first and love will follow.
Marry for love and work for siller.
Marry in May, repent alway.
Marry in Lent, live to repent.
Marry too soon, and you'll repent too late.
Marry your son when you will, your daughter when you can.
More belongs to marriage than four bare legs in a bed.
Needles and pins, needles and pins:
When a man marries, his trouble begins.
Oh! how many torments lie in the small circle of a wedding ring!
One fool at least in every married couple.
One was never married, and that's his hell; another is, and that's his plague.
One year of joy, another of comfort, and all the rest of content.
Remember, it is as easy to marry a rich woman as a poor one.
Second marriage: Another instance of the triumph of hope over experience. *(S. Johnson)*
She who is born handsome is born married.
Such as marry but to a fair face, tie themselves oft to a foul bargain.
The difference is wide that sheets will not decide.
The first wife is matrimony, the second company, the third heresy.
There as my heart is set, there will I wive. *(Chaucer)*
Though women are angels, yet wedlock's the devil. *(Byron)*
'Tis love alone can make our fetters please.
To get married is to tie a knot with the tongue that you can't undo with your teeth.
We bachelors laugh and show our teeth, but you married men laugh till your heart ache.
We should marry to please ourselves, not other people.
We wedded men live in sorrow and care. *(Chaucer)*
Wedlock's a lane where there is no turning.
Wedlock is a padlock.
When the husband is fire and the wife tow, the devil easily sets all in a flame.
Where there's marriage without love, there will be love without marriage.
Who marries does well; who marries not does better.

Who marries for love without money has good nights and sorry days.
Who wives for dower resigns his own power.
A good marriage should be between a blind wife and a deaf husband. *(Montaigne)*
Always say "No," and so you will never be married. *(French)*
Love is often a fruit of marriage. *(French)*
Marriage is a lottery in which men stake their liberty and women their happiness. *(French)*
Marriage is the only venture open to the cowardly. *(Voltaire)*
Marriages are made in heaven and consummated on earth. *(French)*
No one marries but repents. *(French)*
When a man's friend marries, all is over between them. *(French)*
Women when they marry buy a cat in the bag. *(French)*
An impudent face never marries. *(German)*
Marriage is heaven or hell. *(German)*
The old man who is married bids death to the feast. *(German)*
A poor man who marries a wealthy woman gets a ruler and not a wife. *(Greek)*
Be careful to marry a woman who lives near to you. *(Greek)*
For a young man, not yet; for an old man, never at all. *(Greek)*
I never married and I wish my father never had. *(Greek)*
I prefer a man without money, to money without a man. *(Greek)*
It is not beauty that bewitches bridegrooms but nobleness. *(Greek)*
Let like mate with like. *(Greek)*
Marriage is an evil—but a necessary evil. *(Greek)*
Marry in haste, and repent at leisure. *(Greek)*
Thrice ill-starred is he who marries when he is poor. *(Greek)*
Whichever you do, you will repent it. *(Greek)*
Go down the ladder when you marry a wife; go up when you choose a friend. *(Hebrew)*
Marriage makes or mars a man. *(Italian)*
No pot so ugly as not to find a cover. *(Italian)*
Humble wedlock is better than proud virginity. *(St. Augustine)*
If you would wed fitly, wed in your station. *(Latin)*
Mind, not body, makes marriage lasting. *(Latin)*
Nothing is better than a single life. *(Horace)*
The first bond of society is marriage. *(Latin)*
Everyone sings as he has the gift, and marries as he has the luck. *(Portuguese)*
Don't praise marriage on the third day, but after the third year. *(Russian)*

The only thing that can hallow marriage is love. *(Tolstoy)*
Why so flushed? I want to get married.—Why so pale? I am married. *(Russian)*
A bonny bride is soon buskit. *(Scottish)*
A man may woo whar he will, but wed whar he is wierd. *(Scottish)*
Better hand loose than an ill tethering. *(Scottish)*
Better wed over the mixen than over the moor. [*i.e. wed nearer home*] *(Scottish)*
If marriages are made in heaven, you have but few friends there. *(Scottish)*
He that goes far to marry goes to be deceived or to deceive. *(Spanish)*
Honest men marry quickly, but wise men not at all. *(Spanish)*
It goes ill with the house when the hen sings and the cock is silent. *(Spanish)*
The day you marry it's either kill or cure. *(Spanish)*
Observe the mother and take the daughter. *(Turkish)*
The marriage ceremony takes only an hour, but its troubles last a lifetime. *(Yiddish)*
When an old man marries a young wife, he becomes young and she old. *(Yiddish)*

MARSHAL

Every French soldier carries a marshal's bâton in his knapsack. *(Napoleon)*

MARTYR

There are as many martyrs for bad causes as for good ones.
Who falls for love of God, shall rise a star. *(Jonson)*
Who perisheth in needless danger is the devil's martyr.
I am very fond of truth, but not at all of martyrdom. *(Voltaire)*
It is the cause, not the death, that makes the martyr. *(French)*
The blood of the martyrs is the seed of the church. *(Tertullian)*
It is the martyrs who create faith rather than faith that creates martyrs. *(Unamuno)*

MASTER

What belongs to the master is forbidden to the slave. *(Arabian)*
No man can serve two masters. *(New Test., Matthew)*
A falling master makes a standing servant.
A master of straw eats a servant of steel.
Better a master be feared than despised.
Early master, long knave.
Everyone is a master and a servant.

He can ill be master that never was scholar.
He that is master must serve.
He that is master of himself will soon be master of others.
He that will not serve one master will have to serve many.
In every art it is good to have a master.
Masters should be sometimes blind and sometimes deaf.
One eye of the master's sees more than ten of the servants'.
One master in a house is enough.
Such mistress, such Nan; such master, such man.
We cannot all be masters. *(Shakespeare)*
The master eats the flesh, the servant must gnaw the bone. *(German)*
Nothing fattens the horse so much as the master's eye. *(Greek)*
Masters' hints are commands. *(Italian)*
The master should bring honor to the house, not the house to its master. *(Cicero)*
The master's face does more than the back of his head. *(Latin)*
As is the master so is his dog. *(Spanish)*
He who has two masters to serve must lie to one of them. *(Spanish)*
If the abbot sings well, the novice is not far behind him. *(Spanish)*
Masters amuse themselves, servants die. *(Turkish)*
Not everyone who sits in the seat of honor is master. *(Yiddish)*

MAXIM

A good maxim is never out of season.
Maxims are the condensed good sense of nations.
The maxims of men disclose their hearts. *(French)*

MAY

A hot May makes a fat church-yard.
May makes or mars the wheat.
He has a very hard heart that does not love in May. *(French)*
Do not leave off your coat till May. *(Spanish)*

MEADOW

A thin meadow is soon mowed.

MEAL

Better be meals many than one too merry.
He fasts enough that has a bad meal.
Two hungry meals make the third a glutton.
All state and nothing on the plate. *(French)*
A good meal is worth hanging for. *(German)*

MEANNESS
Meanness is the parent of insolence.

MEANS
Use the means and God will give the blessing.

MEASURE
Just scales and full measure injure no man. *(Chinese)*
Better twice measured than once wrong. *(Danish)*
Don't measure others' corn by your own bushel.
Good weight and measure is heaven's treasure.
"Measure for Measure." [*Title*]
There is a measure in all things.
Measure yourself by your own foot. *(Latin)*
You can't measure the whole world with your own yardstick. *(Yiddish)*

MEAT
A piece of kid is worth two of a cat.
All meat is not the same in every man's mouth.
God sendeth and giveth both mouth and meat.
Much meat, much maladies.
One man's meat is another man's poison.
That meat tastes best which costs nothing.
To a full belly all meat is bad. *(Italian)*
Where they eat your meat let them pick your bones. *(Spanish)*
Broth made of cheap meat is tasteless. *(Turkish)*

MEDAL
Every medal has its reverse. *(Italian)*

MEDDLING
Every fool will be meddling. *(Old Test., Prov.)*
He who tastes every man's broth sometimes burns his mouth. *(Danish)*
Of little meddling comes great ease.
Put not thy hand between the bark and the tree.
Who meddleth in all things may shoe the gosling.
Never thrust your sickle into another's corn. *(Latin)*

MEDICINE
Starve the measles and nourish the smallpox. *(Chinese)*
A disease known is half cured.
A salve there is for every sore.
An ounce of prevention is worth a pound of cure.

Different sores must have different salves.
If physic do not work, prepare for the kirk.
If the pills were pleasant, they would not want gilding.
Many dishes, many diseases; many medicines, few cures.
Medicines were not meant to live on.
One is not so soon healed as hurt.
Pills must be bolted, not chewed. *(French)*
Strongest maladies need strongest remedies. *(French)*
By opposites opposites are cured. *(Greek)*
It is part of the cure to wish to be cured. *(Latin)*
Like cures like. [*Similia similibus curantur.*] *(Latin)*
Meet the malady on its way. *(Latin)*
No one tries desperate remedies at first. *(Latin)*
Not even medicines can master incurable diseases. *(Latin)*
Nothing hinders a cure so much as frequent change of medicine. *(Latin)*
There are some remedies worse than the disease. *(Latin)*
God who sends the wound sends the medicine. *(Spanish)*
What cures Sancho makes Martha sick. *(Spanish)*

MEDIOCRITY

To mediocrity genius is unforgivable.
Commonplace and cringing, one gets everywhere. *(Beaumarchais)*
Mediocrity is praised in all cases. *(French)*
Mediocrity is safest. *(Latin)*

MEEKNESS

Blessed are the meek: for they shall inherit the earth.
(New Test., Matthew)
Meekness is not weakness.
They can be meek that have no other cause. *(Shakespeare)*

MEETING

Journeys end in lovers meeting. *(Shakespeare)*
Men meet, mountains never.

MELANCHOLY

As melancholy as a cat.
As melancholy as a dog.
If there be a hell upon earth, it is to be found in the melancholy man's heart. *(Burton)*
Melancholy is the nurse of frenzy. *(Shakespeare)*
Melancholy is the pleasure of being sad. *(French)*

MEMORY

All complain of want of memory but none of want of judgment.
Good memories have ill judgments.
Memory, the warder of the brain. *(Shakespeare)*
Memory of happiness makes misery woeful.
Sorrow remembered sweetens present joy.
That which is bitter to endure may be sweet to remember.
The true art of memory is the art of attention.
We have all forgot more than we remember.
Many a man fails to become a thinker for the sole reason that his memory is too good. *(Nietzsche)*
How sweet to remember the trouble that is past! *(Greek)*
There is no greater sorrow than to recall, in misery, the time when we were happy. *(Dante)*
Memory is the treasury and guardian of all things. *(Latin)*

MEND

Either mend or end.
Never too late to mend.

MERCHANT

He is no merchant who always gains. *(Dutch)*
A merchant that gains not, loseth.
He is not a merchant bare,
That hath money, worth, or 'ware.
He that could know what would be dear,
Need be a merchant but one year.
The merchant that loses cannot laugh.
The art of the merchant lies more in getting paid than in making sales. *(Spanish)*

MERCY

Mercy to the criminal may be cruelty to the people. *(Arabian)*
Blessed are the merciful: for they shall obtain mercy. *(New Test., Matthew)*
As you are stout be merciful.
God strikes with his finger, and not with his arm.
Mercy surpasses justice. *(Chaucer)*
Open the bowels of compassion.
The quality of mercy is not strain'd. *(Shakespeare)*
Mercy is better than vengeance. *(Greek)*

Mercy sways the brave. *(Greek)*
Mercy often gives death instead of life. *(Latin)*

MERIT
Merit is worthier than fame.
Nature makes merit and fortune uses it. *(French)*

MERRY
Is any merry? let him sing psalms. *(New Test., James)*
The merry heart maketh a cheerful countenance. *(Old Test., Prov.)*
As merry as a cricket.
Aye be merry as you can,
  For love ne'er delights in a sorrowful man.
It is good to be merry and wise.
It is good to be merry at meat.
It's merry when men meet.
The more the merrier, the fewer the better fare. *(French)*
A merry man lives as long as a sad one. *(Latin)*

MESSENGER
If you want a thing done, go; if not, send.

MIGHT
Either by might or by sleight.
Might overcometh right.
Might and right govern everything; might till right is ready. *(French)*
The reason of the strongest is always the best. *(La Fontaine)*
Where might is master, justice is servant. *(German)*
I proclaim that might is right . . . *(Plato)*
The dolphin's might is useless upon the ground. *(Greek)*

MILK
Don't cry over spilled milk.
If you would live forever, wash milk from your liver.
What is taken in with the milk, only goes out with the soul. *(Russian)*

MILL
An honest miller hath a golden thumb. *(Chaucer)*
As good water goes by the mill as drives it.
In vain does the mill clack if the miller his hearing lack.
No mill, no meal.
The miller grinds more men's corn than one.
The same water that drives the milk decayeth it.

The mill does not grind with the water that is past. *(French)*
The mills of the gods grind slowly, but they grind exceeding small. *(Greek)*
He who gets to the mill gets befloured. *(Italian)*
Much water goes by the mill that the miller knows not of. *(Italian)*
The first at the mill grinds first. *(Italian)*
The mill gains by going, and not by standing still. *(Spanish)*

MIND

A vacant mind is open to all suggestions, as a hollow mountain returns all sounds. *(Chinese)*
A golden mind stoops not to show of dross. *(Shakespeare)*
A strong body makes a mind strong.
Command you may your mind from play.
Fat bodies, lean minds.
God is mind, and God is infinite; hence all is Mind. *(Mrs. Eddy)*
If the brain sows not corn, it plants thistles.
My mind to me a kingdom is. *(Dyer)*
Out of sight, out of mind.
The march of the human mind is slow. *(Burke)*
The mind is free, whate'er afflict the man.
The rust of the mind is the blight of genius.
What is mind? No matter— What is matter? Never mind.
A feeble body enfeebles the mind. *(French)*
In the long run the sword is beaten by the mind. *(Napoleon)*
It is good to rub and polish our minds against those of others. *(Montaigne)*
The mind is the atmosphere of the soul. *(Joubert)*
It is the mind that ennobles, not the blood. *(German)*
Bodies without minds are as statues in the market-place. *(Greek)*
Mind is ever the ruler of the universe. *(Plato)*
Our mind is God. *(Menander)*
The most perfect mind is a dry light. *(Greek)*
So many heads, so many minds. *(Italian)*
A noble mind is free to all men. *(Latin)*
A sick mind cannot endure any harshness. *(Latin)*
A sound mind in a sound body. [*Mens sana in corpore sano.*] *(Latin)*
A wise man will be master of his mind; a fool, its slave. *(Latin)*
All things can corrupt perverted minds. *(Latin)*
An undisturbed mind is the best salve for affliction. *(Latin)*
Anxious minds quake with both hope and fear. *(Latin)*

Bad mind, bad heart. *(Latin)*
Light minds are pleased with trifles. *(Latin)*
Mind moves matter. *(Latin)*
Pain of mind is worse than pain of body. *(Latin)*
Straining breaks the bow, relaxation the mind. *(Latin)*
The contagion of a sick mind affects the body. *(Latin)*
The mind alone cannot be exiled. *(Ovid)*
The mind is the man. *(Latin)*
To relax the mind is to lose it. *(Latin)*
We employ the mind to rule, the body to serve. *(Latin)*

MINUTE

Take care of the minutes and the hours will take care of themselves.

MIRACLE.

Little saints also perform miracles. *(Danish)*
Miracles are the swaddling-clothes of infant churches.
Miracles are to those who believe in them.
They say miracles are past.
Miracles serve not to convert, but to condemn. *(Pascal)*
Things that are mysterious are not necessarily miracles. *(German)*
I should not be a Christian but for the miracles. *(St. Augustine)*
Let the miracle be wrought, though it be by the devil. *(Spanish)*
The sheik's miracles are those of his own telling. *(Turkish)*

MIRROR

The mirror reflects all objects without being sullied. *(Chinese)*
The best mirror is an old friend.
The devil's behind the glass.
What your glass tells you will not be told by counsel.
An ugly maid hates the mirror. *(Yiddish)*
The mirror shows everyone his best friend. *(Yiddish)*

MIRTH

A merry heart doeth good like a medicine. *(Old Test., Prov.)*
A merry host makes merry guests. *(Dutch)*
The end of mirth is the beginning of sorrow. *(Dutch)*
A merry companion on the road is as good as a nag.
An ounce of mirth is worth a pound of sorrow.
In the time of mirth take heed.
Mirth cannot move a soul in agony. *(Shakespeare)*
Mirth makes the banquet sweet.

Mirth prolongeth life and causeth health.
No mirth good but with God.
Always merry is seldom rich. *(German)*
Mirth is hard to feign when the mind is sad. *(Latin)*
Unseasonable mirth turns to sorrow. *(Spanish)*

MISCHIEF
He that mischief hatcheth, mischief catcheth.
Little mischief—too much.
Welcome mischief if thou comest alone.
He prepares evil for himself who plots mischief for others. *(Latin)*

MISER
A miser's money takes the place of wisdom. *(Dutch)*
A miser puts his back and his belly into his pocket.
He gives straw to his dog and bones to his ass.
The devil lies brooding in the miser's chest.
The miser's death is the heir's holiday.
The miser does spoil his coat by scanting a little cloth. *(Shakespeare)*
Niggard father, spendthrift son. *(French)*
The miser and the pig are of no use till dead. *(French)*
The miser is always poor. *(German)*
The wolf is sometimes satisfied, the miser never. *(German)*
What he has is no more use to the miser than what he has not. *(Latin)*
The miser's teeth are frozen together by greed. *(Russian)*
Misers' money goes twice to market. *(Spanish)*
To beg of the miser is to dig a trench in the sea. *(Turkish)*
The rich miser and the fat goat are good after they are dead. *(Yiddish)*

MISERY
Remembering mine affliction and my misery, the wormwood and the gall. *(Old Test., Lament.)*
Misery is but the shadow of happiness. Happiness is but the cloak of misery. *(Lao-Tsze)*
He beareth his misery best that hideth it most.
It is misery enough to have once been happy.
Misery acquaints a man with strange bedfellows. *(Shakespeare)*
Misery loves company.
Tell not misery's son that life is fair.
When misery is highest, help is nighest.
Sacred even to gods is misery. *(Greek)*
It is easy to mock the miserable. *(Latin)*

The wretched are in haste to hear their wretchedness. *(Latin)*
The miseries of the virtuous are the scandal of the good. *(Latin)*

MISFORTUNE

Misfortunes come on wings and depart on foot.
Misfortunes ever claimed the pity of the brave.
Misfortunes never come alone.
Misfortunes tell us what fortune is.
Misfortunes, wood, and hair grow throughout the year.
The misfortunes hardest to bear are those which never come.
When sorrows come, they come not single spies,
  But in battalions. *(Shakespeare)*
By speaking of our misfortunes we often relieve them. *(French)*
He who cannot bear misfortune, is not worthy of good fortune. *(French)*
Misfortunes come on horseback and depart on foot. *(French)*
We all have sufficient strength to bear other people's misfortunes. *(La Rochefoucauld)*
Who has no misfortune is fortunate enough. *(German)*
He who cannot bear misfortune is truly unfortunate. *(Greek)*
It is the nature of mortals to kick a man when he is down. *(Greek)*
Misfortune is friendless. *(Greek)*
There is none misfortune cannot reach. *(Greek)*
He who is the cause of his own misfortune may bewail it himself. *(Italian)*
Misfortune does not always come to injure. *(Italian)*
Fate is not satisfied with inflicting one calamity. *(Latin)*
Learn to see in another's misfortune the ills which you should avoid. *(Latin)*
Misfortunes come unsent for. *(Latin)*
Another's misfortune does not cure my pain. *(Portuguese)*
Welcome misfortune if thou comest alone. *(Spanish)*
When misfortune sleeps, let no one wake her. *(Spanish)*

MISS

An inch in a miss is as good as an ell.

MISTAKE

Mistakes occur through haste, never through doing a thing leisurely. *(Chinese)*
Every man cannot hit the nail on the head.
He who makes no mistakes makes nothing.

Mistakes are often the best teachers.
Mistakes occur in the best regulated families.
Mistakes remembered are not faults forgot.
The shortest mistakes are always the best. *(French)*
Any man may make a mistake; none but a fool will persist in it. *(Latin)*
I can pardon everybody's mistakes but my own. *(Latin)*
Wise men learn by others' mistakes; fools, by their own. *(Latin)*

MISTRESS
Next to the pleasure of making a new mistress is that of being rid of an old one. *(Wycherley)*
He whose mistress squints says she ogles. *(German)*

MOB
A mob is a monster with many hands and no brains.
Who builds on the mob builds on sand. *(Italian)*

MOCKERY
Mocking is catching.
It is never becoming to mock the miserable. *(French)*
Point not the mockery behind the grand pasha's back. *(Turkish)*

MODERATION
Give me neither poverty nor riches. *(Old Test., Prov.)*
Enough is as good as a feast.
In everything there lieth measure.
Measure is medicine.
Stretch your legs according to your coverlet.
The best things carried to excess are wrong.
You never know what is enough unless you know what is more than enough. *(Blake)*
Who wishes to travel far spares his steed. *(French)*
Only moderation gives charm to life. *(German)*
True happiness springs from moderation. *(German)*
Enough is enough for the wise. *(Greek)*
How many things I can do without! *(Socrates)*
Moderation is best. *(Greek)*
Nothing to excess. *(Greek)*
Let him who has enough ask for nothing more. *(Latin)*
Men live better on little. *(Latin)*
The golden rule in life is moderation in all things. *(Latin)*

Things that are moderate last a long while. *(Latin)*
Can we ever have too much of a good thing? *(Spanish)*

MODESTY

Modesty does not long survive innocence.
Modest dogs miss much meat.
Modesty ruins all that bring it to court.
No one can boast of his modesty.
Though modesty be a virtue, bashfulness is a vice.
Everything that is exquisite hides itself. *(French)*
Modesty is the citadel of beauty and of virtue. *(Greek)*
Modesty becomes a young man. *(Latin)*
Modesty cannot be taught, it must be born. *(Latin)*
Modesty forbids what the law does not. *(Latin)*
Modesty, once banished, never returns. *(Latin)*
Rare is agreement between beauty and modesty. *(Latin)*

MONEY

For the love of money is the root of all evil. *(New Test., I Timothy)*
Money answereth all things. *(Old Test., Eccles.)*
A string of cash can but reach to one's heels. *(Chinese)*
He that has no money might as well be buried in a rice tub with his mouth sewn up. *(Chinese)*
Ready money can put anything in stock. *(Chinese)*
One handful of money is stronger than two handfuls of truth. *(Danish)*
When I had money in my purse, I had food in my mouth. *(Danish)*
A fool and his money are soon parted.
A fool may make money, but it needs a wise man to spend it.
A full purse makes a mouth speak.
A golden key opens every lock.
A man without money is a bow without an arrow.
A penny can do more than it may.
Bad money drives out good money *("Gresham's Law.")*
But help me to money and I'll help myself to friends.
Easy come, easy go.
Everyone bastes the fat hog, while the lean one burns.
For lack of money I could not speed.
God send you more wit and me more money.
Good blood makes bad pudding without suet.
Gold alone makes no prosperity.
He that gets money before he gets wit,
Will be but a short while master of it.

He that hath a full purse never wanted a friend.
He that hath no money needeth no purse.
He that serves God for money will serve the devil for better wages.
He that wants money wants everything.
If money goes before, all ways lie open.
If you want to know what God thinks of money, look at the people
he gives it to.
Money begets money.
Money borrowed is soon sorrowed.
Money cures melancholy.
Money in purse will be always in fashion.
Money is a good servant but a bad master.
Money is a good soldier, and will on. *(Shakespeare)*
Money is ace of trumps.
Money is honey, my little sonny,
And a rich man's joke is always funny.
Money is like an arm or a leg—use it or lose it.
Money is like muck, not good except it be spread.
Money is oft lost for want of money.
Money is the best bait with which to fish for man.
Money is welcome though it come in a dirty clout.
Money is wise: it knows its own way.
Money makes a man laugh.
Money makes mastery.
Money makes the old mare trot and the young tit ramble.
Money makes the pot boil.
Money mars, and money makes.
Money's virtue, gold is fate.
Money will do more than my lord's letter.
Muck and money go together.
Put not your trust in money, but put your money in trust.
(O. W. Holmes)
Ready money is a ready remedy.
So we get the chink, we'll bear with the stink.
Store is no sore.
That is but an empty purse that is full of other men's money.
The love of money and the love of learning seldom meet.
The price we pay for money is paid in liberty.
The savor of money is good, howsoever a man comes by it.
The skilfullest, wanting money, is scorned.
There is no companion like money.

To have money is a fear, not to have it, a grief.
What is got under the devil's back is spent under his belly.
Who steals my purse steals trash. *(Shakespeare)*
Would you know what money is? Go borrow some.
He who has no money in his purse, should have honey on his tongue. *(French)*
Ill-gotten wealth never prospers. *(French)*
Lack of money is trouble without equal. *(French)*
Lend not your money to a great man. *(French)*
Money has wings. *(French)*
Money makes dogs dance. *(French)*
Money never comes out of season. *(French)*
Money talks. *(French)*
When it is a question of money, everybody is of the same religion. *(Voltaire)*
If you have money, take a seat; if not, stand on your feet. *(German)*
Mention money, and the world is silent. *(German)*
Money does not get hanged. *(German)*
Money is the soul of business. *(German)*
Blessed is the man who has both mind and money, for he employs the latter well. *(Menander)*
Money is the sinews of affairs. *(Greek)*
Money makes the man. *(Greek)*
The love of money is the mother-city of all evils. *(Diogenes)*
Count not four, till they be in the bag. *(Italian)*
If money be not thy servant, it will be thy master. *(Italian)*
Little and oft fills the purse. *(Italian)*
Money is money's brother. *(Italian)*
Money is round, and rolls away. *(Italian)*
Public money is like holy water: everyone helps himself to it. *(Italian)*
When gold speaks, every tongue is silent. *(Italian)*
Let us despise money. *(St. John Chrysostom)*
Make money, by fair means if you can; if not, by any means money. *(Horace)*
Money amassed with excessive care chokes many. *(Latin)*
Money has no smell. *(Latin)*
Money is both blood and life to men. *(Latin)*
Money is the ruling spirit of all things. *(Latin)*
Money is the sinews of war. *(Latin)*
The love of money grows as money itself grows. *(Latin)*
There is no fortune so strong that money cannot take it. *(Latin)*

You must spend money, if you wish to make money. *(Latin)*
What is infamy, so long as our money is safe! *(Latin)*
Give me money, not advice. *(Portuguese)*
My money, your money, let us go to the tavern. *(Portuguese)*
When money speaks, truth keeps silent. *(Russian)*
A toom [*empty*] purse makes a blate [*bashful*] merchant. (*Scottish*)
Between smith and smith no money passes. *(Spanish)*
He that has money may choose a husband for his daughter. *(Spanish)*
Money soothes more than the words of a cavalier. *(Spanish)*
The best foundation in the world is money. *(Spanish)*
The devil of money has the better end of the staff. *(Spanish)*
The money paid, the work delayed. *(Spanish)*
There is no companion like a penny. *(Spanish)*
If a man's money be white, his face may be black. *(Turkish)*
Money is needed both by monk and dervish. *(Turkish)*
It is easier to make money than to keep it. *(Yiddish)*
Money draws money. *(Yiddish)*
Money buys sugar. *(Yiddish)*
Where you have lost money, there you must look for it. *(Yiddish)*

MONK

The monk responds as the abbot chants. *(French)*
A monk out of his cloister is like a fish out of water. *(Latin)*
Despair makes the monk. *(Latin)*
The habit does not make the monk. *(Latin)*

MONUMENT

Those only deserve a monument who do not need one.
Do not judge the dead by his monument. *(Greek)*
I would rather have men ask why I have no statue than why I have one. *(Greek)*
The monuments of noble men are their virtues. *(Greek)*
Monuments are superfluous: our memory will endure if our lives have deserved it. *(Latin)*

MOON

God save the moon from the wolves.
Oh, swear not by the moon, the inconstant moon. *(Shakespeare)*
The moon does not heed the barking of dogs.
The moon is not seen when the sun shines.
You gazed at the moon, and fell in a gutter.
Moon is made of green cheese. *(Rabelais)*

MORALITY
Morality was made for man, not man for morality.
There are many religions, but only one morality.
Veracity is the heart of morality.
Not the whiteness of years but of morals is to be praised. *(Latin)*

MORNING
An hour in the morning is worth two in the evening.
The morning sun never lasts a day.
The morning to the mountain, the evening to the fountain.
'Tis always morning somewhere in the world.
The morning hour has gold in its mouth. *(German)*
The morning is wiser than the evening. *(Russian)*

MORTALITY
All flesh is grass, and all the goodliness thereof is as the flower of the field. *(Old Test., Isaiah)*
All men are mortal.
All men think all men mortal but themselves.
All that belongs to mortals is mortal. *(Greek)*
All things are born of earth; all things earth takes again. *(Greek)*
Remember that thou art mortal. *(Greek)*

MOSS
A rolling stone gathers no moss. *(French)*

MOTHER
Her children arise and call her blessed. *(Old Test., Prov.)*
Better the child cry than the mother sigh. *(Danish)*
A barren sow was never good to pigs.
A child may have too much of mother's blessing.
A light-heeled mother makes a heavy-heeled daughter.
Men are what their mothers make them.
Mother is the name for God in the lips and hearts of little children. *(Thackeray)*
Mothers' darlings make but milksop heroes.
Only a mother knows a mother's fondness.
She spins well that breeds her children.
Simply having children does not make mothers.
The kick of the dam hurts not the colt.
The mother knows best whether the child is like the father.
What is home without a mother?

Where yet was found a mother
  Who'd give her booby for another? *(Gay)*

Mother's love is ever in its spring. *(French)*

A mother does not hear the music of the dance when her children cry. *(German)*

Who takes the child by the hand takes the mother by the heart. *(German)*

Children are the anchors that hold a mother to life. *(Greek)*

God could not be everywhere and therefore he made mothers. *(Hebrew)*

A bustling mother makes a slothful daughter. *(Latin)*

A mother's love will draw up from the depths of the sea. *(Russian)*

The mother's breath is aye sweet. *(Scottish)*

What is sucked in with mother's milk runs out in the shroud. *(Spanish)*

A mother needs a large apron to cover her children's faults.

No mother has a homely child. *(Yiddish)*

One mother can satisfy ten children, but ten children not one mother. *(Yiddish)*

There is no bad mother or good death. *(Yiddish)*

MOTHER-IN-LAW

Happy is she who marries the son of a dead mother.

The husband's mother is the wife's devil. *(German)*

Give up all hope of peace so long as your mother-in-law lives. *(Latin)*

The cask full, the mother-in-law drunk. *(Spanish)*

The mother-in-law remembers not that she was a daughter-in-law. *(Spanish)*

MOUNTAIN

If you don't scale the mountain, you can't view the plain. *(Chinese)*

Behind every mountain lies a valley. *(Dutch)*

A mountain and a river are good neighbors.

Friends may meet, but mountains greet.

If the mountain will not go to Mohamet, Mohamet must go to the mountain.

Even God cannot make two mountains without a valley between them. *(Gaelic)*

Behind the mountains there are people to be found. *(German)*

The mountain labors, and a ridiculous mouse is born. *(Horace)*

MOURNING

It is better to go to the house of mourning than to go to the house of feasting. *(Old Test., Eccles.)*

He that lacks time to mourn, lacks time to mend.
"Man Was Made to Mourn." [*Title*] *(Burns)*
Nothing dies but something mourns. *(Byron)*
What man so blest but mourns? *(Homer)*

MOUSE
When a mouse has fallen into the meal-sack, he thinks he is the miller himself. *(Dutch)*
A dead mouse feels no cold.
A mouse, in time, may bite in two a cable.
A mouse must not think to cast a shadow like an elephant.
Don't make yourself a mouse, or the cat will eat you.
I gave the mouse a hole, and she is become my heir.
It had need be a wily mouse that should breed in a cat's ear.
No house without mouse.
The mouse that hath one hole is quickly taken.
It is a poor mouse that sits on the meal-sack and does not gnaw. *(German)*
It is not the mouse but the hole that does the injury. *(German)*
If you are a mouse, don't follow frogs. *(Italian)*
The mouse does not leave the cat's home with a belly full. *(Italian)*
When a building is about to fall, all the mice desert it. *(Latin)*

MOUTH
Out of the abundance of the heart the mouth speaketh. *(Old Test., Eccles.)*
A foul mouth must be provided with a strong back. *(Danish)*
A cool mouth and warm feet live long.
A lying mouth is a stinking pit.
A wise head makes a close mouth.
Open thy mouth that I may know thee.
The heart of the fool is in his mouth, but the mouth of the wise man is in his heart.
Mouth and heart are wide apart. *(German)*
Two eyes, two ears, and only one mouth. *(German)*
Mouth shut and eyes open. *(Italian)*
A closed mouth catches no flies. *(Spanish)*
The mouth that says "yes" says "no." *(Spanish)*
The mouth is not sweetened by saying, "Honey, honey." *(Turkish)*
If the mouth did not have to eat, the head would wear gold. *(Yiddish)*
Let your ears hear what your mouth says. *(Yiddish)*
You can't shut the whole world's mouth. *(Yiddish)*

Your ear to everyone, your hand to a friend, but your mouth only to your wife. *(Yiddish)*

MOVE

Great bodies move slowly.

MUCH

Never too much of a good thing.

Too much breaks the bag.

Too much water drowned the miller.

Too much of a thing nauseates. *(Latin)*

Much never costs little. *(Spanish)*

MUD

Mud chokes no eels.

Muddy springs will have muddy streams.

When a man falls into the mud, the more he flounders the more he fouls himself. *(Italian)*

He who is in the mud likes to pull another into it. *(Spanish)*

MUM

Mum is counsel.

Mum's the word.

MULE

Mules don' kick 'cordin' to no rule. *(American Negro)*

The mule long keeps a kick in reserve for its master. *(French)*

He who wants a mule without fault must walk on foot. *(Spanish)*

MURDER

Thou shalt not kill. *(Old Test., Exodus)*

Murder, like talent, seems occasionally to run in families. *(G. H. Lewes)*

Murder may pass unpunish't for a time,
But tardy justice will o'ertake the crime. *(Dryden)*

Murder will out.

One murder makes a villain, millions a hero.

Many who do not murder would like the power to do it. *(Latin)*

The guilt of murder is the same, whether the victim be renowned or obscure. *(Latin)*

MUSIC

A lamentable tune is sweet music to a woeful mind.

Heard melodies are sweet, but those unheard
Are sweeter. *(Keats)*

Music hath charms to soothe the savage breast. *(Congreve)*
Music helps not the toothache.
Music is essentially useless, as life is. *(Santayana)*
Music is the brandy of the damned. *(G. B. Shaw)*
Music is the eye of the ear.
Music is the only sensual pleasure without vice. *(S. Johnson)*
Music is the poor man's Parnassus. *(Emerson)*
Music is the speech of angels. *(Carlyle)*
Music tells no truths.
Music—the only universal tongue.
What passion cannot music raise and quell? *(Dryden)*
Music does not fill the stomach. *(French)*
The man who has music in his soul will be most in love with the loveliest. *(Plato)*
Music is the medicine of a troubled mind. *(Latin)*
Where there's music there can't be mischief. *(Spanish)*

NAIL

Drive the nail that will go.
Hit the nail on the head.
Nail is driven out by nail.
The horseshoe that clatters wants a nail. *(Spanish)*

NAME

A good name is rather to be chosen than great riches. *(Old Test., Prov.)*
The name of the Lord is a strong tower. *(Old Test., Prov.)*
A good name keeps its luster in the dark.
An ill wound is cured, not an ill name.
Give a dog an ill name and hang him.
If you have the name, you may as well enjoy the game.
Take away my good name and take away my life.
What's in a name? that which we call a rose
By any other name would smell as sweet. *(Shakespeare)*
Who has a bad name is half hanged. *(Italian)*
Don't name your child before it is born. *(Yiddish)*

NAPLES

See Naples and then die. *(Italian)*

NARROWNESS

God keep me from the man who has but one thing in mind.
Beware of the man of one book. *(Latin)*

NATION

Nations, like men, have their infancy.
That nation is worthless which does not joyfully stake everything in defense of her honor. *(Schiller)*

NATURE

The heavens declare the glory of God, and the firmament sheweth his handiwork. *(Old Test., Psalms)*

By nature all men are alike, but by education widely different. *(Chinese)*

About nature consult nature herself. *(Bacon)*
Accuse not nature; she hath done her part. *(Milton)*
It can't be nature, for it is not sense.
Nature draws more than ten oxen.
Nature is a volume of which God is the author.
Nature is the true law.
Nature must obey necessity.
Nature never did betray the heart that loved her. *(Wordsworth)*
Nature pardons no mistake.
Nature passes nurture.
Nature, the vicar of Almightie God. *(Chaucer)*
Nature, to be commanded, must be obeyed. *(Bacon)*
Nature will have its course.
Nature's rules have no exceptions.
No men sleep so soundly as they that lay their heads upon Nature's lap.
One touch of nature makes the whole world kin. *(Shakespeare)*
The volume of nature is the book of knowledge.
Where man is not, nature is barren. *(Blake)*
Drive away nature, it comes back apace. *(French)*
Everything unnatural is imperfect. *(French)*
Nature forms us for ourselves, not for others. *(French)*
Nature has always had more power than education. *(French)*
The truth of nature lies hidden in mines and caverns. *(Greek)*
What is natural is never disgraceful. *(Greek)*
What belongs to nature lasts to the grave. *(Italian)*
Everyone follows the inclination of his own nature. *(Latin)*
It is hard to change nature. *(Latin)*
Live according to nature. *(Latin)*
Nature abhors a vacuum. *(Latin)*
Nature does not proceed by leaps. *(Latin)*
Nature does nothing in vain. *(Latin)*
Nature is the art of God. *(Latin)*
Never can custom conquer nature. *(Latin)*
Never does Nature say one thing and Wisdom another. *(Latin)*
Though you drive out nature with a fork, it will still return. *(Latin)*

NEAR

Near the coat, but nearer the skin.
The nearest the dearest. *(German)*
The tunic is nearer than the frock. *(Latin)*

NEAT

As neat as a new pin.

NECESSITY

Necessity breaks iron.
Necessity does everything well.
Necessity is the argument of tyrants; it is the creed of slaves. *(Pitt)*
Necessity makes an honest man a knave.
Necessity never made a good bargain.
We do what we must, and call it by the best names. *(Emerson)*
He made a virtue of necessity. *(French)*
Necessity is a violent school-mistress. *(French)*
Stern is the visage of necessity. *(Schiller)*
Even the gods do not fight against necessity. *(Greek)*
Every act of necessity is disagreeable. *(Greek)*
Necessity has no law. *(Greek)*
Necessity will teach a man, however stupid, to be wise. *(Greek)*
The force of necessity is irresistible. *(Greek)*
A wise man never refuses anything to necessity. *(Latin)*
Necessity is the last and strongest weapon. *(Latin)*
Necessity is the mother of invention. *(Latin)*
Necessity knows no shame. *(Latin)*
Necessity makes even the timid brave. *(Latin)*
We give necessity the praise of virtue. *(Latin)*
You cannot escape necessities; but you can conquer them. *(Latin)*
A man driven by necessity does as much as thirty. *(Spanish)*
Necessity urges desperate measures. *(Spanish)*

NEED

There is no need to blow what does not burn you. *(Danish)*
Need makes greed.
Need makes the naked man run.
Need makes the naked quean spin.
Need makes the old wife trot.
Need teaches things unlawful. *(Latin)*
Need breaks iron; poverty breaks locks. *(Yiddish)*
Need sharpens the brain. *(Yiddish)*

NEEDLE

One person can thread a needle better than two. *(American Negro)*
A needle is not sharp at both ends. *(Chinese)*
Like a needle in a haystack.
Needle and thread are half clothing. *(Spanish)*

NEIGHBOR

Thou shalt love thy neighbor as thyself. *(Old Test., Levit.)*
A hedge between keeps friendship green.
Every man's neighbor is his looking-glass.
Love your neighbor, yet pull not down your hedge.
We can live without our friends, but not without our neighbors.
You must ask your neighbor if you shall live in peace.
We are nearer neighbors to ourselves than whiteness to snow. *(French)*
Love thy neighbor. *(Thales)*
It is not as thy mother says, but as thy neighbors say. *(Hebrew)*
He who has a good neighbor has a good morning. *(Italian)*
A bad neighbor brings bad luck. *(Latin)*
My neighbor's hen lays more eggs than mine. *(Spanish)*
The bad neighbor gives a needle without thread. *(Spanish)*
What my neighbor eats does my stomach no good. *(Spanish)*
Neighbor's right, God's right. *(Turkish)*
Better a good neighbor than a bad relative. *(Yiddish)*

NEPHEW

To whom God gave no sons, the devil gives nephews. *(Italian)*

NEST

Destroy the nests and the birds will fly away.

NET

In vain the net is spread in the sight of any bird. *(Old Test., Prov.)*
When there is no fish in one spot, cast your net in another. *(Chinese)*
A new net won't catch an old bird. *(Danish)*
All is fish that comes to his net.
The bird avoids the net that shows too plainly. *(Latin)*

NEUTRAL

Who can ride upon two saddles is a neutral. *(German)*

NEW

There is nothing new ["*no new thing*"] under the sun.
(Old Test., Eccles.)

Everything new is fine.
New lords, new laws.
Of a new prince, new bondage.
There is nothing new but what has been forgotten. *(German)*

NEWS

As cold water to a thirsty stone, so is good news from a far country. *(Old Test., Prov.)*
Good news may be told at any time, but ill, in the morning.
He was scant of news who told his father was hanged.
Ill news comes apace.
Ill news comes often on the back of worse.
Stay a little and news will find you.
The messenger of good news is an object of benevolence.
When a dog bites a man, that is not news, but when a man bites a dog, that is news. *(J. B. Bogart)*
He comes too early who brings bad news. *(German)*
He knocks boldly who brings good news. *(Italian)*
No news is good news. *(Italian)*
Bad news is always true. *(Spanish)*

NIGHT

The night cometh, when no man can work. *(New Test., John)*
Watchman, what of the night? *(Old Test., Isaiah)*
He that runs in the night stumbles.
Most men are begotten in the night.
Night is the mother of thoughts.
The longest night will have an end.
The night is a cloak for sinners.
What is done by night appears by day.
The night is long to one kept awake by pain. *(French)*
What I take from my nights I add to my days. *(French)*
The night is no man's friend. *(German)*
By night comes counsel to the wise. *(Greek)*
Black night broods over the deep. *(Vergil)*

"NO"

"No" is a good answer when given in time. *(Danish)*
My "No" is as good as your "Yes." *(Italian)*

NOBILITY

He is noble that hath noble conditions.
The more noble, the more humble.

True nobility is exempt from fear. *(Shakespeare)*
Noblesse oblige. (French)
A noble soul alone can attract noble souls. *(Goethe)*
Common natures pay with what they do, noble ones with what they are. *(Schiller)*
The nobly born must nobly meet their fate. *(Greek)*
Born to consume the fruits of the earth. *(Latin)*
Virtue alone is true nobility. *(Latin)*

NOD
A nod from a lord is a breakfast for a fool.
A nod is as good as a wink. *(French)*
A nod for a wise man, and a rod for a fool. *(Hebrew)*

NOISE
De noise of de wheels don' measure de load in de wagon. *(American Negro)*
Great cry and little wool.
The ass that brays most eats least.
The noisy crow eats less carrion.
The bleating lamb loses his dinner. *(French)*
He that loves noise must buy a pig. *(Spanish)*

NORTH
Cold weather and knees come out of the north.

NOSE
Keep your nose out of another's mess. *(Danish)*
A red nose makes a ragged back.
Follow thy nose, and thou wilt be there presently.
He that has a great nose thinks everybody is speaking of it.
Hold your nose to the grindstone.
Men suffer themselves to be led by their noses like brute beasts.
Your nose betrays what porridge you love.
Who blows his nose too hard makes it bleed.
A long nose never spoiled a handsome face. *(French)*
Cleopatra's nose: had it been shorter, the whole aspect of the world would have been altered. *(Pascal)*
If you have lost your nose put your hand before the place. *(Italian)*
To cut off your nose to spite your face. *(Latin)*
Let everyone pick his own nose. *(Russian)*

NOTHING

Blessed be nothing when the tax-gatherer comes around.
Fair fall nothing once by the year.
Nothing have, nothing crave.
Nothing will come of nothing.
Something has some savor, but nothing has no flavor.
There's nothing new, and there's nothing true, and it don't signify. *(Cornish Proverb)*
They that have nothing need fear to lose nothing.
Where nothing's in, nothing can come out.
He goes safely who has nothing. *(French)*
Nothing can be made of nothing. *(Latin)*

NOVELTY

The novelty of noon is out of date by night.

NOW

Now or never.

NUDITY

Naked came I out of my mother's womb, and naked shall I return thither. *(Old Test., Job)*
The nakedness of woman is the work of God. *(Blake)*
Naked was I born, naked I am, I neither win nor lose. *(Spanish)*

NURSE

With seven nurses a child will be without eyes. *(Russian)*

NUT

He that would eat the kernel must crack the nut. *(Latin)*

OAK

An oak is not felled at one stroke.
Every oak has been an acorn.
Oaks may fall when reeds brave the storm.
Heart of oak. *(Spanish)*

OATH

An unlawful oath is better broke than kept.
As false as dicers' oaths. *(Shakespeare)*
It is great sin to swear unto sin,
  But greater sin to keep a sinful oath. *(Shakespeare)*
Oaths are but words, and words but wind.
Oaths are the fossils of piety. *(Santayana)*
An oath and an egg are soon broken. *(Greek)*
Children are to be deceived with comfits and men with oaths. *(Greek)*
I write a woman's oaths in water. *(Greek)*
My tongue has sworn it, but my mind is unsworn. *(Greek)*
Oaths are not surety for the man, but the man for the oaths. *(Greek)*
A true word needs no oath. *(Turkish)*

OBEDIENCE

Give obedience where 'tis truly owed. *(Shakespeare)*
Let them obey that know not how to rule. *(Shakespeare)*
Obedience alone gives the right to command. *(Emerson)*
Obedience is the courtesy due kings. *(Tennyson)*
Obedience is the key to every door.
Best reign who first well hath obeyed. *(Milton)*
Even though a god, I have learnt to obey the times. *(Greek)*
Learn to obey before you command. *(Greek)*
Obedience is the mother of success, the wife of safety. *(Greek)*
No one can rule except one who can be ruled. *(Latin)*

Obedience is yielded more readily to one who commands gently. *(Latin)*

What the law demands, give of your own free will. *(Latin)*

OBSERVATION

Standers-by see more than gamesters.

Observation, not old age, brings wisdom. *(Latin)*

OBSTINATE

A stubborn heart shall fare evil at the last. *(Apocrypha)*

He can never be good that is not obstinate.

He will not give an inch of his will, for an ell of his thrift.

OBSTACLE

Obstacles increase desire. *(French)*

OCCASION

Occasion is bald behind.

OCCUPATION

Absence of occupation is not rest. *(Cowper)*

Let thy occupations be few. *(Greek)*

Constant occupation prevents temptation. *(Italian)*

The vices of leisure are dispersed by occupation. *(Latin)*

OFFENSE

No offense taken where none is meant.

The offender never pardons. *(Italian)*

Neither give offense to others, nor take offense from them. *(Latin)*

OFFICE

All offices are greasy. *(Danish)*

The king's cheese goes half away in parings.

Office without pay makes thieves. *(German)*

Office tests the man. *(Latin)*

OLD

A man is as old as he feels; a woman as old as she looks.

An old cloak makes a new jerkin.

An old man in a house is a good sign.

Old bees yield no honey.

Old foxes want no tutors.

Old wood to burn, old horse to ride, old books to read, old wine to drink.

You can't teach an old dog new tricks.
You can't catch old birds with chaff.
Old cattle breed not. *(French)*
Old friends, old wine, and old gold are best. *(French)*
He who does not wish to become old may hang himself when young. *(German)*
Old camels carry young camels' skins to the market. *(Hebrew)*
An old man has the almanac in his body. *(Italian)*
As a man grows older, he grows colder. *(Yiddish)*

OLIVE
Call me not olive till you see me gathered. *(Italian)*

OMEN
Coming events cast their shadows before. *(Campbell)*
It is a bad sign when a man in a sweat shivers. *(Latin)*

ONCE
Once upon a time is no time. *(German)*

ONE
One foot is better than two crutches.
One link broken, the whole chain is broken. *(German)*
One swallow does not make a summer. *(Greek)*

OPEN
An open door may tempt a saint.

OPINION
How long halt ye between two opinions? *(Old Test., I Kings)*
A difference of opinion alienates only little minds.
A man may wear opinion on both sides, like a leather jerkin.
Error of opinion may be tolerated where reason is left free to combat it. *(Jefferson)*
He that complies against his will,
Is of his own opinion still. *(Butler)*
It is difference of opinion that makes horse-races. *(Mark Twain)*
Men are never so good or so bad as their opinions.
Opinion in good men is but knowledge in the making. *(Milton)*
Opinion's but a fool, that makes us scan
The outward habit by the inward man. *(Shakespeare)*
Opinion is determined by feeling, not by intellect.
So many heads, so many opinions.
Some men plant an opinion they seem to eradicate.

That is true which all men say.
The foolish and the dead alone never change their opinions.
The man who never alters his opinion is like standing water, and breeds reptiles of the mind. *(Blake)*
Vain opinion all doth sway.
We are all slaves of opinion.
Opinion is of force enough to make itself be expounded at the expense of life. *(Montaigne)*
Opinion is the queen of the world. *(Pascal)*
The clash of opinion brings sparks of light. *(French)*
Those who never retract their opinions love themselves more than they love truth. *(French)*
That man is best who considers everything for himself. *(Greek)*
Wind puffs up empty bladders; opinion, fools. *(Greek)*
A man's own opinion is never wrong. *(Italian)*
So many men, so many opinions. *(Latin)*

OPPORTUNITY

A man must make his opportunity as oft as find it. *(Bacon)*
An occasion lost cannot be redeemed.
An opportunity well taken is the only weapon of advantage.
Hoist your sail when the wind is fair.
Keep thou from the opportunity, and God will keep thee from sin.
Let down your buckets where you are.
Opportunities are seldom labeled.
Opportunity is whoredom's bawd.
Opportunity makes the thief.
Strike while the iron is hot.
Take opportunity by the forelock.
There is a tide in the affairs of men
Which taken at the flood leads on to fortune. *(Shakespeare)*
We must take the current when it serves,
Or lose our ventures. *(Shakespeare)*
Who lets occasion pass will find her bald behind.
He who seizes the right moment is the right man. *(Goethe)*
Know your opportunity. *(Greek)*
Opportunity is a god. *(Greek)*
He who will not when he may, may not when he will. *(Latin)*
Let us snatch our opportunity from the day. *(Horace)*
Pluck with quick hand the fruit that passes. *(Ovid)*
When fair occasion calls, 'tis fatal to delay. *(Latin)*

OPPRESSION

He that oppresseth the poor reproacheth his maker. *(Old Test., Prov.)*

Oppression causeth rebellion.

OPTIMISM

God's in his Heaven—
All's right with the world! *(Browning)*

All is for the best in the best of possible worlds. *(Voltaire)*

Everything that is, is reasonable. *(Hegel)*

Whatever is, is right. *(Greek)*

There is still sunshine on the wall. *(Spanish)*

ORATORY

He is a good orator who convinces himself.

A man becomes an orator; he is born eloquent. *(French)*

An orator's virtue is to speak the truth. *(Greek)*

Orators are driven by their weakness to noise, as lame men take to horses. *(Cicero)*

ORDER

Let all things be done decently and in order. *(New Test., I Corinth.)*

Set thine house in order. *(Old Test., Isaiah)*

A place for everything and everything in its place. *(Smiles)*

Good order is the foundation of all good things.

Order is Heav'n's first law . . . *(Pope)*

ORPHAN

A fatherless child is half an orphan; a motherless child, a whole orphan. *(Yiddish)*

ORTHODOXY

Orthodoxy is my doxy, heterodoxy is your doxy. *(Warburton)*

OVER

If you can't go over, you must go under. *(Yiddish)*

OWL

The owl is not counted the wiser for living retiredly.

OWN

Every sow to her own trough.

OWNER

A pig that has two owners is sure to die of hunger.

OX

As an ox goeth to the slaughter. *(Old Test., Prov.)*

The ox knoweth his owner, and the ass his master's crib. *(Old Test., Isaiah)*

Thou shalt not muzzle the mouth of the ox that treadeth out the corn. *(New Test., I Corinth.)*

If an ox won't drink, you cannot make him bend his neck. *(Chinese)*

Who leads an ox to drink must first wet his own feet. *(Chinese)*

Old oxen have stiff horns. *(Danish)*

An ox is taken by the horns, and a man by the tongue.

If the ox fall, whet your knife.

It depends upon whose ox is gored. *(Noah Webster)*

The ox when weariest treads surest.

Where shall the ox go, but he must labor?

An old ox makes a straight furrow. *(Italian)*

Don't beat the ox for not giving milk. *(Russian)*

He who greases his cart-wheels helps his oxen. *(Spanish)*

The ox without a bell is soon lost. *(Spanish)*

The ox knows not his own strength. *(Yiddish)*

OXFORD

Oxford—the home of lost causes.

OYSTER

He was a bold man that first ate an oyster.

It is the sick oyster which possesses the pearl.

The oyster is a gentle thing,
And will not come unless you sing.

"P's" and "Q's"
Mind your P's and Q's.

PACE
It is the pace that kills.

PACT
Straw should make no pact with fire. *(Russian)*

PAIN
Where a man feels pain he lays his hand. *(Dutch)*
A man of pleasure is a man of pains. *(Young)*
An hour of pain is as long as a day of pleasure.
Faint is the bliss that never passed thro' pain.
Great pain and little gain will make a man soon weary.
Great pains quickly find ease.
If pains be a pleasure to you, profit will follow.
Pain is forgotten when gain comes.
Pain is the price that God putteth upon all things.
Pains are the wages of ill pleasures.
Past pain is pleasure.
Sweet is pleasure after pain. *(Dryden)*
Those who do not feel pain seldom think that it is felt. *(S. Johnson)*
Nothing gives pleasure but that which gives pain. *(Montaigne)*
Great pains cause us to forget the small ones. *(German)*
Pleasure reaches its limit in the removal of all pain. *(Epicurus)*
There is a pleasure akin to pain. *(Greek)*
Every pain, but not heart pain;
  Every ache, but not headache. *(Hebrew)*
Sweet is the pleasure that springs from another's pain. *(Ovid)*
No matter which finger you bite, it will hurt. *(Russian)*
Naething is got without pains but dirt and lang nails. *(Scottish)*

PAINT

For whom does the blind man's wife paint herself? *(Spanish)*

PAINTING

On painting and fighting look afar off.

The love of gain never made a painter, but it has marred many.

Good painting is like good cooking: it can be tasted, but not explained. *(French)*

A picture is a poem without words. *(Latin)*

PARADISE

Paradise is for those who command their anger. *(The Koran)*

He that will enter into Paradise must come with the right key.

Some may perchance, with strange surprise,
  Have blundered into Paradise. *(F. Thompson)*

One cannot enter Paradise in spite of the saints. *(Italian)*

Paradise and hell can be had in this world. *(Yiddish)*

PARDON

It is more noble to pardon than to punish. *(Arabian)*

Pardon is the choicest flower of victory. *(Arabian)*

Never ask pardon before you are accused.

No penny, no pardon.

Pardon all but thyself.

Pardon makes offenders.

Pardoning the bad is injuring the good.

Where no fault is, there needs no pardon.

PARENT

Honor thy father and thy mother. *(Old Test., Exodus)*

My son, hear the instruction of thy father, and forsake not the law of thy mother. *(Old Test., Prov.)*

If parents want honest children, they should be honest themselves.

Everything is dear to its parent. *(Greek)*

Honor the gods, reverence parents. *(Greek)*

The virtue of parents is a great dowry. *(Latin)*

No fathers or mothers think their children ugly. *(Spanish)*

Parents can give everything but common sense. *(Yiddish)*

PARIS

Paris is worth a mass. *(Henri IV)*

PARNASSUS

Parnassus has no gold mines in it.

PARTING

The best of friends must part.
To part is to die a little. *(French)*

PARTNER

He who takes a partner takes a master. *(French)*

PASSION

A man in passion rides a horse that runs away with him.
Glowing coals sparkle oft.
He is a governor that governs his passions, and he a servant that serves them.
If passion drives, let reason hold the reins.
One passion doth expel another still.
We are ne'er like angels till our passion dies.
The end of passion is the beginning of repentance.
What Reason weaves is by Passion undone. *(Pope)*
When passion entereth at the fore-gate, wisdom goeth out of the postern.
Where passion is high, there reason is low.
All passions are extinguished with old age. *(French)*
All the passions are sisters. *(French)*
The passions are merely different kinds of self-love. *(La Rochefoucauld)*
The passions are the only orators who always persuade. *(La Rochefoucauld)*
Great passions are incurable diseases: the very remedies make them worse. *(Goethe)*
It is a harder lot to be a slave to one's passion than to tyrants. *(Greek)*
Passions are good servants and bad masters. *(Greek)*
Govern your passions, or they will govern you. *(Latin)*

PAST

Let bygones be bygones.
Let all things passed pass.
Not heaven itself upon the past has power. *(Dryden)*
The best prophet of the future is the past. *(Byron)*
The mill cannot grind with the water that is past.
The Present is the living sum-total of the whole Past. *(Carlyle)*

Today is yesterday's pupil.
This is denied even to God: the power to undo the past. *(Greek)*
What is past, even the fool knows. *(Greek)*
Nothing is certain except the past. *(Latin)*

PATCH
The best patch is off the same cloth. *(Spanish)*
If you don't lay a small patch, you'll have a big hole. *(Yiddish)*

PATERNITY
It is a wise child that knows his own father.
It is a wise father that knows his own child. *(Shakespeare)*

PATH
Every path hath a puddle.
Better a path than a hole. *(German)*
A beaten path is a safe one. *(Latin)*

PATIENCE
Be patient toward all men. *(Apocrypha)*
Ye have heard of the patience of Job. *(New Test., James)*
An ounce of patience is worth a pound of brains. *(Dutch)*
Beware the fury of a patient man. *(Dryden)*
Grain by grain, the hen fills her belly.
He preacheth patience that never knew pain.
He that can have patience can have what he will.
He that hath patience hath fat thrushes for a farthing.
How poor are they that have not patience! *(Shakespeare)*
Let patience grow in your garden.
Our patience will achieve more than our force.
Patience is a plaster for all sores.
Patience is a virtue. *(Chaucer)*
Patience is pale cold cowardice in noble breasts. *(Shakespeare)*
Patience is sorrow's salve.
Patience is the best medicine there is for a sick man.
Patience is a drink to kill the Giant Despair.
Patience opens all doors.
Patience perforce is medicine for a mad horse.
Patience under old injuries invites new ones.
Patience, which is the leech of all offense . . . *(Gower)*
Patience with poverty is all a poor man's remedy.
Patient men win the day. *(Chaucer)*

Sufferance is a sovereign virtue.
Though God take the sun out of heaven, yet we must have patience.
Though patience be a tired mare, yet she will plod. *(Shakespeare)*
What signifies patience, if you can't find it when you want it?
He that has patience may compass anything. *(French)*
Patience!—in patience there is safety. *(French)*
Patience is bitter, but its fruit is sweet. *(French)*
Patience is the art of hoping. *(French)*
Patience is the virtue of asses. *(French)*
Patience devours the devil. *(German)*
The world is for him who has patience. *(Italian)*
Every misfortune is subdued by patience. *(Latin)*
Have patience, and endure. *(Latin)*
Patience provoked often turns to fury. *(Latin)*
The patient overcome. *(Latin)*
What cannot be removed, becomes lighter through patience. *(Latin)*
Whosoever hath not patience, neither doth he possess philosophy. *(Sadi) (Persian)*
Have patience, Cossack, thou wilt come to be a hetman. *(Russian)*
Patience, and shuffle the cards. *(Spanish)*
With patience and time the mulberry becomes a silk gown. *(Spanish)*
Patience is the key to Paradise. *(Turkish)*
Vengeance with patience becomes wine. *(Turkish)*
If you can't go through evil, you will never live to enjoy the good. *(Yiddish)*

PATRIOTISM

When a nation is filled with strife, then do patriots flourish. *(Chinese)*
A patriot is a fool in ev'ry age. *(Pope)*
He loves his country best who strives to make it best. *(Ingersoll)*
Patriotism is the last refuge of a scoundrel. *(S. Johnson)*
To make us love our country, our country ought to be lovely. *(Burke)*
He dies a glorious death who dies for his country. *(Greek)*
He serves me most who serves his country best. *(Greek)*
It is sweet and glorious to die for one's native land. *(Latin)*
A good citizen owes his life to his country. *(Russian)*

PAUPER

The pauper fears no robbery. *(Yiddish)*
When a pauper eats a chicken, either he is sick—or the chicken is. *(Yiddish)*

PAY

Pay me that thou owest. *(New Test., Matthew)*
A good payer is master of another man's purse.
An ill payer never wants an excuse.
Every man must pay his scot.
He is well paid that is well satisfied.
He that cannot pay, let him pray.
He that pays last never pays twice.
He who pays the piper may call the tune.
Pay as you go, and keep from small score.
Pay beforehand, and your work will be behindhand.
Pay day comes every day.
They take a long day that never pay.
He need say nothing about the score who pays nothing. *(French)*
Never give the skin when you can pay with the wool. *(German)*
Who cannot pay with money, must pay with his body. *(Latin)*
Corn him well, he'll work the better. *(Scottish)*
Sair cravers are aye ill payers. *(Scottish)*
A good paymaster needs no surety. *(Spanish)*
Good demander—bad payer. *(Yiddish)*

PEACE

Blessed are the peacemakers. *(New Test., Matthew)*
How beautiful upon the mountains are the feet of him that bringeth good tidings, that publisheth peace. *(Old Test., Isaiah)*
Peace, peace; when there is no peace. *(Old Test., Jerem.)*
The peace of God which passeth all understanding. *(New Test., Phil.)*
Peace feeds, war wastes; peace breeds, war consumes. *(Danish)*
A disarmed peace is weak.
Better a lean peace than a fat victory.
Better an egg in peace than an ox in war.
By wisdom peace, by peace plenty.
He that will not have peace, God give him war.
In peace prepare for war.
Peace begins just where ambition ends.
Peace hath her victories no less renown'd than war. *(Milton)*
Peace is always beautiful. *(Whitman)*
Peace makes plenty.
Peace without victory. *(W. Wilson)*
Where there is peace, God is.

Who gives a nation peace, gives tranquility to all.
You must ask your neighbor if you shall live in peace.
Hear, see, and be silent, if you would live in peace. *(French)*
Peace and a little. *(French)*
Peace at any price. *(French)*
When a man finds no peace within himself, it is useless to seek it elsewhere. *(French)*
Peace without truth is poison. *(German)*
In His will is our peace. *(Dante)*
Fame will be won in peace as well as in war. *(Latin)*
Fair peace is becoming to men; fierce anger belongs to beasts. *(Latin)*
Peace is liberty in tranquility. *(Latin)*
They make a desert and call it peace. *(Tacitus)*
Peace and patience and death with penitence. *(Spanish)*
Where there is peace there is blessing. *(Yiddish)*

PEACOCK
The peacock hath fair feathers but foul feet.
The pride of the peacock is the glory of God. *(Blake)*

PEARL
Neither cast ye your pearls before swine. *(New Test., Matthew)*
Pearls are not good to eat or drink. *(Chinese)*
Pearls on your neck—stones on your heart. *(Yiddish)*

PEASANT
. . . a bold peasantry, their country's pride,
When once destroyed, can never be supplied. *(Goldsmith)*
Better a healthy peasant than a sickly king. *(German)*
The peasant is a peasant though he sleep till mid-day. *(German)*
A rich peasant, like a shaggy dog, only keeps himself warm with his money. *(Roumanian)*
If the thunder is not loud, the peasant forgets to cross himself. *(Russian)*
Set a peasant on horseback, and he forgets God and man. *(Spanish)*
Peasant erect is taller than peasant on bended knee. *(Turkish)*

PEDANT
An artist may visit a museum, but only a pedant can live there. *(Santayana)*
It smells of the lamp. *(Greek)*

PEDIGREE

The pedigree of honey does not concern the bee. *(E. Dickinson)*
Who asks after the pedigree of a swine he is going to kill?
Ask not after a good man's pedigree. *(Spanish)*

PEN

A goose quill is more dangerous than a lion's paw.
A sword less hurt does than a pen.
Pen and ink is wit's plough.
The pen is mightier than the sword.
You don't need a golden pen to write upon dirt.
The pen scratches; the paper is silent. *(Russian)*
The pen is the tongue of the mind. *(Spanish)*

PENNY

One penny in the money-box makes more noise than when it is full. *(Dutch)*
A bad penny always comes back.
A penny is sometimes better spent than spared.
A penny saved is a penny gained.
Account not that work slavery
That brings in penny savory.
Better penny in silver than any brother.
Every penny that's saved is not gotten.
In for a penny, in for a pound.
Penny and penny laid up will be many.
Penny wise and pound foolish.
Take care of the pennies and the pounds will take care of themselves.
The smith and his penny are always black.
What is not wanted is dear at a penny.
One cannot have a good penny with bad ware. *(French)*
A penny in pocket is better than a ducat in the chest. *(German)*

PEOPLE

No doubt but ye are the people, and wisdom shall die with you. *(Old Test., Job)*
Folks are better than angels.
The Lord prefers common-looking people. That is the reason he made so many of them. *(Lincoln)*
The mob has many heads but no brains.
The people pay with ingratitude.
The tyranny of a multitude is a multiplied tyranny. *(Burke)*

They who have put out the people's eyes, reproach them of their blindness. *(Milton)*
To worship the people is to be worshipped. *(Bacon)*
The public! How many fools does it take to make a public? *(Chamfort)*
Those three intractable beasts: the owl, the serpent, and the people. *(Demosthenes)*
Trust not the many-minded populace. *(Greek)*
I hate the vulgar herd and hold it far. *(Horace)*
It is easy to go over to the crowd. *(Latin)*
No man who depends upon the caprice of the ignorant rabble can be accounted great. *(Cicero)*
Nothing is so uncertain as the judgments of the mob. *(Latin)*
The fickle mob . . . [*Mobile vulgus.*] *(Latin)*
The mob tramples on the coward. *(Latin)*
The people—docile to the yoke. *(Latin)*
The safety of the people shall be the highest law. *(Latin)*
The views of the mob are neither bad nor good. *(Latin)*
The voice of the people is the voice of God. [*Vox populi, Vox Dei.*] *(Alcuin)*

PERFECTION
Be ye therefore perfect, even as your Father which is in heaven is perfect. *(New Test., Matth.)*
Trifles make perfection, and perfection is no trifle. *(Michelangelo)*

PERFUME
They that smell least, smell best.
He smells best that smells of nothing. *(Latin)*

PERSEVERANCE
God is with those who persevere. *(Arabian)*
For a just man falleth seven times and riseth up again. *(Old Test., Prov.)*
By perseverance the snail reached the ark.
He that can stay, obtains.
It's dogged as does it.
Little strokes fell great oaks.
Persevere and never fear.
Slow and steady wins the race.
Troy was not taken in a day.
Link by link the coat of mail is made. *(French)*
Paris was not built in a day. *(French)*

In time a mouse will gnaw through a cable. *(German)*
Persevere, and preserve yourself for better days. *(Latin)*
An oak is not felled at one blow. *(Spanish)*

PERSONALITY

As I am, so I see.
What is commonest, cheapest, nearest, easiest is Me. *(Whitman)*
Sancho Panza by name is my own self, if I was not changed in the cradle. *(Cervantes)*

PERSUASION

By long forbearance is a prince persuaded. *(Old Test., Prov.)*
The persuasion of the fortunate sways the doubtful.

PERVERSE

Perverseness makes one squint-eyed.
All things can corrupt perverted minds. *(Latin)*

PESSIMIST

A man who thinks everybody as nasty as himself. *(G. B. Shaw)*
A pessimist is one who has to live with an optimist.

PETER

Peter in, and Paul out.
Praise Peter but don't find fault with Paul.
To rob Peter, and give it Paul, it were not alms but great sin.

PHILANTHROPY

Be not weary in well-doing. *(New Test., II Thessal.)*
Blessed is he that considereth the poor. *(Old Test., Psalms)*
I was eyes to the blind, and feet was I to the lame. *(Old Test., Job)*
Feel for others—in your pocket.
He who bestows his goods upon the poor,
Shall have as much again, and ten times more. *(Bunyan)*
Mankind will not be reasoned out of the feelings of humanity. *(Blackstone)*
Not what we give, but what we share
For the gift without the giver is bare. *(Lowell)*
The hands that help are holier than the lips that pray. *(Ingersoll)*
The most acceptable service of God is doing good to man. *(Franklin)*
We praise those who love their fellow-men. *(Aristotle)*
I am a man, and nothing human can be indifferent to me. *(Terence)*
In nothing do men more nearly approach the gods than in doing good to their fellow-men. *(Cicero)*

What good thing you do, do not defer it. *(Latin)*
What is done for another is done for oneself. *(Latin)*
Only those live who do good. *(Tolstoy)*
Wipe the nose of your neighbor's son, and take him into your house. *(Spanish)*

PHILOSOPHY

Adversity's sweet milk, philosophy. *(Shakespeare)*
All men are philosophers, to their inches.
Be a philosopher; but amidst all your philosophy, be still a man. *(Hume)*

For there was never yet philosopher
That could endure the toothache patiently. *(Shakespeare)*
In earthly mire philosophy may sleep.
Many talk like philosophers and live like fools.
Philosophers dwell in the moon.
Philosophy will clip an angel's wings. *(Keats)*
There are more things in heaven and earth, Horatio,
Than are dreamt of in your philosophy. *(Shakespeare)*
Clearness marks the sincerity of philosophers. *(French)*
Philosophy is doubt. *(Montaigne)*
Let the philosopher be wise for himself. *(Greek)*
Philosophy is the highest music. *(Plato)*
No statement is too absurd for philosophers to make. *(Latin)*
Philosophy does the going, and wisdom is the goal. *(Latin)*
Philosophy, the mother of the arts. *(Latin)*
The true medicine of the mind is philosophy. *(Latin)*
To enjoy freedom, be the slave of philosophy. *(Latin)*

PHYSICIAN

Every man is a fool or a physician at forty.
God heals, and the physician hath the thanks.
If physic do not work, prepare for the kirk.
Physician, heal thyself.
Honor a physician before thou hast need of him. *(Hebrew)*
That city is in a bad case, whose physician has the gout. *(Hebrew)*
He is a fool that makes his physician his heir. *(Latin)*
More danger from the physician than from the disease. *(Latin)*

PICTURE

Pictures are the books of the unlearned.
A picture is a poem without words. *(Latin)*

PIE

Better some of a pudding than none of a pie.

PIETY

No piety delays the wrinkles. *(Latin)*
Piety is the foundation of all the virtues. *(Latin)*

PIG

Young pigs grunt as old pigs grunted before them. *(Danish)*
If you pull one pig by the tail, all the rest squeal. *(Dutch)*
Feed a pig and you'll have a hog.
You cannot make a silk purse out of a sow's ear.
When the pig is offered, hold up the poke.
A pig's life—short and sweet. *(French)*
Old pigs have hard snouts. *(German)*
He that has but one pig easily fattens it. *(Italian)*
The lazy pig does not eat ripe pears. *(Italian)*
The pig prefers mud to clean water. *(Latin)*
A pig's tail will never make a good arrow. *(Spanish)*
Give a pig a finger, and he wants the whole hand. *(Yiddish)*
Let a pig into your garden, and you can't get rid of him. *(Yiddish)*

PILGRIM

Pilgrims seldom come home saints.

PILLOW

Our pillow should be our counsellor. *(Latin)*

PILOT

The best pilots are ashore. *(Dutch)*
A pilot is not chosen for riches but for his knowledge.
Everyone can navigate in fine weather. *(Italian)*
Reward not a sleeping pilot. *(Latin)*

PINCH

Everyone knows where the shoe pinches.

PINE

The pine wishes herself a shrub when the axe is at her root.

PIPER

Give the piper a penny to play, and two pence to leave off.
Pipers don't pay fiddlers.
You will have to pay the piper.

PISS
He that pisseth against the wind, wets his shirt. *(Italian)*

PIT
Who diggeth a pit shall fall therein. *(Old Test., Prov.)*

PITCH
He that touches pitch shall be defiled. *(Apocrypha)*

PITCHER
Little pitchers have great ears.
The pitcher goes so often to the well, that it is broken at last.
Whether the pitcher strike the stone, or the stone the pitcher, woe to the pitcher. *(Spanish)*

PITY
He that hath pity on the poor lendeth to the Lord. *(Old Test., Prov.)*
Foolish pity mars a city.
For pity runneth soon in gentle heart. *(Chaucer)*
He that pities another remembers himself.
Pity and need make all flesh kin.
Pity is akin to love.
Wherever we meet misery we owe pity.
He who would have others pity him must pity others. *(Yiddish)*

PLACE
A place for everything and everything in its place. *(Smiles)*
All things have their place, knew we how to place them.
At a round table there's no dispute of place.
Sit in your place, and none can make you rise.
The place is dignified by the doer's deed. *(Shakespeare)*
Those to whom everybody allows the second place, have an undoubted title to the first. *(Swift)*
You cannot be in two places at once.
Wherever MacGregor sits is the head of the table.
There is no greater immorality than to occupy a place you cannot fill. *(Napoleon)*
It is not the places that grace men, but men the places. *(Greek)*
Each man has his own place. *(Latin)*
Nothing is more annoying than a low man in a high place. *(Latin)*

PLAGIARISM

If every bird takes back its own feathers, you'll be naked.
Originality is often undetected plagiarism.
Perish those who said our good things before us. *(Latin)*

PLAIN

As plain as a pikestaff.
As plain as the nose on a man's face.
Plain dealing is more praised than practiced.
Call a spade a spade. *(Italian)*

PLANT

He who plants a walnut tree expects not to eat of the fruit.
Plant the crabtree where you will, it will never bear pippins.
Pluck not where you never planted.

PLAY

As good play for nothing as work for nothing.
Play, women, and wine undo men laughing.
The last act crowns the play.
The play's the thing. *(Shakespeare)*
He plays best who wins. *(French)*
The play is not worth the candle. *(French)*
It is not an art to play, but it is a very good art to leave off play. *(Italian)*

PLEASE

He that all men will please shall never find ease.
He that please all and himself too,
Undertakes what he cannot do.
We that live to please must please to live. *(S. Johnson)*
He had need rise betimes that would please everybody. *(French)*
You can't please all the world and his father. *(French)*
I would rather please one good man than many bad. *(Latin)*
By whatever gifts you can please, please. *(Latin)*
Do not care how many, but whom, you please. *(Latin)*
Jupiter himself cannot please everybody. *(Latin)*

PLEASURE

If you long for pleasure, you must labor hard to get it. *(Chinese)*
After pleasant scratching comes painful smarting. *(Danish)*
Fly the pleasure that bites tomorrow.
Follow pleasure and it will flee thee: flee it, and it will follow thee.

"For my own pleasure" as the man said when he struck his wife.
God made all pleasures innocent. *(C. Norton)*
He that loves pleasure, must for pleasure fall. *(Marlowe)*
Men for one pleasure a thousand griefs prove.
Never pleasure without repentance.
No pleasure without pain.
Perils commonly ask to be paid in pleasure. *(Bacon)*
Pleasure makes the hours seem short.
Pleasure's a sin, and sometimes sin's a pleasure. *(Byron)*
Pleasures, while they flatter, sting.
Punish not thyself with pleasure.
Sweet is pleasure after pain. *(Dryden)*
Who will in time present from pleasure refrain,
  Shall in time to come more pleasure obtain.
Stolen pleasures are sweet.
Short pleasure, long lament. *(French)*
A wise man resists pleasures, a fool is a slave to them. *(Greek)*
Consider not pleasures as they come but as they go. *(Greek)*
Pleasure is the greatest incentive to vice. *(Greek)*
Pleasures are transient, honors are immortal. *(Greek)*
Pleasure is frail like a dewdrop; while it laughs, it dries. *(Tagore)*
His own special pleasure attracts each one. *(Latin)*
It is rarity that gives zest to pleasure. *(Latin)*
Pleasures are the baits of evil. *(Latin)*
Pleasures in moderation relax. *(Latin)*
The human mind runs downhill from toil to pleasure. *(Latin)*
There is no pleasure unalloyed. *(Latin)*

PLENTY
My cup runneth over. *(Old Test., Psalms)*
As plenty as blackberries.
He who of plenty will take no heed,
  Shall find default in time of need.
His bread is buttered on both sides.
Plenty is no dainty.
Plenty makes dainty.

PLOUGH
No man, having put his hand to the plough, and looking back, is fit
  for the kingdom of God. *(New Test., Luke)*
A plough that works, shines. *(Dutch)*
God speed the plough.

He that by the plough would thrive, himself must either hold or drive.
It is folly to put the plough in front of the oxen. *(French)*
Plough deep and you will have plenty of corn. *(Spanish)*

POACHER
An old poacher makes the best keeper.

POCKET
The longest road is the road to the pocket. *(Yiddish)*
Money burns a hole in the pocket.

POET
Those who err follow the poets. *(The Koran)*
All poets are mad. *(Burton)*
I sound my barbaric yaup over the roofs of the world. *(Whitman)*
One may be a poet without versing . . .
The poet is the truest historian.
The poet's eye in a fine frenzy rolling . . . *(Shakespeare)*
True poets are the guardians of the state.
It is not good to be the poet of a village. *(German)*
Beggar is jealous of beggar, and poet of poet. *(Greek)*
Poets utter great and wise things which they do not themselves understand. *(Plato)*
A poet is born, not made. *(Latin)*
He does not write whose verses no one reads. *(Latin)*
It costs less to keep a lion than a poet: the poet's belly is more capacious. *(Juvenal)*
The irritable tribe of poets. *(Horace)*
To a poet even a rush may be vocal. *(Turkish)*

POETRY
A poem should not mean
But be. *(MacLeish)*
No Muse is proof against a golden shower.
Oh, love will make a dog howl to rhyme.
Poetry fettered fetters the human race. *(Blake)*
Poetry, the language of the gods.
Poetry, the queen of arts.
The finest poetry was first experience. *(Emerson)*
The true poem is the poet's mind. *(Emerson)*
Poetry is the natural language of all worship. *(French)*
Poetry is truth in its Sunday clothes. *(French)*

Poetry forbids victorious deeds to die. *(German)*
Indignation leads to the making of poetry. *(Juvenal)*
Let your poem be kept nine years. *(Horace)*
Poetry is devil's wine. *(St. Augustine)*

POINT
De point of de pin is de easiest to fin'. *(American Negro)*

POISON
In poison there is physic. *(Shakespeare)*
One drop of poison infecteth the whole tun of wine.
The coward's weapon, poison.
They love not poison that do poison need. *(Shakespeare)*
Where the bee sucks honey, the spider sucks poison.
Poison drives out poison. *(Italian)*
What does not poison, fattens. *(Italian)*
One man's meat is another's poison. *(Latin)*
Poison is drunk from cups of gold. *(Latin)*
When the Fates will, two poisons work for good. *(Latin)*
Wicked poisons lurk in sweet honey. *(Latin)*

POLITENESS
A civil denial is better than a rude grant.
One never loses anything by politeness.
Politeness does not pay the bill.
Politeness is to do and say
The kindest things in the kindest way.
Politeness smooths wrinkles. *(French)*
Hat in hand goes through the land. *(German)*
Politeness is what warmth is to wax. *(German)*
Put your hand twice to your bonnet for once to your pouch. *(Scottish)*

POLITICS
All political parties die at last by swallowing their own lies. *(Arbuthnot)*
All politics is Apple Sauce. *(Will Rogers)*
An honest politician is one who, when he is bought, will stay bought. *(S. Cameron)*
Few politicians die, and none resign. *(Jefferson)*
For politicians neither love nor hate. *(Dryden)*
It is not best to swap horses while crossing a stream. *(Lincoln)*
Old politicians chew on wisdom past. *(Pope)*

Party is the madness of the many for the gain of the few. *(Pope)*
Politics makes strange bedfellows.
Public office is a public trust.
There is no gambling like politics. *(Disraeli)*
Vain hope, to make people happy by politics. *(Carlyle)*
When great questions end, little parties begin.
You can't adopt politics as a profession and remain honest. *(L. M. Howe)*
Office will show the man. *(Greek)*
Man is a political animal. *(Aristotle)*
Politics—a rotten egg; if broken open, it stinks. *(Russian)*

POMP

All our pomp the earth covers.

POOR

The poor ye always have with you. *(New Test., Matth.)*
A poor man has few acquaintances. *(Danish)*
A lamb is as dear to the poor man as an ox to the rich.
A poor man's shilling is but a penny.
As poor as a church mouse.
As poor as Job.
Every poor man is counted a fool.
God help the poor, for the rich can help themselves.
God help the rich, for the poor can beg.
He is poor indeed who can promise nothing.
Poor and content is rich and rich enough.
Poor men seek meat for their stomachs; rich men stomach for their meat.
Poor men's tables are soon spread.
The dainties of the great are the tears of the poor.
The devil wipes his tail with the poor man's pride.
The poor pay for all.
He is too poor to buy a rope to hang himself. *(German)*
The poor must dance as the rich pipe. *(German)*
The poor sing free throughout the world. *(German)*
Whoso stoppeth his ear at the cry of the poor, shall cry himself and not be heard. *(Hebrew)*
Poor men do penance for rich men's sins. *(Italian)*
Not he who has little, but he who wishes for more, is poor. *(Latin)*
A poor man is hungry after eating. *(Portuguese)*

The poor man has his crop destroyed by hail every year. *(Spanish)*
Poor without debt is better than a prince. *(Turkish)*

POPE

We cannot all be pope of Rome. *(German)*
After one pope another is made. *(Italian)*
Being a man I may come to be Pope. *(Spanish)*
He that has the Pope for his cousin need not fear hell fire. *(Spanish)*
The corpse of the pope takes up no more room than the sacristan's. *(Spanish)*

POPULARITY

God will not love thee less, because men love thee more.
Popularity is glory in copper pieces. *(French)*
When one has a good table, he is always right. *(French)*
The popularity of a bad man is as treacherous as himself. *(Latin)*
When Fortune favors us, Popularity bears her company. *(Latin)*

PORRIDGE

He that eats most porridge shall have most meat.

PORT

Any port in a storm.
The worse the passage, the more welcome the port.

PORTION

A portionless dame sits long at hame.

POSITION

He sits not sure that sits too high.
Sit in your place, and none can make you rise.

POSSESSION

As having nothing, and yet possessing all things. *(New Test., II Corin.)*
Is it not lawful for me to do what I will with mine own? *(New Test., Matthew)*
Unto everyone which hath shall be given. *(New Test., Luke)*
Papa's having and mamma's having is not like having oneself. *(Chinese)*
A bird in the hand is worth two in the bush.
All strive to give to him who already has.
An ill-favored thing, sir, but mine own. *(Shakespeare)*
Bliss in possession will not last.
Much will have more.

Possession is nine points of the law.
We give to the rich and take from the poor.
Would ye both eat your cake and have your cake?
Everything goes to him who wants nothing. *(French)*
I carry all my possessions with me. *(Greek)*
Him that is in possession God helps. *(Italian)*
All possessions of mortals are mortal. *(Latin)*
No man can swim ashore and carry his baggage with him. *(Latin)*
To each his own. *(Latin)*
To have may be taken from us; to have had, never. *(Latin)*
What is not ours charms more than our own. *(Latin)*
What is thine own hold as thine own. *(Latin)*
What you have, hold. *(Latin)*
You can never consider that as your own which can be changed. *(Latin)*
So much as you have, so much are you sure of. *(Spanish)*
You must leave your possessions behind, when God summons. *(Yiddish)*

POSTERITY

People will not look forward to posterity, who never look backward to their ancestors. *(Burke)*
Posterity pay for the sins of their fathers. *(Latin)*

POT

A pot that belongs to many is ill stirred and worse boiled.
A watched pot never boils.
Every potter praises his own pot.
Little pot is soon hot.
One pot sets another boiling.
The earthen pot must keep off the brass kettle.
The pot calls the kettle black.
The weaker goeth to the pot.
When the pot boils over it cools itself.
Who boils his pot with chips makes his broth smell of smoke.
A cracked pot never fell off the hook. *(Italian)*

POVERTY

Blessed be ye poor: for yours is the kingdom of God. *(New Test., Luke)*
He that hath pity upon the poor lendeth unto the Lord. *(Old Test., Prov.)*
The destruction of the poor is their poverty. *(Old Test., Prov.)*
The life of the poor is the curse of the heart. *(Apocrypha)*

The poor is hated even of his own neighbors. *(Old Test., Prov.)*
A man guilty of poverty easily believes himself suspected. *(S. Johnson)*
Bare walls make giddy housewives.
Bear wealth: poverty will bear itself.
Better die a beggar than live a beggar.
Come away! Poverty's catching.
He can give little to his servant that licks his knife.
He must stoop that hath a low door.
His purse and his palate are ill met.
If thou be poor, thy brother hateth thee, ... *(Chaucer)*
It is easier to praise poverty than to bear it.
Light purse, heavy heart.
Little goods, little cares.
My poverty, not my will consents. *(Shakespeare)*
Patience with poverty is all a poor man's remedy.
Poor folks are glad of porridge.
Poor folks' friends soon mistake them.
Poor men go to heaven as soon as the rich.
Poverty breeds strife.
Poverty is no sin.
Poverty is no vice—but an inconvenience.
Poverty is not a shame, but the being ashamed of it is.
Poverty is the mother of all the arts.
Poverty is the mother of health.
Poverty is the Muse's patrimony. *(Burton)*
Poverty is the worst guard to chastity.
Poverty makes strange bedfellows.
Poverty parteth fellowship.
Riches come better after poverty than poverty after riches.
Slow rises worth by poverty oppressed. *(S. Johnson)*
The devil dances in an empty pocket.
The rich feast, the poor fast;
  The dogs dine, the poor pine.
There is no virtue that poverty destroyeth not.
What can a poor man do but love and pray?
When the wolf comes in at the door, love flies out at the window.
Who doth sing so merry a note
  As he that cannot change a groat?
Honest poverty is thinly sewn. *(French)*
If you are poor, distinguish yourself by your virtues; if rich, by your good deeds. *(French)*

Poverty is a sort of leprosy. *(French)*
The poor man is never free; he serves in every country. *(Voltaire)*
Everyone likes to wipe his shoes on poverty. *(German)*
Poverty is the daughter of laziness. *(German)*
All the days of the poor are evil. *(Hebrew)*
A poor man is not believed, though he speak the truth. *(Greek)*
Contented poverty is an honorable estate. *(Greek)*
It is better to endure poverty than the arrogance of the rich. *(Greek)*
Nothing is more luckless than a poor man. *(Greek)*
Painless poverty is better than embittered wealth. *(Greek)*
Poverty—the mother of temperance. *(Greek)*
The gods protect the poor. *(Greek)*
Fortune takes least from him to whom she has given least. *(Latin)*
He who has made a fair compact with poverty is rich. *(Latin)*
It is natural for a poor man to count his flock. *(Latin)*
Money is very slow to come where there is poverty. *(Latin)*
No man should praise poverty but he who is poor. *(St. Bernard)*
No one lives so poor as he is born. *(Latin)*
Poverty is a hateful blessing. *(Latin)*
Poverty is safe; riches, exposed to danger. *(Latin)*
Poverty is the mother of crime. *(Latin)*
Poverty—the mother of manhood. *(Latin)*
Remember to bear patiently the burden of poverty. *(Latin)*
The body is well, but the purse is sick. *(Latin)*
The man who has lost his purse will go wherever you wish. *(Latin)*
The penniless traveler may sing before thieves. *(Latin)*
The poor man is despised everywhere. *(Latin)*
The poor, wishing to imitate the powerful, perish. *(Latin)*
There are many things which ragged men dare not say. *(Latin)*
To have nothing is not poverty. *(Latin)*
We do not praise poverty, but him whom poverty cannot bend. *(Latin)*
The poor sing, the rich listen. *(Russian)*
We will do anything for the poor man except get off his back. *(Tolstoy)*
Poverty is no sin, but it is a branch of roguery. *(Spanish)*
There are only two families in the world, the Haves and the Have-Nots. *(Cervantes)*
Poverty is a shirt of fire. *(Turkish)*
Poverty and sloth are brothers. *(Yiddish)*
Poverty is no disgrace—but it is no great honor either. *(Yiddish)*
The first place poverty lies down on, is the face. *(Yiddish)*

POWDER
If you can't stand the smell of powder, don't go to war. *(Yiddish)*

POWER
The powers that be are ordained of God. *(New Test., Romans)*
Power goes before talent. *(Danish)*
He hath no power that hath no power to use.
If you would be powerful, pretend to be powerful.
Increase of power begets increase of wealth.
Power weakeneth the wicked.
The greater the power, the more dangerous the abuse. *(Burke)*
The love of power may be as strong in the heart of a peasant as of a prince.
Unlimited power corrupts the possessor. *(Pitt)*
Who can do as he pleases, commands when he entreats. *(French)*
A partnership with the powerful is never safe. *(Latin)*
Lust of power is the strongest of all passions. *(Latin)*
Power acquired by guilt was never used for a good purpose. *(Latin)*
Power passes to the best from the inferior. *(Latin)*
The highest power may be lost by misrule. *(Latin)*
Who is too powerful seeks power beyond his power. *(Latin)*
Mickle power—mickle enemies. *(Scottish)*
For sovereign power all laws are broken. *(Spanish)*
Power on my head, or the raven on my corpse. *(Turkish)*

PRACTICE
Practice well if you would excel. *(Chinese)*
Practice is everything. *(Greek)*
Practice makes perfect. *(Latin)*
Hand in use is father of lear. *Scottish)*

PRAISE
Out of the mouths of babes and sucklings thou hast perfected praise. *(New Test., Matthew)*
A man's praise in his own mouth doth stink.
Approbation from Sir Hubert is praise indeed.
Damn with faint praise. *(Pope)*
Every man praises his own wares.
Faint praise is akin to abuse.
Forbear to mention what thou canst not praise.
Good things should be praised.
He that praises publicly will slander privately.

He that praiseth himself spattereth himself.
He wants worth who dares not praise a foe. *(Dryden)*
He who loves praise loves temptation.
He who praises everybody praises nobody.
I will praise any man that will praise me.
In their own merits modest men are dumb.
Let every man praise the bridge he goes over.
Neither praise nor dispraise thyself: thy actions serve the turn.
Old praise dies unless you feed it.
Our praise are our wages.
Praise a fair day at night.
Praise a fool, and you water his folly.
Praise is but the shadow of virtue.
Praise is deeper than the lips.
Praise is not pudding.
Praise little—dispraise less.
Praise makes good men better and bad men worse.
Praise the child, and you make love to the mother.
Praise the sea, but keep on land.
Praise to the face is open disgrace.
Praise undeserved is satire in disguise.
Praise without profit puts little into the pot.
Self-praise is no recommendation.
The praise of a fool is incense to the wisest of us.
A man's accusations of himself are always believed, his praises never. *(Montaigne)*
An honest man is hurt by praise unjustly bestowed. *(French)*
The art of praising began the art of pleasing. *(Voltaire)*
The refusal of praise is a wish to be praised twice. *(La Rochefoucauld)*
Usually we praise only to be praised. *(La Rochefoucauld)*
One has only to die to be praised. *(German)*
Self-praise and self-dispraise are alike absurd. *(Greek)*
The most pleasing of all sounds—that of your own praise. *(Greek)*
A part of a man's praise may be told in his presence; the whole, in his absence. *(Hebrew)*
A man commends himself in praising that which he loves. *(Latin)*
Be sparing in praising, and more so in blaming. *(Latin)*
He who praises himself will soon find someone to deride him. *(Latin)*
I am pleased to be praised by one whom everyone praises. *(Latin)*
In doing what we ought we deserve no praise. *(Latin)*
Praise yourself daringly, something always sticks. *(Latin)*

Unless new praise arises, even the old is lost. *(Latin)*
We are all imbued with the love of praise. *(Latin)*
I praise loudly, I blame softly. *(Russian)*
Every pedler praises his own needles. *(Spanish)*
Praise yourself, Basket, for I want to sell you. *(Spanish)*
Self-praise debases. *(Spanish)*
He who praises himself must have bad neighbors. *(Yiddish)*
It is not befitting to praise yourself—but it does no harm. *(Yiddish)*

PRAYER

All things, whatsoever ye ask in prayer, believing, ye shall receive. *(New Test., Matthew)*
Ask, and it shall be given you; seek and ye shall find; knock, and it shall be opened unto you. *(New Test., Matthew)*
The prayer of faith shall save the sick. *(New Test., James)*
Watch and pray. *(New Test., Mark)*
Your Father knoweth what things ye have need of, before you ask Him. *(New Test., Matthew)*
A seraph may pray for a sinner,
  But a sinner must pray for himself. *(C. M. Dickinson)*
And Satan trembles when he sees
  The weakest saint upon his knees. *(Cowper)*
Common people do not pray; they only beg. *(G. B. Shaw)*
Danger is sauce for prayers.
God warms his hands at man's heart when he prays. *(Masefield)*
He who ceases to pray ceases to prosper.
Heaven would often be unjust if it answered our prayers.
More things are wrought by prayer
  Than this world dreams of. *(Tennyson)*
No man ever prayed heartily without learning something. *(Emerson)*
Pray devoutly, but hammer stoutly.
Prayer ardent opens Heaven. *(Young)*
Prayer is a wish turned heavenwards.
Prayer should be the key of the day, and the lock of the night.
Prayers and provender hinder no journey.
Prayers plow not! Praises reap not! *(Blake)*
They never sought in vain that sought the Lord aright. *(Burns)*
When the gods wish to punish us, they answer our prayers. *(Wilde)*
Who goes to bed, and doth not pray,
  Maketh two nights to every day.
Who rises from prayer a better man, his prayer is answered. *(Meredith)*

Whoso will pray, he must fast and be clean,
  And fat his soul, and make his body lean. *(Chaucer)*

Who prays without trust cannot hope to have his prayers answered. *(French)*

A grateful thought toward Heaven is a complete prayer. *(German)*

The fewer the words the better the prayer. *(German)*

To pray well is the better half of study. *(Luther)*

Do not pray for yourself: you do not know what will help you. *(Greek)*

Long tarries destiny, but comes to those who pray. *(Greek)*

Who hearkens to the gods, to him the gods give ear. *(Greek)*

A god, when angry, is moved by the voice of prayer. *(Latin)*

A short prayer enters heaven. *(Latin)*

Do not waste time in praying. *(Ovid)*

Fear drives to prayer. *(Latin)*

Nothing costs so much as what is bought by prayers. *(Seneca)*

Prayers travel faster when said in unison. *(Latin)*

Rather go rob with good men than pray with bad. *(Portuguese)*

A prayer of a dog does not reach heaven. *(Spanish)*

If you pray for another, you will be helped yourself. *(Yiddish)*

Prayers go up and blessings come down. *(Yiddish)*

PREACHER

A good example is the best sermon.

An ounce of practice is worth a pound of preaching.

He that will not be saved needs no preacher.

If the beard were all, the goat might preach.

More vacant pulpits would more converts make. *(Dryden)*

None preaches better than the ant, and she says nothing.

Only the sinner has a right to preach.

Preach not because you have to say something, but because you have something to say.

Preachers say, Do as I say, not as I do.

The parson knows enough who knows a Duke. *(Cowper)*

It is bad preaching to deaf ears. *(German)*

There are many preachers who don't hear themselves. *(German)*

A fool is he who comes to preach or prate,
  When men with swords their right and wrong debate. *(Italian)*

It is easy preaching to the fasting with a full belly. *(Italian)*

Practice yourself what you preach. *(Latin)*

He preaches well that lives well. *(Spanish)*

PRECEDENT
As well to create good precedents as to follow them. *(Bacon)*
The more ancient the abuse the more sacred it is. *(Voltaire)*

PRECIOUS
Precious salve in small boxes. *(French)*

PRECOCIOUS
Early ripe, early rotten.
What ripens fast does not last.
Precocious youth is a sign of premature death. *(Latin)*

PREDICTION
He that would know what shall be, must consider what hath been.

PREJUDICE
A prejudice is a vagrant opinion without visible means of support. *(Bierce)*
It is never too late to give up our prejudices. *(Thoreau)*
Prejudice is the child of ignorance.
Drive out prejudices by the door, they will come back by the window. *(French)*
Prejudices are kings of the vulgar herd. *(Voltaire)*

PREMATURE
Boil not the pap until the child is born.
Count not your chickens before they are hatched.
Don't shout until you are out of the woods.
Don't cry fried fish before they are caught. *(Italian)*
Don't sell the bear's skin before you have killed the bear. *(Italian)*

PREPAREDNESS
A man-of-war is the best ambassador. *(Cromwell)*
Have not thy cloak to make when it begins to rain.
One sword keeps another in the sheath.
Who carries a sword, carries peace. *(French)*
He who is not prepared today, will be less so tomorrow. *(Latin)*
If you want peace, be prepared for war. *(Latin)*
Forewarned, forearmed; to be prepared is half the victory. *(Spanish)*

PRESENT
No time like the present.
The present is big with the future. *(French)*

The present alone can make no man wretched. *(Latin)*
Better an egg today than a hen tomorrow. *(Latin)*

PRESS

When the press is free and every man able to read, all is safe. *(Jefferson)*
Three hostile newspapers are more to be feared than a thousand bayonets. *(Napoleon)*

PREVENTION

An ounce of prevention is better than a pound of cure.

PRICE

Corn and horn go together.
Every man has his price. *(Walpole)*
Not how cheap, but how good.
The highest price a man can pay for a thing is to ask for it.
Things of greatest profit are set forth with least price.
What you do not need is dear at a farthing. *(Latin)*
What costs little is valued less. *(Spanish)*

PRIDE

Pride goeth before destruction, and a haughty spirit before a fall . . . *(Old Test., Prov.)*
When pride cometh, then cometh shame. *(Old Test., Prov.)*
The pride of the poor does not endure. *(Danish)*
A man may be poor in purse, yet proud in spirit.
A proud mind and a beggar's purse agree not well together.
As proud as a peacock.
As proud as a pig with two tails.
As proud as Lucifer.
He that is proud eats up himself.
Overdone pride makes naked side.
Pride and gout are seldom cured throughout.
Pride and grace dwell never in one place.
Pride and poverty are ill met, yet often seen together.
Pride breakfasted with plenty, dined with poverty, and supped with infamy.
Pride costs us more than hunger, thirst, and cold.
Pride dines upon vanity, sups on contempt.
Pride goes before, shame follows after.
Pride had rather go out of the way than go behind.
Pride in prosperity turns to misery in adversity.

Pride is as loud a beggar as want, and a great deal more saucy.
Pride is at the bottom of all great mistakes.
Pride is the cause of allë woe. *(Gower)*
Pride is the sworn enemy to content.
Pride may lurk under a threadbare cloak.
Pride that dines on vanity sups on contempt.
Pride will have a fall; for pride goeth before and shame cometh after.
Shame is Pride's cloak. *(Blake)*
The Devil's darling sin is pride that apes humility. *(Coleridge)*
The devil wipes his tail with the poor man's pride.
The pride of the rich makes the labor of the poor.
The proud hate pride—in others.
The proud will sooner lose than ask the way.
When pride rides, shame lacqueys.
One may be humble out of pride. *(Montaigne)*
Pride and conceit were the original sin of man. *(French)*
When pride is in the saddle, mischief is on the crupper. *(French)*
Peacock, look at your legs. *(German)*
Pride is the mask of one's own faults. *(Hebrew)*
An avenging god pursues the proud. *(Latin)*
He who is on horseback no longer knows his own father. *(Russian)*
You a lady, I a lady, who will put the sow out of doors? *(Spanish)*
But yesterday out of the shell, today he despises the shell. *(Turkish)*
God is the enemy of the proud. *(Turkish)*

PRIEST

Bad priests bring the devil into the church.
Every man is a priest in his own house.
Like priest, like people.
Once have a priest for an enemy, good-bye to peace.
Parish priest forgetteth that ever he was clerk.
Priests pray for enemies but princes kill. *(Shakespeare)*
The priest is always with the herd and against the individual.
The priest should live by the altar. *(French)*
What village priest would not like to be pope? *(French)*
Priests pay each other no tithes. *(German)*
The quarrel of priests is the devil's jubilee. *(German)*
Give the priest a drink, for the clerk is thirsty. *(Italian)*
That priest is a fool who decries his relics. *(Italian)*
When the priest visits you, do not rejoice; he will soon begin to beg. *(Russian)*

PRINCE

Put not your trust in princes. *(Old Test., Psalms)*

All the virtues of the prince are so many misfortunes to the wicked. *(Chinese)*

The blemish of the prince who has forfeited his word can never be removed. *(Chinese)*

A begging prince, what beggar pities not? *(Shakespeare)*

Many princes sin with David, but few repent with him.

Of a new prince, new bondage.

The prince that is feared of many must fear many.

The vices of a prince draw shoals of followers.

The punishment of bad princes is to be thought worse than they are. *(French)*

As the prince fiddles, the subjects must dance. *(German)*

The hand of the prince is as great as his territory. *(German)*

Princes have long arms. *(Italian)*

A prince's greatest virtue is to know his own. *(Latin)*

Princes are mortal, the commonwealth is eternal. *(Latin)*

PRISON

No man loveth his fetters, be they made of gold.

Prisons are built with stones of law, brothels with bricks of religion. *(Blake)*

Whilst we have prisons it matters little which of us occupies the cells. *(G. B. Shaw)*

Stone walls do not a prison make,
Nor iron bars a cage . . . *(Lovelace)*

PROCRASTINATION

"One of these days" is none of these days.

Never put off till tomorrow what can be done today.

Procrastination is the thief of time. *(Young)*

The procrastinating man is ever struggling with ruin. *(Greek)*

By and by never comes. *(Latin)*

While we are postponing, life speeds by. *(Latin)*

PRODIGAL

A returning prodigal is not to be exchanged for gold. *(Chinese)*

A prodigal is no man's foe but his own.

The prodigal robs his heir, the miser, himself.

PROFIT

For profits small as pinheads they run from east to west. *(Chinese)*

Everyone fastens where there is gain.

He bought the fox-skin for three pence and sold the tail for a shilling.
He will go to hell for the house profit.
Look to the main chance.
Profit is better than fame.
What's none of my profit shall be none of my peril.
He who eats the meat, let him pick the bone. *(Spanish)*

PROGRESS
He who moves not forward goes backward. *(German)*

PROHIBITION
Forbidden fruit is sweet. *(Old Test., Genesis)*
Forbid us thing, that thing desyren we. *(Chaucer)*
Forbidden ware sells twice as dear.
Stolen sweets are best.
Things forbidden have a secret charm. *(Greek)*

PROMISE
Promise is a promise, dough you make it in de dark er de moon. *(American Negro)*
In the land of promise a man may die of hunger. *(Danish)*
A man apt to promise is apt to forget.
A promise to men in grief is lightly broken.
An acre of performance is worth a whole land of promise.
Great promise, small performance.
He never broke his hour that kept his day.
He who gives fair words feeds you with an empty spoon.
I will not change a cottage in possession for a kingdom in reversion.
Promise is debt.
Promise is most given when the least is said.
Promise and pie-crust are made to be broken.
They promise mountains, and perform molehills.
Vows made in storms are forgotten in calms.
Things promised are things due. *(French)*
We promise according to our hopes, and perform according to our fears. *(La Rochefoucauld)*
A promised dollar is not worth half. *(German)*
Who makes no promises has none to perform. *(German)*
The righteous promise little and perform much; the wicked promise much and perform not even a little. *(Hebrew)*
Fair promises bind fools. *(Italian)*
He loses his thanks who promises and delays. *(Latin)*

Many promises impair confidence. *(Latin)*
Don't put it in my ear, but in my hand. *(Russian)*
To promise—a thing of the lord; to fulfill—a thing of the slave. *(Russian)*
Take heed, girl, of the promise of a man, for it will run like a crab. *(Spanish)*

PROOF
Prove all things; hold fast that which is good. *(New Test., I Thess.)*
One must not hang a man by his looks.
What is now proved was once only imagined.
Who proves too much proves nothing. *(French)*
The event proves the act. *(Latin)*
The proof of the pudding is in the eating. *(Spanish)*

PROPERTY
If a man own land, the land owns him.
Property assures what toil acquires.
Property has its duties as well as its rights.
Property is theft. *(Proudhon)*
I don't care how, as long as I get it. *(Latin)*

PROPHECY
God has granted to every people a prophet in his own tongue. *(The Koran)*
A prophet is not without honor, save in his own country, and in his own house. *(New Test., Matthew)*
Beware of false prophets, which come to you in sheep's clothing but inwardly they are ravening wolves. *(New Test., Matthew)*
He is the best diviner who conjectures well. *(Greek)*
It is surprising that an augur can see an augur without smiling. *(Latin)*

PROPOSE
Man proposes, God disposes. *(Latin)*

PROSPERITY
In the day of prosperity be joyful, but in the day of adversity consider. *(Old Test., Eccles.)*
When prosperity smiles, beware of its guiles. *(Dutch)*
Adversity is easier borne than prosperity forgot.
He who swells in prosperity, will shrink in adversity.
In prosperity, caution; in adversity, patience.
Plenty is the child of peace.

Prosperity destroys fools, and endangers the wise.
Prosperity discovers vice; adversity, virtue.
Prosperity is a great teacher; adversity, a greater.
Prosperity's the very bond of love. *(Shakespeare)*
Prosperity lets go the bridle.
Prosperity is a feeble reed. *(French)*
Prosperity makes few friends. *(French)*
In prosperity no altars smoke. *(Italian)*
Adversity reveals genius, prosperity hides it. *(Latin)*
Prosperity makes friends, adversity tries them. *(Latin)*
Prosperity proves the fortunate, adversity, the great. *(Latin)*
The prosperous man is never sure that he is loved for himself. *(Latin)*
We are corrupted by prosperity. *(Latin)*
Prosperity forgets father and mother. *(Spanish)*

PROVERB
Proverbs are the daughters of daily experience. *(Dutch)*
A proverb is the wit of one and the wisdom of many.
Patch grief with proverbs. *(Shakespeare)*
Nothing is so senseless as a general maxim. *(Macaulay)*
Proverbs are the wisdom of the streets.
Proverbs lie on the lips of fools.
The genius, wit, and spirit of a nation are discovered in its proverbs. *(Bacon)*
The proverb is something musty. *(Shakespeare)*
The wise make proverbs and fools repeat them.
When a poor man makes a proverb he does not break it. *(German)*
A short saying often contains much wisdom. *(Greek)*
A proverb is a short sentence based on long experience. *(Spanish)*
There is no proverb which is not true. *(Spanish)*

PROVIDENCE
God never sendeth mouth but he sendeth meat.
God provides for him that trusteth.
God send water in that well that people think will never go dry.
God sendeth cold after clothes.
If you leap into a well, Providence is not bound to fetch you out.
Providence cares for every hungry mouth.
Providence is better than rent.
Providence provides for the provident.
There's a divinity that shapes our ends,
  Rough-hew them as we will. *(Shakespeare)*

There is a special providence in the fall of a sparrow.
God tempers the wind to the shorn lamb. *(French)*
Providence is always on the side of the strongest battalions. *(Voltaire)*
The ways of the gods are full of providence. *(Greek)*
Providence assists not the idle. *(Latin)*
God builds the nest of the blind bird. *(Turkish)*
He who gives us teeth will give us bread. *(Yiddish)*

PROVISION
Lay up for a rainy day.
The first years of a man's life must make provision for the last.

PRUDENCE
The prudent man looketh well to his going. *(Old Test., Prov.)*
The prudent seldom err. *(Chinese)*
Use another's foot to kick a dog. *(Chinese)*
A stitch in time saves nine.
Advisement is good before the need. *(Chaucer)*
An ounce of prudence is worth a pound of gold.
Better to go on foot than ride and fall.
Beware of a mule's hind foot, a dog's tooth, and a woman's tongue.
Cast not out the foul water till you bring in the clean.
Commend the sea, but keep thyself ashore.
Early and provident fear is the mother of safety.
Grasp not at much, for fear thou losest all.
Great estates may venture more,
  But little boats must keep near shore.
He that goes barefoot must not plant thorns.
I shall cut my coat after my cloth.
It is always good to have two irons in the fire.
It is good to have a hatch before the door.
Praise the mountains, but love the plains.
Precaution is better than cure.
Prudence is a rich, ugly old maid, courted by Incapacity. *(Blake)*
Prudence is God taking thought for oxen. *(Emerson)*
Prudence is of no service unless it be prompt.
Prudence keeps life safe, but does not often make it happy.
(S. Johnson)
Put your trust in God, and keep your powder dry. *(Cromwell)*
Take things always by their smooth handle.
Venture not all in one bottom.
Whose house is of glass must not throw stones at another's.

Prudence is always in season. *(French)*
Chance fights ever on the side of the prudent. *(Greek)*
A prudent man does not make the goat his gardener. *(Hungarian)*
Have more strings to thy bow than one. *(Latin)*
He is free from danger who is on guard, even when he is safe. *(Latin)*
I prefer silent prudence to loquacious folly. *(Cicero)*
Prudence is the first thing to desert the wretched. *(Latin)*
That should be long considered which can be decided but once. *(Latin)*
We accomplish more by prudence than by force. *(Latin)*
Who fears all snares falls into none. *(Latin)*
Colts by falling and lads by losing grow prudent. *(Spanish)*
Look before you leap. *(Spanish)*
Take heed of an ox before, an ass behind, and a monk on all sides. *(Spanish)*
Venture not all your eggs in one basket. *(Spanish)*
Call the bear "Uncle" till you are safe across the bridge. *(Turkish)*

PRYING
Pry not into the affairs of others.
Who is always prying has a dangerous life. *(Spanish)*

PUBLIC
He who serves the public hath but a scurvy master.

PUN
A pun is the cheapest form of wit.
He that would make a pun would pick a pocket.

PUNCTUALITY
Punctuality is the soul of business.
Punctuality is the politeness of kings. *(French)*

PUNISHMENT
A whip for the horse, a bridle for the ass, and a rod for the fool's back. *(Old Test., Prov.)*
He that spareth the rod hateth his son. *(Old Test., Prov.)*
All punishment is mischief. *(Bentham)*
Corn is cleansed with wind, and the soul with chastening.
He that chastises one, amendeth many.
He that would hang his dog gives out first that he is mad.
Men are not hanged for stealing horses, but that horses may not be stolen.

Punishment is lame, but it comes.
The power of punishment is to silence, not to confute. *(S. Johnson)*
Who punishes one threatens a hundred. *(French)*
The mills of the gods grind slowly, but they grind exceeding small. *(Greek)*
Disgrace does not lie in the punishment, but in the crime. *(Italian)*
The sword of heaven is not in haste to smite,
Nor yet doth linger. *(Dante)*
Let the punishment be equal with the offense. *(Latin)*
Let the ruler be slow to punish, swift to reward. *(Latin)*
Let those who have deserved their punishment bear it patiently. *(Latin)*
One day brings the punishment which many days demand. *(Latin)*
Punishment follows close on guilt. *(Latin)*

PURITY

Blessed are the pure in heart: for they shall see God. *(New Test., Matthew)*
Unto the pure all things are pure. *(New Test., Titus)*
The sun, which passeth through pollutions, and itself remains as pure as before. *(Bacon)*
The stream is always pure at its source. *(French)*

PURPOSE

A good archer is known not by his arrows but by his aim.
As good do nothing as to no purpose.
Pursue worthy aims. *(Greek)*
Slight not what is near through aiming at what is far. *(Greek)*
When a man does not know what harbor he is making for, no wind is the right wind. *(Latin)*

PURSE

Gold is gold though it be in a rogue's purse. *(Danish)*
A full purse never lacks friends.
A heavy purse makes a light heart.
A light purse makes a heavy heart.
All is not gain that is put in the purse.
An empty purse fills the face with wrinkles.
Be it for better, be it for worse,
Do you after him that beareth the purse.
He that hath no money needeth no purse.

He that in his purse lacks money,
  Hath in his mouth much need of honey.
Let your purse be your master.
That is but an empty purse that is full of other men's money.
Who steals my purse steals trash. *(Shakespeare)*
According to your purse, let your mouth speak. *(French)*
Open your purse, and I will open my mouth. *(Portuguese)*
A purse without money is only a piece of leather. *(Yiddish)*

QUACK

Quackery gives birth to nothing; gives death to all things. *(Carlyle)*

Trust not yourself to a quack when you are sick. *(Latin)*

QUALITY

Every man has the defects of his qualities.

There never was a good knife made of bad steel.

QUARREL

A quarelsome man has no good neighbors.

Brawling booteth not.

Fall not out with a friend for a trifle.

In a false quarrel there is no true valor. *(Shakespeare)*

Paintings and fightings are best seen at a distance.

Quarrels do not live long.

Quarrels never could be long,
 If on one side only lay the wrong.

Quarrelsome dogs get dirty coats.

The world is too narrow for two fools a-quarreling.

Those who in quarrels interpose,
 Must often wipe a bloody nose.

Thrice is he armed that hath his quarrel just. *(Shakespeare)*

When we quarrel, how we wish we had been blameless!

Wranglers never want words.

Quarrels do not last long if the wrong is only on one side. *(French)*

It takes two to make a quarrel. *(Greek)*

Avoid quarrels caused by wine. *(Latin)*

Quarrel makes agreement more precious. *(Latin)*

QUENCH

Foul water as soon as fair will quench hot fire.

QUESTION

Ask me no questions and I'll tell you no fibs. *(Goldsmith)*
Every why has a wherefore.
He that nothing questioneth, nothing learneth.
Never answer a question until it is asked.
Question for question is all fair.
Questions are never indiscreet. Answers sometimes are. *(O. Wilde)*
Hard questions must have hard answers. *(Greek)*
To beg the question. *(Greek)*
Avoid a questioner, for he is also a tattler. *(Horace)*
It is not every question that deserves an answer. *(Latin)*

QUICK

Quickly come, quickly go.
Quick at meat, quick at work.
Quick and good go not well together. *(German)*

QUIET

Better is a dry morsel, and quietness therewith, than a house full of sacrifices with strife. *(Old Test., Prov.)*
In quietness and confidence shall be your strength. *(Old Test., Isaiah)*
Study to be quiet. *(New Test., I Thess.)*
A little with quiet is the only diet.
Anything for a quiet life.
Quiet sow, quiet mow.
Sometimes quiet is an unquiet thing. *(Latin)*

QUIT

God Almighty hates a quitter. *(S. Fessenden)*
He quits his place well that leaves his friend there.

QUOTATION

Next to the originator of a sentence is the first quoter of it.
Some for renown on scraps of wisdom dote,
And think they grow immortal as they quote. *(Pope)*
The wisdom of the wise, and the experience of the ages . . .
A fine quotation is a diamond on the finger of a man of wit, and a pebble in the hand of a fool. *(French)*
I quote others only the better to express myself. *(Montaigne)*

R

RACE

The race is not to the swift nor the battle to the strong. *(Old Test., Eccles.)*

The race is got by running.

RAGE

Rage furnishes no weapon. *(Latin)*

Rage is a brief insanity. *(Latin)*

RAGS

Better go to heaven in rags than to hell in embroidery.

Rags are royal raiment when worn for virtue's sake.

RAIN

He sendeth rain on the just and on the unjust. *(New Test., Matthew)*

A coming shower your shooting corns presage.

For a morning rain, leave not your journey.

Much rain wears the marble.

Rain before seven—fine before eleven.

St. Swithin's day, if it does rain,
  For forty days it will remain.

Small rain lays great dust.

When God wills, no wind but brings rain.

When it rains, it rains on all alike.

It never rains but it pours. *(French)*

After rain, fair weather. *(Greek)*

A heavy shower is soon over. *(Italian)*

One already wet does not feel the rain. *(Turkish)*

RAINBOW

The rainbow shall be a covenant between me and the earth. *(Old Test., Genesis)*

The rainbow at night is the sailor's delight.
Where the rainbow rests is a crock of gold.

RAKE
A reformed rake makes the best husband.
Every woman is at heart a rake. *(Pope)*

RANK
The rank is but the guinea's stamp,
  The man's the gowd for a' that. *(Burns)*
There is rank of mind as well as of birth.

RASHNESS
A rash man provokes trouble, but is no match for it when it comes. *(Chinese)*
Rashness is not valor.
Rashness is not always fortunate. *(Latin)*

RAT
A good rat will not injure the grain near its own hole. *(Chinese)*
An old rat easily finds a hole. *(Dutch)*
Rats desert a sinking ship.
Rats do not play tricks with kittens. *(Spanish)*
The rat that has but one hole is soon caught. *(Spanish)*

RAVEN
The young ravens are beaked like the old. *(Dutch)*
The raven doth not hatch a lark.
The raven said to the rook, "Stand away, black coat!"
He pardons ravens but storms at doves. *(Latin)*
Rarer even than a white raven. *(Latin)*
Bring up a raven, and it will peck out your eyes. *(Spanish)*

REACH
A man's reach should exceed his grasp,
  Or what's a Heaven for? *(Browning)*
What you cannot reach you must not want. *(Yiddish)*

READING
Make it plain upon tables, that he may run that readeth it. *(Old Test., Habak.)*
As well expect to grow stronger by always eating as wiser by always reading. *(J. Collier)*

Give a man a pipe he can smoke,
  Give a man a book he can read. *(J. Thomson)*
I love to lose myself in other men's minds. *(Lamb)*
Let blockheads read what blockheads wrote.
Life is too short for reading inferior books.
No man can read with profit what he cannot learn to read with pleasure.
Read, and you will know.
Read, mark, learn, and inwardly digest. *(Bk. Com. Prayer)*
Reading furnishes the mind only with materials of knowledge. *(Locke)*
Reading is seeing by proxy. *(H. Spencer)*
Reading is sometimes an ingenious device for avoiding thought. *(Helps)*
Reading maketh a full man. *(Bacon)*
The art of reading is to skip judiciously.
'Tis the good reader that makes the good book. *(Emerson)*
He that I am reading seems always to have the most force. *(Montaigne)*
To love to read is to exchange hours of ennui for hours of delight. *(Montesquieu)*
It is not wide reading but useful reading that tends to excellence. *(Greek)*
Beware of the man of one book. *(Italian)*
As you read it out, it begins to grow your own. *(Latin)*
In reading of many books is distraction. *(Latin)*
Much, but not many. *(Latin)*
Read not to swallow all, but only what you have use for. *(Ibsen)*
Letters enter with the blood. *(Spanish)*

REAP
A good reaper deserves a good sickle.
Reap where he hath not sown.

READY
He who is not ready today will be less so tomorrow. *(Latin)*

REASON
A man without reason is a beast in season.
And reason panders will. *(Shakespeare)*
"Because" is a woman's reason.
Every man's reason is every man's oracle.
Few have reason; most have eyes.
Good reasons must of force give place to better. *(Shakespeare)*

Harken to reason, or she will be heard.
He that will not reason is a bigot.
Hear reason, or she'll make you feel her.
Neither rhyme nor reason.
O strange excuse
When reason is the bawd to lust's abuse. *(Shakespeare)*
Reason binds the man.
Reason laboreth will.
Reason lies between the spur and the bridle.
Reason rules all things.
Reason rules the wise man and cudgels the fool.
The will of man is by his reason swayed.
We may take Fancy for a companion, but must follow Reason as our guide. *(S. Johnson)*
What Reason weaves, by Passion is undone. *(Pope)*
When Reason preaches, if you don't hear her, she'll box your ears.
Who doth not use his reason is a tame beast; who abuses it, a wild one.
It is not necessary to believe things in order to reason about them. *(Beaumarchais)*
The reason of the strongest is always the best. *(French)*
We have not enough strength to follow reason absolutely. *(La Rochefoucauld)*
Reason does not come before years. *(German)*
Be led by reason. *(Greek)*
Reason is not measured by size or height. *(Greek)*
Reason—the choicest gift bestowed by heaven. *(Greek)*
Unto the good, their reason ever is a good. *(Greek)*
If you wish to subject all things to yourself, subject yourself to reason. *(Latin)*
Nothing can be lasting when reason does not rule. *(Latin)*
Reason—the light and lamp of life. *(Latin)*
What is now reason was formerly impulse. *(Latin)*

REBEL
"Rebel" is the name that tyranny gives to a patriot.
Rebels in Cork are patriots in Madrid. *(T. Moore)*
Rebellion to tyrants is obedience to God.
The devil was the first o' th' name
From whom the race of rebels came. *(Butler)*
Who draws his sword against his prince must throw away the scabbard.

REBUKE
Open rebuke is better than secret hatred.

RECEIVER
The receiver is as bad as the thief.

RECKON
Always count the cost.
He that reckons without his host must reckon twice.
Misreckoning is no payment.
Pay the reckoning overnight, and you shall not be troubled in the morning.
Reckon not your chickens before they are hatched.
The fairer the hostess, the fouler the reckoning.
A short reckoning makes long friendship. *(Italian)*
Wine and roast? Yes, yes! Count the bill. Woe, woe! *(Turkish)*

RED
As red as a fox.
As red as a rose.
As red as blood.

REED
Thou trusted in the staff of this broken reed. *(Old Test., Eccles.)*
Lean not on a reed.
Where there are reeds, there is water.

REFORM
Every generation needs regeneration.
Every reform movement has a lunatic fringe. *(T. Roosevelt)*
It is never too late to mend.
Let each reform himself and not his neighbor.
Never came reformation in a flood. *(Shakespeare)*
Reform must come from within, not from without. *(Card. Gibbons)*
To innovate is not to reform.
Him who reforms, God assists. *(Spanish)*

REFUSE
Who refuses, muses. *(French)*
Some refuse roast meat, and later long for the smoke of it. *(Italian)*
A reason for refusing is never wanting to the miser. *(Latin)*
He who refuses nothing will soon have nothing to refuse. *(Latin)*

It is kindness to refuse immediately what you intend to delay. *(Latin)*
Who gives a doubtful hope, refuses. *(Latin)*
Who refuses courteously grants half our suit. *(Latin)*
Nay ["no"] has the same number of letters as *aye* ["si"]. (Spanish)

REGRET

Beware of Had I wist!

For of all sad words of tongue or pen,
The saddest are these: "It might have been!" *(Whittier)*

The mind longs for what it has missed. *(Latin)*

RELATIVES

Dine with thy aunt, but not every day.
A little more than kin, and less than kind. *(Shakespeare)*
Much kindred, much trouble. *(French)*
Let us have florins and we shall find cousins. *(Italian)*
Curse on account with relatives. *(Spanish)*
My teeth are nearer than my kindred. *(Spanish)*
If you love your wife, you must love her relatives. *(Yiddish)*
You recognize your relatives when they get rich. *(Yiddish)*

RELIGION

Every religion is good that teaches man to be good. *(Paine)*
In religion, as in friendship, they who profess most are the least sincere.
Many have quarreled about religion that never practiced it.
One religion is as true as another. *(Burton)*
Religion can bear no jesting.
Religion hath no landmarks.
Religion hides many mischiefs from suspicion. *(Marlowe)*
Religion is a stalking-horse to shoot other fowl.
Religion is in the heart, not in the knee.
Religion is the best armor in the world, but the worst cloak.
Religion is the elder sister of philosophy. *(Landor)*
Religion should be the rule of life, not a casual incident of it. *(Disraeli)*
Religion without joy is no religion. *(Parker)*
The religion of one age is the poetry of the next. *(Emerson)*
The religion of one seems madness unto another.
There is only one religion, though there are a hundred versions of it. *(G. B. Shaw)*
To be furious in religion is to be irreligiously religious. *(Penn)*

We have just enough religion to make us hate, but not enough to make us love, one another. *(Swift)*
What excellent fools religion makes of men! *(B. Jonson)*
A religious life is a struggle and not a hymn. *(French)*
All false religion is in conflict with nature. *(Rousseau)*
Religion is the opium of the people. *(Marx)*
A profitable religion never wants proselytes. *(Italian)*
A man without religion is like a beast without a bridle. *(Latin)*
There is no age which religion does not become. *(Erasmus)*
All religion relates to life, and the life of religion is to do good. *(Swedenborg)*

REMEDY

Our remedies oft in ourselves do lie,
Which we ascribe to heaven. *(Shakespeare)*
The remedy is worse than the disease.
There is a remedy for all things but death.
There is a remedy for everything, could men find it.
When remedies are needed, sighing avails not. *(Italian)*
If there be a remedy, why worry? *(Spanish)*
If there be no remedy, why worry? *(Spanish)*

REMEMBER

Remember Lot's wife. *(New Test., Matthew)*
We have all forgotten more than we remember.
That is pleasant to remember which was hard to endure. *(Italian)*

REMINDER

A good Jew needs no reminder; to a bad Jew it is of no use. *(Yiddish)*

REMORSE

Remorse begets reform.
Remorse is memory awake.
Remorse, the fatal egg by pleasure laid. *(Cowper)*

REMOVE

Remove not the ancient landmarks which thy fathers have set. *(Old Test., Eccles.)*
Three removes are as bad as a fire.
Plants oft removed never thrive. *(German)*

RENT

Plough or plough not, you must pay the rent. *(Spanish)*
The owner has one house; the renter, a thousand. *(Turkish)*

REPAIR
It is better to repair the beginning than the end. *(German)*
Everything may be repaired except the neckbone. *(Italian)*
He who does not repair a gutter has a whole house to repair. *(Spanish)*

REPENTANCE
The sinning is the best part of repentance. *(Arabian)*
Joy shall be in heaven over one sinner that repenteth . . .
(New Test., Luke)

A death-bed repentance seldom reaches to restitution.
Amendment is repentance.
Do as little as you can to repent of.
He goes far that never returns.
He that repents of his own act, either is, or was, a fool.
It is never too late to repent.
Repentance comes too late.
Repentance is but want of power to sin. *(Dryden)*
Repentance is good, but innocence better.
Repentance is the virtue of weak minds.
Repentance is the whip for fools.
There's no repentance in the grave.
When all is gone, repentance comes too late.
Repentance costs dear. *(French)*
The madness is short, repentance long. *(German)*
A noble mind disdains not to repent. *(Greek)*
No power can absolve the impenitent. *(Dante)*
He who repents his sins is almost innocent. *(Latin)*

REPROACH
The sting of a reproach is the truth of it.

REPROOF
Open rebuke is better than secret love. *(Old Test., Prov.)*
Reprove not a scorner, lest he hate thee; rebuke a wise man, and he will love thee. *(Old Test., Prov.)*
Who reproves the lame must go upright. *(Danish)*
A smart reproof is better than smooth deceit.
Reprove others but correct thyself.
Reproof never does a wise man harm.

REPUTATION
A good name endureth forever. *(Apocrypha)*
A good name is better than precious ointment. *(Old Test., Eccles.)*

A good name is rather to be chosen than great riches. *(Old Test., Prov.)*
Woe unto you, when all men shall speak well of you! *(New Test., Luke)*
A good name keeps its luster in the dark.
A good reputation is a fair estate.
A wounded reputation is seldom cured.
Good name in man and woman . . .
Is the immediate jewel of their soul. *(Shakespeare)*
He that hath an ill name is half hanged.
Men have their reputation by distance.
No man was written out of reputation but by himself.
Read not my blemishes in the world's report. *(Shakespeare)*
Reputation crackt is Venice-glass broke.
Reputation is commonly measured by the acre.
Take away my good name, and take away my life.
The contempt of good reputation is called impudence.
The solar system has no anxiety about its reputation. *(Emerson)*
'Tis better never to be named than to be ill spoken of.
A great reputation is a great noise; the more there is made, the farther off it is heard. *(Napoleon)*
Get a good name, and you may lie a-bed. *(French)*
How many worthy men have we seen survive their own reputation? *(Montaigne)*
A good name covers theft. *(German)*
An honorable reputation is a sacred patrimony. *(Latin)*
Reputation is the life of the mind as breath is the life of the body. *(Latin)*
A man had better die than lose his good name. *(Turkish)*

RESIGNATION

Not my will, but thine, be done. *(New Test., Luke)*
I am tied to the stake, and I must stand the course. *(Shakespeare)*
It's no use crying over spilt milk.
To kiss the rod. *(French)*
Do not kick against the pricks. *(Greek)*
Take no sorrow of the thing lost which may not be recovered. *(Greek)*
Let that please man which has pleased God. *(Latin)*

RESOLUTION

Be resolved, and the thing is done. *(Chinese)*
Without resolution a man must make his living by the sweat of his brow. *(Chinese)*

He who resolves suddenly repents at leisure.
Never tell your resolution beforehand.
Resolve, and thou art free.
The road to resolution lies by doubt.
Set a stout heart to a steep hill-side.
The native hue of resolution
Is sicklied o'er with the pale cast of thought. *(Shakespeare)*

RESPECTABILITY
Least is he marked that does as most men do.
Men are respectable only as they respect.
The more things a man is ashamed of, the more respectable he is. *(G. B. Shaw)*
One of the greatest misfortunes of respectable people is that they are cowards. *(Voltaire)*

RESPONSIBLE
That which a man causes to be done by another he does himself. *(Latin)*

REST
Come unto me, all ye who labor and are heavy laden, and I will give you rest. *(New Test., Matthew)*
Absence of occupation is not rest.
Men tire themselves in pursuit of rest.
Rest and success are fellows.
Rest is for the dead.
Sleep after toil, port after stormy sea.
Rest a while and run a mile. *(French)*
Too much rest itself becomes a pain. *(Greek)*
A field that has rested gives a bountiful crop. *(Latin)*
God has given us this repose. *(Latin)*
The fertile field becomes sterile without rest. *(Spanish)*
Rest is won only by work. *(Turkish)*

RETREAT
He that fights and runs away
May live to fight another day. *(Butler)*
Flying men often meet their fate. *(Latin)*

RETRIBUTION
And with what measure ye mete, it shall be measured to you again. *(New Test., Matthew)*

Eye for eye, tooth for tooth, hand for hand, foot for foot.
(*Old Test., Deuter.*)
He that diggeth a pit shall fall into it. (*Old Test., Eccles.*)
They have sown the wind, and they shall reap the whirlwind.
(*Old Test., Hosea*)
Whatsoever a man soweth, that shall he also reap.
(*New Test., Galatians*)
Whoso sheddeth man's blood, by man shall his blood be shed.
(*Old Test., Genesis*)
As he brews, so shall he drink.
As you make your bed, so shall you lie in it.
Every man's judgment returns to his own door.
For 'tis the sport to have the engineer
  Hoist with his own petar. (*Shakespeare*)
He that plants thorns must not expect to gather roses.
He that sows iniquity shall reap sorrow.
Heat not a furnace for your foe so hot that you may singe yourself.
Men must reap the things they sow. (*Shelley*)
The biter should be bit.
The ways of the gods are slow, but mighty at last to fulfil. (*Greek*)
As you salute you will be saluted. (*Italian*)
Let them fall into the snare which they have laid. (*Latin*)
The camel set out to get him horns, and was shorn of his ears. (*Latin*)
We are paid in our own coin. (*Latin*)
You have mixed the mess, and you must eat it up. (*Latin*)
His Martinmas comes to every pig. (*Spanish*)
Many go out for wool, and come home shorn. (*Spanish*)

RETURN
He runneth far that never turneth again.
Let us return to our muttons. (*French*)

REVENGE
Vengeance is mine; I will repay, saith the Lord. (*New Test., Romans*)
A brave revenge ne'er comes too late.
A man that studieth revenge keeps his own wounds green. (*Bacon*)
Can vengeance be pursued further than death? (*Shakespeare*)
Had I revenged every wrong,
  I had not worn my skirts so long.
Have ye him on the hip.
He meditates revenge who least complains.

He that will venge every wrath,
  The longer he liveth the less he hath.
It costs more to revenge injuries than to bear them.
Living well is the best revenge.
Revenge is a dish that should be eaten cold.
Revenge is a kind of wild justice. *(Bacon)*
Revenge is a morsel for God.
Revenge is profitable, gratitude is expensive. *(Gibbon)*
Revenge proves its own executioner.
The noblest vengeance is to forgive.
The whirligig of time brings in its vengeance. *(Shakespeare)*
There's small revenge in words, but words may be greatly revenged.
To forget a wrong is the best revenge.
To revenge is no valor, but to bear. *(Shakespeare)*
Vengeance is sweet.
Vengeance, though it comes with leaden feet, strikes with iron hands.
Revenge is a luscious fruit which you must leave to ripen. *(French)*
Revenge is sweeter far than flowing honey. *(Greek)*
Swift vengeance waits on wrong. *(Greek)*
Arise from my ashes, unknown avenger! *(Vergil)*
Revenge is a confession of pain. *(Latin)*
To be revenged on an enemy is to obtain a second life. *(Latin)*
Vengeance lies open to patient craft. *(Latin)*
If you want to be revenged, hold your tongue. *(Spanish)*

REVOLUTION

Every revolution was first a thought in one man's mind. *(Emerson)*
Repression is the seed of revolution.
Revolutions never go backwards.
Do you suppose, then, that revolutions are made with rose-water? *(Chamfort)*
Revolutions are not about trifles, but spring from trifles. *(Aristotle)*

REWARD

The laborer is worthy of his reward. *(New Test., I Timothy)*
Desert and reward seldom keep company.
He was very wise who first gave a reward.
Service without reward is punishment.
The deed is everything, the glory naught. *(Goethe)*
The prize is not without dust. *(Latin)*
The reward of a thing rightly done is to have done it. *(Latin)*

RICH

He heapeth up riches and knoweth not who shall gather them. *(Old Test., Psalms)*

He that maketh haste to be rich shall not be innocent. *(Old Test., Prov.)*

If riches increase, set not your heart upon them. *(Old Test., Prov.)*

It is easier for a camel to go through the eye of a needle, than for a rich man to enter into the Kingdom of God. *(New Test., Matthew)*

Riches fly away as an eagle toward heaven. *(Old Test., Prov.)*

Great wealth implies great loss. *(Lao-Tsze)*

He who hastens to be rich incurs peril. *(Chinese)*

To gain wealth is easy; to keep it, hard. *(Chinese)*

De rich git richer and de po' git children. *(American Negro)*

A man is rich in proportion to the number of things he can afford to let alone. *(Thoreau)*

A man of wealth is dubbed a man of worth. *(Pope)*

A man that keeps riches and enjoys them not, is like an ass that carries gold and eats thistles.

A rich man ought to have a strong stomach.

A rich rogue is like a fat hog
Who does never good till as dead as a log.

As the carle riches, he wretches.

Better rich in God than rich in gold.

But Satan now is wiser than of yore,
And tempts by making rich, not making poor. *(Pope)*

Excess of wealth is the cause of covetousness.

For one rich man content, there are a hundred not.

God help the rich, the poor can beg.

Great wealth and content seldom live together.

He is not fit for riches who is afraid to use them.

He is rich enough that needeth neither to flatter nor to borrow.

He is rich, not that hath much, but that coveteth least.

He is wise that is rich.

He may love riches that wanteth them, as much as he that hath them.

If our wealth commands us, we are poor indeed.

Ill fares the land, to hastening ills a prey,
Where wealth accumulates, and men decay. *(Goldsmith)*

It is better to live rich than to die rich.

Knowledge makes one laugh, but wealth makes one dance.

Lay not up for yourselves treasures upon earth where moth and rust doth corrupt. *(New Test., Matthew)*
No man was ever as rich as all men ought to be.
No man's fortune can be an end worthy of his being. *(Bacon)*
Now I have got an ewe and a lamb, everyone cries, Welcome, Peter.
Rich men have no faults.
Rich men's spots are covered with money.
Riches are but the baggage of virtue.
Riches are for spending.
Riches are gotten with pain, kept with care, and lost with grief.
Riches oft bring harm and ever fear.
Riches rule the roast.
Small riches hath most rest,
In greatest seas most sorest is tempest.
Superfluous wealth can buy superfluities only. *(Thoreau)*
The pride of the rich makes the labors of the poor.
The learned pate ducks to the golden fool. *(Shakespeare)*
The pleasures of the rich are bought with the tears of the poor.
The rich are rather possessed by their money than possessors. *(Burton)*
The rich man's wealth is most enemy unto his health.
Wealth is a good servant, a very bad mistress. *(Bacon)*
Wealth makes wit waver.
Without a rich heart, wealth is an ugly beggar. *(Emerson)*
I never knew a silent rich man. *(French)*
Riches serve wise men, but command a fool. *(French)*
The richest man carries nothing away with him but his shroud. *(French)*
God commonly gives riches to such gross asses to whom he gives nothing else that is good. *(Luther)*
Rich men are everywhere at home. *(German)*
The rich can eat with only one mouth. *(German)*
No just man ever became rich all at once. *(Greek)*
Riches cover a multitude of woes. *(Greek)*
Wealth breeds satiety; satiety, outrage. *(Greek)*
At the door of the rich are many friends. *(Hebrew)*
Everyone is a kin to the rich man. *(Italian)*
He that never fails never grows rich. *(Italian)*
To be rich, one must have a relation at home with the devil. *(Italian)*
Virtue and riches seldom settle on one man. *(Italian)*
Wealth is not his who has it, but his who enjoys it. *(Italian)*
A golden bit does not make a better horse. *(Latin)*

A great fortune is a great slavery. *(Latin)*
A rich man is either a rogue, or a rogue's heir. *(Latin)*
Among us most sacred of all is the majesty of wealth. *(Latin)*
As money grows, greed for greater riches follows after. *(Latin)*
Common sense among men of fortune is rare. *(Latin)*
He enjoys riches most who needs them least. *(Latin)*
He is rich enough who does not want bread. *(Latin)*
He who wants riches, wants them at once. *(Latin)*
Morals are corrupted by the worship of riches. *(Latin)*
Riches either serve or govern the possessor. *(Latin)*
Riches, the incentives to evil, are dug out of the earth. *(Latin)*
So he be rich, even a barbarian pleases. *(Latin)*
The house laughs with silver. *(Latin)*
The shortest way to riches is by contempt of riches. *(Latin)*
We all ask whether he is wealthy; none, whether he is good. *(Latin)*
We must spurn riches, the diploma of slavery. *(Latin)*
Wealth excuses folly. *(Latin)*
Wealth lightens not the heart and care of man. *(Latin)*
Riches—sin before God; poverty—sin before men. *(Russian)*
Riches can solder up abundance of flaws. *(Spanish)*
The foolish sayings of the rich pass for wise saws. *(Spanish)*
Pawn your last shirt—only to be rich. *(Yiddish)*
Would you become rich? Be a pig for seven years. *(Yiddish)*

RIDDLE
The Sphinx must solve her own riddle. *(Emerson)*
Beware of the riddle of the young boys. *(Greek)*

RIDICULE
He who laughs, and is himself ridiculous, bears a double share of ridicule.
Jeerers must be content to taste of their own broth.
Mockery is the fume of little hearts. *(Tennyson)*
Ridicule is the test of truth.
Scoffing cometh not of wisdom.
There are few who would not rather be hated than laughed at.
Mockery is often poverty of wit. *(French)*

RIDICULOUS
From the sublime to the ridiculous is but a step. *(French)*
Who are serious in ridiculous things, will be ridiculous in serious affairs. *(Latin)*

RIDING
Before you mount, look at the girth. *(Dutch)*
Better ride an ass that carries me than a horse that throws me.
If two men ride a horse, one must ride behind.
When you ride a young colt, see your saddle be well girt.
He who rides the mule shoes her. *(French)*
Better badly mounted than proud on foot. *(German)*
He who knows the road can ride at full trot. *(Italian)*

RIGHT
A fool must now and then be right by chance. *(Cowper)*
A man in the right with God on his side is in the majority. *(Beecher)*
As right as a ram's horn.
As right as my leg.
As right as rain.
Be sure you're right, then go ahead. *(Crockett)*
Excess of right is no wrong.
Hew to the line of right, let the chips fly where they may. *(Conkling)*
I would rather be right than President. *(Clay)*
If mankind had wished for what is right, they might have had it long ago.
No one is always right.
Right wrongs no man.
The greatest right is the right to be wrong.
They are slaves who dare not be
In the right with two or three. *(Lowell)*
Two blacks do not make a white;
Two wrongs do not make a right.
We are not satisfied to be right, unless we can prove others to be wrong.
What rights are his that dare not strike for them? *(Tennyson)*
Whatever is, is right. *(Pope)*
When everyone is wrong, everyone is right. *(French)*
Right is with the strongest. *(German)*
Right is better than law. *(Greek)*
Better to do right without thanks, than wrong without punishment. *(Latin)*
I see the right and approve it, yet I follow the wrong. *(Ovid)*
Right or wrong, it's our house up to the roof. *(Spanish)*
Where force prevails, right perishes. *(Spanish)*

RIGHTEOUSNESS

Be not righteous over-much, neither make thyself over-wise. *(Old Test., Eccles.)*

Righteousness exalteth a nation. *(Old Test., Prov.)*

The righteous shall flourish as the palm tree. *(Old Test., Psalms)*

RING

Don't put your finger into too tight a ring. *(Italian)*

RIPE

Soon ripe, soon rotten. *(Latin)*

RISING

Early to bed and early to rise,
  Makes a man healthy, wealthy, and wise.

Go to bed with the lamb and rise with the lark.

He that hath the name to be an early riser may sleep till noon.

He that riseth first is first dressed.

The early bird catches the worm.

The early bird gets the late one's breakfast.

Wherefore should master rise before the hens have laid the eggs?

Who rises late must trot all day.

Heaven's help is better than early rising. *(Spanish)*

RISK

He that cannot abide a bad market, deserves not a good one.

It is better to risk, than to delay overmuch.

RIVALRY

Heaven cannot brook two suns, nor earth two masters. *(Greek)*

Rivalry is good for mortals. *(Greek)*

RIVER

A thousand years hence, the river will run as it did.

Rain added to a river that is rank
  Perforce will force it overflow its bank. *(Shakespeare)*

Rivers need a spring.

Follow the river and you'll get to the sea. *(French)*

Where the river is deepest it makes least noise. *(Italian)*

ROAD

Any road leads to the end of the world.

It's a long run that never turns.

Keep the common road and thou art safe.
The beaten road is the safest.
What is the use of running, when you're on the wrong road?
The nearer the inn, the longer the road. *(German)*
I will find a road or make one. *(Hannibal)*

ROB
To rob a robber is not robbery. *(French)*

ROGUE
It is easier to fill a rogue's belly than his eyes. *(Danish)*
A rogue in grain is a rogue amain.
Give a rogue enough rope and he will hang himself.
When rogues fall out, honest men come by their own.
One rogue is usher to another. *(Greek)*
When a rogue kisses you—count your teeth. *(Hebrew)*

ROLLING
A rolling stone gathers no moss.

ROME
You may not sit in Rome and strive with the Pope.
All roads lead to Rome. *(Italian)*
Where the Pope is, Rome is. *(Italian)*
All things at Rome have their price. *(Latin)*
By her own wealth is haughty Rome brought low. *(Latin)*
Outside the Church of Rome there is no salvation. *(St. Cyprian)*
Rome was not built in a day. *(Latin)*
When you are in Rome, do as the Romans. *(Latin)*
St. Peter is very well at Rome. *(Spanish)*
To Rome for everything. *(Spanish)*

ROPE
Name not a rope in the house of him that was hanged.
The rope breaks where it is thinnest. *(Yiddish)*

ROSE
He that plants thorns must never expect to gather roses. *(Arabian)*
A rose is sweeter in the bud than full blown.
Better be stung by a nettle than pricked by a rose.
No rose without a thorn.
The fairest and the sweetest rose
 In time must fade and beauty lose.

When we want to have more roses, we must plant more trees.
You may shatter the vase, but the scent of the rose stays.
Roses and maidens soon lose their bloom. *(German)*
An onion will not produce a rose. *(Latin)*
When the rose dies, the thorn is left behind. *(Latin)*
Roses smell sweet, but they have thorns. *(Yiddish)*

ROTTEN
It is the rotten limb that must be lopped.
There is small choice in rotten apples.
Every pomegranate has its rotten pit. *(Latin)*
The rotten apple infects its neighbors. *(Latin)*

ROUGH
Take the rough with the smooth.

RUBBISH
Rubbish is only matter out of place.
A dealer in rubbish sounds the praise of rubbish. *(Latin)*

RUIN
Babylon is fallen, is fallen. *(Old Test., Isaiah)*
Going to ruin is silent work.
Men moralize among ruins.
The road to ruin is always in good repair; the travelers pay the expense of it.

RULE
No rule is so good as the rule of thumb, if it hit.
The exception proves the rule.
There is no rule without an exception. *(Spanish)*

RULER
Who made thee a ruler and a judge over us? *(New Test., Acts)*
He that hath a fellow-ruler hath an over-ruler.
Iron hand in velvet glove. *(French)*
He who is to be a good ruler must first have been ruled. *(Greek)*
Let the ruler be slow in punishing, swift in rewarding. *(Latin)*
The desire to rule is stronger than all the other passions. *(Latin)*
Unjust rule never endures. *(Latin)*

RUMOR
Rumor doth double, like the voice and echo,
The number of the fear'd. *(Shakespeare)*

Rumor is a great traveler.
In calamity any rumor is believed. *(Latin)*
There is nothing among men swifter than rumor. *(Latin)*

RUN
Who runs is followed. *(Dutch)*
He may ill run that cannot go.
He runs far that never returns.
He that runs in the dark may well stumble.
No use running when you're on the wrong road.
You must learn to creep before you run.
It is not enough to run: one must start in time. *(French)*

RUSSIAN
Scratch a Russian, and you'll find a Tartar. *(French)*

RUST
Better to wear out than to rust out.
The brightest blades grow dim with rust.
If I rest, I rust. *(Luther)*

SABBATH
The Sabbath was made for man, and not man for the Sabbath. *(New Test., Mark)*
Even the sinners in Hell have rest on the Sabbath. *(Yiddish)*

SACK
Bind the sack before it be full.
Old Sacks want much patching.
A full sack pricks up its ears. *(Italian)*
Every man must carry his own sack to the mill. *(Italian)*
Nothing can come out of a sack but what is in it. *(Italian)*

SADDLE
A saddle fits more backs than one.
Always put the saddle on the right horse.
On his own saddle one rides the safest. *(German)*
He that eats his fowl alone must saddle his horse alone. *(Spanish)*

SAFETY
Be wary then; best safety lies in fear. *(Shakespeare)*
He that's secure is not safe.
He who goes the lowest builds the safest.
It is man's perdition to be safe, when he ought to die for the truth.
Out of this nettle, danger, we pluck this flower, safety. *(Shakespeare)*
Safe is the word.
There is always safety in valor.
There is nothing like being on the safe side. *(Latin)*
He is safe from danger who is on guard even when safe. *(Latin)*
Safety lies in the middle course. *(Latin)*
The only safety for the conquered is to expect no safety. *(Latin)*
What is safe is distasteful; in rashness there is hope. *(Latin)*

SAIL

Hoist your sail when the wind is fair.

You must shift your sail with the wind. *(Italian)*

SAINT

Blessed in the sight of the Lord is the death of his saints. *(Old Test., Psalms)*

A saint in crape is twice a saint in lawn. *(Pope)*

A saint is a skeptic once in every twenty-four hours. *(Emerson)*

All are not saints that go to church.

Like saint, like offering.

The saint who works no miracles has few pilgrims.

The tears of the Saints more sweet by far
  Than all the songs of sinners are *(Herrick)*

The way of this world is to praise dead saints and persecute living ones.

They are not all saints who use holy water.

To every saint his own candle.

A young Saint, an old Devil. *(French)*

Saint cannot, if God will not. *(French)*

The saint's day over, good-bye to the saint. *(French)*

The river passed, the saint forgotten. *(Italian)*

A saint sleeps not on soft beds. *(Roumanian)*

When the fields yield not, the saints have not. *(Spanish)*

SALT

If the salt have lost his saltness, wherewith will ye season it? *(New Test., Mark)*

Help me to salt, help me to sorrow.

It is a foolish bird that stayeth the laying of salt on her tail.

Of all smells, bread; of all tastes, salt.

Salt seasons all things.

A man must eat a peck of salt with his friend before he knows him. *(Latin)*

Spilt salt is never all gathered. *(Spanish)*

SALVATION

I know that my Redeemer liveth. *(Old Test., Job)*

A man may be damned for despairing to be saved.

The fearless man is his own salvation.

Salvation is from God only. *(Latin)*

The knowledge of sin is the beginning of salvation. *(Latin)*

SATAN
Don't play with Satan. *(Yiddish)*

SAUCE
What's sauce for the goose is sauce for the gander.
You spoil a good dish with ill sauce.

SAVING
A penny saved is a penny gained.
For age and want save while you may:
No morning sun lasts a whole day.
Of saving cometh having.
Penny and penny laid up will be many.
Penny wise and pound foolish.
Saving is getting.
Who saves, saves for the cat. *(Italian)*
Saving comes too late when you get to the bottom. *(Latin)*
Prepare in youth for your old age. *(Yiddish)*
What you don't store up in this world, you can't take with you to a future world. *(Yiddish)*
What you save is, later, like something found. *(Yiddish)*

SAYING
Easier said than done.
Little said is soonest mended.
Say no ill of the year till it is past.
Saying and doing are two things.
What is said cannot be unsaid.

SCAB
Scabby heads love not the comb.
A scab is a scab, even if you smear honey on it. *(Yiddish)*

SCALD
Scald not your lips in another man's pottage.

SCALE
A false scale is hated even by God. *(Yiddish)*

SCANDAL
Tell it not in Gath, publish it not in the streets of Askelon. *(Old Test., II Samuel)*
A gossip speaks ill of all and all of her.
Common fame is mostly to blame.

For the greatest scandal waits on greatest state. *(Shakespeare)*
Gossip is a vice enjoyed vicariously.
Gossips are frogs—they drink and talk.
In the case of scandal, the receiver is as bad as the thief.
Scandal's the sweetener of a female feast. *(Cowper)*
Scandal will not rub out like dirt when it is dry.
That abominable tittle-tattle,
  Which is the cud chewed by human cattle. *(Byron)*
The more you are talked about, the less powerful you are. *(Disraeli)*
That which passes out of one mouth, passes into a hundred ears.
It is at home, not in public, one washes his dirty linen. *(French)*
The opposite of gossip is often the truth. *(French)*
They say. What do they say? Let them say. *(Greek)*
There is nothing that can't be made worse by telling. *(Latin)*

SCAR
A scar nobly got is a good livery of honor. *(Shakespeare)*
He jests at scars that never felt a wound. *(Shakespeare)*
The generous motive dignifies the scar. *(Greek)*

SCATTER
Scatter with one hand, gather with two.

SCHOLAR
The ink of the scholar is more sacred than the blood of the martyr. *(Arabian)*
The scholar who cherishes the love of comfort is not fit to be deemed a scholar. *(Confucius)*
A scholar at court is an ass among apes.
He can ill be master that never was scholar.
John has been to school to learn to be a fool. *(French)*
The greatest scholars are not the wisest men. *(Latin)*
Who robs a scholar robs the public. *(Spanish)*

SCHOOL
Don't tell tales out of school.

SCIENCE
Human science is uncertain guess. *(Prior)*
Much science, much sorrow.
Science is organized knowledge. *(Spencer)*
Science is the topography of ignorance. *(O. W. Holmes)*

The dismal science. [*i.e. economics*] *(Carlyle)*
The science of fools with long memories. [*i.e. heraldry*]
The science of sciences. [*i.e. philosophy*]
Wonder is the seed of science.
Science is for those who learn; poetry for those who know. *(French)*
Science is nothing but perception. *(Plato)*
Science is nothing but good sense and reason. *(Polish)*
Science is a cemetery of dead ideas. *(Unamuno)*
Science is madness, if good sense does not cure it.

SCOLD
Husbands are in heaven whose wives scold not.

SCORN
Scorn at first makes after-love the more. *(Shakespeare)*
Scornful dogs eat dirty puddings.

SCOT
As hard-hearted as a Scot of Scotland.
Much may be made of a Scotsman if he be caught young. *(S. Johnson)*

SCOUNDREL
Every man over forty is a scoundrel. *(G. B. Shaw)*
Grease a scoundrel's boots, and he'll say you're going to burn them. *(French)*

SCRATCH
I scratch where it itches.
Itch and ease may no man please.
Scratch me and I'll scratch you.
Thou makest me claw where it itcheth not . . .
'Tis better than riches to scratch when it itches.
You'll scratch a beggar before you die.
Let him that itches scratch himself. *(French)*
Mules may ease each other's itch. *(Latin)*

SCULPTURE
Every block does not make a Mercury. *(Latin)*

SEA
All the rivers run into the sea; yet the sea is not full. *(Old Test., Eccles.)*
He that is at sea has not the winds in his hand. *(Danish)*
A passage perilous maketh a port pleasant.
All water runs to the sea.

And seas but join the regions they divide. *(Pope)*
Being on sea, sail; being on land, settle.
In a calm sea every man is a pilot.
Let him who knows not how to pray go to sea.
Praise the sea, but keep on land.
The sea and the air are common to all.
The sea hath no king but God alone.
The sea refuses no river.
The shore has perils unknown to the deep.
They scorn the strand who sail upon the sea.
The sea is today as it was on the first day of creation. *(French)*
The trident of Neptune is the scepter of the world. *(French)*
Every sea is sea. *(Greek)*
The loud-resounding sea. *(Homer)*
The sea washes away all human ills. *(Greek)*
Even the sea, great as it is, grows calm. *(Italian)*
Anyone can hold the helm when the sea is calm. *(Latin)*
Hug the shore . . . let others keep to the deep. *(Latin)*
The hungry sea is fatal to the sailors. *(Latin)*
The seaman sets his sails to suit the wind. *(Latin)*
When the sea is calm the careless sailor takes his ease. *(Latin)*

SEASON
Everything is good in its season.

SECRET
De cow-bell can't keep a secret. *(American Negro)*
Nothing is secret that shall not be made manifest. *(New Test., Luke)*
Stolen waters are sweet, and bread eaten in secret is pleasant.
(Old Test., Prov.)
The secret things belong unto the Lord our God. *(Old Test., Deut.)*
A secret is a weapon and a friend.
He only is secret who never was trusted.
He who tells a secret is another's servant.
If my shirt knew my design, I'd burn it.
If you would keep your secret from an enemy, tell it not to a friend.
Secret path marks secret foe.
The sun discovers the filth under the white snow.
There is no secrecy comparable to celerity. *(Bacon)*
There is no secret time will not reveal.
Three may keep a secret if two of them are dead.

A secret between two is a secret of God; a secret among three is everybody's secret. *(French)*

We confide our secret through friendship, but it escapes through love. *(French)*

When a secret is revealed, it is the fault of the man who confided it. *(French)*

Give up the smallest part of a secret, and the rest is no longer in your power. *(German)*

No one knows better than I where my shoe pinches. *(Greek)*

Secrecy is the seal of speech. *(Greek)*

Two things a man cannot hide: that he is drunk, and that he is in love. *(Greek)*

Do not speak of secret matters in a field that is full of little hills. *(Hebrew)*

Thy secret is thy prisoner; if thou let it go, thou art a prisoner to it. *(Hebrew)*

There is a skeleton in every house. *(Italian)*

If you wish another to keep your secret, first keep it yourself. *(Latin)*

Leave to concealment what has long been concealed. *(Latin)*

Sooner will men hold fire in their mouths than keep a secret. *(Latin)*

You are to be pitied when you have to conceal what you wish to tell. *(Latin)*

Confide a secret to a dumb man, and he will speak. *(Russian)*

A secret fire is discovered by the smoke. *(Spanish)*

Do not tell your secrets behind a wall or a hedge. *(Spanish)*

He who keeps his own secret avoids much mischief. *(Spanish)*

After nine months the secret comes out. *(Yiddish)*

SEE

Better to be blind than to see ill.

I can see as far into a millstone as another man.

One is not bound to see more than he can.

Seeing is believing.

There is a time to wink as well as to see.

Seldom seen, soon forgotten.

Who sees with the eye of another is as blind as a mole. *(German)*

SEEK

Seek, and ye shall find; knock, and it shall be opened unto you. *(New Test., Matthew)*

Seek till you find.

Seek your salve where you got your sore.

Who seeks what he should not, finds what he would not. *(German)*
Those who seek cake lose their bread. *(Yiddish)*

SEEM
Be what you seem, and seem what you are.
Things are seldom what they seem.

SELF
I am as God made me.
I celebrate myself, and sing myself. *(Whitman)*

SELF-CONCEIT
There is more hope of a fool, than of him that is wise in his own conceit. *(Old Test., Prov.)*
Stand up, cent, and let the dollar sit down.
The goslings would lead the geese to grass. *(French)*

SELF-CONFIDENCE
Self-confidence is the first requisite to great undertakings.
All my hope for all my help is myself. *(Montaigne)*
Let every man's hope be in himself. *(Latin)*

SELF-CONSCIOUS
He that has a great nose thinks everybody is speaking of it.

SELF-CONTROL
He is strong who conquers others; he who conquers himself is mighty. *(Lao-Tsze)*
Few are fit to be entrusted with themselves.
Keep yourself within yourself. *(Shakespeare)*
Rule lust, temper tongue, and bridle the belly.
Thrice noble is he who is king of himself.
He conquers twice who conquers himself in victory. *(Latin)*
I am myself my own commander. *(Latin)*

SELF-DEFENSE
Self-defense is Nature's eldest law. *(Dryden)*

SELF-DENIAL
The more a man denies himself, so much the more will he receive from the gods. *(Horace)*

SELF-DEPENDENCE
Every tub must stand on its own bottom.

SELF-DEPRECIATION

He that makes himself dirt is trod on by the swine.
Who makes himself a sheep will be eaten by the wolves.
Him who makes a mouse of himself, the cats will eat. *(German)*
He who makes himself a dove is eaten by the hawks. *(Italian)*

SELF-HELP

He that performs his own errand, saves his messenger's hire. *(Danish)*
Command your man, and do it yourself.
Every man for himself, and the devil take the hindmost.
Every miller draws water to his own mill.
God gives the milk, but not the pail.
God reaches us good things by our own hands.
If you want a thing well done, do it yourself.
Paddle your own canoe.
Self do, self have.
When it rains pottage, you must hold up your dish.
Call Minerva to aid, but bestir yourself. *(Greek)*
God helps them that help themselves. *(Latin)*
Hope in the Lord, but exert yourself. *(Russian)*

SELF-INTEREST

He knows on which side his bread is buttered.
He that owns the cow goes nearest the tail.

SELF-KNOWLEDGE

Every man is best known to himself.
Full wise is he that can himselven know. *(Chaucer)*
Know then thyself, presume not God to scan;
  The proper study of mankind is Man. *(Pope)*
Lord deliver me from myself.
We know what we are, but know not what we may be. *(Shakespeare)*
Know yourself. *(Greek)*
Whoso knoweth himself shall find the kingdom of heaven. *(Greek)*
I know myself better than any doctor can. *(Ovid)*
Live within yourself, and you will discover how small a stock there is. *(Latin)*
What you think of yourself is much more important than what others think of you. *(Latin)*
The knowledge of thyself will preserve thee from vanity. *(Spanish)*

SELF-LOVE

He that falls in love with himself, will have no rivals.
Self-love is a busy prompter.

Self-love is a mote in every man's eye.
Self loves itself best.
To love oneself is the beginning of a life-long romance. *(O. Wilde)*
Offended self-love never forgives. *(French)*
Self-love is the greatest of all flatterers. *(La Rochefoucauld)*
Self-love makes more libertines than love. *(Rousseau)*
Self-love never dies. *(Voltaire)*
Every living creature loves itself. *(Latin)*
Every man is sorry for himself. *(Latin)*
I am myself my own nearest of kin. *(Latin)*

SELF-PRAISE
He dwells far from neighbors that is fain to praise himself.
He that praiseth himself, spattereth himself.
Self-praise stinks in the nostrils.
Self-praise is no recommendation. *(Latin)*

SELF-PRESERVATION
Self-preservation is the first law of nature.
The order of the day
  Is—prey on others, or become a prey.
A drowning man would catch at razors. *(Italian)*

SELF-RESPECT
Self-respect is the corner-stone of virtue.
Respect yourself most of all. *(Greek)*

SELF-SACRIFICE
Present your bodies a living sacrifice, holy, acceptable unto God.
(New Test., Romans)
He who is ready to sacrifice himself, will not hesitate to sacrifice another.

SELF-TORTURE
He that is ill to himself will be good to nobody.

SELFISHNESS
Close sits my shirt, but closer my skin.
Every man for himself and God for us all.
He cares not whose child cry, so his laugh.
He is unworthy to live who lives only for himself.
He is a fool that will forget himself.

He set my house on fire only to roast his eggs.
No man is born unto himself alone;
  Who lives unto himself, he lives to none.
We always took care of number one.
He that lives not somewhat in others, lives little to himself. *(Montaigne)*
Virtues lose themselves in self-interest, as streams lose themselves in the sea. *(La Rochefoucauld)*
The world is ruled by interest alone. *(German)*
Everyone is eloquent in his own cause. *(Latin)*
I today, you tomorrow. *(Latin)*
My tunic is nearer to me than my mantle. *(Latin)*
No one is second to himself. *(Latin)*
Self is the first object of charity. *(Latin)*
The primary and sole foundation of virtue or of the proper conduct of life is to seek our own profit. *(Spinoza)*
Every old woman blows under her own kettle. *(Spanish)*
Every person for his own skin. *(Turkish)*

SELL
Sell me dear and measure me fair.
You must sell as markets go.
Who will sell a blind horse, praises the feet. *(German)*
Don't sell the skin of the bear in the woods. *(Yiddish)*
Every seller praises his wares. *(Yiddish)*

SEND
Send not a cat for lard. *(Italian)*

SENSE
Where sense is wanting, everything is wanting.
Common sense is not so common. *(French)*
God send you mair sense and me mair siller. *(Scottish)*
Borrowed sense is of no use. *(Yiddish)*

SERENITY
After a storm comes a calm.
Keep cool: it will be all one in a hundred years.
Serene amidst the savage waves. *(Latin)*

SERMON
It is a blind goose that comes to the fox's sermon.
Funeral sermon—lying sermon. *(German)*

SERVANT

As with the servant, so with his master. *(Old Test., Isaiah)*
Is thy servant a dog, that he should do this great thing? *(Old Test., II Kings)*
He that is greatest among you shall be your servant. *(New Test., Matth.)*
Masters, give unto your servants that which is just and equal. *(New Test., Coloss.)*
Well done, thou good and faithful servant . . . *(New Test., Matth.)*
A devoted old servant cancels the name of master.
A servant and a cock should be kept but a year.
A servant is his master's money.
A servant is known by his master's absence.
A servant that is diligent, honest, and good,
  Must sing at his work like a bird in the wood.
A servingman's wife may starve for hunger.
A sleepy master makes his servant a lout.
Bad servants wound their masters' fame.
Choose none for thy servant who has served thy betters.
For master and servant oft changing is loss.
Grandfather's servants are never good.
Great men's servants think themselves great.
He can give little to his servant that licks his knife.
He that has no servant must serve himself.
I will not keep a dog and bark myself.
If you pay not a servant his wages, he will pay himself.
If you would have good servants, see that you be good masters.
Let thy maidservant be faithful, strong, and homely.
Never in the way, and never out of the way.
Servants should put on patience when they put on a livery.
Few men have been admired by their servants. *(Montaigne)*
If the servant grows rich and the master poor, they are both good for nothing. *(German)*
Who wishes to be ill-served, let him keep many servants. *(Italian)*
Do not be too ready to believe a wife complaining of servants. *(Latin)*
Every great house is full of saucy servants. *(Latin)*
It is the master that shames me, not the servitude. *(Latin)*
So many servants, so many enemies. *(Latin)*
Take care that you do not let your servant excel you in doing right. *(Latin)*
The tongue of a bad servant is his worst part. *(Latin)*

The truest report comes from a man's servants. *(Latin)*
Do not stuff your servant with bread, and he won't ask for cheese. *(Spanish)*
The lazy servant takes eight steps to avoid one. *(Spanish)*
The servant wench that has a mother in town swoons seven times a day. *(Spanish)*

SERVICE

Unwilling service earns no thanks. *(Danish)*
All service is the same with God. *(Browning)*
Good service is great enchantment.
He that serves everybody is paid by nobody.
In heaven they scorn to serve, so now in hell they reign. *(Fletcher)*
Service is no inheritance.
Service without reward is punishment.
Small service is true service while it lasts. *(Wordsworth)*
They also serve who only stand and wait. *(Milton)*
They serve God well who serve his creatures.
Serve like a serf or fly like a deer. *(French)*
He who serves is preserved. *(Latin)*
Proffered service stinks. *(Latin)*
He who serves is not free. *(Spanish)*

SERVITUDE

Every man basteth the fat hog.
Learn to lick betimes; you know not whose tail you may go by.
Many kiss the hand they wish cut off.
They kiss the hand by which they are oppressed. *(Latin)*
Every man bows to the bush he gets bield of. *(Scottish)*

SEVILLE

Who has not seen Seville has not seen a wonder. *(Spanish)*

SHADOW

Our days on the earth are as a shadow. *(Old Test., Chron.)*
A little man may cast a great shadow.
Catch not at the shadow, and lose the substance.
Even shadows have their shadows too.
Every light has its shadow.
Some there be that shadows kiss;
  Such have but a shadow's bliss. *(Shakespeare)*
Think not thy own shadow longer than that of others.

To fight with a shadow is a vain and useless act.
All we that live are but vain shadows, unsubstantial dreams. *(Sophocles)*
We are but dust and shadow. [. . . *pulvis et umbra.*] *(Horace)*
The longer shadows fall from the lofty mountains. *(Latin)*
The setting sun doubles the lengthening shadows. *(Latin)*

SHAKE
All that shakes falls not. *(French)*

SHAME
Shame lasts longer than poverty. *(Dutch)*
He that has no shame has no conscience.
I never wonder to see men wicked, but I often wonder not to see them ashamed. *(Swift)*
In shame there is no comfort but to be beyond shame.
Man is a beast when shame stands off from him.
Past shame, past grace.
Shame arises more from fear of men than of God.
Shame in a kindred cannot be avoided.
Shame is as it is taken.
Shame is the eldest daughter of uncleanness.
Shame lost, honor lost.
Shame stings sharpest of the worms in hell.
Shame to them that think shame.
There smites nothing so sharp nor smelleth so sour as shame.
Where shame is there is fear. *(Milton)*
Where there is yet shame, there may in time be grace.
It is the crime that makes the shame, and not the scaffold. *(Corneille)*
None but the shamefaced lose. *(French)*
Shame take him that shame thinketh.
[*Honi soit qui mal y pense.*] *(French)*
On shameful things shame everywhere attends. *(Greek)*
The eyes are the abode of shame. *(Greek)*
There is no shame but thinking makes it so. *(Greek)*
Who has no shame, all the world is his own. *(Italian)*
I count him lost who is lost to shame. *(Latin)*
It is a shame to be shameless. *(Latin)*
It is easier to bear shame than annoyance. *(Latin)*
It is false shame that covers unhealed wounds. *(Latin)*
Shame is shame, whether you think so or not. *(Latin)*
Shame once gone does not return. *(Latin)*
The worst shame is the shame of poverty. *(Latin)*

There is hope of salvation where there is shame. *(Latin)*
In the land of the naked, people are ashamed of clothes. *(Russian)*
Who has no shame before men, has no fear of God. *(Yiddish)*

SHARE
He who shareth honey with the bear hath the least part.
Share and share alike.

SHARP
Beware how you give any edged tool
  Unto a young child and unto a fool.
It is ill jesting with edged tools.
The finest edge is made with the blunt whetstone.

SHAVE
A bald head is soon shaved.
A beard well lathered is half shaved. *(Spanish)*

SHEEP
The sheep has no choice when in the jaws of the wolf. *(Chinese)*
As good be hanged for a sheep as a lamb.
As soon goes the young lamb to the market as the old ewe.
Better give the wool than the sheep.
Good pastures make fat sheep.
If one sheep leap o'er the dyke, all the rest will follow.
It is a foolish sheep that makes the wolf his confessor.
It is hard to have wolf full and wether whole. *(Chaucer)*
Shear sheep that have them.
The black sheep is the perilous beast.
The dust raised by the sheep does not choke the wolf.
The sheep does not bite the wolf. *(German)*
A mild sheep is sucked by every lamb. *(Italian)*
Every time the sheep bleats it loses a mouthful. *(Italian)*
He that makes himself a sheep is eaten by the wolf. *(Italian)*
The death of the wolf is the health of the sheep. *(Italian)*
A good shepherd must fleece his sheep, not flay them. *(Latin)*
One scabbed sheep will mar a whole flock. *(Latin)*
Every sheep with his fellow. *(Spanish)*
He who has sheep has fleeces. *(Spanish)*

SHIP
A great ship asks deep waters.
A ship is ever in need of repairing.

Launch not a splendid ship on a ha'p'orth o' tar.
Rats will desert a sinking ship.
Ships fear fire more than water.
Your ships are the wooden walls. *(Themistocles)*
He who steadies himself between two ships will be drowned. *(Russian)*
Two captains sink the ship. *(Turkish)*

SHIPWRECK
A wreck on shore is a beacon at sea. *(Dutch)*
He who has suffered shipwreck, fears to sail upon the sea.
He who will not be ruled by the rudder, must be ruled by the rock.
'Tis double death to drown in ken of shore. *(Shakespeare)*
They make glorious shipwreck who are lost in seeking worlds. *(Lessing)*
A common shipwreck is a consolation to all. *(Latin)*
Each man makes his own shipwreck. *(Latin)*
He wrongly accuses Neptune, who makes shipwreck a second time. *(Latin)*

SHOE
The younger brother's wife copies the shoes made by the elder brother's wife. *(Chinese)*
Not every wood will make wooden shoes. *(Danish)*
All feet tread not in one shoe.
Better cut the shoe than pinch the feet.
He that looks after dead men's shoes, may chance to go barefoot.
The shoe will hold with the sole.
To each foot his own shoe. *(French)*
Let not the shoe be too large for a foot. *(Latin)*
You cannot put the same shoe on every foot. *(Latin)*
Each knows where the shoe pinches him. *(Spanish)*

SHOEMAKER
A hale cobbler is better than a sick king.
Mock not the cobbler for his black thumbs.
The shoemaker makes a good shoe because he makes nothing else. *(Emerson)*
Who is worse shod than the shoemaker's wife?
When we see a man with bad shoes, we say it is no wonder, if he is a shoemaker. *(Montaigne)*
Let not the cobbler go beyond his last. *(Latin)*

SHOP
Keep thy shop and thy shop will keep thee.

SHORT
An inch too short is as bad as an ell.
Short and sweet.
Short boughs, long vintage.

SHOOT
A chance shot will kill the devil.
A miss is as good as a mile.
One does not always hit what he aims at. *(French)*
He is a bad shot who cannot find an excuse. *(German)*
It is not enough to aim: you must hit. *(Italian)*
Shoot not beyond the mark. *(Latin)*

SHREW
Govern a horse with a bit and a shrew with a stick. *(Danish)*
Every man can rule a shrew save he that hath her.
It is better to marry a shrew than a sheep.
Little peace where the hen crows and the cock is mute. *(Italian)*

SHROUD
Shrouds are made without pockets. *(Yiddish)*

SICKNESS
Sickness is every man's master. *(Danish)*
Be long sick, that you may be soon hale.
He who never was sick dies the first fit.
Sickness comes on horseback, but goes away on foot.
Sickness soaks the purse.
That sick man is not to be pitied who hath his cure in his sleeve.
The chamber of sickness is the chapel of devotion.
The sick man is free to say all. *(Italian)*
In time of sickness the soul collects itself anew. *(Latin)*
Sickness shows us what we are. *(Latin)*

SIGH
Never sigh, but send.
Sighs are the natural language of the heart.
The sighing of a contrite heart. *(Bk. Com. Prayer)*

SIGHT
We see through a glass darkly. *(New Test., I Corinth.)*
Out of sight, out of mind.
The sight of a man hath the force of a lion.

We see things not as they are, but as we are.
One man does not see everything. *(Greek)*
Seeing is believing. *(Latin)*
They come to see, they come to be seen. *(Latin)*
You can see farther into a millstone than he. *(Spanish)*

SILENCE
Speech is oft repented, silence never. *(Danish)*
Be checked for silence, but never taxed for speech. *(Shakespeare)*
Better to remain silent and be thought a fool, than to speak out and remove all doubt. *(Lincoln)*
Even silence may be eloquent.
He hasn't a word to throw at a dog.
He is not a fool who knows when to hold his tongue.
He must have leave to speak that cannot hold his tongue.
He that speaks sows, and he that holds his peace gathers.
Little said is soonest mended.
Mum is counsel.
Silence catches a mouse.
Silence is a fine jewel for a woman, but it's little worn.
Silence is more eloquent than words.
Silence is the mother of Truth.
Silence is wisdom, when speaking is folly.
Silence may do good, and can do little harm.
Silence seldom hurts.
The rest is silence. *(Shakespeare)*
There is a time for speaking and a time for being still. *(Caxton)*
When you have nothing to say, say nothing.
Wise men say nothing in dangerous times.
Let him now speak, or else hereafter forever hold his peace. *(Bk. Com. Prayer)*
Do you wish people to think well of you? Don't speak. *(French)*
It is sad when men have neither wit to speak, nor judgment to hold their tongues. *(French)*
Silence is safest for one who distrusts himself. *(French)*
Silence is the wit of fools. *(French)*
Silent people are dangerous. *(French)*
Speech is silver, silence is golden. *(French)*
The silence of the people is a warning for the king. *(French)*
Better silent like a fool, than talk like a fool. *(German)*
No one betrays himself by silence. *(German)*

All things except silence bring repentance. *(Greek)*
Be silent, or let thy words be worth more than silence. *(Greek)*
In silence God brings all to pass. *(Greek)*
No wisdom like silence. *(Greek)*
Silence is gain to many of mankind. *(Greek)*
Silence is man's chief learning. *(Greek)*
Silence is true wisdom's best reply. *(Greek)*
If a word be worth one shekel, silence is worth two. *(Hebrew)*
Keep shut the door of thy mouth even from the wife of thy bosom. *(Hebrew)*
Silence is a healing of all ailments. *(Hebrew)*
Deep vengeance is the daughter of deep silence. *(Alfieri)*
Silence was never written down. *(Italian)*
Beware of a silent dog and still water. *(Latin)*
Hear, see, and be silent, if you wish to live in peace. *(Latin)*
If the crow could feed in silence, he would have more meat and less quarreling. *(Latin)*
Let a fool hold his tongue, and he will pass for a sage. *(Latin)*
Silence gives consent. *(Latin)*
Silence is taught by life's misfortune. *(Latin)*
To silence another, first be silent yourself. *(Latin)*
Who is silent is strong. *(Latin)*
God rights the man that keeps silent. *(Persian)*
Silence is also speech. *(Yiddish)*

SILVER

Bad silver will buy only old sow's flesh. *(Chinese)*
A silver key can open an iron lock.
Silver will have a silver sound.
A silver hammer breaks an iron door. *(French)*

SIMPLICITY

Nature hangs out a sign of simplicity in the face of a fool.
Nothing is more simple than greatness . . . *(Emerson)*
Oh! What a power has white simplicity! *(Keats)*
Blissful are the simple, for they shall have much peace. *(Latin)*
O holy simplicity. *(John Huss)*

SIN

Be sure your sin will find you out. *(Old Test., Numbers)*
Fools make a mock of sin. *(Old Test., Prov.)*
God be merciful to me, a sinner. *(New Test., Luke)*

He that is without sin among you, let him cast the first stone.
(*New Test., John*)

The wages of sin is death. (*New Test., Romans*)
The way of transgressors is hard. (*Old Test., Prov.*)
Woe unto them that draw iniquity with cords of vanity . . .
(*Old Test., Isaiah*)

The son pays the father's debt of sin. (*Chinese*)
A sinful heart makes feeble hand.
Every man carries the bundle of his sins upon his own back.
Every sin brings its punishment with it.
Fear nothing but sin.
Few love to hear the sins they love to act.
God pardons those who through frailty sin. (*Herrick*)
I am a man more sinned against than sinning. (*Shakespeare*)
Little sins make room for great.
Men are punished *by* their sins, not *for* them.
Naught that delights is sin. (*B. Jonson*)
Nip sin in the bud.
Old sin makes new shame.
One leak will sink a ship; and one sin will destroy a sinner. (*Bunyan*)
Sin that is hidden is half forgotten.
Sins are not known till they be acted.
Some rise by sin, and some by virtue fall. (*Shakespeare*)
The blackest sin is cleared with absolution. (*Shakespeare*)
The cat shuts its eyes while it steals cream.
The longer thread of life we spin,
The more occasion still to sin. (*Herrick*)
The sin is not in the sinning, but in being found out.
The sins ye do by two and two, ye must pay for, one by one. (*Kipling*)
Without knowledge there is no sin.
A sin confessed is half forgiven. (*French*)
God hardens the hearts of sinners. (*French*)
Sin writes histories; goodness is silent. (*Goethe*)
Who is not ashamed of his sins, sins double. (*German*)
All that defiles comes from within. (*Greek*)
The gods visit the sins of the fathers upon the children. (*Greek*)
There is a sin of omission as well as of commission. (*Greek*)
Commit a sin thrice, and you will think it allowable. (*Hebrew*)
There is no death without sin. (*Hebrew*)
He does not sin who sins without intent. (*Latin*)
He who does not forbid sin when he can, encourages it. (*Latin*)

Sin can be well-guarded, but cannot be free from anxiety. *(Latin)*
The sins committed by many pass unpunished. *(Latin)*
To sin is human; but to persevere in sin is satanic. *(St. Chrysostom)*
One does not sin with the mind, but with the will. *(Russian)*
For a fresh sin a fresh penance. *(Spanish)*
Take away the motive, and the sin is taken away. *(Spanish)*
The righteous sometimes pay for the sinners. *(Spanish)*
Who sins and mends, commends himself to God. *(Spanish)*

SINCERITY
Be what thou seemest.
From the teeth forward.
I want to see you shoot the way you shout. *(T. Roosevelt)*
Sincerity gives wings to power.
The sincere alone can recognize sincerity.

SING
Each bird loves to hear itself sing.
The bird that can sing and will not sing, must be made to sing.
Sing before breakfast, and you'll cry before night. *(French)*
Some sing who are not merry. *(Italian)*
He who sings frightens away his ills. *(Spanish)*
He who sings in summer will weep in winter. *(Yiddish)*

SIP
Blow first, and sip afterwards. *(Latin)*

SIT
He sits well who can rise without help. *(Danish)*
As good sit still as rise up and fall.
He sits not sure who sits too high.
He that comes first may sit where he will.
Sit on your thumb till more room do come.
Let's get up and see whether we're sitting properly. *(Russian)*

SKELETON
The skeleton at the feast.
The skeleton in the closet.

SKILL
All things require skill but an appetite.
Skill and confidence are an unconquered army.
Skill to do comes of doing.

Skilled hands eat trout.
Skill is stronger than strength. *(French)*
He who has an art has everywhere a part. *(Italian)*

SKIN
Can the Ethiopian change his skin, or the leopard his spots?
(Old Test., Jerem.)

A fair skin covers a crooked mind.
It is good sleeping in a whole skin.
The skin is nearer than the shirt. *(French)*
You are come off now with a whole skin. *(Spanish)*

SKY
There is no relying on a starry sky.
If the sky fall, we shall catch larks. *(French)*
It becomes wearisome to watch the arch of heaven. *(Vergil)*
If the sky falls, the pots will be broken. *(Spanish)*

SLANDER
He that repeateth a matter separateth very friends. *(Old Test., Prov.)*
The mouth that belieth slayeth the soul. *(Apocrypha)*
For slander lives upon succession,
  Forever housed where it gets possession. *(Shakespeare)*
I hate the man who builds his name
  On ruins of another's fame. *(Gay)*
If slander be a snake, it is a winged one—it flies as well as creeps.
If the ball do not stick to the wall, yet it will leave some mark.
If you slander a dead man, you stab him in his grave.
It may be a slander but it is no lie.
Lay it on; some of it will stick.
Slander flings stones at itself.
Slander is a shipwreck by a dry tempest.
Slander that is raised is ill to fell.
Slander—the foulest whelp of Sin.
Slander, whose sting is sharper than a sword's. *(Shakespeare)*
Squint-eyed Slander plies unhallowed tongue.
Tale-bearers are just as bad as the tale-makers.
The man who despises slander, deserves it.
The truth is no slander.
We slander through vanity more often than through malice.
(La Rochefoucauld)

A generous heart repairs a slanderous tongue. *(Homer)*

Speak no ill of a friend, nor even of an enemy. *(Greek)*
The most dangerous of wild beasts: a slanderer; of tame ones: a flatterer. *(Greek)*
Slander slays three persons: the speaker, the spoken to, and the spoken of. *(Hebrew)*
Thy friend has a friend, and thy friend's friend has a friend, so be discreet. *(Hebrew)*
Destruction and spite are received with eager ears. *(Latin)*
Slander always finds an easy entrance to ignoble minds. *(Latin)*
Slander is canine eloquence. *(Latin)*
Slander leaves a scar behind it. *(Latin)*
You make no repute for yourself when you publish another's secret fault. *(Persian)*

SLAVERY

Am I not a man and brother? *(Wedgwood's motto)*
As the slave departs the man returns.
Better the devil's than a woman's slave.
Corrupted freemen are the worst of slaves.
Give a slave a rod, and he'll beat his master.
He that is one man's slave is free from none.
If slavery is not wrong, nothing is wrong. *(Lincoln)*
Slavery is a weed that grows in every soil.
The blow that liberates the slave sets the master free. *(Roche)*
The distinguishing sign of slavery is to have a price, and to be bought for it. *(Ruskin)*
The thrall in person may be free in soul. *(Tennyson)*
Where slavery is, there liberty cannot be; and where liberty is, there slavery cannot be. *(Sumner)*
Slavery is as ancient as war, and war as human nature. *(Voltaire)*
Freedom—the name of virtue; slavery—of vice. *(Greek)*
None can be free who is a slave to his passions. *(Greek)*
Retain a free mind, though a slave, and slave thou shalt not be. *(Greek)*
Slavery enchains a few; more enchain themselves to slavery. *(Latin)*
The foulest death rather than the fairest slavery. *(Latin)*

SLEEP

The sleep of a laboring man is sweet. *(Old Test., Eccles.)*
Who goes fasting to bed will sleep but lightly. *(Dutch)*
A man is not always asleep when his eyes are shut.

He is so wary that he sleeps like a hare, with his eyes open.
He that sleeps feels not the tooth-ache.
Let sleeping dogs lie.
One hour's sleep before midnight is worth three afterwards.
Quiet sleep feels no foul weather.
Sleep is better than medicine.
Sleep is a short death; death, a longer sleep.
Sleep that knits up the ravell'd sleave of care. *(Shakespeare)*
Sleep will not be commanded.
Sweet are the slumbers of the virtuous man.
The sleeping fox catches no poultry.
There will be sleeping enough in the grave.
He sleeps enough who does nothing. *(French)*
He who sleeps wants no dinner. *(French)*
I never sleep comfortably except when I am at sermon . . . *(Rabelais)*
Blessed are the sleepy, for they shall soon drop off. *(German)*
Sleep, to be truly enjoyed, must be interrupted. *(German)*
Sleep to the sick is half health. *(German)*
It is not fitting for a man of counsel to sleep the whole night through. *(Greek)*
No one when asleep is good for anything. *(Greek)*
Sleep anticipates his brother, Death. *(Greek)*
Sleep is the only medicine that gives ease. *(Greek)*
Five hours of sleep a traveler, seven a scholar, eight a merchant, and eleven every knave. *(Italian)*
He who sleeps catches no fish. *(Italian)*
I sleep for myself; I work, I know not for whom. *(Italian)*
He sleeps well who knows not that he sleeps ill. *(Latin)*
Let your midday sleep be short or none at all. *(Latin)*
Six hours for a man, seven for a woman, eight for a fool. *(Latin)*
Sleep after dining is not good. *(Latin)*
Sleep makes the darkness brief. *(Latin)*
Sleep vanishes before the house of care. *(Latin)*
You can sleep on both ears. [*i.e. in security*] *(Latin)*
Blessings on him that first invented sleep. *(Cervantes)*
He who sleeps much learns little. *(Spanish)*
Sleep is the best cure for waking troubles. *(Spanish)*
While we are asleep, we are all equal. *(Spanish)*
As you are rocked to sleep so do you sleep. *(Yiddish)*
Even the one-eyed man must sleep. *(Yiddish)*
He who sleeps late has short days. *(Yiddish)*

SLIP
Better slip with foot than tongue.
Every slip is not a fall.
He stands not surely that never slips.
There's many a slip 'twixt cup and lip. *(Greek)*

SLOTH
The slothful man hideth his hand in his bosom. *(Old Test., Prov.)*
Sloth is the beginning of vice. *(Dutch)*
Sloth, like rust, consumes faster than labor wears.
Sloth must breed a scab.
Sloth turneth the edge of wit.
The slothful man is the beggar's brother.
A slothful man never has time. *(Italian)*
Sloth is the key to poverty. *(Spanish)*

SLOW
As well too forward as too slow.
Be slow to promise, quick to perform.
Slow and steady wins the race.
Slow at meat, slow at work.
Slow but sure.
The slower you go, the quicker you'll get there. *(Yiddish)*

SLUGGARD
Go to the ant, thou sluggard; consider her ways and be wise. *(Old Test., Prov.)*

SMALL
A small cloud may hide both sun and moon. *(Danish)*
A small hurt in the eye is a great one.
A small sore wants not a great plaster.
Small things make base men proud. *(Shakespeare)*
Small axes fell great trees. *(German)*
A small coin in a big jar makes a great noise. *(Hebrew)*

SMILE
A man without a smiling face must not open a shop. *(Chinese)*
A smile is a light in the window of a face which shows that the heart is at home.
A smile recures the wounding of a frown. *(Shakespeare)*
A tender smile is sorrow's only balm.
He surest strikes that smiling gives the blow.

One may smile, and smile, and be a villain. *(Shakespeare)*
There's daggers in men's smiles. *(Shakespeare)*

SMITH
The smith and his penny are both black.
The smith's mare and the cobbler's wife are always the worst shod.

SMOKE
No smoke without some fire.
Smoke rises only from large blocks of wood. *(Russian)*
Secret fire is discerned by its smoke. *(Spanish)*

SNAKE
It is the bright day that brings forth the adder.
Put a snake in your bosom, and it will sting when it is warm.
Serpents lie where flowers grow.
Take heed of the snake in the grass.
When you see a snake, never mind where he came from.
Who sees the lurking serpent steps aside.
A snake deserves no pity. *(Yiddish)*

SNEER
Who can refute a sneer? *(Paley)*
Without sneering, teach the rest to sneer. *(Pope)*

SNEEZE
He hath sneezed thrice; turn him out of the hospital.
He's a friend at a sneeze: the most you can get out of him is a God bless you.

SNOW
A snow year, a rich year.
Snow is the poor man's fertilizer.
Whether you boil snow or pound it, you can have but water of it.
Where are the snows of yesteryear? *(Villon)*

SNUG
As snug as a bug in a rug.

SOCIETY
All the world and his wife.
If from society we learn to live,
'Tis solitude should teach us how to die. *(Byron)*
Man seeketh in society comfort, use, and protection. *(Bacon)*

Man was formed for society.
No society can ever be as large as one man. *(Emerson)*
Society is no comfort to one not sociable.
Solitude is often the best society.
What will Mrs. Grundy say? *(T. Morton)*
Society is as ancient as the world. *(French)*
Society is the union of men and not the men themselves. *(Montesquieu)*
The wise man flees society for fear of being bored. *(French)*
Custom and convention govern society. *(Greek)*
Man is a social animal. *(Latin)*

SOLDIER
A soldier's but a man; a life's but a span;
Why, then, let a soldier drink. *(Shakespeare)*
All soldiers run away, madam. *(Wellington)*
I never expect a soldier to think. *(G. B. Shaw)*
On becoming soldiers, we have not ceased to be citizens.
Soldiers are citizens of death's gray land. *(Sassoon)*
Soldiers in peace are like chimneys in summer.
The greatest general is he who makes the fewest mistakes. *(Napoleon)*
The worse the man, the better the soldier. *(Napoleon)*
A young soldier, an old beggar. *(German)*
An army, like a serpent, travels on its belly. *(Frederick)*
A good soldier talks of success, not of failure. *(Greek)*
What makes the real general, is to have clean hands. *(Greek)*
The soldiers fight, and the kings are heroes. *(Hebrew)*
A soldier, fire, and water soon make room for themselves. *(Italian)*
It is the blood of the soldier that makes the general great. *(Italian)*
A beaten soldier fears a reed. *(Japanese)*
For a soldier there is nothing left of a man after death but a corpse. *(Latin)*
No faith and no honor in men who follow camps. *(Latin)*
All are not soldiers who go to the wars. *(Spanish)*
The soup makes the soldier. *(Spanish)*

SOLITUDE
Woe to him that is alone when he falleth . . . *(Old Test., Eccles.)*
A solitude is the audience-chamber of God. *(Landor)*
He travels the fastest who travels alone.
Solitude is the best nurse of wisdom.
They are never alone that are accompanied with noble thoughts.

Woe unto him that cannot bear to be alone.
Solitude is within us. *(French)*
A solitary man is either a brute or an angel. *(Italian)*
One would not be alone, even in Paradise. *(Italian)*
I am never less alone than when alone. *(Latin)*
The strongest man in the world is he who stands alone. *(Ibsen)*

SOMETHING

Something is better than nothing.
When one is getting something, one is losing nothing. *(Spanish)*

SON

A wise son maketh a glad father; but a foolish son is the heaviness of his mother. *(Old Test., Prov.)*
A son pays his father's debts. *(Chinese)*
The son disgraces himself when he blames his father. *(Chinese)*
Good wombs have born bad sons. *(Shakespeare)*
He that brings up his son to nothing breeds a thief.
Like father, like son.
That unfeather'd two-legged thing, a son. *(Dryden)*
A lame mule and a stupid son have to endure everything. *(Spanish)*
Every man is the son of his own works. *(Spanish)*
Him to whom God gave no sons the Devil gives nephews. *(Spanish)*
A son who marries gives his wife a contract and his mother a divorce. *(Yiddish)*

SON-IN-LAW

The son-in-law's sack is never full. *(Danish)*
After your daughter is married you can always find sons-in-law a-plenty. *(French)*
He who has gold can choose his son-in-law. *(German)*
I can see by my daughter's face when the devil takes hold of my son-in-law. *(Italian)*
To a son-in-law and a hog you need not show the way but once. *(Spanish)*

SONG

A silly song may be sung in many ways. *(Danish)*
A good song is not the worse for being sung twice.
Let me make a people's songs, and I care not who makes their laws.
Lips only sing when they cannot kiss.
What will a child learn sooner than a song?
Everything ends in songs. *(French)*

That which is not worth saying, is sung. *(Beaumarchais)*
The mouth which is busy with song is not busy with grapes. *(French)*
They sing—they will pay. *(French)*
Any words are good enough for music. *(Greek)*
Song is untouched by death. *(Latin)*
Give in return for old wine, a new song. *(Latin)*
Gloomy cares will be lightened by song. *(Latin)*
Men, when alone, lighten their labor by song, however rude. *(Latin)*
Song is persuasive; let girls learn to sing. *(Latin)*
Song wins grace with the gods above, and with the gods below. *(Latin)*
He who sings scares away his woes. *(Spanish)*
Every new song can be set to an old tune. *(Yiddish)*

SOON
Soon got, soon spent.
Soon hot, soon cold.
Soon learned, soon forgotten.
Soon enough, if well enough. *(Latin)*

SORE
It is ill healing of an old sore.
Rip not up old sores.
Sore upon sore is not salve.
There is a salve for every sore.
Where there is no sore, there is no need of plasters. *(French)*

SORROW
Sorrow hath killed many, and there is no profit therein. *(Apocrypha)*
A day of sorrow is longer than a month of joy. *(Chinese)*
Better two losses than one sorrow.
Earth has no sorrow that Heaven cannot heal.
Fat sorrow is better than lean sorrow.
God send you joy, for sorrow will come fast enough.
Hang sorrow; care'll kill a cat.
Make not two sorrows of one.
Nothing comes to us too soon but sorrow.
Sorrow comes unsent for.
Sorrow is good for nothing but sin.
Sorrow is never long without a dawn of ease.
Sorrow is the eldest child of sin.
Sorrow makes websters spin.

Sorrow will pay no debt.
Sorrows remembered sweeten present joy.
Sorrow's crown of sorrow is remembering happier things. *(Tennyson)*
The busy bee has no time for sorrow.
The longest sorrow finds at last relief
Two in distress make sorrow less.
When sorrows come, they come not single spies,
But in battalions. *(Shakespeare)*
When sorrow is asleep wake it not.
Without the door let sorrow lie.
He gains enough who loses sorrow. *(French)*
A fated sorrow may be lightened with words. *(Latin)*
Small sorrows speak; great ones are silent. *(Latin)*
There is no day without sorrow. *(Latin)*
The wounds of the unhappy endure through the night. *(Latin)*
All sorrows are less with bread. *(Spanish)*
Sing away sorrow. *(Spanish)*
Rejoice not in another's sorrow. *(Turkish)*

SORT
It takes all sorts to make a world. *(Spanish)*

SOUL
For what is a man profited, if he shall gain the whole world, and lose his own soul? *(New Test., Matthew)*
My soul is continually in my hand. *(Old Test., Psalms)*
Soul, thou hast much goods laid up for many years . . . *(New Test., Luke)*
Be careless in your dress if you must, but keep a tidy soul. *(Mark Twain)*
I am the captain of my soul. *(Henley)*
Lay not that flattering unction to your soul. *(Shakespeare)*
Little bodies have great souls.
No seed shall perish which the soul hath sown.
Poor men have no souls.
The body is sooner dressed than the soul.
The body is the workhouse of the soul.
The soul is not where it lives but where it loves.
The soul needs few things, the body many.
There is nothing the body suffers that the soul may not profit by.
This soul, to whom Luther and Mahomet were Prisons of flesh. *(Donne)*

Lack of wealth is easily repaired; but poverty of soul is irreparable. *(Montaigne)*
Animals share with us the privilege of having a soul. *(Pythagoras)*
It is more necessary to cure the soul than the body. *(Greek)*
The soul is immortal and is clothed successively in many bodies. *(Plato)*
There is a divinity within our breast. *(Latin)*
The soul alone renders us noble. *(Latin)*

SOUND
As sound as a bell.
The sound must seem an echo to the sense. *(Pope)*

SOURCE
The stream cannot rise above its source.

SOW
One soweth and another reapeth. *(New Test., John)*
They have sown the wind and they shall reap the whirlwind. *(Old Test., Jerem.)*
He who sows money will reap poverty. *(Danish)*
As they sow, so let them reap.
Early sow, early mow.
He that sows thistles shall reap prickles.
He who sows thorns will never reap grapes.
Sow thin and mow thin.
The early sower never borrows of the late.
Who sows thorns should not go barefoot. *(French)*
Sow with the hand, not from the sack's mouth. *(Greek)*
Nobody sows a thing that will not sell. *(Spanish)*
He who sows here shall reap hereafter. *(Turkish)*
If you sow, things will grow. *(Yiddish)*

SPAIN
All evil comes from Spain; all good from the north.
The Spaniard is a bad servant, but a worse master.
When a Spaniard sings either he is mad or has not a doit. *(Spanish)*

SPARE
He that spareth the rod hateth his son. *(Old Test., Eccles.)*
Better spare at brim than at bottom.
Better spared than ill spent.
Ever spare, ever bare.

Spare your breath to cool your porridge.
Who spares when he is young, may spend when he is old.
Too late to spare when the pocket is bare. *(German)*
He that spares the wicked injures the good. *(Latin)*

SPARK
A spark will set a whole city on fire. *(Arabian)*
The smith has always a spark in his throat.
The spark sleeps in the stone. *(German)*
A little spark kindles a great fire. *(Italian)*

SPARROW
A sparrow is a little bird, yet it has liver and gall all complete. *(Chinese)*
Sparrows should not dance with cranes: their legs are too short. *(Danish)*
Every sparrow to its ear of wheat.
Sparrows fight for corn which is none of their own.

SPEAR
A sharp spear needs no polish. *(African)*
Spears are not made of bulrushes.

SPEECH
Let your speech be always with grace, seasoned with salt. *(New Test., Coloss.)*
Out of the abundance of the heart the mouth speaketh. *(New Test., Matth.)*
Speak after the manner of men. *(New Test., Romans)*
As the man, so is his speech. *(Danish)*
A knavish speech sleeps in a foolish ear. *(Shakespeare)*
Blessed is the man who, having nothing to say, abstains from giving us wordy evidence of the fact. *(George Eliot)*
Discretion of speech is more than eloquence.
Dumb men get no lands.
First think, and then speak.
He cannot speak well that cannot hold his tongue.
He never speaks but his mouth opens.
He that speaks lavishly shall hear as knavishly.
He that speaks me fair and loves me not, I'll speak him fair and trust him not.
He that speaks much is much mistaken.

He that speaks without care shall remember with sorrow.
Hear much, speak little.
If you have no honey in your pot, have some in your mouth.
Least said, soonest mended.
Many speak much who cannot speak well.
More have repented speech than silence.
One may think what he dare not speak.
Say well or be still.
Speak and speed: the close mouth catches no flies.
Speak fitly, or be silent wisely.
Speak for yourself.
Speak that I may see thee.
Speak well of the dead.
Speak well of your friend; of your enemy say nothing.
Speak when you are spoken to.
Speaking without thinking is shooting without aiming.
Speech is the picture of the mind.
Teach your child to hold his tongue; he'll learn fast enough to speak.
That is well spoken that is well taken.
The evil that cometh out of thy mouth flieth into thy bosom.
The true use of speech is to conceal our thoughts.
They talk most who have the least to say.
Who spares to speak doth spare to speed.
Saying is one thing, and doing, another. *(French)*
I disapprove of what you say, but I will defend to death your right to say it. *(Voltaire)*
One speaks little when vanity does not make one speak. *(La Rochefoucauld)*
Use your mouth according to your purse. *(French)*
What the mouth says, the heart may not feel. *(French)*
Much speaking and lying are cousins. *(German)*
Speech is silvern, silence golden. *(German)*
Who says little has little to answer for. *(German)*
A man's character is revealed by his speech. *(Greek)*
It is better to guard speech than to guard wealth. *(Greek)*
Man's speech is like his life. *(Greek)*
Speech is the mirror of action. *(Greek)*
To speak much is one thing, to speak well, another. *(Greek)*
Who knows most speaks light. *(Italian)*
A soft speech has its poison. *(Latin)*
Even the most timid man can deliver a bold speech. *(Latin)*

He speaks in his drink what he thought in his drought. *(Latin)*
It is better to say nothing than not enough. *(Latin)*
It is easy for men to say one thing and think another. *(Latin)*
Speech both conceals and reveals the thoughts of men. *(Latin)*
The man is wise who speaks few things. *(Latin)*
The smooth speeches of the wicked are full of treachery. *(Latin)*
He who speaks, sows; who listens, reaps. *(Russian)*
When a' men speak, nae man hears. *(Scottish)*
He that speaks not, God hears not. *(Spanish)*
He who says what he likes, hears what he does not like. *(Spanish)*
Though the speaker be a fool, let the hearer be wise. *(Spanish)*
He that speaks truth must have one foot in the stirrup. *(Turkish)*

SPEND
Easy come, easy go.
He eats the calf in the cow's belly.
She is one of mine aunts that made nine uncles go begging.
Spend, and God will send; spare, and ever bare.
Spend and you get.
Who spends before he thrives, will bed before he dies.
He that spends more than he is worth, spins a rope for his own neck. *(French)*
Spend one sou less than the clear gain. *(French)*
To spend much and gain little is the sure road to ruin. *(German)*
Through not spending enough we spend too much. *(Spanish)*

SPIDER
The spider lost her distaff, and is ever since forced to draw her thread through her tail.
The spider's web lets the rat escape and catches the fly. *(Spanish)*

SPIN
It is better to spin with Penelope than sing with Helen.
She that gazes much spins not much.
Spin not too fine a thread lest it break in weaving up.
You must spoil before you spin.

SPIRIT
A wounded spirit who can bear? *(Old Test., Prov.)*
Not of the letter, but of the spirit: for the letter killeth, but the spirit giveth life. *(New Test., II Corinth.)*
The spirit indeed is willing, but the flesh is weak. *(New Test., Matth.)*
The spirit illuminates everything. *(Chinese)*

Raise no more spirits than you can conjure down.
Spirits are not finely touch'd but to fine issues. *(Shakespeare)*

SPIT
Who spits against the wind, it fouls his beard. *(Dutch)*
Spit in your hand and take better.
Spit not in the well whose water you may have to drink.
He who spits above himself will have it all in his face. *(Spanish)*

SPITE
There is no spite like that of a proud beggar.
A spiteful cur must be tied short. *(French)*
He'd take one of his own eyes out, only to take both of yours. *(Yiddish)*

SPOIL
Spilt wine is worse than water.
A spoiled child—shod in the cradle, barefoot in the stubble. *(Scottish)*
What you spoil in youth, you can't correct in old age. *(Yiddish)*

SPORT
He that cannot make sport should mar none.
Sport is sweetest when there be no spectators.
The game is not worth the candle. *(French)*
Said in sport, meant in earnest. *(German)*
The strong man's sport is the weak man's death. *(German)*

SPOT
Skill or fortune will efface the spots. *(Danish)*
A spot is most seen on the finest cloth.
Point not at others' spots with a foul finger.
The fairer the paper the fouler the blot.
Are there not spots on the sun? *(French)*

SPRAT
Every sprat nowadays calls itself a herring.

SPRING
In spring time, the only pretty ring time. *(Shakespeare)*
In the spring a young man's fancy lightly turns to thoughts of love. *(Tennyson)*
Spring, the sweet Spring, is the pleasant year's king.
In spring heat returns to the bones. *(Latin)*

SPUR

A spur in the head is worth two in the heel.
Of what use are spurs, if there is no horse. *(Yiddish)*

SPY

Spies are the ears and eyes of princes.
The life of spies is to know, not to be known.

STABLE

A man is not a horse because he was born in a stable.

STAFF

Cross a bridge, then throw the staff away. *(Chinese)*
Cast your staff into the air, and it will fall upon its heavy end. *(Hebrew)*
A staff in the hand is better than a tongue in the mouth. *(Yiddish)*

STAIN

The fairest silk is soonest stained.
A stain on silk leaves the stuff still silk. *(Yiddish)*

STAND

He who stands high sees from afar. *(Danish)*
He that stands may fall.
Standing pools gather filth.
Who moves picks up; who stands dries up. *(Italian)*

STAR

Canst thou bind the sweet influence of Pleiades, or loose the bands of Orion? *(Old Test., Job)*
The morning stars sang together, and all the sons of God shouted for joy. *(Old Test., Job)*
The stars in their courses fought against Sisera. *(Old Test., Judges)*
A man gazing at the stars is at the mercy of the puddles on the road.
He that looks for a star puts out his candle.
He that strives to touch the stars
Oft stumbles at a straw. *(Spenser)*
Hitch your wagon to a star. *(Emerson)*
Stars are not seen by sunrise.
The stars above us govern our conditions. *(Shakespeare)*
The stars are the sentinels of the skies.
The stars that have most glory have no rest.
There be more stars, God wot, than a pair. *(Chaucer)*

These blessed candles of the night. *(Shakespeare)*
Too low they build, who build beneath the stars. *(Young)*
Two stars keep not their motion in one sphere.
The stars rule men, but God rules the stars. *(Latin)*
There is no easy road from the earth to the stars. *(Latin)*
Through hardship to the stars. [*Per aspera ad astra.*] *(Latin)*

START
One starts the hare, another bags it. *(Spanish)*

STARVE
Starve together, eat together.
The sated understand not the pain of the starving. *(Turkish)*

STATE
Better one suffer, than a nation grieve.
The worth of a State is the worth of the individuals composing it. *(J. S. Mill)*
What belongs to the state belongs to nobody.
The foundation of a state is its education of its youth. *(Greek)*

STATISTICS
There are three kinds of lies: lies, damned lies, and statistics. *(Disraeli)*

STEAL
Don't steal if you can't conceal.
He that steals can hide.
He that will steal a pin will steal an ox.
If you steal for others, you shall be hanged yourself.
One man may steal a horse, while another may not look over a hedge.
Stolen fruit is sweetest.
Stolen bread stirs the appetite. *(French)*
Stolen wool does not warm long. *(German)*
Who steals a calf steals a cow. *(German)*
He who steals once is never to be trusted. *(Spanish)*
If the eye did not see, the hand would not steal. *(Yiddish)*

STEP
Step after step the ladder is ascended.
It's the first step that counts. *(French)*
There is but one step from the sublime to the ridiculous. *(French)*
The hardest step is over the threshold. *(Italian)*
Step not on the sleeping serpent. *(Spanish)*

STEP-MOTHER
A step-mother has a hard hand. *(Danish)*
There are as many good step-mothers as white ravens. *(German)*

STICK
A straight stick is crooked in the water.
A stick is a peacemaker. *(French)*
There is no argument like that of a stick. *(Spanish)*

STILL
Be still, and have thy will.
Still waters run deep.
Beware of still water, a still dog, and a still enemy. *(Yiddish)*

STING
Better be stung by a nettle than pricked by a rose.

STINGY
He will dress an egg and give the offal to the poor.
He will not lose the droppings of his nose.
He would skin a louse, and send the hide to market.
She will as soon part with the crock as the porridge.
A stingy man is always poor. *(French)*
He hath left his purse in his other breeks. *(Scottish)*
A rich man who is stingy is the worst pauper. *(Yiddish)*

STITCH
A stitch in time saves nine.

STOMACH
A full stomach praises Lent. *(Danish)*
A good stomach is the best sauce.
A sharp stomach makes short devotion.
The stomach is a bad counsellor. *(German)*
The stomach is easier filled than the eye. *(German)*
The stomach rules the head. *(German)*
It is the stomach that bears the feet. *(Spanish)*
The way to a man's heart is through his stomach. *(Spanish)*

STONE
Who throws a stone above himself may have it fall on his own head.
(Old Test., Prov.)
The stone that everybody spits upon will be wet at last. *(Danish)*

A rolling stone gathers no moss.
A rugged stone grows smooth from hand to hand.
Beware of the stone you stumbled at before.
To kill two birds with one stone.
When the stone leaves the hand it belongs to the devil.
He is not a good mason that refuses any stone. *(Italian)*
The stone sharpens knives but is dull itself. *(Italian)*
The stone that lies in one place becomes covered with moss. *(Yiddish)*

STOOP
He must stoop that hath a low door.
He that will not stoop for a pin will never be worth a point.

STOP
To stop the hand is the way to stop the mouth. *(Chinese)*
One must know when to stop. *(French)*

STORM
A good pilot is best tried in a storm.
After a storm comes a calm.
Any port in a storm.
As the days grow longer, the storms grow stronger.
Every storm hath his calm.
Storms make oaks take deeper root.
The more violent the storm, the sooner it is over. *(Latin)*

STRAIGHT
Straight trees have crooked roots.
The straight can't become straighter. *(Russian)*

STRAIN
Men strain at gnats and swallow camels.

STRAW
Straws show which way the wind blows.
The last straw breaks the camel's back.

STREAM
It is ill striving against the stream.

STRENGTH
Be strong, and quit yourselves like men. *(Old Test., I Samuel)*
As thy days, so shall thy strength be. *(Old Test., Deut.)*
Let your strength be the law of justice. *(Apocrypha)*

My strength is made perfect in weakness. *(New Test., II Corinth.)*
They that wait upon the Lord shall renew their strength.
(Old Test., Isaiah)

. . . it is excellent to have a giant's strength,
But it is tyrannous to use it like a giant. *(Shakespeare)*
Brute strength without reason falls of its own weight. *(Latin)*
He who has great strength should use it lightly. *(Latin)*
Such strength as a man has he should use. *(Latin)*
The stronger always wins. *(Latin)*

STRETCH
Stretch your arms no further than your sleeves will reach.
Stretch your legs according to your coverlet. *(German)*

STRIKE
He that strikes my dog would strike me if he durst.
He that strikes with his tongue must ward with his head.
Many strokes fell great oaks.
Strike while the iron is hot.
Strike—but hear. *(Greek)*
Strike the cold stone, and a hot spark will fly out. *(Yiddish)*

STRIVE
Striving to better, oft we mar what's well. *(Shakespeare)*

STRONG
He must be strong to pull a rope against a stronger. *(Danish)*
The strong one is always right. *(Yiddish)*

STUDY
I would live to study, not study to live. *(Bacon)*
The study of vain things is laborious idleness.
To spend too much time in studies is sloth. *(Bacon)*
Studies grow into habits. *(Latin)*

STUMBLE
A stumble may prevent a fall.
He who stumbles twice over one stone deserves to break his shins.
It is a good horse that never stumbles.
Well may he stumble that chooses a stony way.
Wisely and slow: they stumble that run fast.
Better stumble once than be always tottering. *(French)*
Even a horse who has four legs stumbles. *(Italian)*

STUPID

He is not only dull himself, but the cause of dullness in others.
Nature delights in punishing stupid people. *(Emerson)*
There is no sin but stupidity. *(O. Wilde)*
The fault rests with the gods who have made us stupid. *(French)*
Against stupidity the gods themselves contend in vain. *(Schiller)*

STYLE

Proper words in proper places. *(Swift)*
That's not good language that all understand not.
All styles are good except the boring kind. *(Voltaire)*
Clearness ornaments profound thoughts. *(French)*
The style is the man himself. *(Buffon)*
The style dares not go beyond the genius. *(Petrarch)*
When an old phrase fits the occasion, it is well used. *(Latin)*

SUBMISSION

O calm, dishonorable, vile submission! *(Shakespeare)*
Submission to one wrong brings on another. *(Latin)*

SUBORDINATE

He who rides behind another does not travel when he pleases.

SUCCESS

The race is not to the swift, nor the battle to the strong. *(Old Test., Eccles.)*
If the plow cannot reach it, the harrow can. *(Chinese)*
It is not in mortals to command success.
Life begins only in success.
Nothing is so impudent as success.
Success alters our manners.
Success is a ladder which cannot be climbed with your hands in your pockets.
Success is never blamed.
Success is the child of audacity.
Success makes a fool seem wise.
The many fail, the one succeeds.
The true touchstone of desert—success. *(Byron)*
All succeeds with those who are cheerful. *(French)*
Everything is subservient to success. *(French)*
Nothing succeeds like success. *(French)*
To know how to wait is the great secret of success. *(French)*

Success in men's eyes is God, and more than God. *(Greek)*
Success has many friends. *(Greek)*
Success is the reward of toil. *(Greek)*
Success is the gift of Heaven. *(Greek)*
Either do not attempt it, or succeed. *(Latin)*
Success has brought many to destruction. *(Latin)*
Success leads to insolence. *(Latin)*
We never know when we have succeeded best. *(Unamuno)*

SUFFER
When another man suffers, a piece of wood suffers. *(Arabian)*
Of suffering comes ease.
We by our sufferings learn to prize our bliss. *(Dryden)*
Many suffer for what they cannot help. *(French)*
He who suffers much will know much. *(Greek)*
Suffering, when it climbs highest, lasts not long. *(Greek)*
Present sufferings seem greater than those we dread. *(Latin)*
He that lives long suffers much. *(Spanish)*
Suffer in order to know; toil in order to have. *(Spanish)*
The sufferer becomes a chatterer. *(Turkish)*

SUGAR
Even sugar itself may spoil a good dish.
Where you need sugar, salt will not serve. *(Yiddish)*

SUICIDE
Happy men that have the power to die. *(Tennyson)*
He that hangeth himself on Sunday
Shall hang still uncut down on Monday.
Nine men in ten are suicides. *(Franklin)*
There is no refuge from confession but suicide; and suicide is confession. *(D. Webster)*
'Tis more brave to live than to die.
To be or not to be: that is the question. *(Shakespeare)*
We are in the power of no calamity while death is in our own. *(Sir T. Browne)*
We men are in a kind of prison and must not set ourselves free or run away. *(Plato)*
He dies twice who perishes by his own hand. *(Latin)*
The gods forbid us to leave the world without their command. *(Latin)*
There is but one entrance into life, but many exits. *(Latin)*
Tranquillity can be purchased at the cost of a pin-prick. *(Latin)*

When all the blandishments of life are gone,
The coward sneaks to death, the brave live on. *(Martial, tr. Sewell)*

SUIT

Sue a beggar, and get a louse.
The last suitor wins the maid.

SULTAN

The sultan's interdict lasts three days. *(Turkish)*

SUMMER

A dry summer ne'er made a dear peck.
Do what we can, summer will have its flies.
Sumer is icumen in,
Lhude sing cuccu!
It will not always be summer. *(Greek)*
When the summer is winter, and the winter summer, it is a sorry year. *(Spanish)*

SUN

As thick as motes in the sun-beam. *(Chaucer)*
Clouds, that the sun builds up, darken him.
For the happy the sun seems always to have just set.
He that walketh in the sun shall be tanned.
In every country the sun rises in the morning.
Men honor the rising, rather than the setting sun.
Most men worship the rising sun.
The sun can be seen by nothing but its own light.
The sun is never the worse for shining on a dunghill.
The sun shines on both sides of the hedge.
When the sun is highest he casts the least shadow.
When the sun sets, who doth not look for night? *(Shakespeare)*
When the sun shines let foolish gnats make sport. *(Shakespeare)*
The sun shines for all the world. *(French)*
Though the sun shines, leave not your cloak at home. *(French)*
If the sun shines, I care not for the moon. *(Italian)*
The sun will blind you, if you persist in gazing at it. *(Latin)*
Who would dare say the sun is false? *(Vergil)*
Make hay while the sun shines. *(Spanish)*
The sun shines on rich and poor alike. *(Yiddish)*
The sun that makes linen white, makes the gypsy black. *(Yiddish)*

SUN-DIAL

I number none but the cloudless hours. *(Latin)*

SUPERSTITION

A superstition is a premature explanation that overstays its time.

All people have their superstitions.

Better be dumb than superstitious. *(B. Jonson)*

Sickness and sorrows come and go, but a superstitious soul hath no rest. *(Burton)*

Superstition is godless religion, devout impiety.

Superstition is the religion of feeble minds.

Superstition is the reproof of the Deity. *(Bacon)*

Crush the infamous thing! *(Voltaire)*

Superstition poisons and destroys all peace of mind. *(Latin)*

SUPPER

Light suppers mak lang life days. *(Scottish)*

Go to bed without supper and you'll rise without debt. *(Spanish)*

SUPPORT

He must needs swim that is held up by the chin.

One father can support ten children; ten children cannot support one father. *(Spanish)*

SURE

As sure as eggs is eggs.

Better be sure than sorry.

SURETY

He that hateth surety-ship is sure. *(Old Test., Prov.)*

He that is surety for a stranger shall smart for it. *(Old Test., Prov.)*

Be bail and pay for it.

Act as surety, and ruin is at hand. *(Greek)*

SURGEON

Call not a surgeon before you are wounded.

The best surgeon is he of the soul.

Tender surgeons make foul wounds. *(Italian)*

SURRENDER

Never say die.

SUSPICION

As good steal the horse as look over the hedge.

At the gate where suspicion enters love goes out.

Banish squint suspicion. *(Milton)*
He lives unsafely that looks too near on things.
He that hath suspicion is rarely at fault.
Suspicion absolves faith. *(Bacon)*
Suspicion has double eyes.
Suspicion is no less an enemy to virtue than to happiness. *(S. Johnson)*
Suspicion is the companion of mean souls. *(Paine)*
Suspicion may be no fault, but showing it may be a great one.
Suspicions are like bats that fly only at twilight.
The virtue of a coward is suspicion.
Always suspect that which seems probable. *(French)*
Suspicion is the poison of friendship. *(French)*
Suspicion follows closest on mistrust. *(German)*
He that is in fault is in suspicion. *(Italian)*
The hawk suspects the snare, and the pike the covered hook. *(Latin)*
The losing side is full of suspicion. *(Latin)*

SWALLOW
One swallow does not make spring, nor does one fine day. *(Greek)*
One swallow does not make summer. *(Spanish)*

SWAN
The jealous swan, against his death that singeth. *(Chaucer)*

SWAP
Don't swap horses when you are crossing a stream. *(Lincoln)*

SWEAR
Damn braces. Bless relaxes. *(Blake)*
He that sweareth deep, sweareth like a lord.
He will swear a dagger out of sheath.
He will swear the devil out of hell.
He will swear through an inch board.
He will swear till he's black in the face.
When I swear, it is only by God. *(Montaigne)*
To swear is unbecoming to a man of sense. *(Latin)*
He's swearing even when he says nothing. *(Russian)*
He who tells the truth saves himself the trouble of swearing. *(Yiddish)*

SWEEP
Everyone sweeps before his own door. *(French)*
If each one sweeps before his own door, the whole street is clean. *(Yiddish)*
When the house is swept, what was lost is found. *(Yiddish)*

SWEET

Better short and sweet than long and lax.
Every sweet hath its sour.
No sweet without sweat.
Sweet appears sour when we pay.
Sweet meat must have its sour sauce.
Sweetest nut hath sourest rind.
Sweets to the sweet.
Take the sweet with the sour.
The bitter goes before the sweet, and makes the sweet sweeter.
The fly that sips treacle is lost in the sweets.
Things sweet to taste prove in digestion sour. *(Shakespeare)*
What is sweet in the mouth is bitter in the maw.
Who hath bitter in the mouth spits not sweet.
Flee what is sweet, if it can turn to bitterness. *(Latin)*
He deserves not the sweet that will not take the sour. *(Latin)*
Even the sole of a shoe fried in honey is sweet. *(Yiddish)*

SWIM

He may lightly swim that is held up by the chin.
Never venture out of your depth till you can swim.
Swim with the stream.
The best swimmers are the oftenest drowned.

SWINE

Root, hog, or die. *(American)*
Draff is good enough for swine.
Still swine eats all the draff.
You have the wrong sow by the ear.
You cannot make a satin purse of a sow's ear.
Cast not pearls before swine. *(Latin)*

SWORD

They that take the sword shall perish with the sword.
(New Test., Matthew)
Better die with the sword than by the sword.
Good sword has often been in poor scabbard.
He that strikes with the sword shall be beaten with the scabbard.
He who has the longest sword is always thought to be in the right.
One sword keeps another in the sheath.
Scanderbeg's sword must have Scanderbeg's arm.
In olden days the sword ruled all things. *(German)*

The sword knows no friends. *(German)*
Don't stir the fire with a sword. *(Greek)*
Great is the license of the sword. *(Latin)*
Leave not a sword in the hands of a fool. *(Latin)*
Let the sword decide. *(Latin)*
Our right is in our swords. *(Latin)*
Snatch away the sword from one who is in a rage. *(Latin)*
He who plays with a sword plays with the devil. *(Spanish)*
Use not the sword against him who asks forgiveness. *(Turkish)*

SYMPATHY

Rejoice with them that do rejoice, and weep with them that weep. *(New Test., Romans)*
When your own tooth aches, you know how to sympathize with one who has a toothache. *(Chinese)*
No man limps because another is hurt. *(Danish)*
A brother's sufferings claim a brother's pity.
Our sympathy is cold to the relation of distant misery.
People in distress never think that you feel enough.
Sympathy without relief is like mustard without beef.
Other men's ills hang by a hair. *(Spanish)*

SYSTEM

A peg for everything.
A place for everything and everything in its place.

T

TABLE

The table robs more than the thief.

TAILOR

Dull scissors make crooked-mouthed tailors. *(Danish)*

God makes and the tailor shapes.

Let every tailor keep to his goose.

Nine tailors make but one man. [*The "nine tailors" are the nine teller-strokes that ring for the death of a man.*]

The tailor that makes not a knot loseth a stitch.

There is little to sew where tailors are true.

Though the tailor makes the man, the cook yet makes the dishes.

TAKE

Take things always by the smooth handle.

One "Take this" is better than two "You shall have." *(French)*

Take out without putting in, soon comes to the bottom. *(Spanish)*

Who likes to take hates to give. *(Yiddish)*

TALE

Believe not every tale. *(Apocrypha)*

A good tale ill told is marred in the telling.

A good tale is none the worse for being twice told.

A sad tale's best for winter.

A tale never loses in the telling.

A tale twice told is cabbage twice old.

Believe no tales from an enemy's tongue.

In a fair tale may be foul falsity.

Life is as tedious as a twice-told tale. *(Shakespeare)*

Sey forth thy tale, and tarry not the time. *(Chaucer)*

Tell no tales out of school.

The tale runs as it pleases the teller.

There is many a true tale told in jest.
What a tale of a cock and a bull!
It is an irksome thing to tell again a plain-told tale. *(Greek)*
He thinks every old wives' tale to be a truth. *(Latin)*

TALE-BEARER
A dog that fetches a bone will carry one.
Put no faith in tale-bearers.

TALENT
The more talents, the more they will be developed. *(Chinese)*
Hide not your talents, they for use were made.
What's a Sun-dial in the Shade? *(Franklin)*
That one talent which is death to hide . . . *(Milton)*
Let the path be open to talent. *(Napoleon)*
To do easily what is difficult for others is the mark of talent. *(Amiel)*
Talent is developed in retirement; character is formed in the rush of the world. *(Goethe)*
Often the greatest talents lie unseen. *(Latin)*

TALK
The talk of the lips tendeth only to penury. *(Old Test., Prov.)*
A great talker never wants for enemies. *(Chinese)*
Talk does not cook rice. *(Chinese)*
Foolish tongues talk by the dozen.
Great talkers are commonly liars.
He hath tied a knot with his tongue that he cannot untie with his teeth.
He that knows not how to hold his tongue knows not how to talk.
He that talks to himself speaks to a fool.
Least said, soonest mended.
People may come to do almost anything by talking about it.
So much they talked, so very little said.
Talk is but talk; 'tis money buys lands.
Talk often, but never long.
Talk to every woman as if you loved her; to every man as if he bored you. *(O. Wilde)*
The gift of gab.
The greatest talkers, the least doers.
The less people think, the more they talk.
The mill that is always going grinds coarse and fine.
They never taste who always drink;
They always talk who never think. *(Prior)*

To talk without thinking is to shoot without aiming.
When I can't talk sense, I talk metaphor. *(J. P. Curran)*
Much bruit, little fruit. *(French)*
Talk with deliberation, fair and softly, as lawyers go to heaven. *(Rabelais)*
You talk like a book. *(French)*
Let people talk and dogs bark. *(German)*
Much talk, much foolishness. *(Hebrew)*
He who talks much cannot always talk well. *(Italian)*
The talker sows, the listener reaps. *(Italian)*
He that says what he should not, hears what he would not. *(Latin)*
Let your talk be worthy of belief. *(Latin)*
This is idle talk. *(Latin)*
Do not talk Arabic in the house of a Moor. *(Spanish)*
He who talks much is sometimes right. *(Spanish)*
Talk much and err much. *(Spanish)*
Two great talkers will not travel far together. *(Spanish)*

TASTE
Men lose their tempers in defending their tastes. *(Emerson)*
Tastes differ.
Everyone to his taste. *(French)*
Everyone as he likes, as the woman said when she kissed her cow. *(Rabelais)*
Taste is the literary conscience of the soul. *(Joubert)*
There are as many tastes as there are men. *(Latin)*
No disputing about taste. [*De gustibus non est disputandum.*] *(Latin)*
To a depraved taste sweet is bitter. *(Spanish)*
Whether sugar be white or black, it preserves its proper taste. *(Turkish)*

TATTLER
A tattler is worse than a thief.
The tattler's tongue is always dancing a silly jig.

TAXES
All taxes must at last fall upon agriculture. *(Gibbon)*
Taxation without representation is tyranny. *(Otis)*
The power to tax is not the power to destroy. *(Holmes)*
Unnecessary taxation is unjust taxation.
In this world nothing is certain but death and taxes. *(French)*

TEA
Love and scandal are the best sweeteners of tea.
Polly, put the kettle on, we'll all have tea.

TEACH

A teacher should be sparing of his smile.
Bachelors' wives and maids' children are well taught.
Better fed than taught.
Better untaught than ill taught.
He teacheth ill who teacheth all.
He teaches who gives, and he learns who receives.
He that teaches himself has a fool for his master.
He who can, does. He who cannot, teaches. *(G. B. Shaw)*
It is hard to teach an old dog new tricks.
Teach your grandmother to suck eggs.
We loved the doctrine for the teacher's sake.
I do not teach, I only tell. *(Montaigne)*
The Prussian schoolmaster won the battle of Sadowa. *(Von Moltke)*
He is either dead or teaching school. *(Greek)*
If you love instruction you will be well educated. *(Greek)*
The man that has never been flogged has never been taught. *(Greek)*
The same persons telling to the same people the same things about the same things. *(Greek)*
Those having torches will pass them on to others. *(Greek)*
Who teaches, often learns himself. *(Italian)*
While the colt has a tender neck, the trainer teaches him. *(Latin)*

TEARS

A small tear relieves a great sorrow.
A woman's tears are silent orators.
And weep the more because I weep in vain. *(Gray)*
But only human eyes can weep.
Every tear from every eye
  Becomes a baby in eternity. *(Blake)*
How much better it is to weep at joy than to joy at weeping. *(Shakespeare)*
It is as great a pity to see a woman weep as a goose to go barefoot.
Onions can make even heirs and widows weep.
Our funeral tears from diff'rent causes rise. *(Young)*
Tears are the noble language of the eye.
The busy have no time for tears.
The fewer his years, the fewer his tears.
There's no seeing one's way through tears.
Weep not, my wanton, smile upon my knee,
  When thou art old there's grief enough for thee. *(Greene)*

Women laugh when they can and weep when they will.
Women's weapons, water-drops. *(Shakespeare)*
You cannot cleanse your heart with tears.
In youth, one has tears without grief; in age, grief without tears. *(French)*
Tears are the silent language of grief. *(French)*
The tears of the night equal the smiles of the day. *(French)*
Tears soothe suffering eyes. *(German)*
In tears was I born, and after tears I die. *(Greek)*
Tears benefit not the wounded. *(Greek)*
Tears in mortal miseries are vain. *(Homer)*
The tribute of a tear is all I crave. *(Homer)*
Waste not fresh tears over old griefs. *(Euripides)*
Even when the gates of prayer are shut, the gates of tears are open. *(Hebrew)*
He wastes his tears who weeps before the judge. *(Italian)*
Hence those tears. [*Hinc illae lacrimae.*] *(Vergil)*
If you would have me weep, you must first feel grief yourself. *(Horace)*
Nothing dries sooner than a tear. *(Latin)*
Repentant tears wash out the stain of guilt. *(Latin)*
Tears are sometimes as weighty as words. *(Latin)*
There are the tears of things. [*Sunt lacrimae rerum.*] *(Vergil)*
An orphan's tear falls not in vain. *(Russian)*
He loves thee well that makes thee weep. *(Spanish)*
Of what good is a silver cup, if it is filled with tears? *(Yiddish)*
Onion tears do not touch the heart. *(Yiddish)*

TELL
Don't tell everything you know. *(Yiddish)*

TEMPER
To a boiling pot flies come not.
He who loses his temper is in the wrong. *(French)*
He called me scabbed because I will not call him scald. *(Scottish)*

TEMPERANCE
Eat not to dulness; drink not to elevation. *(Franklin)*
Temperance is a bridle of gold.
Temperance is the best medicine.
Temperance is the nurse of chastity.
Temperance consists in foregoing bodily pleasures. *(Latin)*

TEMPLE
The groves were God's first temples. *(Bryant)*
Let nothing vile come into the temple. *(Latin)*
The truest temples are fixed in the heart. *(Latin)*

TEMPTATION
Blessed is the man that endureth temptation. *(New Test., James)*
Lead us not into temptation, but deliver us from evil. *(New Test., Matth.)*
If sinners entice thee, consent thou not. *(Old Test., Prov.)*
Watch and pray, that ye enter not into temptation. *(New Test., Matth.)*
An open box tempts an honest man. *(Dutch)*
A bad padlock invites a picklock.
An open door may tempt a saint.
I can resist everything except temptation. *(O. Wilde)*
I was taken by a morsel, says the fish.
It is easy to keep a castle that was never assaulted.
It is easier to stay out than get out. *(Mark Twain)*
She is good who is close to the fire and does not burn.
Tempt not a desperate man.
The less the temptation the greater the sin.
The tempter or the tempted, who sins most? *(Shakespeare)*
When we do ill, the devil tempts us; when we do nothing, we tempt him.
At an open chest the righteous sin. *(French)*
May God defend me from myself! *(French)*
He who avoids the temptation avoids the sin. *(Spanish)*
Shut your door and you will make your neighbor good. *(Spanish)*
The key to my girdle keeps me good and my neighbor too. *(Spanish)*

TEST
The proof of gold is fire; the proof of woman, gold; the proof of man, a woman.

THANKS
Old thanks are not for new gifts. *(Italian)*
You can't put thanks into your pocket. *(Yiddish)*

THICK
As thick as hops.
As thick as thieves.

THIEF

Look not at thieves eating flesh, but look at them suffering punishment. *(Chinese)*

A thief thinks every man steals. *(Danish)*

There are more thieves than are hanged. *(Dutch)*

A rackless hussy makes many thieves.

A thief knows a thief as a wolf knows a wolf.

A thief passes for a gentleman when stealing has made him rich.

A true man and a thief think not the same.

All are not thieves that dogs bark at.

An old thief deserves a new halter.

Call him a thief, and he will steal.

Change be no robbery.

Every true man's apparel fits your thief. *(Shakespeare)*

Give a thief rope enough and he'll hang himself.

Great thieves hang little ones.

Hang a thief when he's young, and he won't steal when he is old.

He that fears the gallows shall never be a good thief.

He that is once a thief is evermore in danger.

He that shows his purse bribes the thief.

He that steals can hide.

He that steals honey should beware of the sting.

He that will be rich before night may be hanged before noon.

He that will steal an egg will steal an ox.

He will bear it away if it be not too hot or too heavy.

How great his theft who robs himself!

Little thieves are hanged, but great ones escape.

No receiver, no thief.

One thief robs another.

Opportunity makes the thief.

Save a thief from the gallows and he will cut your throat.

Set a thief to catch a thief.

The thief doth fear each bush an officer. *(Shakespeare)*

There is honor among thieves.

When false thieves fall out, true men come to their own.

When it thunders, the thief becomes honest.

He is a thief indeed that robs a thief. *(French)*

The thief cannot find any tree that suits him for a gallows. *(German)*

We hang little thieves and take off our hats to great ones. *(German)*

Every rascal is not a thief, but every thief is a rascal. *(Greek)*

The receiver is as bad as the thief. *(Greek)*

If the thief has no opportunity, he think himself honorable. *(Hebrew)*
The thief is frightened even by a mouse. *(Italian)*
No one shall be a thief with me to help him. *(Latin)*
A man is not born a thief: he dies one. *(Russian)*
A thief doesn't always steal; but always be on your guard against him. *(Russian)*
Every tribe has its thief, every mountain its wolf. *(Russian)*
He who has a son grown up should not call another a thief. *(Spanish)*
If you would make a thief honest, trust him. *(Spanish)*
Stealing would be a nice thing, if thieves were hanged by the girdle. *(Spanish)*
The hole invites the thief. *(Spanish)*
The thief thinks that all men are like himself. *(Spanish)*
Thieves are never rogues among themselves. *(Spanish)*
A thief has long hands and short pockets. *(Yiddish)*
If you need the thief, you cut him down from the gallows. *(Yiddish)*
Not the mouse is the thief, but the hole in the wall. *(Yiddish)*
When thieves fall out, the peasant gets his cow back. *(Yiddish)*

THIN
As thin as Banbury cheese.

THINGS
Things at the worst will sometimes mend.

THIRST
Who has no thirst has no business at the fountain. *(Dutch)*
I came upon no wine
  So wonderful as thirst. *(E. St. V. Millay)*
When they are thirsty, fools would fain have drink. *(Shakespeare)*
Thirst makes wine out of water. *(German)*
The thirsty drink in silence. *(Greek)*
Thirst comes from drinking. *(Italian)*
You look at what I drink and not at my thirst. *(Spanish)*

THISTLE
Thistles are a salad for asses.
If you should plant a thistle in Paradise it would never become a rose. *(German)*

THORN
He that handles thorns shall prick his fingers.
He that scatters thorns, let him not go bare.

The thorn comes into the world point foremost.
Thorns make the greatest crackling.
Without thorns no roses. *(German)*
He knows well where the thorn pricks him. *(Italian)*
Better one thorn plucked out than all remain. *(Latin)*

THOUGHT

And which of you with taking thought can add to his stature one cubit? *(New Test., Luke)*
As he thinketh in his heart, so is he. *(Old Test., Prov.)*
Have no depraved thoughts. *(Confucius)*
A moment's thinking is an hour in words.
A penny for your thoughts.
A thought may take a man prisoner.
Great thoughts reduced to practice become great acts.
He is a fool that thinks not that another thinks.
He never is alone that is accompanied with noble thought.
Give thy thoughts no tongue,
  Nor any unproportion'd thought his act. *(Shakespeare)*
He that thinks amiss concludes worse.
He thinks not well that thinks not again.
I would that my tongue could utter
  The thoughts that arise in me. *(Tennyson)*
If men would think more, they would act less.
No harvest of thought without a seed-time of character.
Nothing is too sacred to be thought about.
One may think that dare not speak.
Our thoughts are often worse than we are.
Say nothing, but think the more.
Strange thoughts beget strange deeds.
The profound thinker always suspects that he may be superficial. *(Disraeli)*
There's more in your head than the comb will take out.
There is nothing either good or bad, but thinking makes it so. *(Shakespeare)*
Things bring thoughts.
Think today and speak tomorrow.
Thought hath good legs.
Thought is a nimble footman.
Thought is often bolder than speech.
Thought once awakened does not slumber.
Thoughts are free from toll.

To speak as the common people, to think as the wise.
Your thoughts close, and your countenance loose.
Great thoughts come from the heart. *(French)*
Man is but a reed, the weakest in nature, but he is a thinking reed. *(Pascal)*
Think much, speak little, and write less. *(French)*
No thought without phosphorus. *(Moleschott)*
Thoughts are toll-free but not hell-free. *(German)*
I pray thee, O God, that I may be beautiful within. *(Socrates)*
Life is thought. *(Greek)*
Second thoughts are wisest. *(Greek)*
Thoughts are mightier than strength of hand. *(Greek)*
First thoughts are not always the best. *(Italian)*
Man is only miserable so far as he thinks himself so. *(Italian)*
Who is never done thinking, never begins doing. *(Italian)*
Good thoughts, even if forgotten, do not perish. *(Latin)*
I think, therefore I am. *(Descartes)*
Thought is free. *(Latin)*
To live is to think. *(Latin)*
Men suffer from thinking more than from anything else. *(Tolstoy)*
To think is to converse with oneself. *(Spanish)*

THREAD
Short flax makes long thread. *(Danish)*
To hang by a thread.
Who holds the thread holds the ball. *(French)*
By the thread we unwind the skein. *(Spanish)*
The thread breaks where it is thinnest. *(Spanish)*

THREAT
Threateners do not fight. *(Dutch)*
A man does not die of threats.
Barking dogs never bite.
He is a fool that makes a wedge of his fist.
He threatens many that hath injured one.
His bark is worse than his bite.
Many a man threatens while he quakes with fear.
There are more men threatened than stricken.
Threatened folk live long.
Threats without power are like powder without ball.
Who cares naught for death cares naught for threats. *(French)*
Who threatens warns. *(German)*

A blow threatened is never given. *(Italian)*
Longer lives he that is threatened than he that is hanged. *(Italian)*
To freemen threats are impotent. *(Latin)*
More are threatened than are stabbed. *(Spanish)*
Threatened folk, too, eat bread. *(Spanish)*

THREE
One's too few and three's too many.
What three know everybody knows. *(Spanish)*

THRIFT
A penny in the purse is better than a friend at court.
A penny saved is twice got.
A pin a day is a groat a year.
A shilling spent idly by a fool, may be picked up by a wiser man. *(Franklin)*
He that will not stoop for a pin will never be worth a pound.
He that will thrive must rise at five;
He that hath thriven may lie till seven.
He who spends all he gets is on his way to beggary.
If you keep a thing for seven years, you are sure to find a use for it at last.
If you put nothing into your purse, you can take nothing out.
It is too late to spare when the bottom is bare.
Of saving cometh having.
Penny and penny laid up will be many.
Spare and have is better than spend and crave.
Take care of the pence, and the pounds will take care of themselves.
Their thrift waxes thin that spend more than they win.
Thrift is the philosopher's stone.
'Tis not all saved that's put in the purse.
Who more than he is worth doth spend,
He makes a rope his life to end.
Who will not lay up a penny shall never have many.
Wise men say, keep somewhat till a rainy day.
Saving is getting. *(Italian)*
If you spend a thing you cannot have it. *(Latin)*

THRONE
No throne without thorn.
The throne is but a piece of gilded wood covered with velvet. *(Napoleon)*

THUNDER

The thunder hath but its clap.
Winter's thunder is the world's wonder.
A bolt does not always fall when it thunders. *(German)*
The god hurls his thunderbolt against the loftiest structure. *(Greek)*

TIDE

The ebb will fetch off what the tide brings in.
The tide turns at low water as well as at high.
There is a tide in the affairs of men,
  Which, taken at the flood, leads on to fortune. *(Shakespeare)*
The tide tarries for no man.
Ebb and flood wait for no man. *(German)*
No animal dies except upon a receding tide. *(Latin)*

TIE

See that you tie so that you can untie. *(Dutch)*
Who ties well unties well. *(Spanish)*

TIGER

He who rides a tiger is afraid to dismount. *(Chinese)*
In painting tigers, one can paint the skin but not the bones. *(Chinese)*
The tiger on the plain is insulted by the dogs. *(Chinese)*
The tiger that has once tasted blood is never sated with the taste of it.
When did the tiger's young ones teach the dam? *(Shakespeare)*
Shun the companionship of the tiger. *(Latin)*

TIME

Time subdues all things. *(Arabian)*
There is a time for all things. *(Old Test., Eccles.)*
Our time is a very shadow that passeth away. *(Apocrypha)*
An inch of time cannot be bought by an inch of gold. *(Chinese)*
There is a time to fish and a time to dry nets. *(Chinese)*
Time is not tied to a post like a horse to a manger. *(Danish)*
Time is God's, not ours. *(Dutch)*
A little time is enough to hatch a great mischief.
A mouse may cut a cable in time.
As good have no time, as make no good use of it.
As time hurts, so does time cure.
Bide for time, for time will no man bide.
But all things hath time.
By losing present time we lose all time.

Cormorant devouring Time. *(Shakespeare)*
Every scrap of a wise man's time is worth saving.
Everything hath its time, and that time must be watched.
For time y-lost, this knowen ye, by no way may recovered be.
Gather ye rose-buds while ye may,
  Old Time is still a-flying. *(Herrick)*
God stands winding His lonely horn,
  And time and the world are ever in flight. *(Yeats)*
He that has most time has none to lose.
He who gains time gains everything.
In time the savage bull doth bear the yoke. *(Shakespeare)*
It will be all the same a hundred years from now.
Let time that makes you homely make you sage.
Lost time is never found again.
Make use of time if you love eternity.
Nought treads so silent as the foot of time.
Take time to be quick.
Take time when time is.
The clock upbraids me with the waste of time. *(Shakespeare)*
There is a time for all things.
Thus the whirligig of time brings in his revenges. *(Shakespeare)*
Time and chance reveal all secrets.
Time and tide wait for no man.
Time enough is little enough.
Time flies over us but leaves its shadow behind.
Time goes on crutches till love have all his rites. *(Shakespeare)*
Time hath a taming hand.
Time heals sorrow.
Time is an herb that cures all diseases.
Time is the greatest innovator. *(Bacon)*
Time is the measure of business, as money is of wares.
Time is the nurse and breeder of all good.
Time is the rider that breaks youth.
Time is . . . Time was . . . Time is past.
Time trieth truth in every doubt.
Time stays not at the fool's leisure.
Time wasted, is existence; used, is life. *(Young)*
Time's waters will not ebb or stay.
To choose time, is to save time.
To save time is to lengthen life.
To things immortal, Time can do no wrong. *(Cowley)*

Who hath time, and tarrieth for time, loseth time.
Who hath time hath life.
You may delay, but time will not.
All the treasures of earth cannot bring back one lost moment. *(French)*
Nothing is so dear and precious as time. *(French)*
Time—sovereign physician of our passions. *(Montaigne)*
The time best employed is that which one wastes. *(French)*
Those who make the worst use of time, most complain of its shortness. *(La Bruyère)*
Man cannot buy time. *(German)*
The clock does not strike for the happy. *(Schiller)*
Time brings roses. *(German)*
Time is man's equal. *(German)*
Time makes hay. *(German)*
Time works wonders. *(German)*
A time to love, and a time to wed, and a time to rest. *(Greek)*
Be ruled by time, the wisest counsellor of all. *(Greek)*
Ever-aging Time teaches all things. *(Aeschylus)*
For the just, Time is the best of champions. *(Greek)*
Take time by the forelock—for she is bald behind. *(Greek)*
The greatest sacrifice is the sacrifice of time. *(Greek)*
The wisest thing is time, for it brings everything to light. *(Greek)*
Time brings everything. *(Greek)*
Time is a gentle deity. *(Greek)*
Time is a river of passing events—a rushing torrent. *(Greek)*
Time is money. *(Greek)*
Time is the soul of the world. *(Greek)*
Time will bring healing. *(Greek)*
For time lost irks him most that knows most. *(Dante)*
The good time comes but once. *(Italian)*
There is no appeal from time past. *(Italian)*
Time is a noiseless file. *(Italian)*
Even as we speak, envious Time has fled. *(Horace)*
Nothing is ours except time. *(Seneca)*
The happier the time, the more quickly it passes. *(Latin)*
The inconstant hour flies on double wings. *(Horace)*
The stream of time glides on smoothly. *(Latin)*
There is no bridle that can curb the flying days. *(Latin)*
Time flies. [*Tempus fugit.*] *(Latin)*
Time is the herald of truth. *(Latin)*
Time is the one loan that no one can repay. *(Latin)*

Time rolls swiftly ahead, and rolls us with it. *(Latin)*
Time softens grief. *(Latin)*
Time stands with impartial law. *(Latin)*
Time that devours all things. *(Latin)*
Time does not bow to you; you must bow to time. *(Russian)*
Nae man can tether time or tide. *(Scottish)*
A hundred years hence we shall all be bald. *(Spanish)*
All in good time. *(Spanish)*
Time and I against any two. *(Spanish)*
Time ripens all things. *(Spanish)*
If the time doesn't suit you, suit yourself to the time. *(Turkish)*
In time even a bear can be taught to dance. *(Yiddish)*
Time is the best doctor. *(Yiddish)*

TIMELINESS
A stitch in time save nine.
He that does his turn in time sits half idle.
Put out your tubs when it is raining.
Set not your loaf till the oven's hot.

TIMES
Be a child o' the times. *(Shakespeare)*
The time is out of joint. *(Shakespeare)*
Other times, other manners. *(French)*

TIMID
He that observeth the wind, shall not sow; and he that regardeth the clouds, shall not reap. *(Old Test., Eccles.)*
He cannot say *bo* to a goose.
Timidity is an enemy to poverty.
Tommy's tears and Mary's fears
Will make them old before their years.
Bashfulness is an ornament to youth, but a reproach to old age. *(Greek)*
Faint-hearted men never erect a trophy. *(Greek)*
The most timorous animals are hardest to train. *(Greek)*
Great empires are not maintained by timidity. *(Tacitus)*
The timid man calls himself cautious, the sordid man, thrifty. *(Latin)*
The timid see dangers which do not exist. *(Latin)*
Who timidly requests invites refusal. *(Latin)*
Faint heart ne'er won fair lady. *(Spanish)*

TIRED
Tired folks are quarrelsome. *(French)*
Who does not tire, achieves. *(Spanish)*

TITLE
Rank is a great beautifier.
The fool or knave that wears a title, lies.
Empty heads love long titles. *(German)*
Of what avail are pedigrees? *(Latin)*
The rank is but the guinea's stamp,
  The man's the goud for a' that. *(Burns)*

TOBACCO
Neither do thou lust after that tawny weed, tobacco.
Tobacco *"hic,"* if a man be well it will make him sick.
Tobacco is the tomb of love. *(Disraeli)*
When smoking began to go out of fashion, learning began to go out of fashion too. *(Porson)*

TODAY
If today will not, tomorrow may.
One today is worth two tomorrows.
Rather an egg today than a hen tomorrow.
Today a man in gold, tomorrow closed in clay.
Today at good cheer, tomorrow on the bier.
Today is yesterday's pupil.
What hapt today to me, tomorrow may to you.
I today, you tomorrow. *(Latin)*
Seize today, trust tomorrow as little as possible. *(Horace)*
What's lost today may be won tomorrow. *(Spanish)*

TOIL
He who toils with pain will eat with pleasure. *(Chinese)*
Nothing is achieved without toil.
Toil is the lot of all. *(Greek)*
Toil is prayer. [*Laborare est orare.*] *(Latin)*

TOMORROW
Boast not thyself of tomorrow; for thou knowest not what a day may bring forth. *(Old Test., Prov.)*
Sufficient unto the day is the evil thereof. *(New Test., Matthew)*
Never put off till tomorrow what you can do today.
No one has ever seen tomorrow.

Tomorrow every fault is to be amended; but that tomorrow never comes.
Tomorrow is a new day.
Tomorrow is an old deceiver, and his cheat never grows stale. *(S. Johnson)*
My country is tomorrow. *(French)*
Tomorrow, tomorrow, not today,
Hear the lazy people say. *(German)*
Who knows aright of tomorrow's fortune? *(Greek)*
As much to the purpose as "Tomorrow I found a horseshoe." *(Spanish)*

TONGUE

A wholesome tongue is the tree of life. *(Old Test., Prov.)*
Keep thy tongue from evil, and thy lips from speaking guile. *(Old Test., Psalms)*
The tongue can no man tame. *(New Test., James)*
The tongue which is yielding, endures; the teeth which are stubborn, perish. *(Chinese)*
He loses least in a quarrel who keeps his tongue in cheek. *(Danish)*
Keep not two tongues in one mouth. *(Danish)*
A good tongue is a good weapon.
A honey tongue, a heart of gall.
A slip of the foot may be soon recovered; but that of the tongue, perhaps never.
A still tongue makes a wise head.
A soft tongue may strike hard.
All tongues are not made of the same flesh.
An ox is taken by the horns and a man by the tongue.
Be not thy tongue thy own shame's orator. *(Shakespeare)*
Foolish tongues talk by the dozen.
He that knows not how to hold his tongue, knows not how to talk.
I shall keep my tongue between my teeth.
It hurteth not the tongue to give fair words.
It is better to play with the ears than with the tongue.
Let not your tongue cut your throat.
Many a man's own tongue gives evidence against his understanding.
Many a man's tongue shakes out his master's undoing. *(Shakespeare)*
The lame tongue gets nothing.
The magic of the tongue is the most dangerous of spells.
The tongue breaketh bone, though itself have none.
The tongue is not steel yet it cuts.

The tongue is the rudder of our ship.
The tongue offends and the ears get the cuffing.
There is no venom to that of the tongue.
Tongue double brings trouble.
Turn your tongue seven times before speaking.
What the heart thinketh the tongue speaketh.
A brain is worth little without a tongue. *(French)*
The wise man's tongue is a shield, not a sword. *(German)*
Let not your tongue outrun your thought. *(Greek)*
The greatest of man's treasures is the tongue. *(Greek)*
The tongue is a sharper weapon than the sword. *(Greek)*
The tongue of mortals is pliant, and the words within it numberless. *(Homer)*
The tongue speaks wisely when the soul is wise. *(Greek)*
What among men is both good and bad? The tongue. *(Greek)*
Train thy tongue to say "I do not know," lest thou be entrapped into falsehood. *(Hebrew)*
Whose heart is narrow, his tongue is large. *(Hebrew)*
He that strikes with his tongue must ward with his head. *(Italian)*
He who has a bad tongue should have good loins. *(Italian)*
One pair of ears draws a hundred tongues. *(Italian)*
Who has a tongue in his head can go all the world over. *(Italian)*
A fool's treasure is in his tongue. *(Latin)*
Hold your tongue. *(Latin)*
The tongue is a wild beast; once let it loose, it is difficult to chain. *(Latin)*
The tongue turns to an aching tooth. *(Latin)*
It is a gude tongue that says nae ill. *(Scottish)*
A long tongue betokens a short hand. *(Spanish)*
The tongue of a bad friend cuts more than a knife. *(Spanish)*
He who holds his tongue saves his head. *(Turkish)*
A man's tongue sometimes leads him to the gallows. *(Yiddish)*
An evil tongue is worse than a heavy hand. *(Yiddish)*
The tongue has no bones but it breaks bones. *(Yiddish)*
The whole world stands on the tip of the tongue. *(Yiddish)*

TOOLS

A good reaper deserves a good sickle.
He can ill pipe that lacketh his upper lip.
He that works without tools is twice tired.
What is a workman without his tools?

TOOTH

The teeth of the puppy are growing while the old dog is gnawing bones. *(Danish)*

An aching tooth is better out than in.

Who hath aching teeth hath ill tenants.

The teeth form a barrier to check wanton words. *(Greek)*

The toothless man envies those that can bite. *(Latin)*

TOWER

The loftiest towers rise from the ground. *(Chinese)*

TOY

There are toys for all ages. *(French)*

TRADE

Every trade has its ways. *(Chinese)*

Small trades make great profits. *(Chinese)*

A jack of all trades, master of none.

A man of many trades begs his bread on Sunday.

A trade is better than service.

Every man to his trade.

He that learns a trade hath a purchase made.

Trade is the mother of money.

Two of a trade seldom agree.

There are no foolish trades; there are only foolish people. *(French)*

He that brings not up his son to some trade makes him a thief. *(Hebrew)*

Everyone finds fault with his own trade. *(Italian)*

He who has a trade may travel through the world. *(Spanish)*

A trade is a shield against poverty. *(Yiddish)*

TRADESMAN

A tradesman who cannot lie may shut up his shop. *(French)*

TRAINING

Train up a child in the way he should go. *(Old Test., Prov.)*

TRANSLATOR

Translators—traitors! [*Tradutori, traditori.*] *(Italian)*

TRAP

The fowler's pipe sounds sweet till the bird is caught.

TRAVEL

From going to and fro in the earth, and from walking up and down in it. *(Old Test., Job)*

A fool wanders; the wise man travels.

A gentleman ought to travel abroad, but dwell at home.

A tired traveler must be glad of an ass, if he have not a horse.

A traveler may lie with authority.

Discreet stops make speedy journeys.

Don't put tricks upon travelers.

Fair and softly goes far in a day.

He travels best that knows when to return.

He travels the fastest who travels alone. *(Kipling)*

He that travels much knows much.

I pity the man who can travel from Dan to Beersheba and cry, "'Tis all barren!" *(Sterne)*

If an ass goes traveling, he'll not come home a horse.

It is not worth while to go round the world to count the cats in Zanzibar. *(Thoreau)*

Journeys end in lovers meeting. *(Shakespeare)*

Meat and matins hinder no man's journey.

'Tis a great journey to the world's end.

Travel makes a wise man better, but a fool worse.

Travel teaches toleration.

Travelers, poets, and liars are three words of one signification.

Traveling makes a man wiser, but less happy.

He who stops at every stone never gets to his journey's end. *(French)*

Who goes and returns makes a good journey. *(French)*

If a goose flies across the sea, there comes back a quack-quack. *(German)*

It is better to turn back than go astray. *(German)*

See one mountain, one sea, one river—and see all. *(Greek)*

A wise traveler never despises his own country. *(Italian)*

He who never leaves his country is full of prejudices. *(Italian)*

On a long journey even a straw is heavy. *(Italian)*

Who goes softly goes safely, and he that goes safely goes far. *(Italian)*

A man need not go away from home for instruction. *(Latin)*

Leave thy home, O youth, and seek out alien shores. *(Petronius)*

The traveler without money will sing before the robber. *(Latin)*

They change their sky, not their soul, who run beyond the sea. *(Horace)*

Fools are aye fond o' flittin', and wise men o' sittin'. *(Scottish)*

He travels safest in the dark night who travels lightest. *(Spanish)*
He who takes the wrong road must make his journey again. *(Spanish)*

TREACHERY

Treachery lurks in honeyed words. *(Danish)*
He covers me with his wings, and bites me with his bill.
It is the bright day that brings forth the adder. *(Shakespeare)*
Take heed of him that by the back thee claweth.
The silence of a friend is sometimes treachery.
More are guilty of treachery through weakness than through a studied design to betray. *(La Rochefoucauld)*
Betrayers are hated even by those whom they benefit. *(Latin)*
Treachery, in the end, betrays itself. *(Latin)*

TREASON

A subtle traitor needs no sophistry. *(Shakespeare)*
No religion binds men to be traitors.
Treason doth never prosper. What's the reason?
Why, if it prosper, none dare call it treason. *(Harrington)*
Treason is not inherited.
The treason is loved, but the traitor is hated. *(Italian)*
A traitor is a coward. *(Turkish)*

TREE

In the place where the tree falleth, there it shall be. *(Old Test., Eccles.)*
The ax is laid unto the root. *(New Test., Matthew)*
The tree is known by his fruit. *(New Test., Matthew)*
If the roots are deep, no fear that the wind will uproot the tree. *(Chinese)*
When the tree falls, the shade is gone. *(Chinese)*
High trees give more shade than fruit. *(Dutch)*
A short tree stands long.
A tree is a nobler object than a prince in his coronation robes. *(Pope)*
As the twig is bent, the tree's inclined.
Great trees are good for nothing but shade.
Great trees keep down little ones.
He that betaketh him to a good tree hath good shade.
I will bend the tree while it is a wand.
Only at trees bearing fruit do people throw stones.
Only God can make a tree. *(Kilmer)*
Shake the tree when the fruit is ripe.
Straight trees have crooked roots.

The highest tree hath the greatest fall.
The tree falls not at the first stroke.
The tree that God plants, no winds hurt it.
The tree will wither long before it fall.
When the tree is fallen, all go with their hatchets.
An old tree is hard to straighten. *(French)*
The highest trees have the most reason to dread the thunder. *(French)*
As the tree, so the fruit. *(German)*
Great trees give more shade than fruit. *(Italian)*
The best trees are the most beaten. *(Italian)*
The tree is not to be judged by its bark. *(Italian)*
A twig in time becomes a tree. *(Latin)*
He is a fool who looks at the fruit of a tree and does not measure its height. *(Latin)*
When the tree is down, everybody gathers wood. *(Latin)*
Good fruit never comes from a bad tree. *(Portuguese)*
A young tree bends; an old one breaks. *(Yiddish)*
The apple falls near the apple tree. *(Yiddish)*

TRIAL
He whose father is a judge goes safe to trial.

TRICK
He has as many tricks as a dancing bear.
I know a trick worth two of that.
Tricks are either knavish or childish.
There are tricks in every trade.

TRIFLE
He that contemneth small things, will perish by little and little. *(Apocrypha)*
The journey of a thousand miles begins with one step. *(Chinese)*
An acorn one day proves an oak.
Children and Princes will quarrel for trifles.
Great businesses turn on a little pin.
Great floods flow from simple sources.
He that shuns trifles must shun the world.
I see day at this little hole.
Little drops of water, little grains of sand,
  Make the mighty ocean and the pleasant land. *(J. F. Carney)*
Many little leaks sink a ship.
Many smallë maken a great. *(Chaucer)*

Many strokes overthrow great oaks.
Small things make base men proud. *(Shakespeare)*
Men are led by trifles. *(French)*
Trifles console us because trifles distress us. *(Pascal)*
We are tortured to death by pin-point wounds. *(French)*
Practice yourself in little things. *(Greek)*
The gods give small things to the small. *(Greek)*
From a little spark may burst a mighty flame. *(Italian)*
Even by small things are great ends helped. *(Latin)*
Frivolous minds are won by trifles. *(Latin)*
It is degrading to make difficulties of trifles. *(Latin)*
Small things befit a small man. *(Latin)*
There will grow from straws a mighty heap. *(Latin)*

TROUBLE

Man is born unto trouble, as the sparks fly upward. *(Old Test., Job)*
Shut your doors and sit in your house, yet trouble will fall from the skies. *(Chinese)*
Don't cross the bridge till you get to it.
He is worth no weal that can bide no woe.
He that seeks trouble never misses it.
Horns and gray hairs do not come by years.
I have brought an ill comb to my own head.
In for a penny, in for a pound.
In trouble to be troubled is to have your trouble doubled.
Let's fear no storm before we feel a shower.
Let your trouble tarry till its own day comes.
Never meet trouble half-way.
Never trouble trouble till trouble troubles you.
Out of the frying-pan into the fire.
Send not to market for troubles.
The troubles hardest to bear are those that never come.
They who have nothing to trouble them, will be troubled at nothing.
Things with trouble attained are long retained.
To such as fear, is trouble ever dead?
Sweet is the remembrance of troubles when you are in safety. *(Greek)*
We must seek some other cause than the gods for our troubles. *(Greek)*
Who troubles others has not rest himself. *(Italian)*
Forgetting trouble is the way to cure it. *(Latin)*
Let each man turn his mind to his own troubles. *(Latin)*
Trouble is to man what rust is to iron. *(Yiddish)*

TROY

Troy was not took in a day.
By trying the Greeks got into Troy. *(Greek)*
The Trojans became wise too late. *(Latin)*
Troy fell because Cassandra was not believed. *(Latin)*

TRUST

In God we trust; all others cash. *(American)*
Put not your trust in princes. *(Old Test., Eccles.)*
Eat a peck of salt with a man before you trust him.
He that trusts to borrowed ploughs, will have his land lie fallow.
He who trusteth not is not deceived.
I will trust him no farther than I can throw a millstone.
I sell nothing on trust till tomorrow.
If you trust before you try,
  You may repent before you die.
In God is our trust. *(Key)*
In trust is treason.
In trust is truth.
Living on trust is the way to pay double.
Never trust him whom you have wronged.
Never trust to a broken staff.
Put your trust in God, but keep your powder dry. *(Cromwell)*
To be trusted is a greater compliment than to be loved.
Trust begets trust.
Trust is the mother of deceit.
Trust me, but look to thyself.
Trust not a great weight to a slender thread.
Trust not a horse's heel, nor a dog's tooth.
Trust not him that once hath broken faith.
Trust not to rotten planks.
Swim on, and don't trust. *(French)*
Trust, but not too much. *(German)*
"Trust-well" rides away with the horse. *(German)*
Who mistrusts most should be trusted least. *(Greek)*
From those I trust, God guard me; from those I mistrust, I will guard myself. *(Italian)*
It is equally an error to trust all men or no man. *(Latin)*
Trust in God, but mind your business. *(Russian)*
Trust not a horse on the road and a wife at home. *(Yiddish)*

TRUTH

Truth is better than gold. *(Arabian)*

Buy the truth and sell it not. *(Apocrypha)*

Truth is mighty and will prevail. *(Apocrypha)*

What is truth? said jesting Pilate; and would not stay for an answer. *(New Test.) [Bacon]*

Ye shall know the truth, and the truth shall make you free. *(New Test., John)*

The words of truth are always paradoxical. *(Lao-Tsze)*

Better suffer for truth than prosper by falsehood. *(Danish)*

To withhold truth is to bury gold. *(Danish)*

A lie travels round the world while Truth is putting on her boots.

A truth-teller finds the doors closed against him.

A truth that's told with bad intent
Beats all the lies you can invent. *(Blake)*

Against truth falsehood hath no might.

All great truths begin as blasphemies. *(G. B. Shaw)*

All truth is precious and divine;
Too rich a pearl for carnal swine. *(Butler)*

All truths are not to be told.

An innocent truth can never stand in need of a guilty lie.

As true as God is in heaven.

As true as steel.

Be so true to thyself, as thou be not false to others. *(Bacon)*

Children and fools speak true.

Craft must have clothes, but truth loves to go naked.

Every man seeks for truth, but God only knows who has found it. *(Chesterfield)*

Face to face the truth comes out.

Fair fall truth and daylight.

Follow not truth too near the heels lest it dash out thy teeth.

God offers to every man his choice between truth and repose. *(Emerson)*

Half the truth is often a great lie.

He that trusts in a lie shall perish in truth.

Many a true word hath been spoken in jest.

Naked truth needs no shift.

None but a fool distasteful truth will tell. *(Dryden)*

Oil and truth will come to the surface.

Speak no more than the truth; utter no less.

Speaking truth is like writing fair, and only comes by practice.

That is true which all men say.
The greater the truth the greater the libel.
The man who finds a truth lights a torch.
The truth is mighty and will prevail.
The truth is the best advocate.
The truth shows best being naked.
The truth will out.
Truth can never be told so as to be understood, and not be believed. *(Blake)*
Truth crushed to earth shall rise again. *(Bryant)*
Truth fears no colors.
Truth finds foes where it makes none.
Truth forever on the scaffold . . . *(Lowell)*
Truth gives wings to strength.
Truth hath a quiet breast.
Truth hath always a fast bottom.
Truth is a means, not an end.
Truth is afraid of nothing but concealment.
Truth is . . . stranger than fiction. *(Byron)*
Truth is the anvil which has worn out many a hammer.
Truth is eternal, and the son of heaven.
Truth is that which a man troweth.
Truth is the highest thing that man may keep. *(Chaucer)*
Truth is truth to the end of reckoning.
Truth lies at the bottom of a well.
Truth makes all things plain.
Truth makes the devil blush.
Truth needs no memory.
Truth needs not the foil of rhetoric.
Truth never grows old.
Truth never hurts the teller.
When in doubt, tell the truth. *(Mark Twain)*
I am very fond of truth, but not at all of martyrdom. *(Voltaire)*
In too much disputing the truth is lost. *(French)*
Individuals may perish; but truth is eternal. *(French)*
Man is ice for truth, fire for falsehood. *(La Fontaine)*
Some truths are not for all men at all times. *(French)*
'Tis possible if true. *(French)*
Truth alone wounds. *(French)*
We know the truth not only by the reason but also by the heart. *(Pascal)*

What is true by lamplight is not always true by sunlight. *(French)*
In the mountains of truth you never climb in vain. *(Nietzsche)*
One must not say all that is true. *(German)*
To fool the world, tell the truth. *(Bismarck)*
Truth gives a short answer; lies go round about. *(German)*
Truth may be suppressed, but not strangled. *(German)*
Nature has buried truth at the bottom of the sea. *(Greek)*
No man has seen pure truth. *(Greek)*
No man was ever harmed by truth. *(Greek)*
"Plato is dear to me, but dearer still is truth." *(Greek)*
Simple are the words of truth. *(Greek)*
The truth is always the strongest argument. *(Greek)*
The truth is bitter to fools. *(Greek)*
Truth breeds hatred. *(Greek)*
Truth is the pleasantest of sounds. *(Plato)*
Truth is heavy; few therefore can bear it. *(Hebrew)*
A little truth makes the whole lie pass. *(Italian)*
He who would speak the truth must keep a sharp lookout. *(Italian)*
It is truth that makes a man angry. *(Italian)*
Speak the truth and shame the devil. *(Italian)*
Truth may languish but can never perish. *(Italian)*
I am conquered by truth. *(Latin)*
It is right to yield to the truth. *(Latin)*
Nothing is truer than the truth. *(Latin)*
Time discovers truth. *(Latin)*
Truth conquers all things. *(Latin)*
Truth (flows) in wine. [*In vino veritas.*] *(Latin)*
Truth hates delays. *(Latin)*
Truth is often attended with danger. *(Latin)*
Truth is often eclipsed but never extinguished. *(Latin)*
Truth is the daughter of Time. *(Latin)*
Truth seeks no corner. *(Latin)*
To utter great truths is no easier than to lie. *(Russian)*
The truth may stretch but will not break. *(Spanish)*
Truth before peace. *(Unamuno)*
Truth is God's daughter. *(Spanish)*
Truth tramples on a lie as oil on water. *(Spanish)*
In truth is right. *(Turkish)*
A half truth is a whole lie. *(Yiddish)*
Everyone loves the truth, but not everyone tells it. *(Yiddish)*
The truth may be told, even about one's own father. *(Yiddish)*

TRY

If at first you don't succeed, try, try again.
Try the ice before you venture on it.

TURN

Turn about is fair play.

TURNIP

There is no getting blood out of a turnip. *(Italian)*

TWIG

A twig in time becomes a tree.
As the twig is bent, the tree's inclined.
Birchen twigs break no ribs.

TWINS

For the pauper, twins are like a fifth wheel to the wagon. *(Yiddish)*

TWO

Two are the masters of one. *(Danish)*
Two dry sticks will kindle a green one.
Two eyes can see more than one.
Two heads are better than one.
Two in distress make sorrow less.
Two watermelons cannot be held under one arm. *(Turkish)*

TYRANT

A tyrant is most tyrant to himself.
A tyrant is the best sacrifice to Jupiter. *(Burton)*
He who allows the oppression shares the crime.
Resistance to tyrants is obedience to God. *(Jefferson)*
When law ends, tyranny begins.
Clever tyrants are never punished. *(Voltaire)*
Is there no tyrant but the crowned one? *(Chénier)*
Slaves would be tyrants if the chance were theirs. *(French)*
Tremble, ye tyrants, for ye cannot die! *(Delille)*
Happy the tyrant who dies in bed. *(Greek)*
One tyrant helps another tyrant. *(Greek)*
Tyranny is a lovely eminence, but there is no way down from it. *(Solon)*
Tyrants are a money-loving race. *(Sophocles)*
What is more cruel than a tyrant's ear? *(Juvenal)*

UGLY

If all the world were ugly, deformity would be no monster.
No one blames a man for being ugly. *(Greek)*

UNCERTAINTY

All between the cradle and the coffin is uncertain.
Between the hand and the lip the morsel may slip.
There's many a slip 'twixt the cup and the lip.

UNDERSTANDING

I shall light a candle of understanding in thine heart, which shall not be put out. *(Apocrypha)*
With all thy getting, get understanding. *(Old Test., Prov.)*
Give it an understanding but no tongue. *(Shakespeare)*
"Put Yourself in His Place." [*Title*] *(Reade)*
Understanding is the wealth of wealth.
The understanding is ever the dupe of the heart. *(French)*
Each one brings his understanding to market. *(German)*
What we do not understand we do not possess. *(Goethe)*
What is not understood is always marvelous. *(Latin)*

UNITY

Three, if they unite against a town, will ruin it. *(Arabian)*
A threefold cord is not quickly broken. *(Old Test., Eccles.)*
Behold, how good and how pleasant it is for brethren to dwell together in unity. *(Old Test., Psalms)*
He that is not with me is against me. *(New Test., Matthew)*
The lone sheep is in danger of the wolf.
United we stand, divided we fall. *(G. P. Morris)*
We must all hang together, or we shall all hang separately. *(Franklin)*
Weak things united become strong.

All for one, and one for all. *(Dumas)*
Strength united is greater. *(Latin)*
Two are an army against one. *(Latin)*
Union gives strength to the humble. *(Latin)*
A sheaf without a sheaf-band is straw. *(Russian)*

UNIVERSE
A grain of sand includes the universe. *(Coleridge)*
Space is the stature of God. *(Joubert)*
The universe is a thought of God. *(Schiller)*
All that is in tune with thee, O Universe, is in tune with me. *(M. Aurelius)*
The sum total of all sums total is eternal. *(Lucretius)*

UNIVERSITY
A university is a place where pebbles are polished and diamonds are dimmed. *(Ingersoll)*
Alma mater. [Fostering mother.] *(Latin)*

UNKNOWN
Everything unknown is taken for magnificent. *(Latin)*

UNLUCKY
If I dealt in shrouds, people would stop dying. *(Arabian)*
He was cursed in his mother's belly that was killed by a cannon.
If it rained soup, I'd have a fork instead of a spoon.
He falls on his back and breaks his nose. *(French)*
If I were a hatter, people would be born without heads. *(German)*
If I went to sea, I should find it dry. *(Italian)*

UNWELCOME
As welcome as snow in harvest.
As welcome as water into a ship.
As welcome as water into one's shoes.
His room is better than his company.
He threw my coat out the door, and I happened to be in it. *(Yiddish)*

UPRIGHT
The upright never grow rich in a hurry. *(Danish)*
An empty bag cannot stand upright.

USE
The used key is always bright.
Use is second nature.

A used plough shines; standing water stinks. *(German)*
The iron ring is worn out by constant use. *(Latin)*
Use makes the craftsman. *(Spanish)*
What's in use wants no excuse. *(Spanish)*

USEFUL
To everything its use. *(Latin)*
Unless what we do is useful, glory is vain. *(Latin)*
What is useful cannot be base. *(Latin)*

USELESS
Nothing is useless to a person of sense. *(French)*
He who is of no use to himself is of no use to anyone else. *(Yiddish)*

USURY
A usurer is one of the evangelists of Lucifer. *(Dutch)*
To borrow on usury brings sudden beggary.

VACUUM
Nature abhors a vacuum. *(Latin)*

VALLEY
He that stays in the valley shall never get over the hill.

VALOR
Immoderate valor swells into a fault.
Our valors are our best gods.
The better part of valor is discretion.
There is always safety in valor.
True valor is fire; bullying is smoke.
Valor that parleys is near yielding.
When valor preys on reason,
  It eats the sword it fights with. *(Shakespeare)*
Valor has its limits like the other virtues. *(Montaigne)*
The valorous to the valorous, the wise to the wise. *(Greek)*
Valor would cease to be a virtue if there were no injustice. *(Greek)*
All honor to you in your valor. *(Latin)*
In valor there is hope. *(Latin)*
Valor flourishes by a wound. *(Latin)*
Valor grows by daring; fear, by holding back. *(Latin)*
Valor not founded on prudence is rashness. *(Spanish)*

VANITY
Vanity of vanities; all is vanity. *(Old Test., Eccles.)*
Verily every man at his best state is altogether vanity.
(Old Test., Psalms)
Woe unto them that draw iniquity with cords of vanity . . .
(Old Test., Isaiah)
The cow rails at the pig for being black. *(Chinese)*

An ounce of vanity spoils a hundred-weight of merit.
Every man thinks his own geese swans.
The pomps and vanities of this wicked world. *(Bk. Com. Prayer)*
The pot calls the kettle black.
The vain man makes a merit of misfortune.
There was never yet fair woman but she made mouths in a glass. *(Shakespeare)*
Vanity backbites more than malice.
Vanity is the food of fools.
Vanity is the pride of Nature.
Vanity, like murder, will out.
"We hounds killed the hare," quoth the dog.
"What a dust we kicked up," said the fly to the car-wheels.
Why does the blind man's wife paint herself?
Make not thy tail broader than thy wings. *(French)*
Vanity has no greater foe than vanity. *(French)*
What makes the vanity of other people insupportable is that it wounds our own. *(La Rochefoucauld)*
Vanity ruins more women than love. *(French)*
Every man thinks his own copper gold. *(German)*
I see the vanity through the holes of thy coat. [*Ref. to Cynics*] *(Greek)*
Life without vanity is almost impossible. *(Tolstoy)*
"Your feet are crooked, your hair is good for nothing," said the pig to the horse. *(Russian)*
The kettle calls the sauce-pan smutty. *(Turkish)*

VARIETY

Variety creates an appetite.
Variety is the mother of enjoyment.
Variety is the soul of pleasure.
Variety is the spice of life.
Variety is sweet in all things. *(Greek)*

VENGEANCE

Vengeance should always pursue crime. *(Arabian)*
The noblest vengeance is to forgive.
Vengeance is wild justice.
Vengeance has no foresight. *(French)*
Vengeance is the pleasure of the gods. *(French)*
Vengeance should be left to women. *(Italian)*

VENISON

All flesh is not venison.

VENOM

No viper so little but hath its venom.

In the tail lies the venom. *(French)*

VENTURE

Throw a brick to allure a gem. *(Chinese)*

He has put all his eggs in one basket.

He that dare not venture must not complain of ill luck

He that would catch fish must venture his bait.

Many ventures make a full freight.

Never venture out of your depth till you can swim.

Nothing venture, nothing have.

Venture a small fish to catch a great one.

Venture not all in one bottom.

Ventures make men and ventures break men.

He that ventures not fails not. *(French)*

Boldly ventured is half won. *(German)*

Who ventures nothing has no luck. *(Spanish)*

VENUS

. . . the source and well of weal and woe. *(Gower)*

Venus smiles not in a house of tears. *(Shakespeare)*

All the race of men obey the eternal sway of Venus. *(Greek)*

Cruel mother of the Cupids. *(Latin)*

VESSEL

Do not look upon the vessel, but upon what it holds. *(Hebrew)*

VICE

He who plunges into vice is like one who rolls from the top of a precipice. *(Chinese)*

Betwixt two vices every virtue lies.

Concealed goodness is a sort of vice.

Every vice hath a cloak and creepeth in under the mask of a virtue.

If you swallow vice it will rise badly in your stomach.

Let thy vices die before thee.

Lordly vices require lordly estates.

Neither our virtues nor our vices are our own. *(S. Johnson)*

Never open the door to a little vice lest a great one enter with it.

One vice begets another.

Our pleasant vices are made the whip to scourge us. *(Shakespeare)*
Private vices are public benefits. *(de Mandeville)*
Search others for their virtues, thyself for thy vices.
The gods are just, and of our pleasant vices make instruments to plague us. *(Shakespeare)*
The proudest vice is ashamed to wear its own face long.
The vices are never so well employed as in combating one another.
The virtues of society are the vices of the saints. *(Emerson)*
Vice is a monster of so frightful a mien,
As to be hated needs but to be seen. *(Pope)*
Vice is its own punishment.
Vice itself lost half its evil, by losing all its grossness.
Vice knows she's ugly, so puts on her mask.
Vice makes virtue shine.
Vice should not correct sin.
Vices are learned without a master.
Virtue in distress, and vice in triumph
Make atheists of mankind. *(Dryden)*
Virtue is never aided by a vice.
Virtue itself turns vice, being misapplied. *(Shakespeare)*
What maintains one vice would bring up two children. *(Franklin)*
Where vice goes before, vengeance follows after.
A man must either imitate the vicious or hate them. *(Montaigne)*
I prefer an accommodating vice to an obstinate virtue. *(Molière)*
Our virtues are most frequently but vices in disguise. *(La Rochefoucauld)*
The vice which offends no one is not really a vice. *(Montaigne)*
We please more often by our vices than by our virtues. *(La Rochefoucauld)*
When our vices leave us, we flatter ourselves with the credit of having left them. *(La Rochefoucauld)*
Great abilities produce great vices as well as virtues. *(Greek)*
The vicious obey their passions as slaves do their masters. *(Greek)*
One hates not the person but the vice. *(Italian)*
All vices are less serious when they are open. *(Latin)*
Fools, in avoiding vice, run to the opposite extreme. *(Latin)*
If vice were profitable, the virtuous man would be the sinner. *(Latin)*
Learning virtue means unlearning vice. *(Latin)*
No vice remains within bound. *(Latin)*
The good hate vice because they love virtue. *(Latin)*
The greatest virtues are only splendid vices. *(St. Augustine)*

The road to vice is not only downhill, but steep. *(Latin)*
To flee vice is the beginning of virtue. *(Latin)*
Vice is nourished by concealment. *(Latin)*
Vices creep into our hearts under the name of virtues. *(Latin)*
We bear with accustomed vices; we reprove those that are new. *(Latin)*
We make a ladder of our vices, if we trample them underfoot. *(St. Augustine)*
After one vice a greater follows. *(Spanish)*

VICISSITUDE
Here today and gone tomorrow.

VICTORY
The harder matched, the greater victory.
To whom God will, there be the victory!
Victory and defeat are each of the same price.
Victory—or Westminister Abbey. *(Nelson)*
There are some defeats more triumphant than victories. *(Montaigne)*
He who has victory, has right. *(German)*
Often the victor triumphs but to fall. *(Greek)*
Such another victory, and we are undone. *(Pyrrhus)*
He conquers twice who upon victory conquers himself. *(Latin)*
Victory does not like rivalry. *(Latin)*
Woe to the vanquished! [*Vae victis!*] *(Latin)*

VILLAGE
Small town, great renown. *(Rabelais)*
There is more harm in the village than is dreamt of. *(Spanish)*

VILLAIN
O villain, villain, smiling, damned villain. *(Shakespeare)*
Where villainy goes before, vengeance follows after.
Anoint a villain and he will prick you. *(French)*
At an ambuscade of villains, a man does better with his feet than with his hands. *(Spanish)*

VINEGAR
More flies are caught with a drop of honey than with a cask of vinegar. *(Dutch)*
He cries wine and sells vinegar.
Beware of vinegar made of sweet wine. *(Italian)*

VIRTUE

Heaven wills that virtue be proved by trials. *(Arabian)*
Where there is not virtue, there can be no liberty. *(Arabian)*
All the virtues are in peril when filial piety is attacked. *(Chinese)*
Virtue is not hereditary. *(Chinese)*
Virtue is not left to stand alone. *(Chinese)*
Virtue is the base for the prosperity of an empire. *(Chinese)*
With virtue one may conquer the world. *(Chinese)*
Whether I am praised or blamed, I can advance in virtue. *(Chinese)*
A man that hath no virtue in himself, ever envieth virtue in others.
Assume a virtue, if you have it not. *(Shakespeare)*
He cannot be virtuous that is not rigorous.
He is ill clothed who is bare of virtue.
Men's evil manners live in brass,
  Their virtues we write in water. *(Shakespeare)*
Sell not virtue to purchase wealth.
Some rise by sin and some by virtue fall. *(Shakespeare)*
Sweet are the slumbers of the virtuous man.
The virtue which requires to be ever guarded is scarcely worth the sentinel. *(Goldsmith)*
There is no road or ready way to virtue.
Virtue alone has majesty in death. *(Young)*
Virtue alone is an estate.
Virtue and happiness are mother and daughter.
Virtue and sense are one.
Virtue and trade are the best inheritance for children.
Virtue dwells not in the tongue but in the heart.
Virtue finds no friends.
Virtue is a jewel of great price.
Virtue is a stronger guard than brass.
Virtue is bold and goodness never fearful.
Virtue's but a word; Fortune rules all.
Virtue is choked with foul ambition. *(Shakespeare)*
Virtue is its own reward.
Virtue is the first title to nobility.
Virtue is the fount whence honor springs. *(Marlowe)*
Virtue itself 'scapes not calumnious strokes. *(Shakespeare)*
Virtue never grows old.
Virtue seldom walks forth without Vanity at her side.
Birth is nothing where virtue is not. *(French)*

The virtues and vices are put in motion by interest. *(La Rochefoucauld)*
Virtue alone is the sign of a noble soul. *(French)*
Virtue debases itself in justifying itself. *(Voltaire)*
Virtue is the health of the soul. *(Joubert)*
Virtue often trips and falls on the sharp-edged rock of poverty. *(French)*
Virtue is always in a minority. *(French)*
Virtue must be followed for its own sake. *(French)*
Virtue and vice cannot dwell under the same roof. *(German)*
Virtue flourishes in misfortune. *(German)*
The perfect good is the exercise of virtue. *(Greek)*
Virtue is harmony. *(Greek)*
Virtue is the path of praise. *(Greek)*
Virtue of itself is sufficient for happiness. *(Greek)*
Virtue passes current all over the world. *(Greek)*
Virtue proceeds through toil. *(Greek)*
Virtue has no greater enemy than wealth. *(Italian)*
Conquer by means of virtue. *(Latin)*
He who dies for virtue does not perish. *(Latin)*
Honor is the reward of virtue. *(Latin)*
I wrap myself in my virtue. *(Latin)*
In virtue are riches. *(Latin)*
It is impossible for fortune to conquer virtue. *(Latin)*
It is virtue to flee vice. *(Latin)*
No one can be happy without virtue. *(Latin)*
No way is barred to virtue. *(Latin)*
Of less worth than gold is silver; than virtue, gold. *(Latin)*
Through virtue lies the road to peace. *(Latin)*
Virtue even in rags will keep warm. *(Latin)*
Virtue is doubly pleasing in one whose form is beautiful. *(Vergil)*
Virtue is nothing if not difficult. *(Latin)*
Virtue is praised, and starves. *(Latin)*
Virtue lives beyond the grave. *(Latin)*
Virtue may be gay, yet with dignity. *(Latin)*
Virtue overcomes envy. *(Latin)*
Virtue unites man with God. *(Latin)*
Virtue, when concealed, has no value. *(Latin)*
Virtue withers without opposition. *(Latin)*
You make a virtue of necessity. *(Latin)*
Poverty does not destroy virtue, nor wealth bestow it. *(Spanish)*

VISION

I have multiplied visions and used similitudes. *(Old Test., Hosea)*

Your old men shall dream dreams, your young men shall see visions. *(Old Test., Joel)*

Where there is no vision, the people perish. *(Old Test., Prov.)*

Vision is the art of seeing things invisible. *(Swift)*

VISIT

Fish and visitors smell in three days.

Friendship increases by visiting friends, but by visiting seldom.

If you'd lose a troublesome visitor, lend him money.

Visits should be short, like a winter's day;
  Lest you're too troublesome, hasten away.

VOICE

A still small voice. (*Old Test., I Kings*)

His voice is as the sound of many waters. (*New Test., Revelation*)

His voice is Jacob's voice, but the hands are the hands of Esau. *(Old Test., Genesis)*

The voice of him that crieth in the wilderness. *(Old Test., Isaiah)*

A loud voice bespeaks a vulgar man.

Her voice was ever soft, Gentle, and low, an excellent thing in woman. *(Shakespeare)*

There is no index of character so sure as the voice.

All voice, and beyond that, nothing. *(Latin)*

The living voice moves. *(Latin)*

The voice of the people is the voice of God. [*Vox populi, vox Dei.*] *(Latin)*

He who has no voice in the valley will have none in the council. *(Spanish)*

VOTE

Among free men there can be no successful appeal from the ballot to the bullet. *(Lincoln)*

The right of election is the very essence of the constitution. *("Junius")*

Universal suffrage is the government of a house by its nursery. *(Bismarck)*

VOW

Men's vows are women's traitors. *(Shakespeare)*

The vow that binds too strictly snaps itself.

Vows are made in storms and forgotten in calms.
Vows were ever brokers to defiling. *(Shakespeare)*

VULGAR

A thing is not vulgar merely because it is common.
Vulgarity is simply the conduct of other people. *(O. Wilde)*
Vulgarity defiles fine garments more than mud. *(Latin)*

WAGER
A wager is a fool's argument.

WAGES
He cannot lead a good life who serves without wages. *(Italian)*

WAGON
The wagon must go whither the horses draw it. *(Danish)*
Hitch your wagon to a star. *(Emerson)*
The empty wagon must make way for the full one.

WAIT
Learn to labor and to wait. *(Longfellow)*
Patient waiters are no losers.
Serene I fold my hands and wait. *(Burroughs)*
They also serve who only stand and wait. *(Milton)*
When you do not know what to do—wait.
Who longest waits most surely wins.
Everything comes to those who can wait. *(French)*
"Wait" is a hard word to the hungry. *(German)*
He who can wait obtains what he wishes. *(Italian)*
Seven never waited for one. *(Russian)*
The future belongs to him who knows how to wait. *(Russian)*
He who waits for another man's platter has a cold meal. *(Spanish)*

WALK
First creep, and then go.
Before supper, walk a little; after supper, do the same. *(Latin)*
It is solved by walking. *(Latin)*

WALL
When a wall is cracked and lofty, its fall will be speedy. *(Chinese)*
It is bad to lean against a falling wall. *(Danish)*

Hedges have eyes and walls have ears.
A white wall is the fool's paper. *(Italian)*

WANT
He that wants money, means, and content is without three good friends.
I want what I want when I want it.
Man wants but little here below, nor wants that little long.
On the ends of wants, wants grow.
Our real wants in a small compass lie.
The more one has, the more one wants.
Want is the mother of industry.
Want makes strife 'twixt man and wife.
Wit's whetstone is want.
Everything goes to him who does not want it. *(French)*
He that wants the kernel must crack the nut. *(French)*
To have no wants is divine . . . *(Socrates)*
Want too oft betrays the tongue to lies. *(Greek)*
He who wants a good deal must not ask for a little. *(Italian)*
Bad is want which is born of plenty. *(Latin)*
He is not in want who has no desires. *(Latin)*
Those who want much are always much in want. *(Latin)*
Everyone must speak of his wants, be he where he will. *(Spanish)*
If you can't get what you want, you must want what you get. *(Yiddish)*

WANTON
As wanton as a calf with two dams.
He has an ill look among lambs.

WAR
Let not him that girdeth on his harness boast himself as he that putteth it off. *(Old Test., I Kings)*
In war it is best to tie your horse to a strange manger. *(Danish)*
A just war is better than an unjust peace.
Clothe thee in war: arm thee in peace.
For what can war but endless war still breed? *(Milton)*
Force and fraud are in war the two cardinal virtues. *(Hobbes)*
He that is not in the wars is not out of danger.
He that preaches war is the devil's chaplain.
O war! thou son of hell! *(Shakespeare)*
Pride, pomp, and circumstance of glorious war! *(Shakespeare)*

The angel, Pity, shuns the walks of war.
The first blow is as much as two.
There are few die well that die in a battle.
There never was a good war nor a bad peace.
War is death's feast.
War is hell. *(Sherman)*
War is the child of pride.
War is the trade of kings. *(Dryden)*
War makes thieves, and peace hangs them.
War never leaves where it found a nation. *(Burke)*
War seldom enters but where wealth allures.
Wars bring scars.
When Greek meets Greek then comes the tug of war.
When war begins, the devil makes hell bigger.
Who is afraid of wounds must not go to war.
God is on the side of the big battalions. *(French)*
The right of war: let him take who can take. *(French)*
Better pointed bullets than pointed speeches. *(Bismarck)*
It is a bad war from which no one returns. *(German)*
In war it is not permitted to make a mistake twice. *(Greek)*
Money is the sinews of war. *(Greek)*
The War-god hates those who hesitate. *(Greek)*
To die or conquer are the terms of war. *(Greek)*
War does not spare the brave, but the coward. *(Greek)*
War loves to seek its victims in the young. *(Greek)*
He who has land has war. *(Italian)*
The fear of war is worse than war itself. *(Italian)*
War begun—hell unchained. *(Italian)*
A wise man should try everything before resorting to war. *(Latin)*
Dying is more honorable than killing. *(Seneca)*
Gold and riches—the causes of war. *(Latin)*
Little reason is there in arms. *(Latin)*
Mind avails most in war. *(Latin)*
War is sweet to those who have not experienced it. *(Latin)*
Wars, hateful to mothers. *(Horace)*
When war is raging, the laws are dumb. *(Latin)*
Who asks whether the enemy were defeated by strategy or valor? *(Vergil)*
Yield, ye arms, to the toga. *(Cicero)*
After the war many heroes present themselves. *(Roumanian)*
Talk of the war, but do not go to it. *(Spanish)*

The last argument of kings. *(Spanish)*
A dead man makes no war. *(Yiddish)*

WARE

Bad ware is never cheap.
Good wares make a quick market.
Pleasing ware is half sold.
When the wares are gone, shut up the shop windows.
Good ware was never dear. *(Italian)*

WARM

He will burn his house to warm his hands.
Up to thirty, warmth from a wife; after thirty, warmth from drink; in the end, not even the oven. *(Russian)*

WARNING

He was slain that had warning, not he that took it.
Once warned, twice armed.
Stop—Look—Listen! *(R. R. Upton)*
Beware! I am here. *(Latin)*
Forewarned is forearmed. *(Latin)*
The tempest threatens before it comes; houses creak before they fall. *(Latin)*

WASH

Dirty water does not wash clean. *(Danish)*
For washing his hands none sell lands.
The laundress washeth her own smock first.
Wash your hands often, your feet seldom, your head never.
Dirty linen should be washed at home. *(French)*
All will come out in the washing. *(Spanish)*
It's a waste of soap to wash the ass's head. *(Spanish)*
You can wash only the body, but not the soul. *(Yiddish)*

WASHINGTON

A citizen, first in war, first in peace, and first in the hearts of his countrymen. *(H. Lee)*
The Father of his Country. *(American)*

WASTE

Wasted his substance with riotous living. *(New Test., Luke)*
He sprinkles incense on a dunghill.
He that keeps not crust nor crumb, shall ever want some.

Spare at the spigot and let out at the bunghole.
The waste of plenty is the resource of scarcity.
Waste brings woe.
Waste is not grandeur.
Waste not, want not.
Wilful waste brings woeful want.

WATCH

A watched kettle never boils.
Good watch prevents misfortune.
Harm watch, harm catch.
To him that watches, everything is revealed. *(Italian)*

WATER

As water spilt on the ground, which cannot be gathered up again. *(Old Test., II Samuel)*
Drink waters out of thine own cistern. *(Old Test., Prov.)*
The waters wear the stones. *(Old Test., Job)*
Unstable as water, thou shalt not excel. *(Old Test., Genesis)*
The water that bears the boat is the same that swallows it up. *(Chinese)*
In still water are the largest fish. *(Danish)*
The water runs while the miller sleeps. *(Danish)*
Foul water will quench fire.
He seeks water in the sea.
Honest water which ne'er left men i' the mire. *(Shakespeare)*
It is not safe to wade in unknown water.
Smooth runs the water where the brook is deep.
The mill cannot grind with the water that is past.
The water that comes from the same spring cannot be fresh and stale both.
Under water—famine; under snow—bread.
We never know the worth of water till the well is dry.
There is not any worse water than water that sleeps. *(French)*
Still waters run deep. *(German)*
Where water has been, water will come again. *(German)*
The noblest of the elements is water. *(Greek)*
When water chokes you, what can you drink to wash it down? *(Greek)*
A glass of water is sometimes worth a tun of wine. *(Italian)*
Far water does not put out near fire. *(Italian)*
He that would have pure water must go to the fountain head. *(Italian)*
Running water carries no poison. *(Italian)*
Still water breeds vermin. *(Italian)*

Where least expected, water breaks forth. *(Italian)*
Beware of a silent dog and still water. *(Latin)*
From a pure source pure water comes. *(Latin)*
No verses can please long, or live, which are written by water-drinkers. *(Horace)*
Water comes to the mill from afar. *(Portuguese)*
Water washes everything. *(Portuguese)*
However foul it be, never say, "Of this water I will not drink." *(Spanish)*
On dry land even brackish water is good. *(Spanish)*
Don't pour out the dirty water before you have clean. *(Yiddish)*

WAY
Half the way to know the way.
The way to Babylon will never bring you to Jerusalem.
There is no short cut of way, without some ill delay.
The longest way round is the shortest way home. *(Italian)*

WEAK
The weaker goeth to the pot.
The weakest goes to the wall. *(Shakespeare)*
To be weak is to be miserable.
Weak things united become strong.
Willows are weak, but they bind the faggot.
The weakest must hold the candle. *(French)*
Every man has his weak side. *(Greek)*
In a just cause the weak overcome the strong. *(Greek)*

WEALTH
Wealth gotten by vanity is diminished. *(Old Test., Prov.)*
Wealth maketh many friends; but the poor is separated from his neighbors. *(Old Test., Prov.)*
A great fortune in the hands of a fool is a great misfortune.
A great fortune is a great slavery.
A man's wealth is his enemy.
Bear wealth; poverty will bear itself.
Command your wealth, else it will command you.
Great wealth and content seldom live together.
He is most loved who has most bags.
He who multiplies riches multiplies cares.
Ill fares the land, to hastening ills a prey,
Where wealth accumulates and men decay. *(Goldsmith)*
Ill-gotten wealth never prospers.

Little wealth, little care.
Wealth and content are not always bed-fellows.
Wealth is best known by want.
Wealth is crime enough to him that's poor.
Wealth maketh worship.
Where there is wealth friends abound.
A great estate is not gotten in a few hours. *(French)*
Ill gotten, ill spent. *(French)*
The wealth of the mind is the only true wealth. *(Greek)*
Men make wealth and women preserve it. *(Italian)*
Wealth conquered Rome after Rome had conquered the world. *(Italian)*
Wealth is not his that has it, but his that enjoys it. *(Italian)*
The lust for wealth can never bear delay. *(Latin)*
Gear is easier gotten than guided. *(Scottish)*
Of lawful wealth the devil takes the half; of unlawful, the whole and the owner too. *(Turkish)*
Just as it's bad to be rich, it's no joy to be a pauper either. *(Yiddish)*

WEAPON
They who fight with golden weapons are sure to prove their right. *(Dutch)*
A weapon is an enemy even to its owner. *(Turkish)*

WEAR
Everything is the worse for wearing.
It is better to wear out than to rust out.

WEATHER
Fair weather cometh out of the north. *(Old Test., Job)*
A foul morn may turn to a fine day.
A green Christmas makes a fat churchyard.
Change of weather is the discourse of fools.
Expect not fair weather in winter from one night's ice.
Farewell frost, fair weather next.
Hail brings frost with its tail.
In fair weather prepare for foul.
It never rains, but it pours.
It never thunders, but it rains.
No weather is ill, if the wind be still.
The evening red, and the morning gray,
Is the sign of a fair day.

To a child all weather is cold.
Praise a fine day at night. *(German)*
After clouds a clear sun. *(Latin)*
On a hot day muffle yourself the more. *(Spanish)*
Everybody talks about the weather, but nobody does anything about it. *(Mark Twain)*

WEDDING

One wedding begets another.
Winter and wedlock tames man and beast.
After a wedding, a circumcision ceremony. *(Yiddish)*

WEDGE

A blunt wedge can do what a sharp axe cannot.
One wedge drives another. *(German)*

WEED

A good garden may have some ill weeds.
An ill weed grows apace.
Evil weed is soon grown.
He that bites on every weed must needs light on poison.
No garden without its weeds.
On fat land grow foulest weeds.
One ill weed mars a mess of pottage.
The frost hurts no weeds.
Weeds need no sowing.
Weeds never die. *(German)*
The weed o'ergaes the corn. *(Scottish)*

WEEP

Better the cottage where one is merry than the palace where one weeps. *(Chinese)*
Better children weep than old men.
He who loves you well makes you weep.
Learn weeping, and thou shalt gain laughing.
Onions can make even heirs and widows weep.
To weep overmuch for the dead is an affront to the living.
When the vulture dies, the hen does not weep. *(German)*
He who weeps from the heart can provoke even the blind to tears. *(Russian)*
Weeping makes the heart grow lighter. *(Yiddish)*

WEIGHT
Great weights hang on small wires.
Weight and measure save a man toil. *(Spanish)*

WELCOME
As welcome as flowers in May.
Do not outstay your welcome.
Such a welcome, such a farewell.
Welcome ever smiles, and farewell goes out sighing. *(Shakespeare)*
Welcome is the best dish in the kitchen.
He who brings is welcome. *(German)*
Welcome is the best cheer. *(Greek)*
Who comes seldom is welcome. *(Italian)*

WELL (noun)
Dig a well before you are thirsty. *(Chinese)*
Drawn wells are seldom dry.
When the well is dry we know the worth of water.
It is a bad well into which one must put water. *(German)*
Don't throw a stone into a well from which you have drunk. *(Yiddish)*
Even a well can be pumped dry. *(Yiddish)*

WELL (adv.)
All is well that ends well.
Let well enough alone.

WHEEL
Don't speak to the man at the wheel.
I want to see the wheels go round.
The wheel has come full circle.
The wheel that does the squeaking is the one that gets the grease.
The wheel that turns gathers no rust.
The worst wheel of the cart makes the most noise.
There are wheels within wheels.
Crazy wheels run longest. *(German)*
A fifth wheel to a cart is but an encumbrance. *(Spanish)*
The hind wheel of a carriage will pass where the fore wheel has passed. *(Turkish)*

If you grease the wheel, it won't squeak. *(Yiddish)*

WHETSTONE
A whetstone can't cut, but it makes tools that can.

WHIP

A whip for a fool and a rod for a school.
An old coachman loves the crack of a whip. *(German)*
Whip me in the market-place provided it is not known at home. *(Spanish)*
Who does not whip the child does not mend the youth. *(Spanish)*
A whip is found to beat a horse. *(Yiddish)*

WHISPER

What is whispered in your ear is often heard a hundred miles off. *(Chinese)*
He who whispers, lies. *(Danish)*
The whisperer's tongue is worse than the serpent's tooth. *(Latin)*
What is whispered in your ear tell not to your husband. *(Spanish)*

WHITE

A crow is never the whiter for washing herself often.

WHORE

Water in a jar does not become sour milk, and a whore does not repent. *(Arabian)*
A young whore, an old saint.
A whore paints to put out a sign that she is to let.
As common as the pavement to every man that walketh.
In silk and scarlet walks many a harlot.
Once a whore, and ever a whore.
There is no need of a ferret to catch a harlot.
When dying sinners, to blot out their score,
Bequeath the church the leavings of a whore. *(Young)*
Whores' curses are blessings.
A whore and a buffoon fare ill in their old age. *(Spanish)*
He who has one foot in a brothel has another in a hospital. *(Spanish)*
Spit in a whore's face, and she'll say it's raining. *(Yiddish)*

WHY

Every "why" has its "because."

WICKED

He that rebuketh the wicked getteth a blot. *(Old Test., Prov.)*
My lips shall not speak wickedness, nor my tongue utter deceit. *(Old Test., Job)*
Let the wicked forsake his way . . . *(Old Test., Isaiah)*
The triumphing of the wicked is short. *(Old Test., Prov.)*

The way of the wicked is as darkness. *(Old Test., Prov.)*
The wicked are snared in the work of their own hands.
The wicked flee when no man pursueth. *(Old Test., Prov.)*
There is no peace unto the wicked. *(Old Test., Prov.)*
Wickedness proceedeth from the wicked. *(Old Test., I Sam'l)*
Ye have ploughed wickedness, ye have reaped iniquity.
(Old Test., Hosea)
The wicked shun the light as the devil shuns the cross. *(Dutch)*
A wicked companion invites us all to hell.
A wicked man is afraid of his own memory.
A wicked man is his own hell.
The wicked heart fears God only when it thunders.
Wickedness with beauty is the devil's hook baited.
All wickedness comes of weakness. *(Rousseau)*
The happiness of the wicked glides away like a stream. *(Racine)*
Never was the wicked wise. *(Greek)*
The majority are wicked. *(Greek)*
The wicked ears are deaf to wisdom's call. *(Greek)*
Wicked men cannot be friends. *(Greek)*
He who brings aid to the wicked, grieves for it later. *(Latin)*
No man ever became wicked all at once. *(Latin)*
No man is so wicked as to wish to appear wicked. *(Latin)*
The safe way to wickedness is always through wickedness. *(Latin)*
The success of the wicked entices many more. *(Latin)*
The sun shines even on the wicked. *(Latin)*
The wickedness of a few is the calamity of all. *(Latin)*
God bears with the wicked, but not forever. *(Spanish)*

WIDOW

The rich widow's tears soon dry. *(Danish)*
A widow must be a mourner.
A widow of doubtful age will marry almost any sort of a white man.
(H. Greeley)
Be wary how you marry one that hath cast her rider.
He that woos a widow must take time by the forelock.
Long a widow weds with shame.
Marry a widow before she leaves mourning.
Never marry a widow unless her first husband was hanged.
Sorrow for a husband is like a pain in the elbow—sharp and short.
Who marries a widow and two daughters marries three thieves.
Widows are always rich.

One can with dignity be wife and widow but once. *(French)*

A rich widow weeps with one eye and laughs with the other. *(Portuguese)*

A buxom widow must be either married, buried, or shut up in a convent. *(Spanish)*

He that marries a widow will have a dead man's head thrown in his dish. *(Spanish)*

In the widow's house there's no fat mouse. *(Turkish)*

Better a young widow than an old maid. *(Yiddish)*

WIFE

The wife is the keeper of her husband's soul. *(Arabian)*

A prudent wife is from the Lord. *(Old Test., Prov.)*

A virtuous woman is a crown to her husband. *(Old Test., Prov.)*

Giving honor unto the wife as the weaker vessel. *(New Test., I Peter)*

It is not good that man should be alone. *(Old Test., Genesis)*

She looketh well to the ways of her household, and eateth not the bread of idleness. *(Old Test., Prov.)*

The contentions of a wife are a continual dropping. *(Old Test., Prov.)*

Whoso findeth a wife findeth a good thing. *(Old Test., Prov.)*

A vicious wife and an untoward sow no laws can govern. *(Chinese)*

A young wife should be in her house but a shadow and an echo. *(Chinese)*

A cheerful wife is the joy of life.

A dead wife under the table is the best goods in a man's house. *(Swift)*

A fair wife without a fortune is a fine house without furniture.

A good wife and health are man's best wealth.

A light wife doth make a heavy husband.

A man must ask his wife's leave to thrive.

A man's best fortune or his worst is a wife.

A nice wife, and a back door, oft do make a rich man poor.

A wife is not to be chosen by the eye only.

All are good maids, but whence come the bad wives?

An expensive wife makes a pensive husband.

An obedient wife commands her husband.

An undutiful daughter will prove an unmanageable wife.

As the goodman saith, so say we;
As the good wife saith, so it must be.

As the market goes, wives must sell.

Bare walls make gadding housewives.

Better a portion in a wife than with a wife.

Better be an old man's darling than a young man's slave.

Blind men's wives need no paint.
Choose a house made and a wife to make.
Choose a wife rather by your ear than your eye.
Discreet wives have neither eyes nor ears.
Every man can rule an ill wife but him that has her.
Good wives and private soldiers should be ignorant. *(Wycherley)*
Hanging and wiving go by destiny. *(Butler)*
He fasts enough whose wife scolds all dinner time.
He has great need of a wife that marries Mama's Darling.
He knows little who will tell his wife all he knows.
He makes a false wife that suspects a true.
He that has a wife has a master.
He that hath a wife and children hath given hostages to fortune. *(Bacon)*
He that hath a wife hath strife.
He that kisses his wife in the market-place shall have enough to teach him.
He that loses his wife and a farthing, hath a great loss of his farthing.
He that marries a wife must pay her debts.
He that takes a wife takes care.
He that tells his wife news is but newly married.
Here lies my wife: here let her lie!
  Now she's at rest, and so am I. *(Dryden)*
How much the wife is dearer than the bride!
Husband, don't believe what you see, but what I tell you.
Husbands are in heaven whose wives chide not.
If the hen does not prate, she will not lay.
If you give your wife a yard, she'll take an ell.
If you make your wife an ass, she will make you an ox.
In choosing a wife and buying a sword we ought not to trust another.
It's a good horse that never stumbles,
  And a good wife that never grumbles.
It is a sweet sorrow to bury a termagant wife.
Man's best possession is a loving wife.
Many blame the wife for their own thriftless life.
Next to no wife, a good wife is best.
Suspicion, Discontent and Strife,
  Come in for dowry with a wife. *(Herrick)*
The calmest husbands make the stormiest wives.
The clog of all pleasure, the luggage of life,
  Is the best can be said for a very good wife. *(Rochester)*

The cunning wife makes her husband her apron.
The foot on the cradle, the hand on the distaff—a sign of a good housewife.
The only comfort in my life is that I never yet had wife.
The wife is the key of the house.
The wife that expects to have a good name,
Is always at home, as if she were lame.
The wife that loves the looking-glass hates the saucepan.
'Tis hard to wive and thrive both in a year.
What a pity it is that nobody knows how to manage a wife but a bachelor! *(G. Colman)*
What the good wife spares, the cat eats.
Who hath a fair wife needs more than two eyes.
Wives are young men's mistresses, companions for middle age, and old men's nurses. *(Bacon)*
Wives may be merry and honest too. *(Shakespeare)*
Wives must be had, whether good or bad.
You may beat the devil into your wife, but you'll never bang him out again.
Empty rooms make giddy housewives. *(French)*
Let not the hen talk and the cock be silent. *(French)*
Man has found remedies against all poisonous creatures, but none was yet found against a bad wife. *(Rabelais)*
A bad wife is the shipwreck of her husband. *(German)*
A poor man who takes a rich wife has a ruler, not a wife. *(German)*
A young wife is an old man's post-horse to the grave. *(German)*
Fire, water, and a bad wife are three great evils. *(German)*
No fellow is so poor that he has not a wife on his arm. *(German)*
The dead wife and the living sheep make a man rich. *(German)*
The nobleman finds a wife easier than the peasant. *(German)*
To choose a wife two heads are not enough. *(German)*
When the wife rules the house, the devil is the man-servant. *(German)*
Who has a bad wife is poor in the midst of riches. *(German)*
He who is cursed with an ugly wife sees darkness when he lights the evening lamp. *(Greek)*
The bitterest morsel of human life is a bad wife. *(Greek)*
A good wife is a good gift. *(Hebrew)*
A man can only find real delight in one wife. *(Hebrew)*
A wife speaks and spurs. *(Hebrew)*
Every evil, but not an evil wife. *(Hebrew)*
Gnaw the bone which is fallen to thy lot. *(Hebrew)*

Go down the ladder when you marry a wife; go up when you choose a friend. *(Hebrew)*
If your wife is little, stoop to her. *(Hebrew)*
When the wife is asleep, the basket is asleep also. *(Hebrew)*
As you would have a daughter, so choose a wife. *(Italian)*
Every man has a good wife and a bad trade. *(Italian)*
For a wife and a horse go to your neighbor. *(Italian)*
Grief for a dead wife lasts to the door. *(Italian)*
If the wife sins, the husband is not innocent. *(Italian)*
A virtuous wife rules her husband by obeying him. *(Latin)*
Caesar's wife must be above suspicion. *(Latin)*
His wife wore the breeches. *(Latin)*
Never have dealings with other men's wives. *(Latin)*
The bed that holds a wife is never free from wrangling. *(Latin)*
The better the man, the less good will he get out of his wife. *(Juvenal)*
The husband of an ugly wife is better blinded. *(Persian)*
An unscolded wife, like an uncut millstone, does not go easily. *(Roumanian)*
A wife is not a guitar; you can't play on her and then hang her on the wall. *(Russian)*
Choose neither a wife nor linen by candle-light. *(Spanish)*
Every married man should think his wife the one good woman in the world. *(Spanish)*
He who does not honor his wife dishonors himself. *(Spanish)*
The first wife is a broom; the second, a lady. *(Spanish)*
The old wife, if she do not serve for a pot, serves for a cover. *(Spanish)*
A dumb wife curses, not with her mouth, but with her hands. *(Yiddish)*
A wife and a horse should not be loaned. *(Yiddish)*
A wife is good for the body but not for the soul. *(Yiddish)*
If the wife wears the pants, the husband must rock the cradle. *(Yiddish)*
The devil will take away everything but a bad wife. *(Yiddish)*
The first wife is like a dog; the second, like a cat; the third, like a pig. *(Yiddish)*
The wife has the labor-pains, and the husband celebrates the circumcision. *(Yiddish)*
Why does the bear dance? Because he has no wife. *(Yiddish)*

WILD

A wild goose never laid a tame egg.
Every man must sow his wild oats.

WILFUL

A wilful man had need be very wise.
A wilful man never wants woe.
As wilful as a pig; he'll neither lead nor drive.
He that doth what he will, doth not what he ought.
Wilfulness is more terrible than slavery. *(Russian)*

WILL

Not my will, but thine, be done. *(New Test., Luke)*
The will of even a common man cannot be taken away from him. *(Confucius)*
A man's will is his heaven. *(Danish)*
He that complies against his will
  Is of his own opinion still. *(Butler)*
He wants wit that wants resolved will. *(Shakespeare)*
Let not thy will roar, when thy power can but whisper.
Take the will for the deed.
The will is the man.
Where there's a will, there's a way.
Will is the cause of woe.
Will will have will though will woe win.
Will without reason is blind, and against reason, is mad.
When the will is ready, the feet are light. *(French)*
He who is firm in will molds the world to himself. *(Goethe)*
No one can rob us of our free will. *(Epictetus)*
The man who has the will to undergo all labor may win to any goal. *(Greek)*
There is nothing good or evil save in the will. *(Greek)*
The will cannot be compelled. *(Latin)*

WILLING

A willing heart adds feather to the heel.
All lay the load on the willing horse.
Nothing is troublesome that we do willingly.
He that cannot is always willing. *(Italian)*
He that will does more than he can. *(Portuguese)*

WILLOW

We hanged our harps upon the willows . . . *(Old Test., Psalms)*
Willows are weak yet serve to bind other wood. *(Italian)*

WIN

Either win the horse or lose the saddle.
He plays best that wins.

They laugh that win.
Easy won is easy lost. *(German)*

WIND
If the wind blows it enters every corner. *(Arabian)*
The wind bloweth where it listeth. *(New Test., John)*
They have sown the wind and they shall reap the whirlwind.
(Old Test., Hosea)
Every wind is against a leaky ship. *(Danish)*
A little wind kindles; much puts out the fire.
An ill wind that bloweth no man good.
As the wind blows seek your shelter.
Every wind bloweth not down the corn.
High winds blow on high hills.
Ill blows the wind that profits nobody. *(Shakespeare)*
Puff not against the wind.
The sharper the blast, the shorter it will last.
The wind keeps not always in one quarter.
The wind is not in your debt though it fill your sail.
To a crazy ship all winds are contrary.
When the wind serves, all aid.
You can't catch the wind in a net.
God tempers the wind to the shorn lamb. *(French)*
One can't hinder the wind from blowing. *(French)*
The pilot cannot calm the winds. *(Greek)*
Wind puffs up empty bladders; opinion, fools. *(Greek)*
Not every wind shakes down the nut. *(Italian)*
If the wind will not serve, take to the oars. *(Latin)*
It is easy to set the sails to propitious winds. *(Latin)*
It is folly to complain of the fickleness of the wind. *(Latin)*
They who plough the sea do not carry the winds in their hands. *(Latin)*
Wind and fortune are not lasting .*(Spanish)*

WINE
Its sinfulness is greater than its use. *(The Koran)*
There is a devil in every berry of the grape. *(The Koran)*
Corn shall make the young men cheerful, and new wine the maids.
(Old Test., Zechariah)
Drink no longer water, but use a little wine for thy stomach's sake.
(New Test., I Timothy)
Look not thou upon the wine when it is red, . . .
At the last it biteth like a serpent. *(Old Test., Prov.)*

Neither do men put new wine into old bottles. *(New Test., Matthew)*
Wine . . . causes the lips of those that are asleep to speak.
(Old Test., Song of Songs)
Wine is a mocker, strong drink is raging. *(Old Test., Prov.)*
Wine that maketh glad the heart of man. *(Old Test., Psalms)*
Wine enters the stomach, and business grows ripe in the brain.
(Chinese)
Truth and folly dwell in the wine cask. *(Danish)*
Good wine praises itself. *(Dutch)*
Counsels in wine seldom prosper.
Good wine engendereth good blood.
Good wine makes a bad head and a long story.
Good wine needs no bush.
If sack and sugar be a fault, God help the wicked! *(Shakespeare)*
It is a good wind that blows a man to the wine.
Love of a woman and a bottle of wine
  Are sweet for a season, but last for a time.
Milk says to wine, "Welcome, friend!"
No matter the vessel so the wine in it be good.
Old wood to burn, old wine to drink.
Season the wood never so well, the wine will taste of the cask.
Spilt wine is worse than water.
Take counsel in wine, but resolve afterwards in water.
The best wine comes out of an old vessel.
The wine in the bottle does not quench thirst.
When wine enters, modesty departs.
When wine sinks, words swim.
Wine and wenches empty men's purses.
Wine and youth are fire upon fire.
Wine by the savor and bread by the heat.
Wine ever pays for his lodging.
Wine gives us liberty, love takes it away.
Wine makes us princes, love makes us beggars. *(Wycherley)*
Wine makes all sorts of creatures at table.
Wine turns a man inside outside.
Wine washes off the daub.
Wine whets the wit. [*cf.* "*Wine in, wit out.*"]
Women and wine do make a man
  A doting fool all that they can.
You cannot know wine by the barrel.
Since the wine is drawn it must be drunk. *(French)*

The best wine has its lees. *(French)*
Wine is the milk of old men. *(French)*
Wine poured out is not wine swallowed. *(French)*
Wine wears no breeches. [*i.e. discloses the man*] *(French)*
Wine will not keep in a foul vessel. *(French)*
Women, money, and wine have their pleasure and their poison. *(French)*

No one so wise but wine makes a fool of him. *(German)*
Of what use is the cup of gold if the wine be sour? *(German)*
Who loves not woman, wine, and song,
  Remains a fool his whole life long. *(Voss)*
Bronze is the mirror of the form; wine, of the heart. *(Greek)*
I like best the wine another pays for. *(Greek)*
Inflaming wine dulls the noble heart. *(Greek)*
Where there is no wine there is no love. *(Greek)*
Wine to the poet is a winged steed . . . *(Greek)*
Strong is the vinegar of sweet wine. *(Italian)*
Thick wine is better than clear water. *(Italian)*
When the wine is in, the wit is out. *(Italian)*
Bacchus opens the gate of the heart. *(Latin)*
Bacchus scatters carking cares. *(Latin)*
Give, in return for old wine, a new song. *(Latin)*
In wine there is truth. [*In vino veritas.*] *(Latin)*
The master's wine is in the butler's gift. *(Latin)*
Wine carries no rudder. *(Latin)*
Wine is a cunning wrestler: it catches you by the feet. *(Latin)*
Wine gives courage and makes men apt for passion. *(Latin)*
Wine has drowned more men than the sea. *(Latin)*
Wine is one thing; drunkenness another. *(Latin)*
Wine kindles wrath. *(Latin)*
I wonder often what the Vintners buy
  One half so precious as the stuff they sell. *(Omar Khayyám)*
Wine in excess keeps neither secrets nor promises. *(Spanish)*

WINK

A wink's as good as a nod.
Although I wink, I am not blind.
Hard must he wink that shuts his eyes from heaven.
There's a time to wink as well as to see.
When most I wink, then do mine eyes see best. *(Shakespeare)*
You may wink and choose.

WINTER

A green winter makes a fat churchyard.
Every mile is two in winter.
If Winter comes, can Spring be far behind? *(Shelley)*
It is a hard winter when one wolf eats another.
Winter draws out what summer laid in.
Winter eateth what summer getteth.
Winter is summer's heir.
Winter thunder makes summer wonder.

WISDOM

In much wisdom is much grief. *(Old Test., Eccles.)*
So teach us to number our days, that we may apply our hearts unto wisdom. *(Old Test., Psalms)*
The fear of the Lord is the beginning of wisdom. *(Old Test., Prov.)*
The price of wisdom is above rubies. *(Old Test., Job)*
The wisdom of this world is foolishness with God. *(New Test., I Corinth.)*
Wisdom giveth life to them that have it. *(Old Test., Eccles.)*
Wisdom is justified of her children. *(New Test., Matthew)*
When wisdom fails, luck helps. *(Danish)*
That is good which is wisdom in the end. *(Dutch)*
A flow of words is no proof of wisdom.
In wisdom's ranks he stands the first,
Who stands prepared to meet the worst.
Learn wisdom by the follies of others.
The doors of wisdom are never shut.
'Tis wisdom sometimes to seem a fool.
What is not wisdom is danger.
Wisdom and goodness to the vile seem vile. *(Shakespeare)*
Wisdom asks fruit, but folly flowers.
Wisdom goes not always by years.
Wisdom in a poor man is a diamond set in lead.
Wisdom is a good purchase though we pay dear for it.
Wisdom is not finally tested in the schools. *(Whitman)*
Wisdom is oftentimes nearer when we stoop
Than when we soar. *(Wordsworth)*
Wisdom is the wealth of the wise.
Wisdom rides on the ruins of folly.
Wisdom sails with wind and tide.
An ounce of luck is worth a pound of wisdom. *(French)*
Man's chief wisdom consists in knowing his follies. *(La Rochefoucauld)*

The gods laugh at the wisdom of men. *(French)*
Wisdom is to the soul what health is to the body. *(French)*
The wise seek wisdom, the fool has found it. *(German)*
Too much wisdom is folly. *(German)*
Wisdom is only found in truth. *(Goethe)*
Wisdom is the mother of all arts. *(German)*
In youth and beauty wisdom is but rare. *(Homer)*
That man is wisest who realizes that his wisdom is worthless. *(Socrates)*
The mark of wisdom is to read the present aright. *(Greek)*
Wisdom adorns riches and shadows poverty. *(Greek)*
Wisdom comes by suffering. *(Greek)*
Wisdom never lies. *(Greek)*
He that has grown to wisdom does not hurry. *(Italian)*
Learn wisdom by the folly of others. *(Italian)*
Not by age but by capacity is wisdom attained. *(Latin)*
There is often wisdom under a shabby cloak. *(Latin)*
To flee from folly is the beginning of wisdom. *(Latin)*
Wisdom at proper times will forget. *(Latin)*
Wisdom first teaches what is right. *(Latin)*
Wisdom is always an overmatch for strength. *(Latin)*
Wisdom is the conqueror of fortune. *(Latin)*
Wisdom is the only liberty. *(Latin)*
The wise man hides his wisdom; the fool displays his foolishness. *(Yiddish)*

WISE

A wise man is strong; yea, a man of knowledge increaseth strength. *(Old Test., Prov.)*
Be ye therefore wise as serpent, and harmless as doves. *(New Test., Matthew)*
The children of this world are in their generation wiser than the children of light. *(New Test., Luke)*
Woe unto them that are wise in their own eyes, and prudent in their own sight. *(Old Test., Isaiah)*
The wise man does not lay up treasure. *(Lao-Tsze)*
A wise man is a great wonder.
A wise man is out of the reach of fortune.
A wise man turns chance into good fortune.
A wise man's loss is his secret.
A word to the wise is sufficient.
All countries are a wise man's home.
Be wise with speed:
A fool at forty is a fool indeed. *(Young)*

He is wise enough that can keep himself warm.
He is wise that hath enough wit for his own affairs.
He is wise that is ware in time.
He that is wise by day is no fool by night.
He seemeth wise with whom all things thrive.
If things were done twice, all would be wise.
It is easy to be wise after the event.
None is born wise or learned.
Some folks are wise—and some are otherwise.
The greatest clerks be not the wisest men. *(Chaucer)*
We are wiser than we know. *(Emerson)*
When one is wise, two are happy.
Young men are made wise; old men become so.
A wise man is not wise in everything. *(French)*
Better be mad with all the world than wise alone. *(French)*
It is easier to be wise for others than for yourself. *(French)*
It is not wise to be wiser than is necessary. *(French)*
The wisest man is he who does not think he is so. *(French)*
A wise man—a strong man. *(German)*
The wise man has long ears and a short tongue. *(German)*
He is not wise who is not wise for himself. *(Greek)*
How cautious are the wise! *(Homer)*
It takes a wise man to recognize a wise man. *(Greek)*
The wise learn many things from their foes. *(Greek)*
Who consorts with the wise will become wise. *(Greek)*
When wise men play the fool, they do it with a vengeance. *(Italian)*
Dare to be wise. *(Latin)*
It becomes all wise men to confer and converse. *(Latin)*
No man is wise enough by himself. *(Latin)*
No man is the only wise man. *(Latin)*
No man was ever wise by chance. *(Latin)*
No one is wise at all times. *(Latin)*
The wise man strikes twice against the same stone. *(Russian)*
Better be wise than rich. *(Spanish)*
He who thinks himself wise has an ass near at hand. *(Spanish)*
What's the good of being wise when foolishness serves? *(Yiddish)*

WISH

When what you wish does not happen, wish for what does happen. *(Arabian)*

I wish I knew the good of wishing.

If a man could have half his wishes, he would double his troubles. *(Franklin)*
If wishes were buttercakes, beggars might bite.
If wishes were horses, beggars would ride.
Like our shadows
  Our wishes lengthen as our sun declines. *(Young)*
Mere wishes are silly fishes.
Not what we wish, but what we want.
Thy wish was father to that thought. *(Shakespeare)*
Wishers and woulders ben small house holders.
Wishes never filled the bag.
Wishes were ever fools. *(Shakespeare)*
Wishes won't wash dishes.
After the doing, wishing is in vain. *(French)*
We cannot wish for what we don't know. *(French)*
What one has wished for in youth, in old age one has in abundance. *(Goethe)*
The evil wish is most evil to the wisher. *(Greek)*
Wish not for soft things, lest thou earn the hard. *(Greek)*
Who has no money must have no wishes. *(Italian)*
With wishing comes grieving. *(Italian)*
Men easily believe what they wish to believe. *(Latin)*
If things are not as you wish, wish them as they are. *(Yiddish)*
You can't get rich by wishing. *(Yiddish)*

WIT
All the wit in the world is not in one head.
An ounce of wit is worth a pound of sorrow.
An ounce of wit that is bought
  Is worth a pound that is taught.
Better a witty fool than a foolish wit. *(Shakespeare)*
Bought wit is best but may cost too much.
Don't set your wit against a child. *(Swift)*
Everyone is witty for his own purpose.
Good wits jump.
Great wits have short memories.
Great wit to madness sure is near allied. *(Dryden)*
Head so little, there is no room for wit; so long, there is no wit for so much room.
I'm poor enough to be a wit. *(Congreve)*
It is not wit to pick a lock and steal a horse; but it is wisdom to let them alone.

Love of wit makes no man rich.
No house is big enough for two wits to live in together.
Plagued with an itching leprosy of wit. *(B. Jonson)*
So many heads, so many wits.
Some are half-wits—two to a wit.
True wit is nature to advantage dress'd,
  What oft was thought, but ne'er so well express'd. *(Pope)*
Nothing more fine than wit, yet nothing more fickle.
Weak men had need be witty.
Wit and wisdom are born with a man.
Wit does not take the place of knowledge.
Wit is folly unless a wise man hath the keeping of it.
Wit is the salt of conversation, not the food.
Wit without an employment is a disease.
You beat your pate, and fancy wit will come:
  Knock as you please, there's nobody at home. *(Pope)*
A man of wit would often be at a loss, were it not for the company of fools. *(La Rochefoucauld)*
I never have any wit until I am below stairs. *(La Bruyère)*
No one shall have wit save we and our friends. *(Molière)*
The wit one wants spoils what one has. *(French)*
Wit sometimes lets us act rudely with impunity. *(La Rochefoucauld)*
Melancholy men are the most witty. *(Greek)*
Every ditch is full of after-wit. *(Italian)*
Wit rules the heavens, discretion guides the skies. *(Tasso)*
Even wit is a burden when it talks too long. *(Latin)*
It is a sort of wit to know how to use the wit of others. *(Latin)*
Want o' wit is waur than want o' siller. *(Scottish)*
Don't put too fine a point to your wit, for fear it should get blunted. *(Cervantes)*

WITCH
Aroint thee, witch, aroint thee! *(Shakespeare)*
They that burn you for a witch lose all their coals.

WITNESS
A madman and a fool are no witnesses.
False folk should have many witnesses.
The thief does not fear a dumb witness. *(Yiddish)*
What you don't see with your eyes, don't witness with your mouth. *(Yiddish)*

WOE

A drop of pleasure for a sea of woe.
O sudden woe, that ever art successor
To wordly bliss! *(Chaucer)*
One woe doth tread upon another's heel . . . *(Shakespeare)*
Woe to the house where there is no chiding.
By telling our woes we often assuage them. *(French)*
Their causes are hidden, but our woes are clear. *(Ovid)*

WOLF

An old wolf is not scared by loud cries. *(Danish)*
A wolf will never make war against another wolf.
Ill herds make fat wolves.
It is a hard winter when one wolf eats another.
The death of the wolf is the health of the sheep.
The life of the wolf is the death of the lamb.
The wolf doth gin before he barketh.
The wolf finds a reason for taking the lamb.
The wolf must die in his own skin.
The wolf sheds his coat once a year, his disposition never. *(Franklin)*
There is a wolf in a lamb's skin.
Though home be homely . . . let us keep the wolf from the door.
Wake not a sleeping wolf. *(Shakespeare)*
When the wolf grows old, the crows ride him.
Who is bred among wolves will learn to howl.
Wolves lose their teeth but not their nature.
For the wolf's flesh, dog sauce. *(French)*
Talk of the wolf, and his tail appears. *(French)*
To tame the wolf you must marry him. *(French)*
The wolf does not weep over the death of the dog. *(German)*
The wolf must pay with his skin. *(German)*
The wolf may lose his teeth, but never his nature. *(Italian)*
I've got a wolf by the ears; I can't let go and I can't hold on. *(Latin)*
He who keeps a wolf-cub will be torn to pieces when the wolf comes for it. *(Persian)*
No matter how much you feed a wolf, he will always return to the forest. *(Russian)*
The wolf will hire himself off very cheaply as a shepherd. *(Russian)*

WOMAN

De wimmen, dey does de talkin' en de flyin'; en de mens, dey does de walkin' en de pryin'. *(American Negro)*

A foolish woman is clamorous. *(Old Test., Prov.)*

A virtuous woman is a crown to her husband. *(Old Test., Prov.)*

A woman is the weaker vessel. *(New Test., I Peter)*

All wickedness is but little to the wickedness of a woman. *(Apocrypha)*

As a jewel of gold in a swine's snout, so is a fair woman which is without discretion. *(Old Test., Prov.)*

It is better to dwell in a corner of the housetop than with a brawling woman in a wide house. *(Old Test., Prov.)*

One man among a thousand have I found; but a woman among all those have I not found. *(Old Test., Eccles.)*

A man's words are like an arrow; a woman's like a broken fan. *(Chinese)*

Out of nine women, one is sure to be affected with jealousy. *(Chinese)*

The tongue of women is their sword, and they take care not to let it rust. *(Chinese)*

The three virtues of a woman: Obey the father, obey the husband, obey the son. *(Chinese)*

A truth-telling woman has few friends. *(Danish)*

An ill-tempered woman is the devil's door-nail. *(Danish)*

Kind words and few are a woman's ornament. *(Danish)*

A cat has nine lives and a woman has nine cats' lives.

A cunning woman is a knavish fool.

A dishonest woman cannot be kept in, and an honest one will not out.

A fair woman and a slashed gown always find some nail in the way.

A handsome woman: English to the neck, French to the waist, Dutch below.

A slighted woman knows no bounds.

A woman, a dog, and a walnut-tree,
The more you beat 'em, the better they be.

A whistling woman and a crowing hen
Is neither fit for God nor men.

A woman and a glass are ever in danger.

A woman can be anything the man who loves her would have her be. *(Barrie)*

A woman is an angel at ten, a saint at fifteen, a devil at forty, and a witch at fourscore.

A woman is to be from her home three times:
When she is christened, married and buried.

A woman that paints puts up a bill to let.
A woman with a past has no future. *(O. Wilde)*
A woman's mind and winter wind change oft.
A woman's oaths are wafers, break with making.
A woman's strength is in her tongue.
A woman's tongue is the last thing about her that dies.
A woman's tongue wags like a lamb's tail.
A woman's work is never at an end.
An artful woman makes a modern saint.
Are women books? Would mine were an Almanack, to change her every year. *(Franklin)*
As great a pity to see a woman cry as a goose go barefoot.
At home like devils, abroad like angels.
Be to her virtues very kind;
Be to her faults a little blind. *(Prior)*
Believe a woman or an epitaph,
Or any other thing that's false. *(Byron)*
Better the devil's than a woman's slave.
Can man be free if woman is a slave? *(Shelley)*
Dally not with other folks' women or money.
Dear bought and far fetched are dainties for ladies.
For half so boldly can there no man
Swear and lyen as a woman can. *(Chaucer)*
Frailty, thy name is woman! *(Shakespeare)*
Geese with geese, and women with women.
Give woman thy whole heart, and she will break it.
He ploughs in sand and sows against the wind,
That hopes for constant love from womankind.
He seldom errs who thinks the worst of womankind.
He that hath a woman hath an eel by the tail.
Hell has no fury like a woman scorned. *(Congreve)*
How hard it is for women to keep counsel! *(Shakespeare)*
I am a woman, needs must I speak. *(Chaucer)*
I'm not denyin' the women are foolish: God Almighty made 'em to match the men. *(Geo. Eliot)*
I hate a dumpy woman. *(Byron)*
I like men who have a future, and women who have a past. *(O. Wilde)*
If women be but young and fair,
They have the gift to know it. *(Young)*
If women were humbler, men would be honester.

Let men say whate'er they will,
  Woman, woman rules them still.
Let not the creaking of shoes nor the rustling of silks betray thy poor heart to woman. *(Shakespeare)*
Let women spin and not preach.
Love well, whip well.
Man born of woman, must of woman die. *(Hood)*
Man has his will—but woman has her way. *(O. W. Holmes)*
Many women, many words.
My only books were woman's looks,
  And folly's all they've taught me. *(T. Moore)*
"No" is no negative in a woman's mouth.
No vengeance like a woman's.
No woman marries a man for God's sake.
Nothing agreeth worse
  Than a lady's heart and a beggar's purse.
O woman! in our hours of ease
  Uncertain, coy, and hard to please. *(Scott)*
One hair of a woman draws more than a team of oxen.
One tongue is enough for a woman.
Please your eye and plague your heart.
She will stay at home, perhaps, if her leg be broke.
Silence is the best ornament of a woman.
The female of the species is more deadly than the male. *(Kipling)*
The happiest women, like the happiest nations, have no history. *(Geo. Eliot)*
The house goes mad when women gad.
The plain ones be as safe as churches. *(T. Hardy)*
The woman that deliberates is lost.
There is no mischief done but a woman is one.
There is no other purgatory but a woman.
There's no music when a woman is in the concert.
There was never yet fair woman but she made mouths in a glass. *(Shakespeare)*
To furnish a ship requireth much trouble,
  But to furnish a woman, the charges are double.
Trust not a woman even when dead.
Two women placed together makes cold weather.
We may live with, but cannot live without 'em.
Were there no women, men might live like gods.
Were it not for gold and women, there would be no damnation.
What attracts us in a woman rarely binds us to her.

What female heart can gold despise?
What cat's averse to fish? *(Gray)*
What woman can resist the force of praise?
When a lady's in the case, all other things give place. *(Gay)*
When an ass climbeth a ladder, you may find wisdom in women.
When fortune favors, still the fair are kind. *(Pope)*
Who is it can read a woman?
Who trusts himself to women or to waves,
Should never hazard what he fears to lose.
Wit and women are two frail things.
Woman ben wise in short avysement. *(Chaucer)*
Woman reduces us all to the common denominator. *(G. B. Shaw)*
Woman will be the last thing civilized by man. *(Meredith)*
Woman! Would that we could fall into her arms without falling into her hands. *(Bierce)*
Woman's counsel is fatal counsel.
Woman's love is writ in water!
Woman's faith is traced on sand!
Women and elephants never forget. *(D. Parker)*
Women and linen show best by candle-light.
Women and music should never be dated. *(Goldsmith)*
Women and princes must trust somebody. *(Selden)*
Women are in churches, saints; abroad, angels; at home, devils.
Women are only children of larger growth. *(Chesterfield)*
Women are the devil's nets.
Women, being the weaker vessel, are ever thrust to the wall. *(Shakespeare)*
Women do most delight in revenge.
Women forgive injuries, but never forget slights.
Women were created for the comfort of men.
Women will have the last word.
Women's jars breed men's wars.
Women's reasons: they would not because they would not.
A man of straw is more worth than a woman of gold. *(French)*
A woman and a melon are hard to choose. *(French)*
A woman who looks much in the glass spins but little. *(French)*
All the reasoning of men is not worth one sentiment of women. *(Voltaire)*
Find the woman. [*Cherchez la femme.*] *(French)*
How unhappy the woman who is loved and virtuous at the same time. *(La Rochefoucauld)*

It is because of men that women dislike each other. *(French)*

One woman drives out another so quickly in Paris, when one is a bachelor. *(de Maupassant)*

The great ambition of women is to inspire love. *(French)*

There is no accounting for the actions of a woman. *(French)*

There was never a mirror that told a woman she was ugly. *(French)*

Women are strong when they arm themselves with their weaknesses. *(French)*

Women have always some mental reservation. *(French)*

Women have no rank. *(Napoleon)*

Women pardon great infidelities more easily than little ones. *(French)*

Women laugh when they can and weep when they will. *(French)*

A bag of fleas is easier to keep watch over than a woman. *(German)*

A handsome woman is always right. *(German)*

A noble man is led far by woman's gentle words. *(Goethe)*

A woman has never spoiled anything through silence. *(German)*

Every woman loves the woman in the mirror. *(German)*

Fortune and women are partial to fools. *(German)*

Priests and women never forget. *(German)*

Put the light out, and all women are alike. *(German)*

The Eternal Feminine draws us upward. *(Goethe)*

There are only two good women in the world: the one is dead, the other not found. *(German)*

With women one should never venture to joke. *(German)*

Women are silver dishes into which we put golden apples. *(German)*

Women are watches that keep bad time. *(German)*

A woman should be good for everything at home, for nothing, abroad. *(Greek)*

A woman should stand by a woman. *(Greek)*

A woman without dower has no liberty to speak. *(Greek)*

He who teaches a woman letters feeds more poison to a terrible asp. *(Menander)*

Nothing is worse than a woman—even a good one. *(Greek)*

Silence gives grace to a woman. *(Sophocles)*

The hearts of women sicken for love more than do the hearts of men. *(Euripides)*

There are many wild beasts on land and in the sea, but the beastliest of all is woman. *(Menander)*

There's nothing in the world worse than a woman—except another woman. *(Aristophanes)*

Woman—a foe to friendship, an unescapable punishment, a necessary evil. *(St. Chrysostom)*

Woman brings to man his greatest blessing and his greatest plague. *(Greek)*

You will find many excuses, for you are a woman. *(Greek)*

A man shall walk behind a lion rather than behind a woman. *(Hebrew)*

A woman of sixty, the same as a girl of six, runs to the sound of the timbrel. *(Hebrew)*

Ten measures of speech descended on the world; women took nine and men one. *(Hebrew)*

A woman can love a poor boy better than a rich dotard. *(Hebrew)*

Ugliness is the guardian of women. *(Hebrew)*

Woman is the handsomest in animal creation. *(Hebrew)*

A beautiful woman smiling, bespeaks a purse weeping. *(Italian)*

A woman at a window, as grapes on the highway. *(Italian)*

A woman is flax, man is fire, the devil comes and blows the bellows. *(Italian)*

Adam must have an Eve to blame for his faults. *(Italian)*

If women were little as they are good,
A pease-cod would make them a gown and a hood. *(Italian)*

In men every mortal sin is venial; in women every venial sin is mortal. *(Italian)*

It is a sad house where the hen crows louder than the cock. *(Italian)*

It is better to irritate a dog than an old woman. *(Italian)*

Mills and women ever want some thing. *(Italian)*

To a foolish woman a violin is more pleasing than a distaff. *(Italian)*

When woman reigns, the devil governs. *(Italian)*

Woman is as fickle as a feather in the wind. [*La donn' è mobile . . .*] *(Italian)*

Women rouge that they may not blush. *(Italian)*

Women's tears are the fountain of craft. *(Italian)*

A woman's tongue is only three inches long, but it can kill a man six feet high. *(Japanese)*

An ugly woman dreads the mirror. *(Japanese)*

A virtuous woman commands her husband by obeying him. *(Latin)*

A wicked woman is a magazine of evils. *(Latin)*

A wise woman is twice a fool. *(Latin)*

A woman dares all things when she loves or hates. *(Latin)*

A woman finds it easier to do ill than well. *(Latin)*

A woman smells sweet when she smells of nothing. *(Latin)*

A woman who meditates alone meditates evil. *(Latin)*
A woman's mind is moved by the meanest gifts. *(Latin)*
All women can be caught; spread but your nets. *(Latin)*
As is the body, so is the soul of tender women frail. *(Latin)*
Every woman thinks herself lovable. *(Latin)*
He who can avoid women, let him avoid them. *(Latin)*
Nothing more unbearable than a wealthy woman. *(Latin)*
Take the first advice of a woman and not the second. *(Latin)*
The woman that spares her lover spares herself too little. *(Latin)*
Those women who grieve least make the most lamentation. *(Latin)*
Two women are worse than one. *(Latin)*
Woman is ever a fickle and changeable thing. *(Vergil)*
Woman is man's confusion. *(Latin)*
Woman's counsel is either too dear or too cheap. *(Latin)*
Women are one and all a set of vultures. *(Latin)*
Women are the gates of hell. *(St. Jerome)*
Women are worthless wares. *(Latin)*
Women beat men in evil counsel. *(Latin)*
A goose, a woman, and a goat are bad things, lean. *(Portuguese)*
Women and glass are always in danger. *(Portuguese)*
A dog is wiser than a woman; he does not bark at his master. *(Russian)*
Beat a woman with a hammer and you'll make gold. *(Russian)*
Better a de'il than a daw. *(Scottish)*
Her prentice han' she tried on man,
  An' then she made the lasses, O. *(Burns)*
A mule and a woman do what is expected of them. *(Spanish)*
A woman and a cherry paint themselves for their own hurt. *(Spanish)*
A woman and a greyhound must be small in the waist. *(Spanish)*
A woman and a hen are soon lost in gadding. *(Spanish)*
A woman of charm is as rare as a man of genius. *(de Madariaga)*
A woman's advice is of little value, but he who won't take it is a fool. *(Cervantes)*
A woman is known by her walking and drinking. *(Spanish)*
A woman's tears and a dog's limping are not real. *(Spanish)*
Between a woman's *Yes* and *No*
  There is not room for a pin to go. *(Spanish)*
He is a fool who thinks by force or skill
  To turn the current of a woman's will. *(Spanish, tr. Tuke)*
He that does not love a woman sucked a cow. *(Spanish)*
Tell a woman she's beautiful and the devil will tell it to her ten times. *(Spanish)*

The more a woman admires her face, the more she ruins her house. *(Spanish)*

The woman who dresses well draws her husband from another woman's door. *(Spanish)*

The woman in finery, the house in filth, but the doorway swept. *(Spanish)*

What a woman wills, God wills. *(Spanish)*

Woman is made of glass. *(Spanish)*

A dog is faithful, women never. *(Turkish)*

Believe one word in forty that a woman speaks. *(Turkish)*

Woman, like good wine, is a sweet poison. *(Turkish)*

Women have long hair and short wits. *(Yiddish)*

WONDER

A wonder lasts but nine days.

Wonder is involuntary praise. *(Young)*

Wonder is the daughter of ignorance.

Wonder—which is the seed of knowledge. *(Bacon)*

Wonders will never cease.

Wonder is the first cause of philosophy. *(Aristotle)*

To wonder at nothing. [*Nil admirari.*] *(Latin)*

WOOD

Chop your own wood, and it will warm you twice.

He that fears leaves, let him not go into the wood.

Never cry hallo till you are out of the woods.

Wood half burned is easily kindled.

Ye cannot see the wood for the trees.

The axe goes to the wood from whence it borrowed its helve. *(Hebrew)*

Even the gods dwelt in the woods. *(Vergil)*

In a moment the ashes are made, but a forest is a long time growing. *(Latin)*

It is foolish to carry timber to the wood. *(Latin)*

WOOING

A man chases a woman until she catches him. *(American)*

A man shall win us best with flattery. *(Chaucer)*

Barkis is willin'! *(Dickens)*

Blessed is the wooing that is not long a-doing.

He that would the daughter win,
Must with the mother first begin.

If I am not worth the wooing, I surely am not worth the winning. *(Longfellow)*

Men are April when they woo, December when they wed. *(Shakespeare)*

She's beautiful, and therefore to be woo'd:
She is a woman, therefore may be won. *(Shakespeare)*

The last suitor wins the maid.

The surest way to hit a woman's heart is to take aim kneeling. *(Jerrold)*

The weather is fine when folks are courting.

The wooing was a day after the wedding.

Who could not win the mistress wooed the maid. *(Pope)*

Who wooed in haste and means to wed at leisure. *(Shakespeare)*

For Nature framed all women to be won. *(Tasso)*

Employ soft flatteries, and words which delight the ear. *(Ovid)*

Flee, and she follows; follow, and she'll flee. *(Martial)*

A man may woo where he will, but he will wed where his hap is. *(Scottish)*

Sunday's wooin' draws to ruin. *(Scottish)*

Faint heart ne'er won fair lady. *(Spanish)*

WOOL

Much cry and little wool.

Many go out for wool and come home shorn. *(Spanish)*

WORD

A word fitly spoken is like apples of gold in pictures of silver. *(Old Test., Prov.)*

A word spoken in due season, how good it is! *(Old Test., Prov.)*

Be not rash with thy mouth . . . let thy words be few. *(Old Test., Eccles.)*

By thy words thou shalt be condemned. *(New Test., Matthew)*

He multiplieth words without knowledge. *(Old Test., Job)*

He that hath knowledge spareth his words. *(Old Test., Prov.)*

Heaven and earth shall pass away, but my words shall not pass away. *(New Test., Matthew)*

How forcible are right words! *(Old Test., Job)*

The words of the wise are as goads. *(Old Test., Eccles.)*

Who is this that darkeneth counsel by words without knowledge? *(Old Test., Job)*

He who lightly assents will seldom keep his word. *(Chinese)*

In a multitude of words there will surely be error. *(Chinese)*

Sincere words are not grand. *(Chinese)*
Without knowing the force of words, it is impossible to know men. *(Confucius)*
Words are the voice of the heart. *(Chinese)*
A man's word is his honor. *(Danish)*
Big words seldom go with good deeds. *(Danish)*
It is bitter fare to eat one's own words. *(Danish)*
Better one living word than a hundred dead. *(Dutch)*
Evil words corrupt good manners. *(Dutch)*
Take a horse by his bridle and a man by his word. *(Dutch)*
A blow with a word strikes deeper than a blow with a sword.
A fool and his words are soon parted.
A good word costs no more than a bad one.
A kind word leads the cow into the stable.
A man of words and not of deeds
  Is like a garden full of weeds.
A word and a stone let go cannot be called back.
A word before is worth two behind.
A word hurts more than a wound.
A word in earnest is as good as a speech.
A word once spoken, revokèd cannot be.
A word spoken is an arrow let fly.
All food is good to eat but all words are not fit to speak.
An acute word cuts deeper than a sharp weapon.
An honest man's word is as good as his bond.
Bare words buy no barley.
Bare words make no good bargain.
Be not the first by whom the new are tried,
  Nor yet the last to lay the old aside. *(Pope)*
Cool words scald not the tongue.
Evening words are not like to morning.
Fair words break no bones.
Fair words butter no parsnips.
Fair words fat few.
Fair words fill not the belly.
Fair words hurt not the tongue.
Fair words make fools.
Fair words make me look to my purse.
Fair words will not make the pot play.
Feeble deeds are vainer far than words.
Few words but to effect.

Fine words dress ill deeds.
Fine words will not keep a cat from starving.
From words to deeds is a great space.
Good words and ill deeds deceive wise and fools.
Good words anoint a man, ill words kill a man.
Good words are better than bad strokes.
Good words are good cheap.
Good words are worth much and cost little.
Good words cool more than cold water.
Good words fill not a sack.
Good words without deeds are rushes and reeds.
Great talkers are never great doers.
He that is lavish of words is a niggard in deed.
Honey in the mouth saves the purse.
I have no words: My voice is in my sword. *(Shakespeare)*
I'll make you eat your words.
Ill deeds are doubled with an evil word.
Ill words are bellows to a slackening fire.
It is as folk do, not as folk say.
Just deeds are the best answer to injurious words. *(Milton)*
Let thy actions to thy words accord.
Men of few words are the best men.
More sharp word than sword.
One ill word asketh another.
Our words are our own if we keep them within.
Our words have wings but fly not when we would.
Saying and doing have quarreled and parted.
Sharp words make more wounds than surgeons can heal.
Smooth words make smooth ways.
Soft words break no bones.
Soft words hurt not the mouth.
Soft words win hard hearts.
Sooner said than done.
Syllables govern the world. *(Selden)*
The word must be cousin to the deed.
The words of Mercury are harsh after the songs of Apollo. *(Shakespeare)*
They don't break bones, nor give black eyes.
Things were first made, then words.
Trust on the deed and not in gay speeches. *(Lyly)*
Use soft words and hard arguments.

Well done is better than well said.
What is word but wind?
When the word is out, it belongs to another.
Words are but holy as the deeds they cover. *(Shelley)*
Words are but wind, but blows, unkind.
Words and feathers the wind carries away.
Words are less needful to sorrow than to joy.
Words are like leaves, and where they most abound,
Much fruit of sense beneath is rarely found. *(Pope)*
Words are wise men's counters; they are the money of fools. *(Hobbes)*
Words pay no debts.
Words that weep, and tears that speak. *(Cowley)*
Words without thoughts never to heaven go. *(Shakespeare)*
Words, words, mere words, no matter from the heart. *(Shakespeare)*
For mad words, deaf ears. *(French)*
It is not as far from the heart to the mouth, as it is from the mouth to the hand. *(French)*
Word by word the book is made. *(French)*
Words repeated have, as another sound, another sense. *(French)*
A good word always finds its man. *(German)*
A good word stills great anger. *(German)*
Men's words are ever bolder than their deeds. *(German)*
Do not go forth on the gale with every sail set into an ocean of words. *(Greek)*
Every word is vain that is not completed by deed. *(Greek)*
It befits the brave to combat ill with words. *(Homer)*
Loyal words have the secret of healing grief. *(Menander)*
Whatsoever word you speak, that you will also hear.
Winged words. *(Homer)*
Words are the physician of a mind diseased. *(Aeschylus)*
Words provoke to senseless wrath. *(Greek)*
Words will build no walls. *(Greek)*
If a word be worth one shekel, silence is worth two. *(Hebrew)*
The words of the good are like a staff in a slippery place. *(Hebrew)*
Words are the daughters of earth, and deeds are the sons of heaven. *(Hindu)*
A good word for a bad one is worth much and costs little. *(Italian)*
Fair words—but look to your purse. *(Italian)*
Fair words won't feed a cat. *(Italian)*
Smooth words do not flay the tongue. *(Italian)*
A meaningless torrent of words. *(Latin)*

A word to the wise is sufficient. *(Latin)*
Empty words—sound without thought. *(Vergil)*
Fair words make fools fain. *(Latin)*
Few words, but those from the heart. *(Latin)*
Prove your words by your deeds. *(Latin)*
Smooth words in place of gifts. *(Latin)*
The word once spoken flies beyond recall. *(Latin)*
Why should I spare words? They cost nothing. *(Latin)*
Words a foot and a half long. [*Sesquipedalia verba.*] *(Horace)*
Words don't chink. *(Latin)*
A common word is always correct. *(Polish)*
A word isn't a bird; if it flies out you'll never catch it again. *(Russian)*
The spoken word cannot be swallowed. *(Russian)*
A good word extinguishes more than a pail full of water. *(Spanish)*
It's a long step from saying to doing. *(Spanish)*
Sugared words prove bitter. *(Spanish)*
Many words: an unsound heart. *(Turkish)*
One honest word is better than two oaths. *(Turkish)*
A word does not make a hole in the head. *(Yiddish)*
Better one word before than two after. *(Yiddish)*
Words should be weighed, not counted. *(Yiddish)*

WORK

Establish thou the work of our hands upon us. *(Old Test., Psalms)*
Every man's work shall be made manifest. *(New Test., I Corinth.)*
In the sweat of thy brow shalt thou eat bread. *(Old Test., Genesis)*
If any would not work, neither should he eat. *(New Test., II Thess.)*
Man goeth forth unto his work and to his labor until the evening. *(Old Test., Psalms)*
The night cometh when no man can work. *(New Test., John)*
Your work and labor of love. *(New Test., Hebrews)*
Never was good work done without much trouble. *(Chinese)*
A work ill done must be twice done.
After working like horses, don't fight like dogs.
All work and no play makes Jack a dull boy.
As good play for nought as work for nought.
Blessed is he who has found his work; let him ask no other blessedness. *(Carlyle)*
For men must work and women weep . . . *(Kingsley)*
Get thy spindle and thy distaff ready, and God will send thee flax.
Great gain makes easy work.

He that works after his own manner, his head aches not at the matter.
If you live without work, you must live without food.
It is working that makes a workman.
It will go all in your day's work.
Man hath his daily work of body and mind appointed.
Men work but slowly that have poor wages.
No pains, no gains.
No sweat, no sweet.
Slow work produces fine goods.
The result tests the work. *(Washington)*
There is no substitute for hard work. *(Edison)*
They must hunger in frost that will not work in heat.
Think of ease, but work on.
Wanting to work is so rare a merit that it should be encouraged. *(Lincoln)*
Work bears witness who does well.
Work first and then rest.
Work is something you want to get done; play is something you just like to be doing.
Everyone will be judged by his works. *(French)*
Our best friend is ever work. *(French)*
The sick man is not to be pitied who has a remedy in his sleeve. *(Montaigne)*
Work is worship. *(French)*
Good material is half the work. *(German)*
Sour work—sweet sleep. *(German)*
Where there are too many there is little work. *(German)*
Work has a bitter root but sweet fruit. *(German)*
A work well begun is half done. *(Greek)*
Light is the task when many share the toil. *(Homer)*
The gods sell us all good things for hard work. *(Greek)*
To generous souls, every task is noble. *(Euripides)*
Work is no disgrace: the disgrace is idleness. *(Greek)*
Great is work which lends dignity to man. *(Hebrew)*
He who would rest must work. *(Italian)*
It is not the long day but the heart that does the work. *(Italian)*
When I die, may I be taken in the midst of work. *(Ovid)*
Finish the work you have set yourself. *(Latin)*
Many hands make light work. *(Latin)*
To labor is to pray. [*Laborare est orare.*] (*Latin*)
Work is the sustenance of noble minds. *(Seneca)*

Work done expects money. *(Portuguese)*
He who does not kill hogs will not get black puddings. *(Spanish)*
Girn when ye bind, and laugh when ye loose. *(Scottish)*
Fools and bairns should not see half-work done. *(Scottish)*

WORKMAN

The laborer is worthy of his hire. *(New Test., Matthew)*
A workman is known by his chips.
An ill workman quarrels with his tools.
Good workmen are seldom rich.
Work makes the workman.
He who has money to throw away, let him employ workmen and not stand by.

WORLD

World without end. *(Old Test., Isaiah)*
A man may know the world without leaving his own home. *(Lao-Tsze)*
The world likes to be cheated. *(Dutch)*
"A Mad World, My Masters." [*Title*]
A world where nothing is had for nothing.
All the world and his wife. *(Swift)*
All the world's a stage,
And all the men and women merely players . . . *(Shakespeare)*
Be wisely worldly, be not worldly wise. *(Quarles)*
Do well and right, and let the world sink. (*Herbert*)
He that best understands the world, least likes it.
How full of briars is this working-day world! *(Shakespeare)*
How weary, stale, flat and unprofitable,
Seem to me all the uses of this world. *(Shakespeare)*
It is a world to see.
Knowledge of the world is to be acquired only in the world, not in the closet. *(Chesterfield)*
Let the world pass.
Let the world slide.
Let the world slip.
Let the world wag.
So goeth the world: now woe, now weal. *(Chaucer)*
The best thing in the world is to live above it.
The created world is but a small parenthesis in eternity. *(Sir T. Browne)*
The gown is his that wears it, and the world his that enjoys it.

The more a man drinketh of the world, the more it intoxicateth. *(Bacon)*

The world's a bubble.
The world's a prophecy of worlds to come.
The world is a wheel, and it will all come round right.
The world is as you take it.
The world is much the same everywhere.
The world is too much with us. *(Wordsworth)*
The world meets nobody half-way.
The world runs on wheels.
The world was all before them. *(Milton)*
The world was made at one cast.
The world was never less beautiful though viewed through a chink or knothole. *(Thoreau)*
The world, which took six days to make, is like to take six thousand to make out. *(Sir T. Browne)*
The world will, in the end, follow only those who have despised as well as served it. *(S. Butler)*
They enjoy the world most who admire it least.
'Tis a wicked world and we make part of it.
What is this world? A snare to snare the soul.
Why, then, the world's mine oyster,
Which I with sword will open. *(Shakespeare)*
Half the world does not know how the other half lives. *(Rabelais)*
The world is but a perpetual see-saw. *(Montaigne)*
The world is wiser than it was. *(French)*
Take the world as it is, not as it ought to be. *(German)*
I am a citizen of the world. *(Diogenes)*
A falling world might crush, but it could not intimidate me. *(Petrarch)*

Come, follow me, and leave the world to its babblings. *(Dante)*
Of this world each man has as much as he takes. *(Italian)*
The world is a beautiful book, but of little use to him who cannot read it. *(Goldoni)*
The world is governed with little brains. *(Italian)*
The world is a ladder for some to go up and some down. *(Italian)*
The verdict of the world is conclusive. *(St. Augustine)*
The whole world is the temple of the immortal gods. *(Seneca)*
You must either imitate or loathe the world. *(Latin)*
The world is a bride superbly dressed,
Who weds for dowry must pay his soul. *(Hafiz)*

In the world there must be of all sorts. *(Spanish)*
Lord of the Universe! Climb down from heaven, and look at the world you made! *(Yiddish)*
The whole world is like a dream. *(Yiddish)*

WORM

Tread on a worm and it will turn.
Worm's food is fine end of our living.
Worms wind themselves into our sweetest flowers. *(Cowper)*
Every worm has his hole. *(Yiddish)*

WORRY

A hundred load of thought will not pay one of debt.
It will be all one a hundred years hence.
Worry is the interest we pay on trouble before it is due.
Nothing in the affairs of men is worthy of great anxiety. *(Plato)*
What I don't know doesn't worry me. *(Yiddish)*

WORSHIP

For where two or three are gathered together in my name, there am I in the midst of them. *(New Test., Matthew)*
There may be worship without words.
They that worship God merely from fear,
Would worship the devil too, if he appear.

WORST

Provide for the worst; the best will save itself.
Things at the worst will mend.
The worst is always the present. *(French)*
It is best to know the worst at once. *(Latin)*
The corruption of the best produces the worst. *(Latin)*

WORTH

All good things are cheap; all bad are very dear.
As well worth it, as a thief is worth a rope.
Not worth a button.
Not worth a cress.
Not worth a fig.
Not worth a fly.
Not worth a groat.
Not worth a haddock.
Not worth a haw.
Not worth a leek.

Not worth a nutshell.
Not worthy to unbuckle his shoes.
Slow rises worth, by poverty depress'd. *(S. Johnson)*
The worth of a thing is what it will bring.
Worth makes the man, and want of it the fellow. *(Pope)*
So much is a man worth as he esteems himself. *(French)*
Things are only worth what one makes them worth. *(French)*
Everything is worth what its purchaser will pay for it. *(Latin)*
Great things cannot be bought for small sums. *(Latin)*
Hidden worth differs little from buried indolence. *(Horace)*
What is not needed is dear at an obol. *(Latin)*
Worthy things happen to the worthy. *(Latin)*
The worth of a thing is known by its want. *(Spanish)*
The worth of good is not known but by experience. *(Turkish)*

WOUND
If you can't heal the wound, don't tear it open. *(Danish)*
A green wound is soon healed.
A wound heals but the scar remains.
A private wound is deepest.
He jests at scars that never felt a wound. *(Shakespeare)*
None can speak of a wound with skill, if he hath not a wound felt.
Small wounds, if many, may be mortal.
The wound that bleedeth inwardly is the most dangerous.
There is no balm for every wound.
They that are afraid of wounds must not come near a battle.
What wound had ever heal but by degree? *(Shakespeare)*
Wounds cannot be cured without searching.
Old wounds easily bleed. *(German)*
A wound foreseen pains the less. *(Italian)*
He that would heal a wound must not handle it. *(Italian)*
Unbending the bow does not heal the wound. *(Italian)*
Fools, through false shame, conceal their wounds. *(Latin)*
Re-open not a wound once healed. *(Latin)*
Too late I grasp my shield when wounded. *(Ovid)*
Wounds pain most when grown old. *(Spanish)*
The knife's wound heals; the tongue's, never. *(Turkish)*
Pour not salt on my wound! *(Yiddish)*

WREN
Wrens may prey where eagles dare not perch.

WRETCHED

Let him be wretched who thinks himself so. *(Spanish)*

WRINKLE

An old wrinkle never wears out.

Wrinkles should merely indicate where smiles have been. *(Mark Twain)*

Wrinkles disfigure a woman less than ill nature. *(French)*

WRITING

Oh that mine adversary had written a book! *(Old Test., Job)*

What I have written, I have written. *(New Test., John)*

Written with a pen of iron, and with the point of a diamond. *(Old Test., Jerem.)*

All writing comes by the grace of God. *(Emerson)*

Either write things worth reading, or do things worth writing. *(Franklin)*

Learn to write well, or not to write at all.

Let him be kept from paper, pen, and ink;
So may he cease to write, and learn to think. *(Prior)*

Like author, like book.

Look in thy heart and write. *(Sidney)*

No man but a blockhead ever wrote except for money. *(S. Johnson)*

This will help to boil the pot.

True ease in writing comes from art, not chance. *(Pope)*

What comes from the heart goes to the heart.

Write with the learned, pronounce with the vulgar. *(Franklin)*

You write with ease to show your breeding,
But easy writing's curst hard reading. *(Sheridan)*

In every author let us distinguish the man from his works. *(Voltaire)*

If you want to be a good writer, write. *(Greek)*

Writing is the language of the hand. *(Hebrew)*

Choose a subject, ye who write, suited to your strength. *(Horace)*

His powers betray the writer. *(Ovid)*

The incurable itch of writing possesses many. *(Juvenal)*

Some fling books on the world as if they were fritters. *(Cervantes)*

He who can't write says the pen is bad. *(Yiddish)*

WRONG

What is wrong today won't be right tomorrow. *(Dutch)*

Better suffer than do ill.

Do wrong once and you'll never hear the end of it.

He that doth what he should not, shall feel what he would not.
Morally wrong can never be politically right.
No wrong without a remedy.
The silent man still suffers wrong.
Truth forever on the scaffold,
  Wrong forever on the throne. *(Lowell)*
Two wrongs don't make a right.
Wrong has no warrant.
Ye lean to the wrong shore.
He who does the wrong forgets it, but not he who receives it. *(Italian)*
The wrong doer never lacks a pretext. *(Italian)*
By bearing old wrongs you provoke new ones. *(Latin)*
Submit to one wrong and another follows. *(Spanish)*

YEAR

A thousand years in thy sight are but as yesterday when it is past. *(Old Test., Psalms)*

One year borrows another year's food. *(Chinese)*
The year has a wide mouth and a big belly. *(Danish)*
All the same a hundred years hence.
The more thy years, the nearer thy grave.
The year doth nothing else but open and shut.
The years teach much which the days never know. *(Emerson)*
Years know more than books.
The ill year comes in swimming. *(French)*
Everything is of the best year. *(Italian)*
Years and sins are always more than owned up to. *(Italian)*
Each passing year robs us of something. *(Latin)*
Nothing is swifter than the years. *(Latin)*
Give us years—troubles come of themselves. *(Yiddish)*
The years of a man's life pass like a dream. *(Yiddish)*

YESTERDAY

And all our yesterdays have lighted fools
The way to dusty death. *(Shakespeare)*
Each day is the scholar of yesterday. *(Latin)*

YOUTH

Let no man despise thy youth. *(New Test., I Timothy)*
Rejoice, O young man, in thy youth; and let thy heart cheer thee in the days of thy youth. *(Old Test., Eccles.)*
Remember now thy creator in the days of thy youth. *(Old Test., Eccles.)*
A youth growing has a wolf in his belly.
Almost everything that is great has been done by youth. *(D'Israeli)*

For young hot colts, being raged, do rage the more. *(Shakespeare)*
Force of juventus, hardy as lion. *(Lydgate)*
God's lambs will play.
Green wood makes a hot fire.
It is better to be a young June-bug than an old bird of paradise. *(Mark Twain)*
My salad days
  When I was green in judgment: cold in blood. *(Shakespeare)*
Reckless youth makes rueful age.
Rule youth well, for age will rule itself.
The days of our youth are the days of our glory. *(Byron)*
The young will sow their wild oats.
The Youth of a Nation are the trustees of Posterity. *(D'Israeli)*
We shall never be younger.
You can't put old heads on young shoulders.
Young fellows will be young fellows.
Youth and white paper take any impression.
Youth comes but once.
Youth's a stuff will not endure. *(Shakespeare)*
Youth is the season of hope.
Youth must dance while the old sit by the fire.
Youth should watch joys and shoot them as they fly. *(Dryden)*
Youth will be served.
Youth will have his course.
If youth knew; if age could. *(French)*
One is young only once. *(French)*
The majority of men employ the first portion of their life in making the other portion miserable. *(La Bruyère)*
Youth is a continual intoxication; it is the fever of reason. *(La Rochefoucauld)*
Youth is drunkenness without wine. *(Goethe)*
Enjoy the season of thy prime. *(Greek)*
The wildest colts make the best horses. *(Greek)*
Whom the gods love die young. *(Greek)*
Youth holds no society with grief. *(Aristotle)*
Goslings lead the geese to grass. *(Italian)*
Youth flies. *(Latin)*
Let us then rejoice, while we are young. [*Gaudeamus igitur . . .*] *(Latin)*
Whilst the morning shines, gather the flowers. *(Latin)*
There die as many lambs as wethers. *(Spanish)*

Z

ZEAL

It is good to be zealously affected always in a good thing. *(New Test., Galat.)*

I do not love a man who is zealous for nothing. *(Goldsmith)*

Zeal is fit only for wise men but is found mostly in fools.

Zeal is like fire; it wants both feeding and watching.

Zeal without knowledge is a fire without a light.

Zeal without knowledge is a runaway horse.

Zeal without knowledge is the sister of folly.

Not too much zeal. *(Talleyrand)*

Zeal is a bad servant. *(French)*

Blind zeal can only do harm. *(German)*

INDEX OF SUBJECTS

A

Ability, 3
Absence, 3
Absent-Minded, 3
Abstinence, 4
Abundance, 4
Abuse, 4
Accident, 4
Accounts, 4
Ache, 4
Acquaintance, 4
Action, 4
Actors, 4
Adam, 5
Adder, 5
Advantage, 5
Adventure, 5
Adversity, 5
Advice, 5-6
Affection, 6
Affliction, 6
Africa, 6
Age, 7-8
Age, The Golden, 8
Agreement, 9
Ague, 9
Ale, 9
Almost, 9
Alms, 9
Alone, 9
Ambition, 9-10
America, 10
Amusement, 10
Ancestry, 11
Angel, 11
Anger, 11-12
Answer, 12
Ant, 12
Antiquity, 13
Anvil, 13
Ape, 13
Appearance, 13-14
Appetite, 14
Applause, 14-15
Apple, 15
Appropriateness, 15
April, 15
Arcadia, 15
Archer, 15
Architecture, 15
Argument, 16
Arm, 16
Arms, 16
Army, 16
Arrogance, 16
Arrow, 16
Art, 16-17
Artist, 17
Ashes, 18
Ask, 18
Aspiration, 18
Ass, 18-19
Atheism, 19
Auction, 20
Audience, 20
August, 20
Authority, 20
Autumn, 20
Avarice, 20
Award, 20

B

Baby, 21
Bacchus, 21
Bachelor, 21
Bad, 21
Bait, 21
Baker, 22
Bald, 22
Barber, 22
Bargain, 22
Bark, 22
Bashful, 22
Bastard, 22
Beans, 23
Bear, 23
Beard, 23
Beast, 23
Beating, 23
Beauty, 23-25
Bed, 25
Bee, 25
Beer, see Ale
Beg, 25
Beggar, 25-26
Begin, 26-27
Behavior, 27
Behind, 27
Belief, 27
Bell, 27-28
Belly, 28
Bend, 28
Benefit, 29
Best, 29
Betray, 29
Better, 29
Beware, 29
Bible, 30
Bid, 30
Bind, 30
Biography, 30
Bird, 30
Birth, 30-31
Bit, 31
Bite, 31
Blab, 31
Black, 31
Blade, 31
Blame, 31
Blessing, 31-32
Blind, 32
Bliss, 32

Blockhead, 32
Blood, 32-33
Blot, 33
Blow, 33
Blowing, 33
Blunder, 33
Blush, 33
Boast, 33-34
Boat, 34
Body, 34
Boldness, 34-35
Bone, 35
Book, 35-36
Boot, 36
Bore, 36
Borrow, 36-37
Boston, 37
Bough, 37
Bourbons, 37
Bow, 37
Boy, 37-38
Brag, 38
Brain, 38
Branch, 38
Brandy, 38
Brave, 38
Bread, 38-39
Breakfast, 39
Breath, 39
Breeding, 39
Brevity, 39
Brew, 39
Bribe, 40
Bride, 40
Bridge, 40
Bright, 40
Brook, 40
Broom, 40
Brother, 40
Build, 41
Bull, 41
Bullet, 41
Bully, 41
Burden, 41
Business, 41-42
Busy, 42
Butter, 43
Butterfly, 43
Buy, 43
Bygone, 43

C

Cabbage, 44
Caesar, 44
Cage, 44
Cake, 44
Calamity, 44
Calf, 44
Calm, 45
Calumny, 45
Camel, 45
Candle, 45
Candor, 45-46
Cap, 46
Cards, 46
Care, 46
Careful, 46
Careless, 46
Caress, 47
Carrion, 47
Cart, 47
Carthage, 47
Case, 47
Cask, 47
Castle, 47
Cat, 47-48
Cat's Paw, 48
Catch, 48
Cause, 48-49
Caution, 49
Cemetery, 49
Censure, 49
Ceremony, 49
Certain, 49
Chaff, 50
Chain, 50
Chair, 50
Chalk, 50
Chance, 50
Change, 50-51
Chaos, 51
Character, 51
Charity, 51-52
Charm, 52
Chastise, 52
Chastity, 52-53
Chatter, 53
Cheap, 53
Cheat, 53-54
Cheerful, 54
Cheese, 54
Cheshire, 54
Chicken, 54
Children, 54-56
Childhood, 56
Chimney, 56
Choice, 56
Chop, 56
Christ, 56
Christianity, 57
Christmas, 57
Church, 57
Circle, 57
Circumstances, 57
City, 57
Civility, 58
Civilization, 58
Clamor, 58
Clay, 58
Cleanliness, 58
Clemency, 58
Clever, 58
Climb, 58-59
Cloak, 59
Clock, 59
Clothes, 59
Cloud, 59
Clown, 59
Clout, 59
Clumsy, 59
Coal, 59
Coat, 60
Cobbler, 60
Cock, 60
Cockroach, 60
Coddle, 60
Cold, 60
Colt, 60
Comfort, 60
Coming, 61
Command, 61
Commerce, 61

Common, 61
Companion, 61
Company, 61-62
Comparison, 62
Compensation, 62
Competition, 62
Complain, 62
Complexion, 63
Compliment, 63
Compromise, 63
Compulsion, 63
Conceal, 63
Conceit, 63
Condition, 63
Conduct, 63
Confession, 63-64
Confidence, 64
Conquer, 64
Conscience, 64-65
Consequence, 65
Conservative, 65
Consistency, 65
Constant, 66
Contemplation, 66
Contempt, 66
Content, 66-67
Contention, 67
Control, 67
Conversation, 67
Convince, 67
Cook, 67
Cooking, 67
Copy, 67
Coquetry, 68
Cord, 68
Corporation, 68
Correction, 68
Corruption, 68
Cosmopolitan, 68
Cost, 68
Counsel, 68
Count, 69
Country, 69
Couple, 69
Courage, 69
Court, 70
Courtesy, 70
Courtier, 70
Courting, 70
Cousin, 70
Cover, 70
Covet, 70-71
Cow, 71
Coward, 71-72
Crab, 72
Craft, 72
Crafty, 72
Crave, 72
Cream, 72
Credit, 72-73
Creditor, 73
Creed, 73
Crime, 73
Cripple, 73
Critic, 73-74
Criticism, 74
Crocodile Tears, 74
Crooked, 74
Cross, 74
Crossing, 74
Crow, 74-75
Crowd, 75
Crown, 75
Cruelty, 75
Crust, 75
Cry, 75
Cuckold, 76
Cuckoo, 76
Cunning, 76
Cup, 76
Cupid, 76
Cur, 76
Cure, 76
Curiosity, 77
Curse, 77
Custom, 77-78
Cut, 78
Cynic, 78

Dainties, 79
Daisy, 79
Dance, 79
Danger, 79-80
Darkness, 80-81
Darling, 81
Daughter, 81
Dawn, 81
Day, 81-82
Deaf, 82
Death, 82-87
Debt, 87-88
Deceit, 88-89
Decency, 89
Decision, 89
Decorum, 89
Deed, 89-90
Deep, 90
Defect, 90
Defense, 90
Defile, 91
Delay, 91
Delight, 91
Demagogue, 91
Demand, 91
Democracy, 91-92
Demure, 92
Deny, 92
Dependence, 92
Descent, 92
Deserving, 92
Desire, 92-93
Despair, 93
Despise, 93
Destiny, 93
Determination, 94
Devil, 94-95
Devotion, 95
Diamond, 95
Dice, 95
Die, 95
Difference, 95
Difficulty, 95-96
Digestion, 96
Dignity, 96
Dilemma, 96
Diligence, 96
Dining, 97
Diplomacy, 97
Directness, 97
Dirt, 97
Disappointment, 97

Discontent, 98
Discord, 98
Discover, 98
Discretion, 98
Discussion, 98
Disease, 98-99
Disgrace, 99
Dishonest, 99
Disillusion, 99
Dislike, 99
Dispute, 99
Distance, 99-100
Distrust, 100
Divide, 100
Divided Interest, 100
Divine, 100
Divorce, 100
Do, 100-101
Doctor, 101-102
Doctrine, 102
Dog, 102-103
Dollar, 104
Donkey, 104
Doomsday, 104
Door, 104
Doubt, 104
Dove, 104
Down, 105
Dowry, 105
Dream, 105
Dress, 105-106
Drift, 106
Drink, 106-107
Drive, 108
Drop, 108
Drown, 108
Drunkenness, 108-109
Due, 109
Dust, 109
Duty, 109
Dwarf, 109

E

Eagle, 110
Ear, 110
Early, 111
Earth, 111
Earthquake, 111
East, 111
Easter, 111
Easy, 111-112
Eat, 112-113
Eavesdropper, 113
Ebb, 113
Echo, 113
Economy, 114
Education, 114-115
Eel, 115
Efficient, 115
Effort, 115
Egg, 115
Egoism, 115-116
Egypt, 116
Elephant, 116
Eloquence, 116
Empty, 116
End, 116-117
Endure, 117
Enemy, 117-118
England, 118-119
Enough, 119-120
Enthusiasm, 120
Envy, 120
Epigram, 121
Epitaph, 121
Equality, 121
Error, 121-122
Escape, 122
Estate, 122
Eternity, 122
Europe, 122
Evidence, 122
Evil, 122-123
Exaggerate, 123
Example, 124
Exception, 124
Excess, 124
Exchange, 124
Excuse, 124
Exertion, 124
Exile, 125
Expectation, 125
Expense, 125
Experience, 125-126
Expert, 126
Explanation, 126
Extravagance, 126
Extreme, 126
Eye, 126-127

F

Face, 128
Fact, 129
Failure, 129
Fair, 129
Fairy, 129
Faith, 129-130
Fall, 130-131
False, 131
Falsehood, 131
Fame, 131-132
Familiarity, 132
Family, 132
Famine, 132
Fanatic, 132
Fancy, 132-133
Far, 133
Farewell, 133
Farming, 133
Fashion, 133-134
Fast, 134
Fasting, 134
Fat, 134-135
Fate, 135
Father, 135-136
Fault, 136-137
Favor, 137
Fear, 138-139
Feast, 139-140
Feather, 140
February, 140
Feeling, 140
Feet, 140
Fence, 140
Fetter, 140
Fiction, 140
Fiddler, 141
Fidelity, 141
Field, 141
Fig, 141

Fight, 141
File, 141
Find, 141
Finger, 142
Fire, 142
First, 143
Fish, 143
Fishing, 143-144
Fist, 144
Fit, 144
Flag, 144
Flat, 144
Flattery, 144-145
Flea, 145-146
Flesh, 146
Flight, 146
Flighty, 146
Fling, 146
Flint, 146
Flock, 146
Flower, 146-147
Fly, 147
Flying, 147
Fog, 147
Follow, 147
Folly, 147-148
Food, 148
Fool, 148-152
Foot, 152
Force, 152
Foreigners, 152
Foresight, 153
Forget, 153
Forgive, 153
Fortune, 153-156
Fox, 156
France, 156
Freedom, 157
Frenchman, 157
Friend, 157-160
Friendship 160-161
Frog, 161
Fruit, 161-162
Full, 162
Funeral, 162
Futility, 162
Future, 162

G

Gain, 163
Gallows, 163-164
Gambling, 164
Garden, 164
Garlic, 165
Garrulity, 165
Genius, 165
Gentle, 165-166
Gentleman, 166
German, 166
Giant, 166
Giddy, 166
Gift, 166-168
Gild, 168
Girl, 168
Giving, 168-170
Glass, 170
Glory, 170
Gluttony, 170-171
Goat, 171
God, 171-174
Gods, 174
Going, 174-175
Gold, 175-176
Golden Age, 176
Golden Rule, 176
Good, 176-177
Goodness, 177
Goose, 177-178
Gossip, 178
Government, 178
Gown, 179
Grace, 179
Gradual, 179
Grapes, 179
Grasp, 179
Grass, 179
Gratitude, 179-180
Grave, 180
Great, 180-181
Greek, 181
Greed, 181
Grief, 181-182
Groom, 182
Growth, 182
Guard, 182
Guess, 182
Guest, 182-183
Guilt, 183
Gullible, 183
Gut, 183

H

Habit, 184
Hail, 184
Hair, 184-185
Half, 185
Hammer, 185
Hand, 185-186
Handsome, 186
Hanging, 186
Happen, 186
Happiness, 187
Hard, 187
Hare, 188
Harm, 188
Harvest, 188
Haste, 188-189
Hat, 189
Hate, 189-190
Have, 190
Hawk, 190-191
Hay, 191
Head, 191
Heal, 191
Health, 191-193
Hear, 193
Heart, 193-194
Heaven, 195-196
Heavy, 196
Hedge, 196
Heel, 196
Heir, 196
Helen of Troy, 196
Hell, 196
Help, 196-197
Hen, 197
Heredity, 197
Heresy, 197
Hermit, 197
Hero, 197-198

Herring, 198
Hesitate, 198
Hide, 198
High, 198
Hill, 198
History, 198
Hobby, 199
Hog, 199
Hole, 199
Holiday, 199
Holy, 199
Home, 199-200
Homer, 200
Honesty, 200-201
Honey, 201
Honor, 201-203
Hook, 203
Hope, 203-204
Horse, 204-206
Hospitality, 206
Hour, 206
House, 206-207
Housekeeper, 207
Howl, 207
Humility, 207-208
Humor, 208
Hunchback, 208
Hunger, 208-209
Hunting, 209
Husband, 209-210
Hypocrite, 210-211

I

Ice, 212
Idea, 212
Ideal, 212
Idleness, 212-214
Idolatry, 214
"If," 214
Ignorance, 214-215
Ill, 215-216
Ill-Gotten, 216
Illegitimate, 216
Illness, 216
Imagination, 216
Imitation, 216
Immoderation, 216
Immortality, 217
Impartiality, 217
Impatience, 217
Impossible, 217-218
Impulse, 218
Inconsistency, 218
Inconvenience, 218
Indecision, 218
Independence, 218-219
Indifference, 219
Industry, 219-220
Infection, 220
Influence, 220
Ingratitude, 220
Inheritance, 220-221
Injury, 221
Injustice, 221
Inn, 221
Innocence, 221
Inquisitive, 221
Insignificant, 222
Insolence, 222
Inspiration, 222
Instinct, 222
Insult, 222
Intelligence, 222
Intention, 222
Invalid, 222
Invention, 223
Invitation, 223
Involved, 223
Irish, 223
Iron, 223
Italy, 223

J

Jack, 224
Jealousy, 224
Jest, 224-225
Jew, 225
Joy, 225
Judge, 226
Judgment, 226-227
June, 227
Jury, 227
Justice, 227-228

Keep, 229
Keeper, 229
Key, 229
Kick, 229
Kin, 229
Kindness, 229-230
King, 230-231
Kiss, 231-232
Kitchen, 232
Kite, 232
Knave, 232-233
Knife, 233
Knowledge, 233-234

L

Labor, 235-236
Lady, 236
Lamb, 236
Lame, 236
Lamp, 236
Land, 237
Lane, 237
Language, 237
Large, 237
Lark, 237
Lass, 237
Last, 237-238
Late, 238
Laugh, 238-239
Law, 239-242
Lawyer, 242-243
Lazy, 243
Leader, 243
Leak, 243
Lean, 243
Leap, 243-244
Learn, 244
Learning, 244-245
Leave, 245

Leg, 245
Leisure, 245
Lend, 245-246
Lenity, 246
Letter, 246
Liar, 246
Libel, 246
Liberty, 246-247
Library, 247
Lie, 247-248
Life, 248-252
Light, 252-253
Lightly, 253
Lightning, 253
Like, 253-254
Lily, 254
Linen, 254
Link, 254
Lion, 254-255
Lip, 255
Listen, 255
Literature, 255
Little, 255
Load, 256
Lock, 256
London, 256
Loneliness, 256
Long, 256
Longing, 256
Look, 256
Lord, 256
Lose, 257
Louse, 257
Love, 257-264
Low, 264
Loyalty, 264
Luck, 264-265
Luxury, 265

M

Machinery, 266
Madness, 266
Mahomet, 266
Magistrate, 267
Maid, 267
Majority, 267
Make, 267-268
Malice, 268
Mammon, 268
Man, 268-271
Manners, 271-272
March, 272
Market, 272
Marriage, 272-276
Marshal, 276
Martyr, 276
Master, 276-277
Maxim, 277
May, 277
Meadow, 277
Meal, 277
Meanness, 278
Means, 278
Measure, 278
Meat, 278
Medal, 278
Meddling, 278
Medicine, 278-279
Mediocrity, 279
Meekness, 279
Meeting, 279
Melancholy, 279
Memory, 280
Mend, 280
Merchant, 280
Mercy, 280-281
Merit, 281
Merry, 281
Messenger, 281
Might, 281
Milk, 281
Mill, 281-282
Mind, 282-283
Minute, 283
Miracle, 283
Mirror, 283
Mirth, 283-284
Mischief, 284
Miser, 284
Misery, 284-285
Misfortune, 285
Miss, 285
Mistake, 285-286
Mistress, 286
Mob, 286
Mockery, 286
Moderation, 286-287
Modesty, 287
Money, 287-290
Monk, 290
Monument, 290
Moon, 290
Morality, 291
Morning, 291
Mortality, 291
Moss, 291
Mother, 291-292
Mother-in-Law, 292
Mountain, 292
Mourning, 292-293
Mouse, 293
Mouth, 293-294
Move, 294
Much, 294
Mud, 294
Mule, 294
Mum, 294
Murder, 294
Music, 294-295

N

Nail, 296
Name, 296
Naples, 296
Narrowness, 296
Nation, 296
Nature, 297
Near, 298
Neat, 298
Necessity, 298
Need, 298
Needle, 299
Neighbor, 299
Nephew, 299
Nest, 299
Net, 299
Neutral, 299
New, 299-300
News, 300

Night, 300
Nobility, 300-301
Nod, 301
Noise, 301
North, 301
Nose, 301
Nothing, 302
Novelty, 302
Now, 302
Nudity, 302
Nurse, 302
Nut, 302

O

Oak, 303
Oath, 303
Obedience, 303-304
Observation, 304
Obstinate, 304
Obstacle, 304
Occasion, 304
Occupation, 304
Offense, 304
Office, 304
Old, 304-305
Olive, 305
Omen, 305
Once, 305
One, 305
Open, 305
Opinion, 305-306
Opportunity, 306
Oppression, 307
Optimism, 307
Oratory, 307
Order, 307
Orphan, 307
Orthodoxy, 307
Over, 307
Owl, 307
Own, 307
Owner, 307
Ox, 308
Oxford, 308
Oyster, 308

P

"P's" and "Q's" 309
Pace, 309
Pact, 309
Pain, 309
Paint, 310
Painting, 310
Paradise, 310
Pardon, 310
Parent, 310
Paris, 310
Parnassus, 311
Parting, 311
Partner, 311
Passion, 311
Past, 311-312
Patch, 312
Paternity, 312
Path, 312
Patience, 312-313
Patriotism, 313
Pauper, 313
Pay, 314
Peace, 314-315
Peacock, 315
Pearl, 315
Peasant, 315
Pedant, 315
Pedigree, 316
Pen, 316
Penny, 316
People, 316-317
Perfection, 317
Perfume, 317
Perseverance, 317-318
Personality, 318
Persuasion, 318
Perverse, 318
Pessimist, 318
Peter, 318
Philanthropy, 318-319
Philosophy, 319
Physician, 319
Picture, 319
Pie, 320
Piety, 320
Pig, 320
Pilgrim, 320
Pillow, 320
Pilot, 320
Pinch, 320
Pine, 320
Piper, 320
Piss, 321
Pit, 321
Pitch, 321
Pitcher, 321
Pity, 321
Place, 321
Plagiarism, 322
Plain, 322
Plant, 322
Play, 322
Please, 322
Pleasure, 322-323
Plenty, 323
Plough, 323-324
Poacher, 324
Pocket, 324
Poet, 324
Poetry, 324-325
Point, 325
Poison, 325
Politeness, 325
Politics, 325-326
Pomp, 326
Poor, 326-327
Pope, 327
Popularity, 327
Porridge, 327
Port, 327
Portion, 327
Position, 327
Possession, 327-328
Posterity, 328
Pot, 328
Poverty, 328-330
Powder, 331
Power, 331
Practice, 331
Praise, 331-333
Prayer, 333-334
Preacher, 334
Precedent, 335

Precious, 335
Precocious, 335
Prediction, 335
Prejudice, 335
Premature, 335
Preparedness, 335
Present, 335-336
Press, 336
Prevention, 336
Price, 336
Pride, 336-337
Priest, 337
Prince, 338
Prison, 338
Procrastination, 338
Prodigal, 338
Profit, 338-339
Progress, 339
Prohibition, 339
Promise, 339-340
Proof, 340
Property, 340
Prophecy, 340
Propose, 340
Prosperity, 340-341
Proverb, 341
Providence, 341-342
Provision, 342
Prudence, 342-343
Prying, 343
Public, 343
Pun, 343
Punctuality, 343
Punishment, 343-344
Purity, 344
Purpose, 344
Purse, 344-345

Quack, 346
Quality, 346
Quarrel, 346
Quench, 346
Question, 347
Quick, 347
Quiet, 347
Quit, 347
Quotation, 347

R

Race, 348
Rage, 348
Rags, 348
Rain, 348
Rainbow, 348-349
Rake, 349
Rank, 349
Rashness, 349
Rat, 349
Raven, 349
Reach, 349
Reading, 349-350
Reap, 350
Ready, 350
Reason, 350-351
Rebel, 351
Rebuke, 352
Receiver, 352
Reckon, 352
Red, 352
Reed, 352
Reform, 352
Refuse, 352-353
Regret, 353
Relatives, 353
Religion, 353-354
Remedy, 354
Remember, 354
Reminder, 354
Remorse, 354
Remove, 354
Rent, 354
Repair, 355
Repentance, 355
Reproach, 355
Reproof, 355
Reputation, 355-356
Resignation, 356
Resolution, 356-357
Respectability, 357
Responsible, 357
Rest, 357
Retreat, 357
Retribution, 357-358
Return, 358
Revenge, 358-359
Revolution, 359
Reward, 359
Rich, 360-362
Riddle, 362
Ridicule, 362
Ridiculous, 362
Riding, 363
Right, 363
Righteousness, 364
Ring, 364
Ripe, 364
Rising, 364
Risk, 364
Rivalry, 364
River, 364
Road, 364-365
Rob, 365
Rogue, 365
Rolling, 365
Rome, 365
Rope, 365
Rose, 365-366
Rotten, 366
Rough, 366
Rubbish, 366
Ruin, 366
Rule, 366
Ruler, 366
Rumor, 366-367
Run, 367
Russian, 367
Rust, 367

Sabbath, 368
Sack, 368
Saddle, 368
Safety, 368
Sail, 369
Saint, 369
Salt, 369

Salvation, 369
Satan, 370
Sauce, 370
Saving, 370
Saying, 370
Scab, 370
Scald, 370
Scale, 370
Scandal, 370-371
Scar, 371
Scatter, 371
Scholar, 371
School, 371
Science, 371-372
Scold, 372
Scorn, 372
Scot, 372
Scoundrel, 372
Scratch, 372
Sculpture, 372
Sea, 372-373
Season, 373
Secret, 373-374
See, 374
Seek, 374-375
Seem, 375
Self, 375
Self-Conceit, 375
Self-Confidence, 375
Self-Conscious, 375
Self-Control, 375
Self-Defense, 375
Self-Denial, 375
Self-Dependence, 375
Self-Depreciation, 376
Self-Help, 376
Self-Interest, 376
Self-Knowledge, 376
Self-Love, 376-377
Self-Praise, 377
Self-Preservation, 377
Self-Respect, 377
Self-Sacrifice, 377
Self-Torture, 377
Selfishness, 377-378
Sell, 378
Send, 378
Sense, 378
Serenity, 378
Sermon, 378
Servant, 379-380
Service, 380
Servitude, 380
Seville, 380
Shadow, 380-381
Shake, 381
Shame, 381-382
Share, 382
Sharp, 382
Shave, 382
Sheep, 382
Ship, 382-383
Shipwreck, 383
Shoe, 383
Shoemaker, 383
Shop, 383
Short, 384
Shoot, 384
Shrew, 384
Shrouds, 384
Sickness, 384
Sigh, 384
Sight, 384-385
Silence, 385-386
Silver, 386
Simplicity, 386
Sin, 386-388
Sincerity, 388
Sing, 388
Sip, 388
Sit, 388
Skeleton, 388
Skill, 388-389
Skin, 389
Sky, 389
Slander, 389-390
Slavery, 390
Sleep, 390-391
Slip, 392
Sloth, 392
Slow, 392
Sluggard, 392
Small, 392
Smile, 392-393
Smith, 393
Smoke, 393
Snake, 393
Sneer, 393
Sneeze, 393
Snow, 393
Snug, 393
Society, 393-394
Soldier, 394
Solitude, 394-395
Something, 395
Son, 395
Son-in-Law, 395
Song, 395-396
Soon, 396
Sore, 396
Sorrow, 396-397
Sort, 397
Soul, 397-398
Sound, 398
Source, 398
Sow, 398
Spain, 398
Spare, 398-399
Spark, 399
Sparrow, 399
Speech, 399-401
Spear, 401
Spend, 401
Spider, 401
Spin, 401
Spirit, 401-402
Spit, 402
Spite, 402
Spoil, 402
Sport, 402
Spot, 402
Sprat, 402
Spring, 402
Spur, 403
Spy, 403
Stable, 403
Staff, 403
Stain, 403
Stand, 403
Star, 403-404
Start, 404
Starve, 404
State, 404
Statistics, 404

Steal, 404
Step, 404
Step-Mother, 405
Stick, 405
Still, 405
Sting, 405
Stingy, 405
Stitch, 405
Stomach, 405
Stone, 405-406
Stoop, 406
Stop, 406
Storm, 406
Straight, 406
Strain, 406
Straw, 406
Stream, 406
Strength, 406-407
Stretch, 407
Strike, 407
Strive, 407
Strong, 407
Study, 407
Stumble, 407
Stupid, 408
Style, 408
Submission, 408
Subordinate, 408
Success, 408-409
Suffer, 409
Sugar, 409
Suicide, 409-410
Suit, 410
Sultan, 410
Summer, 410
Sun, 410
Sun-Dial, 411
Superstition, 411
Supper, 411
Support, 411
Sure, 411
Surety, 411
Surrender, 411
Surgeon, 411
Suspicion, 411-412
Swallow, 412
Swan, 412
Swap, 412
Swear, 412
Sweep, 412
Sweet, 413
Swim, 413
Swine, 413
Sword, 413-414
Sympathy, 414
System, 414

T

Table, 415
Tailor, 415
Take, 415
Tale, 415-416
Tale-Bearer, 416
Talent, 416
Talk, 416-417
Taste, 417
Tattler, 417
Taxes, 417
Tea, 417
Teach, 418
Tears, 418-419
Tell, 419
Temper, 419
Temperance, 419
Temple, 420
Temptation, 420
Test, 420
Thanks, 420
Thick, 420
Thief, 421-422
Thin, 422
Things, 422
Thirst, 422
Thistle, 422
Thorn, 422-423
Thought, 423-424
Thread, 424
Threat, 424-425
Three, 425
Thrift, 425
Throne, 425
Thunder, 426
Tide, 426
Tie, 426
Tiger, 426
Time, 426-429
Times, 429
Timeliness, 429
Timid, 429
Tired, 430
Title, 430
Tobacco, 430
Today, 430
Toil, 430
Tomorrow, 430-431
Tongue, 431-432
Tools, 432
Tooth, 433
Tower, 433
Toy, 433
Trade, 433
Tradesman, 433
Training, 433
Translator, 433
Trap, 433
Travel, 434-435
Treachery, 435
Treason, 435
Tree, 435-436
Trial, 436
Trick, 436
Trifle, 436-437
Trouble, 437
Troy, 438
Trust, 438
Truth, 439-441
Try, 442
Turn, 442
Turnip, 442
Twig, 442
Twins, 442
Two, 442
Tyrant, 442

U

Ugly, 443
Uncertainty, 443
Understanding, 443
Unity, 443-444
Universe, 444

University, 444
Unknown, 444
Unlucky, 444
Unwelcome, 444
Upright, 444
Use, 444-445
Useful, 445
Useless, 445
Usury, 445

V

Vacuum, 446
Valley, 446
Valor, 446
Vanity, 446-447
Variety, 447
Vengeance, 447
Venison, 448
Venom, 448
Venture, 448
Venus, 448
Vessel, 448
Vice, 448-450
Vicissitude, 450
Victory, 450
Village, 450
Villain, 450
Vinegar, 450
Virtue, 451-452
Vision, 453
Visit, 453
Voice, 453
Vote, 453
Vow, 453-454
Vulgar, 454

Wager, 455
Wages, 455
Wagon, 455
Wait, 455
Walk, 455
Wall, 455-456
Want, 456
Wanton, 456
War, 456-458
Ware, 458
Warm, 458
Warning, 458
Wash, 458
Washington, 458
Waste, 458-459
Watch, 459
Water, 459-460
Way, 460
Weak, 460
Wealth, 460-461
Wear, 461
Weapon, 461
Weather, 461-462
Wedding, 462
Wedge, 462
Weed, 462
Weep, 462
Weight, 463
Welcome, 463
Well (noun), 463
Well (adv.), 463
Wheel, 463
Whetstone, 463
Whip, 464
Whisper, 464
White, 464
Whore, 464
Why, 464
Wicked, 464-465
Widow, 465-466
Wife, 466-469
Wild, 469
Wilful, 470
Will, 470
Willing, 470
Willow, 470
Win, 470-471
Wind, 471
Wine, 471-473
Wink, 473
Winter, 474
Wisdom, 474-475
Wise, 475-476
Wish, 476-477
Wit, 477-478
Witch, 478
Witness, 478
Woe, 479
Wolf, 479
Woman, 480-487
Wonder, 487
Wood, 487
Wooing, 487-488
Wool, 488
Word, 488-492
Work, 492-494
Workman, 494
World, 494-496
Worm, 496
Worry, 496
Worship, 496
Worst, 496
Worth, 496-497
Wound, 497
Wren, 497
Wretched, 498
Wrinkle, 498
Writing, 498
Wrong, 498-499

Year, 500
Yesterday, 500
Youth, 500-501

Z

Zeal, 502

INDEX OF AUTHORS

A

Adams, John
(1735-1826)
178
Adams, Samuel
(1722-1803)
118
Addison, Joseph
(1672-1719)
42
Aeschylus
(B.C. 525-456)
8, 17, 196, 428, 491
Aesop
(Fl. B.C. 560)
14, 23
à Kempis
see Thomas à Kempis
Alcott, Amos Bronson
(1799-1888)
35, 58
Alcuin (735-804)
317
Alfieri, Vittorio
(1749-1803)
386
Amiel, Henry Frédéric
(1821-1881)
17, 27, 416
Andersen, Hans Christian (1805-1875)
249
Appleton, Thos. Gold
(1812-1884)
10
Arbuthnot, John
(1667-1735)
30
Aristophanes
(B.C. 448?-380?)
17, 484
Aristotle
(B.C. 384-322)
6, 25, 29, 318, 326, 359, 487, 501
Arnold, Matthew
(1822-1888)
51, 63
Ascham, Roger
(1515-1568)
244
Augustine, [Saint]
(354-430)
42, 130, 164, 173, 215, 275, 283, 325, 449, 495

B

Bacon, Francis
(1561-1626)
7, 11, 13, 15, 19, 24, 27, 34, 35, 46, 49, 66, 74, 76, 138, 154, 157, 158, 164, 191, 230, 233, 241, 246, 266, 297, 306, 317, 323, 335, 341, 344, 350, 358, 359, 361, 373, 393, 407, 411, 412, 427, 439, 467, 468, 487, 495
Barbour, John
(1316-1395)
264
Barère, Bertrand de
(1755-1841)
247
Barrie, Jas. Matthew
(1860-1939)
85, 249, 480
Bayly, Thos. H.
(1797-1839)
3
Beaumarchais, de
[P. A. Caron] (1732-1799)
279, 351, 396
Beaumont and Fletcher
260
Beccaria, C. B. di
(1735-1794)
198
Beecher, Henry Ward
(1813-1887)
102, 363
Bellows, Henry W.
(1814-1882)
17
Bentham, Jeremy
(1748-1832)
343
Bernard, [Saint]
(1091-1153)
252, 330
Bierce, Ambrose
(1842-1914?)
5, 14, 36, 483
"Billings, Josh"
[-H. W. Shaw]
(1839-1913)
215, 233
Bion (c. B.C. 200)
8, 24
Bismarck, O. E. von
(1815-1898)
166, 441, 453, 457
Blackstone, Wm.
(1723-1780)
318
Blake, William
(1757-1827)
9, 17, 18, 67, 82, 90, 91, 92, 110,

147, 149, 151, 161, 165, 213, 233, 286, 297, 302, 306, 315, 324, 333, 337, 342, 412, 418, 439, 440
Bogart, John B. (1845-1921) 300
Borgia, Cesare (1476-1507) 44
Brathwaite, Richard (1588 ?-1675) 16
Bright, John (1811-1889) 119, 237
Brillat-Savarin (1755-1826) 67
Browne, Sir Thomas (1605-1682) 85, 121, 217, 222, 249, 269, 409, 494, 495
Browning, Robert (1812-1889) 18, 136, 153, 187, 249, 307, 349, 380
Bryant, Wm. Cullen (1794-1878) 20, 121, 420, 440
Buffon, Count de (1707-1788) 165, 408
Bulwer-Lytton, Edw. (1803-1873) 14, 129, 259
Bunn, Alfred (1796-1860) 204
Bunyon, John (1628-1688) 93, 207, 318, 387
Burgess, F. Gelett (1866-) 161
Burke, Edmund (1729-1797) 13, 24, 91, 124, 138, 164, 230, 282, 316, 328, 331, 457
Burns, Robert (1759-1796) 35, 84, 90, 109, 187, 229, 250, 264, 271, 293, 333, 349, 430, 486
Burr, Aaron (1756-1836) 240
Burroughs, John (1837-1921) 455
Burton, Robert (1577-1640) 9, 88, 134, 223, 279, 324, 353, 361, 411, 442
Butler, Samuel (1612-1680) 63, 98, 101, 102, 130, 305, 351, 357, 439, 467, 470
Butler, Samuel (1835-1902) 190, 250, 495
Byron, Lord G. G. N. (1788-1824) 5, 49, 126, 131, 133, 182, 210, 225, 238, 250, 260, 274, 293, 311, 323, 371, 393, 408, 440, 481, 501

C

Caesar, Julius (B.C. 102 ?-44) 10, 64, 139, 143
Cameron, Simon (1799-1889) 325
Campbell, Thos. (1777-1844) 44, 99, 305
Campion, Thos. (? -1620) 128
Carlyle, Thos. (1795-1881) 30, 35, 119, 197, 247, 295, 326, 346, 372, 492
Carney, Julia F. (1823-1908) 436
Cato, Marcus (B.C. 234-149) 8, 28, 33, 47, 209
Catullus, Quintus (B.C. 87-54 ?) 133
Caxton, William (1422 ?-1491) 385
Cervantes, Saavedra (1547-1616) 14, 19, 27, 31, 32, 81, 166, 178, 190, 196, 318, 330, 391, 478, 486, 498
Chamfort, S. R. N. (1741-1794) 156, 317, 359
Channing, Wm. E. (1780-1842) 130, 217
Chaucer, Geoffrey (1340 ?-1400) 13, 23, 34, 45, 47, 85, 93, 117, 123, 134, 149, 150, 154, 159, 164, 166, 210, 225, 233, 237, 250, 259, 274, 280, 281, 297, 312, 321, 329, 334, 342, 376, 382, 403, 436, 440, 476, 479, 481, 483, 487, 494
Chénier, A. M. de (1762-1794) 182, 442

Chesterfield, 4th Earl of (1694-1773) 105, 134, 178, 239, 270, 439, 483, 494
Chrysostom, John [Saint] (347?-407) 289, 388, 485
Churchill, Charles (1731-1764) 4
Cibber, Colley (1671-1753) 3, 9
Cicero, Marcus Tullius (B.C. 106-43) 3, 6, 8, 14, 16, 27, 36, 49, 215, 272, 277, 307, 317, 318, 343, 457
Claudian (c. 375) 3
Clay, Henry (1777-1852) 363
Clemens, Sam'l L. (1835-1910) 12, 37, 63, 115, 177, 184, 248, 269, 271, 305, 397, 420, 440, 462, 501
Cohan, Geo. M. (1873-1940) 249
Coke, Sir Edward (1552-1634) 240
Coleridge, Sam'l T. (1772-1834) 65, 121, 140, 187, 212, 249, 337, 444
Colman, George (1762-1836) 468
Colton, Chas. C. (1780-1832) 13, 52
Confucius (B.C. 551-478) 193, 195, 268, 371, 423, 470, 489
Congreve, William (1670-1729) 29, 121, 232, 295, 477, 481
Conkling, Roscoe (1829-1888) 363
Constantine the Great (Reg. 306-337) 57
Cook, Eliza (1818-1889) 114
Corbet, Richard (1582-1635) 129
Corneille, Pierre (1606-1684) 231, 381
Cowley, Abraham (1618-1667) 57, 427, 491
Cowper, William (1731-1800) 10, 52, 57, 119, 137, 147, 172, 209, 210, 262, 304, 333, 334, 354, 363, 371, 496
Crabbe, George (1754-1832) 35
Crockett, "Davy" (1786-1836) 363
Cromwell, Oliver (1599-1658) 230, 335, 342, 438
Curran, John P. (1750-1817) 417
Cyprian, [Saint] (c. 200-258) 365

D

Dante, Alighieri (1265-1321) 6, 17, 104, 195, 204, 280, 315, 344, 355, 428, 495
Danton, Georges J. (1759-1794) 34
D'Avenant, Sir Wm. (1606-1668) 9
Decatur, Stephen (1779-1820) 10, 69
Dekker, Thomas (1570?-1641?) 7, 11
Delille, Jacques (1738-1813) 442
Demosthenes (B.C. 384?-322) 317
Denham, Sir John (1615-1669) 16, 35
DeQuincey, Thomas (1785-1859) 158
Descartes, René (1596-1650) 424
Dickens, Charles (1812-1870) 4, 129, 194, 487
Dickinson, C. M. (1842-1924) 333
Dickinson, Emily (1830-1886) 24, 36, 316
Diderot, Denis (1713-1784) 104

Diogenes
(B.C. 412?-323?)
68, 174, 270, 289, 495
Disraeli, Benjamin
(1804-1881)
5, 7, 35, 63, 65, 261, 267, 273, 326, 353, 371, 423, 430, 500, 501
D'Israeli, Isaac
(1766-1848)
120
Dix, John A.
(1798-1879)
10
Dobson, Henry A.
(1840-1921)
36
Donne, John
(1573-1631)
81, 151, 397
Dryden, John
(1631-1701)
12, 16, 17, 34, 38, 69, 79, 106, 107, 121, 265, 167, 180, 202, 260, 269, 294, 295, 309, 311, 312, 323, 325, 332, 355, 375, 395, 409, 439, 449, 457, 467, 477, 501
Dumas, Alexandre
(1803-1870)
444
Dyer, Edward
(1540-1607)
282

E

Eddy, Mary B. G.
(1821-1910)
99, 122, 282
Edison, Thomas A.
(1847-1931)
165, 493
Einstein, Albert
(1879-　　)
162, 216
Eldon, Lord J. S.
(1751-1838)
68
"Eliot, Geo."
(1819-1880)
399, 481, 482
Elizabeth (Queen)
(1533-1603)
66
Ellis, H. Havelock
(1859-1940)
17, 216
Emerson, Ralph W.
(1803-1882)
7, 10, 13, 17, 18, 24, 36, 49, 56, 65, 73, 91, 114, 126, 129, 131, 138, 158, 161, 165, 173, 174, 181, 189, 192, 197, 202, 212, 227, 233, 237, 266, 269, 295, 298, 303, 324, 333, 342, 350, 353, 356, 359, 331, 362, 369, 383, 386, 394, 403, 408, 417, 439, 449, 455, 476, 498, 500
Epictetus
(c. 60-120)
270, 470
Epicurus
(B.C. 342-270)
309
Erasmus, Gerard D.
(1465-1536)
8, 46, 354
Euclid
(c. 300 B.C.)
115, 244
Euripides
(B.C. 480-406)
8, 419, 484, 493
Evans, Mary Ann
see "Eliot, Geo."

F

Falkland, Viscount
(1610-1643)
244
Fessenden, Samuel
(1847-1908)
347
Fletcher, John
(1579-1625)
4, 180, 380
Fosdick, H. E.
(1878-　　)
190
France, Anatole
(Jacques Anatole Thibaud)
(1844-1924)
74
Francis I (of France)
(1494-1547)
141, 202
Franklin, Benjamin
(1706-1790)
4, 5, 6, 7, 8, 10, 11, 12, 29, 30, 49, 61, 83, 85, 118, 125, 130, 146, 151, 152, 153, 158, 165, 192, 205, 213, 233, 235, 240, 243, 244, 247, 273, 318, 409, 416, 419, 443, 477, 479, 481, 498
Frederick the Great
(1712-1786)
394

G

Gandhi, (Mahatma)
(1869-　　)
251
Gardner, Percy
(1846-1920)
10

Garrick, David
(1717-1779)
119
Gauguin, Paul
(1848-1903)
17, 58
Gay, John
(1685-1732)
242, 249, 259, 292, 389, 483
Gibbon, Edward
(1737-1794)
47, 359, 417
Gibbons, (Cardinal)
(1834-1921)
352
Gilbert, Sir Humphrey
(1539-1583)
195
Goethe, Johann W.
(1749-1832)
13, 14, 15, 27, 34, 51, 122, 151, 165, 169, 194, 198, 237, 239, 251, 253, 262, 270, 272, 301, 306, 311, 359, 387, 416, 443, 470, 475, 484, 501
Goldoni, Carlo
(1707-1793)
33, 495
Goldsmith, Oliver
(1730-1774)
7, 35, 61, 160, 238, 247, 250, 315, 347, 360, 451, 460, 483, 502
Goncourt, Edmond
(1822-1896)
36, 165
Googe, Barnabe
(1540-1594)
3
Gower, John
(1325?-1408)
312, 337, 448
Grant, Ulysses S.
(1822-1885)
240
Granville, Geo.
(1667-1735)
131
Gray, Thomas
(1716-1771)
146, 170, 215, 418, 483
Greeley, Horace
(1811-1872)
465
Greene, Robert
(1560?-1592)
418
Gregory I [Pope]
(540?-604)
119, 130
Grosvenor, C. H.
(1833-1917)
248

H

Hafiz (?-c. 1389)
495
Hale, Nathan
(1755-1776)
10
Halifax, [Lord]
(1633-1695)
50
Hannibal
(B.C. 247-183)
365
Hardy, Thomas
(1840-1928)
482
Harrington, Sir John
(1561-1612)
435
Hawthorne, Nathaniel
(1804-1864)
269
Hazlitt, William
(1778-1830)
181
Heber, Reginald
(1785-1826)
195, 270
Hegel, G. W. F.
(1770-1831)
307
Heine, Heinrich
(1797-1856)
19, 119, 270
Helps, Sir Arthur
(1813-1875)
350
Henley, W. E.
(1849-1903)
135, 397
Henri IV (of France)
(1553-1610)
310
Henry, Patrick
(1736-1799)
195
Herbert, George
(1593-1633)
18, 19, 494
Herrick, Robert
(1591-1674)
105, 232, 267, 369, 387, 427, 467
Hippocrates
(B.C. 460?-377?)
17
Hobbes, Thomas
(1588-1679)
157, 245, 250, 456, 491
Hodgson, Ralph
(1871-)
213
Holmes, Oliver W.
(1809-1894)
37, 248, 288, 371, 417, 482
Homer
(Fl. 1000 B.C.)

Homer—*Continued*
3, 12, 28, 34, 46, 68, 85, 92, 136, 148, 157, 194, 198, 231, 251, 270, 293, 373, 389, 419, 475, 476, 491, 493
Hood, Thomas (1759-1845) 123, 482
Horace (B.C. 65-8) 6, 11, 12, 14, 20, 27, 32, 38, 46, 87, 93, 140, 148, 165, 200, 204, 214, 271, 275, 289, 292, 306, 317, 324, 325, 347, 375, 381, 419, 428, 430, 434, 457, 460, 492, 497, 498
Howe, L. M. (1871-1936) 326
Hoyle, Edmond (1672-1769) 46
Hubbard, Elbert (1859-1915) 17, 65, 85
Hubbard, "Kin" (1860-1930) 153
Hume, David (1711-1776) 20
Huneker, J. G. (1860-1921) 17
Huss, John (1369-1415) 386
Hutcheson, Francis (1694-1746) 187
Hutchinson, John (1674-1737) 4

I

Ibsen, Henrik (1828-1906) 219, 267, 350, 395
Ingersoll, Robt. G. (1833-1899) 19, 121, 165, 215, 313, 318, 444
Innocent III [Pope] (1161-1216) 171
Irving, Washington (1783-1859) 104

J

Jameson, Robert (1774-1854) 6
Jefferson, Thomas (1743-1826) 10, 61, 121, 178, 247, 305, 325, 336, 442
Jerome, [Saint] (340-420) 486
Jerrold, D. W. (1803-1857) 259, 488
Johnson, Samuel (1709-1784) 7, 16, 74, 85, 98, 121, 134, 140, 182, 200, 208, 211, 213, 216, 231, 237, 247, 250, 273, 274, 295, 309, 313, 322, 329, 342, 344, 351, 372, 412, 431, 448, 497, 498
Jonson, Ben (1573-1637) 9, 16, 131, 237,
Jonson, Ben—*Cont'd.* 276, 354, 387, 411, 478
Joubert, Joseph (1754-1824) 159, 216, 227, 230, 282, 417, 444, 452
Julian (Emperor) (331-363) 56
Julius III [Pope] (1443-1513) 178
"Junius" (c. 1760) 230, 453
Junot [Marshal] (1771-1813) 11
Juvenal (c.60-c.140) 8, 20, 25, 26, 34, 39, 195, 201, 324, 325, 442, 469, 498

K

Keats, John (1795-1821) 23, 24, 111, 250, 254, 270, 294, 319, 386
Keble, John (1792-1866) 255
[Kempis] see Thomas à Kempis
Key, Francis Scott (1779-1843) 438
Kierkegaard, S. A. (1813-1855) 252
Kilmer, Joyce (1886-1918) 435

Kingsley, Charles
(1819-1875)
58, 89, 177, 193, 492
Kipling, Rudyard
(1865-1936)
41, 119, 218, 273, 387, 434, 482

L

La Bruyère, Jean de
(1645-1696)
10, 178, 428, 478, 501
La Fontaine, Jean de
(1621-1695)
24, 145, 147, 208, 281, 440
Lamartine, Alphonse de
(1790-1869)
262
Lamb, Charles
(1775-1834)
164, 255, 269, 350
Landor, Walter Savage
(1775-1864)
12, 181, 217, 353, 394
Langland, William
(1330 ?-1400 ?)
24
Lao-tsze
(c. 6th Cent. B.C.)
195, 222, 284, 360, 375, 439, 475, 494
La Rochefoucauld, François, (Duc de)
(1613-1680)
3, 8, 36, 53, 68, 137, 148, 153, 154, 159, 169, 170, 177, 179, 187, 194, 211, 220, 262, 285, 311, 332, 378, 389, 400, 435, 447, 449, 452, 474, 478, 483, 501
Lawrence, James
(1781-1813)
10
Lee, Henry
(1756-1818)
458
Lemaître, F. E. J.
(1853-1914)
74
Lessing, G. E.
(1729-1781)
4, 129, 194, 383
Lewes, Geo. Henry
(1817-1878)
294
Lincoln, Abraham
(1809-1865)
52, 170, 178, 316, 325, 385, 390, 412, 453, 493
Livy [Titus Livius]
(B.C. 59-A.D. 17)
5
Locke, John
(1632-1704)
235, 350
Longfellow, H. W.
(1807-1882)
6, 192, 217, 250, 455, 488
Lovelace, Richard
(1618-1658)
120, 338
Lowell, J. R.
(1819-1891)
91, 169, 190, 318, 363, 440, 499
Lubbock, John
(1834-1913)
17
Lucian
(120 ?-200 ?)
19
Lucretius
(B.C. 96 ?-B.C. 55)
13, 444
Luther, Martin
(1483-1546)
65, 173, 334, 361, 367
Lydgate, John
(1370 ?-1451)
259, 273, 501
Lyly, John
(1554 ?-1606)
4, 490

M

Macaulay, T. B.
(1800-1859)
85, 118, 341
Mackay, Charles
(1814-1889)
120
MacLeish, A.
(1892-)
324
Mandeville, Bernard de
(1670-1733)
449
Mann, Horace
(1796-1859)
114
Marcus Aurelius
(121-180)
444
"Mark Twain"
see Clemens, S. L.
Marlowe, Christopher
(1564-1593)
135, 158, 195, 261, 323, 353, 451
Martial
[M. V. Martialis]
(40 ?-102 ?)
27, 252, 410, 488
Marvell, Andrew
(1621-1678)
180
Marx, Karl
(1818-1883)
354
Masefield, John
(1874-)
10, 187, 249, 333

Maupassant G. de
(1850-1893)
246, 484
Melville, Herman
(1819-1891)
69, 249
Menander
(B.C. 342-290)
5, 272, 282, 289,
484, 491
Mencken, H. L.
(1880-)
133
Meredith, George
(1828-1909)
78, 333, 483
Metternich, Prince von
(1773-1859)
223
Michelangelo
(Buonarroti)
(1475-1564)
17, 25, 244, 317
Middleton, Thomas
(1570 ?-1627)
6
Mill, John Stuart
(1806-1873)
165
Millay, Edna St. V.
(1892-)
422
Milton, John
(1608-1674)
20, 24, 35, 53, 66,
81, 119, 128, 131,
172, 231, 240, 253,
297, 303, 305, 314,
317, 380, 381, 412,
416, 455, 456, 490,
495
Mizner, Addison
(1872-1933)
132
Moleschott, Jacob
(1822-1893)
424
Molière
[Jean B. Poquelin]
Molière—*Continued*
(1622-1673)
33, 89, 166, 449,
478
Montaigne, Michel de
(1533-1592)
8, 27, 28, 36, 46,
48, 53, 169, 184,
210, 241, 251, 265,
275, 282, 306, 309,
319, 332, 337, 347,
350, 375, 378, 379,
383, 398, 412, 418,
428, 446, 449, 450,
493, 495
Montesquieu, L. de
(1689-1755)
151, 157, 178, 198,
350, 394
Montgomery, James
(1771-1854)
79, 207
Moody, D. L.
(1837-1899)
51, 195
Moore, Thos.
(1779-1852)
84, 211, 351, 482
Morris, G. P.
(1802-1864)
443
Morris, William
(1834-1896)
105, 182, 204
Morton, Thos.
(1764 ?-1838)
394
Motley, J. L.
(1814-1877)
265

N

Napoleon Bonaparte
(1769-1821)
19, 114, 118, 165,
218, 223, 262, 282,
Napoleon Bonaparte—
Continued
321, 336, 356, 394,
416, 484
Nash, Ogden
(1902-)
106
Nelson, Lord Horatio
(1758-1805)
119, 450
Newman, John Henry
(1801-1890)
166, 253
Nietzsche, F. W.
(1844-1900)
270, 280, 441
Norton, C. E. S.
(1808-1877)
323
Novalis
(-F von Hardenberg)
(1772-1801)
30, 119

O

Omar, (Caliph)
(582-644)
247
Omar Khayyám
(? -1123)
73, 147, 473
Ossian
(Mythical Bard)
129
Otis, James
(1725-1783)
417
Otway, Thomas
(1652-1685)
180
Overbury, Sir Thomas
(1581-1613)
261
Ovid
[Pub. Ovidius Naso]
(B.C. 43-A.D. 17)
6, 12, 13, 17, 25,

Ovid—*Continued*
27, 36, 38, 41, 53, 127, 168, 185, 194, 201, 204, 214, 215, 263, 283, 306, 309, 334, 363, 376, 479, 488, 493, 497, 498

P

Paine, Thomas (1737-1809) 157, 353, 412
Paley, William (1743-1805) 393
Parker, Dorothy, (1893-) 230, 483
Parker, Theodore (1810-1860) 36, 91, 353
Parnell, Thomas (1679-1718) 83
Pascal, Blaise (1623-1662) 26,116, 123, 173, 194, 233, 247, 270, 283, 301, 306, 424, 437, 440
Payne, J .H. (1791-1852) 199
Penn, William (1644-1718) 20, 247, 353
Periander (c. 600 B.C.) 12, 91
Persius, Flaccus (34-62) 15, 42
Petrarch [Francesco Petrarca] (1304-1374) 263, 408, 495
Petronius, Gaius (? -66) 14, 25, 165, 434
Phaedrus (? -B.C. 70) 14
Phillips, Wendell (1811-1884) 240, 246, 267
Pinckney, C. C. (1746-1825) 10, 90
Pitt, William (1759-1806) 298, 331
Plato (B.C. 428-347) 11, 24, 173, 215, 221, 270, 281, 282, 295, 319, 324, 272, 298, 409, 441, 496
Plautus, Titus Marc. (c. 254-184 B.C.) 6, 27, 32
Pilny (the Elder) (23-79) 36, 214
Plutarch (c. 66) 25, 44
Pope, Alexander (1688-1744) 10, 24, 32, 43, 55, 66, 79, 114, 125, 126, 131, 147, 150, 162, 173, 177, 178, 200, 202, 203, 206, 226, 231, 233, 244, 259, 270, 307, 311, 313, 325, 326, 331, 347, 349, 351, 360, 363, 369, 373, 376, 393, 398, 449, 478, 483, 488, 489, 491, 497, 498
Porson, Richard (1759-1808) 430
Prior, Matthew (1664-1721) 131, 136, 175, 371, 416, 481, 498
Propertius, Sextus (B.C. 50 ?-15 ?) 3
Protagoras (B.C. 481 ?-411) 270
Proudhon, P. J. (1809-1865) 181, 340
Pushkin, A. S. (1799-1837) 264
Pyrrhus (B.C. 381-272) 450
Pythagoras (B.C. 582-500) 398

Q

Quarles, Francis (1592-1644) 195, 196, 494
Quintillian, M. F. (c. 35-95) 17

R

Rabelais, François (1494-1553) 113, 146, 206, 251, 290, 391, 417, 450, 468, 495
Racine, Jean B. (1639-1699) 202, 465
Raleigh, Sir Walter (1552 ?-1618) 53, 84

Reade, Charles
(1814-1884)
140, 443
Richard I
(1157-1199)
119
Richter, Jean Paul
(1763-1825)
262
Roche, Jas. J.
(1847-1908)
390
Rochester (Earl of)
(1647-1680)
467
Rogers, Will
(1879-1935)
325
Roland (Madame)
(1754-1793)
247
Roosevelt, Franklin Delano
(1882-1945)
157
Roosevelt, Theodore
(1858-1919)
352, 388
Roscommon (Earl of)
(1633-1685)
89
Rousseau, Jean-Jacques
(1712-1778)
4, 56, 57, 354, 377, 465
Ruskin, John
(1819-1900)
15, 58, 390
Russell, Bertrand
(1872-)
91

S

Sadi (c. 1200)
188, 313
Sainte-Beuve, C. S.
(1804-1869)
74
Sallust, Caius
(B.C. 86-34)
11
Santayana, George
(1863-)
17, 132, 295, 303, 315
Sappho (c. 610 B.C.)
25, 220
Sassoon, Siegfried
(1886-)
394
Schiller, Fr. von
(1759-1805)
6, 65, 157, 165, 182, 187, 225, 267, 296, 298, 301, 408, 428, 444
Schopenhauer, Arthur
(1788-1860)
217
Scott, Sir Walter
(1771-1832)
9, 88, 482
Sedley, Sir Chas.
(1639-1701)
261
Seeger, Alan
(1888-1916)
84
Selden, John
(1584-1654)
274, 483, 490
Seneca, L. A.
(c. 5-65)
5, 8, 11, 12, 17, 20, 46, 82, 92, 178, 231, 244, 271, 334, 428, 457, 493, 495
Shakespeare, Wm.
(1564-1616)
[*Passim*
Quoted 376 times]
Shaw, Geo. B.
(1856-)
89, 91, 118, 119, 187, 190, 199, 214, 295, 318, 333, 353, 357, 372, 394, 418, 439, 483
Shaw, Henry W.
see "Billings, Josh"
Shelley, P. B.
(1792-1822)
18, 73, 83, 84, 92, 123, 185, 202, 213, 216, 236, 239, 250, 358, 474, 481, 491
Shenstone, Wm.
(1714-1763)
133
Sheridan, R. B.
(1751-1816)
258, 498
Sherman, (Gen.) W. T.
(1820-1891)
457
Sidney, Sir Philip
(1554-1586)
10, 498
Smiles, Samuel
(1812-1904)
307, 321
Smith, Adam
(1723-1790)
269
Smith, Logan P.
(1865-1946)
134
Socrates
(B.C. 469-399)
24, 263, 286, 424, 456, 475
Solon
(c. 600 B.C.)
6, 62, 442
Sophocles
(B.C. 495-406)
8, 381, 442, 484

Spencer, Herbert (1820-1903) 187, 197, 250, 350, 371
Spenser, Edmund (1552-1599) 26, 143, 178, 260, 270, 271, 403
Spinoza, Baruch (1632-1677) 378
Statius, Publ. P. (c. 60-96) 12
Steele, Sir Richard (1672-1729) 15
Sterne, Laurence (1713-1768) 156, 434
Stevenson, R. L. (1850-1894) 192
Sumner, Charles (1811-1874) 390
Swedenborg, Emanuel (1688-1772) 174, 196
Swift, Jonathan (1667-1745) 7, 21, 46, 97, 133, 145, 166, 212, 223, 240, 253, 269, 321, 354, 381, 408, 453, 466, 477, 494
Swinburne, A. C. (1837-1909) 269

T

Tacitus, C. C. (c. 55-c. 117) 3, 5, 53, 165, 315, 429
Tagore, Sir R. (1861-1939) 251, 323
Talleyrand-Périgord (1754-1838) 502
Tasso, Torquato (1544-1595) 478, 488
Taylor, Bert L. (1866-1921) 36
Tennyson, Alfred (1809-1892) 7, 20, 27, 29, 104, 113, 122, 230, 231, 233, 261, 273, 303, 333, 362, 363, 390, 402, 409, 423
Terence, P. A. (c. 180 B.C.) 6, 8, 21, 184, 318
Tertullian, Q. S. (c. 150-230) 27, 49, 75, 142, 218, 276
Thackeray, W. M. (1811-1863) 291
Thales (c. 600 B.C.) 299
Themistocles (c. 514-449 B.C.) 383
Theocritus (c. 280 B.C.) 24
Thomas à Kempis (1380-1471) 52, 208, 245
Thompson, Francis (1859-1907) 310
Thomson, James (1834-1882) 119, 350
Thoreau, Henry David (1817-1862) 51, 81, 122, 187, 198, 219, 245, 335, 360, 361, 434, 495
Tolstoy, L. N. (1828-1910) 25, 122, 130, 132, 242, 276, 319, 330, 424, 447
Trumbull, John (1750-1831) 240
"Twain, Mark" See Clemens, S. L.

U

Unamuno, Miguel de (1864-1936) 218, 264, 372, 409, 441
Upton, R. R. (1868-1935) 458

V

Vergil (P. V. Maro) (B.C. 70-19) 3, 8, 12, 14, 27, 167, 181, 192, 196, 206, 227, 263, 300, 359, 389, 410, 419, 452, 457, 486, 487, 492
Villon, François (1431-1484?) 82, 393
Voltaire [F. M. Arouet] (1694-1778) 11, 17, 36, 71, 119, 138, 157, 159, 164, 173, 194, 208, 221, 231, 262, 265,

Voltaire—*Continued*
275, 276, 289, 307, 330, 332, 335, 342, 357, 377, 390, 400, 408, 411, 440, 442, 452, 483, 498
Von Merchel, W. (1803-1861) 91
Von Moltke, H. C. B. (1800-1891) 418
Voss, J. H. (1751-1826) 473

Waller, Edmund (1606-1687) 261
Walpole, Sir Robert (1676-1745) 40, 134, 336
Walton, Izaak (1593-1683) 143
Warburton, Wm. (1698-1779) 307
Ward, Artemas [C. F. Browne] (1834-1867) 37
Washington, George (1732-1799) 40, 247, 269, 493
Watts, Isaac (1674-1748) 30, 103, 185, 213
Webster, Daniel (1782-1852) 409
Webster, Noah (1758-1843) 237, 308
Wedgwood, Josiah (1730-1795) 390
Wellington, Duke of (1769-1852) 394
Wesley, John (1703-1791) 189
Whistler, J. A. McN. (1834-1903) 16, 105
Whitman, Walt (1819-1892) 34, 128, 172, 217, 269, 314, 318, 324, 375
Whittier, J. G. (1807-1892) 10, 197, 202, 353
Wilcox, Ella W. (1855-1919) 238
Wilde, Oscar (1856-1900) 17, 78, 109, 117, 140, 271, 333, 347, 377, 408, 416, 420, 454, 481
Wilson, Woodrow (1856-1924) 91, 141, 314
Wither, George (1588-1667) 261
Wordsworth, William (1770-1850) 55, 109, 184, 195, 250, 297, 380, 474, 495
Wycherley, William (1640-1716) 33, 467, 472

Y

Yeats, William B. (1865-1939) 427
Young, Edward (1683-1765) 3, 18, 19, 34, 131, 150, 170, 172, 175, 180, 193, 195, 217, 269, 270, 309, 333, 338, 404, 418, 427, 451, 464, 475, 477, 481, 487

Z

Zeno (c. 355 B.C.) 25

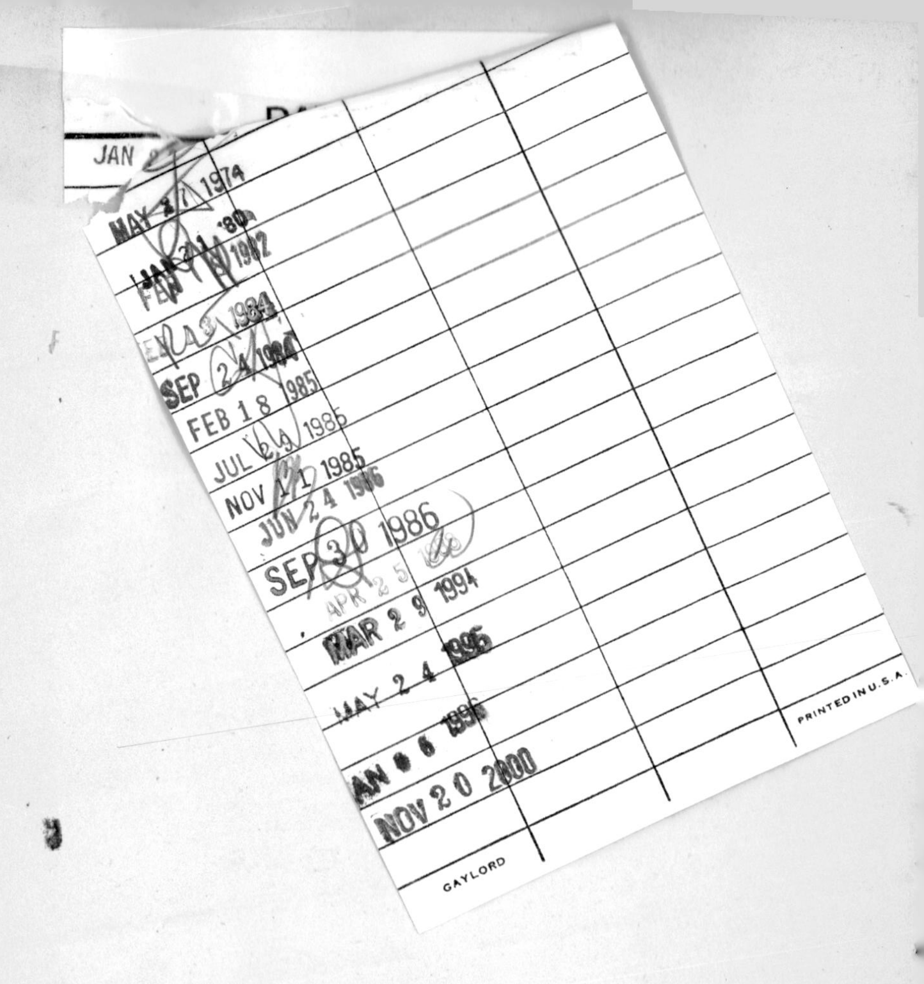

Davidoff, Henry.
A world treasury of proverbs from twenty-five languages: African, Arabic, Chinese [etc.] ... collected by Henry Davidoff. New York, Random House [1946]
2p. ℓ., vii-ixp., 1ℓ., 526p. 24cm.

"First printing."
Bibliography included in foreword.

1.Proverbs. 2.Quotations, English. I.Title.